Third Sector Policy at the Crossroads

The nonprofit sector occupies an ever more central role in economic and social policies. At the same time, nonprofit organizations face increasing public scrutiny and calls for more 'efficiency' and greater 'accountability'.

The sector is confronted with often conflicting demands of new public management, tight budgeting and greater competition. As a result, many nonprofit organizations are feeling more insecure about their role and are searching for a clearer 'identity', trying to understand the specific competencies that set them apart from both government and business firms. In essence, the nonprofit sector is at an important crossroads in its development.

Against this background, this book explores key policy issues:

- Is the nonprofit sector in crisis? What are the common themes and patterns in current policy debates concerning the future of the sector?
- What policy models are being discussed, and what are their implications?
- How can nonprofit organizations negotiate a course between commercialization and tighter government regulation?

Contributions from leading international scholars examine key policy issues across a wide range of developed and developing countries, in both established market economies and economies in transition.

This work will interest not only scholars, practitioners and students working in the nonprofit sector, but also those involved in studying political science, comparative politics, international relations and policy studies.

Helmut K. Anheier (Ph.D. Yale) is Director of the Centre for Civil Society at the London School of Economics, and Reader in the Department of Social Policy. Prior to this he was a Senior Associate and Project Director at Johns Hopkins University, Associate Professor of Sociology at Rutgers University, Director of the Rutgers Centre for Social Science Research, and a Social Affairs Officer at the United Nations. **Jeremy Kendall** is Research Fellow at the Personal Social Services Research Unit, LSE Health & Social Care and the Centre for Civil Society, Department of Social Policy, London School of Economics. He is the Editor of VOLUNTAS, the International Journal of Voluntary and Nonprofit Organizations.

Routledge Studies in the Management of Voluntary and Non-Profit Organizations
Series Editor: Stephen P. Osborne

Third Sector Policy at the Crossroads

An international nonprofit analysis

**Edited by Helmut K. Anheier
and Jeremy Kendall**

London and New York

First published 2001
by Routledge
11 New Fetter Lane, London EC4P 4EE

Simultaneously published in the USA and Canada
by Routledge
29 West 35th Street, New York, NY 10001

Routledge is an imprint of the Taylor & Francis Group

© 2001 editorial material and selection, Helmut K. Anheier and Jeremy
Kendall; individual chapters, the contributors

Typeset in Baskerville by Taylor & Francis Books Ltd
Printed and bound in Great Britain by Biddles Ltd,
Guildford and King's Lynn

All rights reserved. No part of this book may be reprinted or reproduced
or utilised in any form or by any electronic, mechanical, or other means,
now known or hereafter invented, including photocopying and recording,
or in any information storage or retrieval system, without permission in
writing from the publishers.

British Library Cataloguing-in-Publication Data
A catalogue record for this book is available from the British Library.

Library of Congress Cataloging-in-Publication Data
Anheier, Helmut K., 1954–
Third sector policy at the crossroads : an international nonprofit analysis /
Helmut K. Anheier and Jeremy Kendall.
p. cm.
Includes bibliographical references and index.
1. Nonprofit organizations. 2. Non-governmental organizations.
I. Kendall, Jeremy. II. Title.
HD2769.15 .A54 2001
060–dc21   00-069035

ISBN 0–415–21313–4

Contents

Illustrations

Figures

Tables

Boxes

Contributors

Helmut K. Anheier is Director of the Centre for Civil Society at the London School of Economics and Political Science.

Elizabeth T. Boris is Director of the Center on Nonprofits and Philanthropy at the Urban Institute, Washington DC.

Eleanor L. Brilliant is Professor in the School of Social Work, Rutgers University.

Dwight F. Burlingame is Associate Executive Director and Director of Academic Program at the Center on Philanthropy, Indiana University.

Ledivina V. Cariño is Professor and Dean of the National College of Public Administration and Governance, University of the Philippines.

Lisa Carlson is a Research Assistant in the Centre for Civil Society at the London School of Economics and Political Science.

Nicholas Deakin is Visiting Professor in the Centre for Civil Society, London School of Economics and Political Science.

Masayuki Deguchi is Professor at the Graduate University for Advanced Studies (Sokendai), Kanagawa, Japan.

Paul Dekker is Fellow of the Globus Institute of Tilburg University and Researcher at the Dutch Social and Cultural Planning Office.

Adam Habib is Associate Professor in the School of Governance at the University of Durban-Westville, South Africa.

Jeremy Kendall is Research Fellow at the Personal Social Services Research Unit, LSE Health & Social Care and the Centre for Civil Society, London School of Economics and Political Science.

Éva Kuti is Researcher in Voluntary Sector Studies at the Central Statistical Office, Budapest, Hungary.

Diana Leat is International Fellow in Philanthropy at Philanthropy Australia, Melbourne.

José Luis Méndez is General Coordinator of the Unit of Analysis of the Presidency of Mexico.

Joanna Regulska is Professor of Geography and Women's Studies at Rutgers University.

Lester M. Salamon is Director of the Center for Civil Society Studies at the Institute for Policy Studies, Johns Hopkins University.

Rupert Taylor is Associate Professor in the Department of Political Studies at the University of the Witwatersrand, Johannesburg, South Africa.

Jennifer Wolch is Professor of Geography at the University of Southern California.

Julian Wolpert is Professor of Public Affairs at the Woodrow Wilson School of Public and International Affairs, Princeton University.

Annette Zimmer is Professor of Social Policy and Comparative Politics at the University of Münster Institute for Political Science, Germany.

Acknowledgements

We would like to thank the participants of the 1997 VOLUNTAS symposium held at the London School of Economics and Political Science, and in particular colleagues who helped us with the planning of that event, which provided a large part of the material on which this volume is based. Cathy Pharoah, Lester Salamon, Dwight Burlingame, and Virginia Hodgkinson all played a role in this respect. The symposium would have been impossible without Lynne Moulton, who expertly liaised with contributors, as well as taking care of symposium logistics and administration. We are particularly grateful to Charities Aid Foundation (UK), the Nippon Foundation (Japan), the Indiana University Center on Philanthropy (USA) and the International Society for Third Sector Research (ISTR) for providing the financial support for the VOLUNTAS symposium.

Thanks are also due to anonymous referees who gave us valuable suggestions in developing the book proposal, and Steve Osborne, the series editor, for encouraging us to pull together the volume in the first place. We are also grateful to Stuart Hay and Michelle Gallagher at Routledge, who shepherded us once the proposal was accepted, and were remarkably tolerant of our tendency to miss deadlines. In addition, we particularly thank Lisa Carlson for ably managing the final production of the manuscript and helping the various papers over their last hurdles; and Rachel Kerr, who assisted Lisa with the final steps. The usual disclaimers apply.

Finally, we are grateful to ISTR for permission to reproduce chapters 2, 4, 9, 13–17, which correspond to, or are heavily based upon, papers which appeared in VOLUNTAS, ISTR's official journal, in 1999 (special issue co-edited by Jeremy Kendall and Helmut Anheier). We are also grateful to Taylor & Francis Ltd for permission to publish Chapter 10, which is a slightly extended and revised version of a paper published in the *Journal of European Public Policy*, volume 6, no. 2, 1999.

1 Third sector policy at the crossroads

Continuity and change in the world of nonprofit organizations

Helmut K. Anheier, Lisa Carlson and Jeremy Kendall

This volume presents a collection of essays that explore the current policy environment of nonprofit, voluntary or nongovernmental organizations in a broad cross-section of countries. The general underlying thesis guiding both the conception of this volume as well as the structure of individual chapters is the general notion or assessment that the nonprofit sector finds itself at a crucial juncture or crossroads. The reasons why nonprofit sectors seemingly are in crises or facing critical challenges are varied, as the contributions to this volume demonstrate. But a significant factor in most countries is the economic growth the sector experienced in many countries over the last two decades, in particular since 1990, twinned with a possible flattening or even decline in its traditional reliance on volunteers and charitable donations.

These shifts have taken place against a backdrop of mixed messages from governments, with ample supportive rhetoric often not matched, and sometimes even contradicted by, ambivalence in policies and their implementation. These developments, implying both greater economic importance and at least symbolic political recognition, have turned nonprofit organizations from somewhat marginal actors to more central, sometimes even major, policy players. Against this background, the purpose of the present volume is to throw light on the nature of the crossroads confronting the nonprofit sector, and explore the dilemmas, opportunities and problems involved. We suggest that – depending on how policymakers and nonprofit actors will react to these challenges, and what choices they will ultimately make in confronting them – the future development of the nonprofit sector will be set on a different course.

In approaching the nature of these crossroads and challenges, it is useful to recall some basic facts about the significant change in the importance of the third sector in recent years. In 1995, nonprofit organizations accounted for 6.9 per cent of total employment in western Europe and 7.8 per cent in the United States (Salamon *et al.* 1999). Between 1990 and 1995, the sector grew by an average of 24 per cent in major OECD countries like the United States, France, Germany, the Netherlands, Belgium and Japan. In other parts of the world, the economic scale of the sector is significantly lower. The third sector in those countries from Central and Eastern Europe (CEE) represented in this study accounted, on average, for 1.1 per cent of paid employment, with an average of 2.2 per cent for the developing world. Nonetheless, in terms of development financing, nongovernmental organizations (NGOs) have become a major circuit of flows from North to South (Smillie 1994; Lewis 1999; Fowler 1997).

As well as demonstrating economic weight, a core result of much recent empirical work (see Salamon *et al.* 1999) on the importance of the nonprofit sector is simply this: across countries – which otherwise differ significantly in terms of economy, civil society, politics and welfare system – the nonprofit sector has come to receive more attention by policy makers, and has come to occupy a more central role in discussions about the future of economic and social policies in a wide variety of fields. For example, nonprofit organizations figure prominently in current debates about the US (Lipsky and Smith 1993; see Brilliant, Chapter 12 in this volume) and the UK (Deakin 2000; see Deakin, Chapter 3 in this volume) social welfare system.

Nongovernmental organizations are also being recognized as important actors in development projects by the World Bank (2000a; 2000b)[1] and other international bodies such as the EU (Commission of the European Communities 1997). 'Creating' civil society through a network of voluntary associations has become a hallmark of programmes aimed at fostering democracy in Central and Eastern Europe.[2] The third sector has become significantly more important at the international level, and more generally (Meyer *et al.* 1997; Boli and Thomas 1999). In 1990, the Union of International Associations (UIA) listed 22,334 international nongovernmental entities; by 1999/2000, this number increased by 96.8 per cent to 43,958 (UIA 1999/2000).[3] Whereas until the 1980s NGOs played a marginal role at best at major international and intergovernmental conferences, they have had an increasingly high profile in influencing agendas, and in some cases have arguably proved capable of making or breaking the success of international treaties and intergovernmental summits. Examples include the Earth Summit in Rio de Janeiro in 1992, the Copenhagen Social Summit in 1995, the Beijing Women's Conference in 1997, and the 1999 World Trade Organization's meeting in Seattle. Importantly, some countries have decided to include NGO representatives in their national delegations in the run up to, or to see through the implementation of, such agreements. For example, regarding the Copenhagen Social Summit, Germany has involved the nonprofit sector in the so-called 'Copenhagen plus Five' to discuss the progress that has subsequently been made on the world's social agenda.

However, becoming more important and moving from the policy fringes closer to the political centre brings new challenges and opportunities. We have noted already that rhetoric and reality may seem out of kilter in some countries and contexts. And perhaps not surprisingly, with increased economic and political importance comes criticism and competition. Specifically, we find that nonprofit organizations are being made subject to increased public scrutiny, and calls for greater 'efficiency' of operations and greater 'accountability' to public authorities and other constituencies are becoming more frequent. In many ways, the new prominence enjoyed by the nonprofit sector in many countries brings with it greater interest in the performance and regulation of this set of institutions. The Commission on the Future of the Voluntary Sector in the United Kingdom (see chapter by Deakin, this volume), and recent challenges to the tax exempt status of nonprofit organizations in the US Senate are examples of this process (see chapters by Salamon, Wolch, and Brilliant).

Thus the sector sees itself confronted with new, often conflicting demands brought against it in what appears to be an increasingly volatile policy environment. As the chapters in this book show, an increasingly pervasive element of this environment in many countries are 'new public management' imperatives (Hood 1991), involving tight budgeting and competitive bidding and contracting regimes. These emphases are evolving in the context of a general retreat of the state from service provision and welfare responsibility. As a result, many nonprofit organizations are feeling less secure about their role in society at the very time when they have come to occupy a more important role, particularly in service provision. Nonprofit organizations are searching for a clearer 'identity', trying to understand the specific competencies that set them apart from both government and business firms. For example, most of the larger German nonprofit organizations are in the process of examining their mission statements and are involved in a discussion about their core values and areas of true competency. In the UK, the National Council of Voluntary Organizations (NCVO) has launched a Voluntary Sector Foresight Project to help the sector position itself in the future without putting its central values in jeopardy.

Yet it is unclear whether the expansion of the nonprofit sector will continue at all, and if so, at what rate and according to what policy trajectories. We simply have no theory that would help us understand, let alone predict, when the size of the nonprofit sector is at the right level, given economic and social conditions, and when it is either too small or too large. In other words, other than against objectives set in government policies, there is currently no way to gauge theoretically how much of a third sector a country needs. What is more, available economic theories are largely silent on how sustainable expansions are financed, and how potential changes in revenue structures are to be achieved. Tellingly, as Salamon *et al.* (1999) have shown, the expansion of the nonprofit sector in the nine OECD countries for which they could collect time series data was financed largely by fees and charges rather than private donations. These figures raise serious policy questions about the long-term sustainability of the nonprofit form, given recent trends in changes in revenue structure, yet they are difficult to assess theoretically in what they imply for the nonprofit form.

Interestingly, in developed countries, the current tendency towards 'self-reflection' among nonprofit policy makers occurs in a context in which the expansion of the nonprofit sector seems less affected by business cycles and public budget considerations than the rest of the economy. Although data on the long-term economic growth of the nonprofit sector are rare, data from the US (see Hodgkinson *et al.* 1984–96), and Germany (Anheier and Seibel 2000) suggest the absence of ups and downs, a noncyclical nature of expansion. Yet how long and to what level can expansion continue without changing the 'nature' of the nonprofit sector and its relations with government, business and civil society at large?

In developing countries, too, the nonprofit sector finds itself at the crossroads, even though the context and nature of the 'choices' and dilemmas confronting NGOs and other voluntary associations are strikingly different because the limited capabilities of the state and the relationship with overseas actors loom so much larger. Specifically, the sector faces the dual challenge of operating in countries with weak states and fragile, often under-funded public administrations on the one hand, and the complexities and uncertainties of the international donor community on the other. To what extent can and should the third sector compensate for weak governments in the long run? Given that NGOs are becoming ever more part of the way in which international development aid and humanitarian assistance functions, how can they retain their advantage over public agencies and international institutions like the World Bank (see Smillie 1994; Smith 1993)?

The democratization process of the 1980s and 1990s (Linz and Stepan 1996) saw many authoritarian regimes toppled and replaced by often fragile democracies. Governments and NGOs in countries like the Philippines (see Carino, Chapter 16 in this volume), South Africa (see Habib and Taylor, Chapter 17 in this volume), Brazil (Landim 1998) or Ghana (Atingdui *et al.* 1998) found themselves in a somewhat uneasy honeymoon where the relationship between state and third sector involved in some sense a *tabula rasa* in which 'learning by doing' even in such fundamental aspects as constitutional status was the order of the day. Even now, in many cases, basic parameters and principles appear unsettled, creating a climate of considerable uncertainty. In those developing countries which have retained autocratic regimes, restrictive laws regulating nonprofit organizations have often remained in place, as is the case in Egypt (Kandil 1998), and state/NGO relations are frequently tense and adversarial.

At the same time, the third sector in developing countries appears increasingly bifurcated at the local level. In countries that depend heavily on external aid, the bifurcation is between a group of international NGOs, typically originating from OECD countries on the one hand, and a growing and versatile group of indigenous organizations, some of which question the role and power of Northern NGOs, on the other (Fowler 1997; Edwards 1999). The relationship between international and indigenous NGOs is by no means clear cut, and many fault lines exist in the way third sectors are emerging in the context of volatile political and administrative systems. Many thorny questions about legitimacy and representation will continue to come up and are likely to remain at the forefront of NGO/government and NGO/civil society relations in countries of the South. In countries like Brazil (Landim 1998) and Mexico (see Méndez, Chapter 15 in this volume), the bifurcation is also between an older, elite-oriented and elite-dominated segment of schools, hospitals and other service providers, and a more recent segment of local grassroots initiatives and self-help groups among the poor.

The nonprofit sector is facing challenges in transition countries, too. More than a decade after the fall of state socialist regimes, the nonprofit sector remains

fragile and heavily dependent on outside funding (Kuti 1999). The straight trans-
lation of civil society organizations, which emerged in the initial transition
period 1989–91, into functioning nonprofit organizations proved much more
difficult. Although the track record across the region is unequal, in no country
have nonprofit organizations achieved a critical mass and momentum that would
leave their persistence and continued growth a foregone conclusion (see Anheier
and Seibel 1998). Dependencies on outside funding remain high, as does the
politicization of the sector from across the spectrum. Moreover, the philanthropic base of the sector remains weak, as those aware of its cultured
inheritance suggested it would (Dahrendorf 1990), and the relationship with the
generally weak public administration systems are underdeveloped and often
deeply troubled. In short, despite its initial growth and political prominence, the
long-term viability of the third sector in Central and Eastern Europe is not guaranteed. How can the sector simultaneously cultivate a mature and balanced
relationship with the various tiers of the state, whilst cultivating a greater sense of
ownership by, and participation from, the people it seeks to serve? This wide-
ranging challenge is just one of many dimensions to the crossroads confronting
nonprofit organizations in transition economies.

The chapters in this book cover developing and developed countries as well as
transition economies, and taken together address a variety of policy environments. The following overview will examine what crossroads, dilemmas, and
challenges the chapters identify for the nonprofit sector in the various countries
and regions, and what likely options, choices and developments they foresee.

Crossroads, crises, and challenges

Developed market economies

Chapter 2 in this volume, by Lester M. Salamon, represents a clear and wide-
ranging point of departure for the chapters that follow on the situation in
OECD countries. For Salamon, a leading scholar on government/nonprofit relations in the US, it is clear that the American third sector is at a turning point so
pervasive, problematic and fundamental as to amount to a real crisis. The overarching crisis for the US third sector is the result of the cumulative impact of
four distinctive crises:

- A *fiscal* crisis, which reflects continued government financial retrenchment
  and the tight purse of new public management;
- An *economic* crisis, as market organizations infiltrate fields in which third
  sector organizations have traditionally been insulated from competition;
- A crisis of *effectiveness*, resulting *inter alia* from an apparent inability or unwillingness to demonstrate their impact in tackling social problems; and
- A crisis of *legitimacy*, reflecting particularly prevailing misunderstandings
  about the sector's resource base and the character which third sector organizations have themselves misguidedly reinforced.

Taken together, these crises, Salamon suggests, have collectively undermined public confidence in this sector and prompted questions about the basic legitimacy of the special tax and legal benefits it enjoys. Reviewing alternative responses to these cumulative crises, Salamon advocates a strategy of 'renewal'. This would involve better monitoring for evaluative and accountability purposes, the adoption of more creative resourcing options; measures to widen citizen participation; and public education to raise awareness of the sector's symbiotic relationship with government and business as constituted in the status quo.

Jennifer Wolch in Chapter 4 challenges Salamon's renewal strategy for the third sector and advocates instead a decentred third sector. Salamon argues that the nonprofit sector is the core or centre of civil society. According to Wolch, Salamon correctly diagnoses the nonprofit sector's problems but his proposal to 'hold the centre' through sectoral renewal and a partnership model of state/nonprofit relations is problematic. This is the case, she argues, in part because the effects of economic globalization are reducing nation-state autonomy. In addition, fragmentation of social identity in a postmodern era challenges sectoral legitimacy, while devolution and localization of social welfare responsibilities reduces nonprofit effectiveness. On the basis of US evidence, Wolch argues that rather than trying to 'hold the centre', the nonprofit sector should be decentred – away from dominant institutions, powerful groups and privileged places – and join the margins in an effort to weave a new, more humane and inclusive social contract. For Wolch, such structural 'decentring' led by the third sector involves literally relocating to allow local elites to learn from, and be more responsive to, the marginalized people in their communities; dramatically responding to hostile and threatening state actions by struggle, resistance and opposition rather than acquiescent 'collusion'; and in general exhibiting an enhanced willingness to involve socially excluded groups in agenda-setting and governance.

In contrast to Salamon and Wolch, Eleanor L. Brilliant in her chapter 'The American third sector at the end of the twentieth century: public and private revisited' (Chapter 12) asserts that the American third sector is not at a dramatic crisis point, but finds it more elucidating to portray it as a critical turning point or crossroads. She examines four troublesome issues for the future: trends in the size and value of the third sector; changes in public/private relationships and distinctions between the sectors; the concept of civil society; and problems of accountability and abuse. First, policy decisions regarding the third sector are often misguided because the size and value of the third sector is not accurately portrayed in data. Difficulties in data collection and analysis will continue despite cooperation with the Internal Revenue Service, but, she contends, data collection and analysis methods can improve with a new perspective on the size of, rates of growth in, and government expenditures on the third sector.

Second, the distinction between the public, private and nonprofit sectors is ultimately philosophical and not corporeal, especially regarding tax-exempt status. In other words, should private contributions be defined as public money? Third, like Dekker in his chapter on the Netherlands (see below), Brilliant challenges the use of the term 'civil society' as if it were synonymous with the nonprofit sector. Finally, Brilliant argues for greater public debate on the third sector, which will help determine the 'locus of accountability' for nonprofit activity. She also advocates the establishment of another commission, along the lines of the Peterson and Filer Commissions in the 1970s, to review the role of the third sector in the context of its interaction with the public and private sectors. While a public commission has the potential to become bogged down in politics, this issue needs to be tackled at the federal level in order to move beyond the crossroads.

How does the US situation compare to other parts of the developed world? In 'The UK voluntary sector in the new millennium', Nicholas Deakin (Chapter 3) analyses a new pattern of relationships that has emerged in the last decade between the third sector, the state and the market. The rapid expansion of the third sector over the last decade has served to define expectations and enlarge the space within which the sector operates. This 'new voluntary sector', Deakin explains, represents a shift from philanthropy to mutual aid, but maintains, albeit less prominently, the essential characteristics and traditions of the sector – charitable donation and provision of services to the needy. By situating the debate within a broad social and institutional context, Deakin's analysis of the third sector in the UK represents a more holistic view of the changing environment of the third sector as it enters the new millennium. His analysis reflects changes taking place across the developed world, and therefore allows for a much wider comparison.

In his chapter on the Dutch nonprofit sector, Paul Dekker highlights the ambiguous nature of the sector in the Netherlands compared to the US and the UK (Chapter 5). Many of the trends in those countries – contract culture consolidation, loss of youth involvement in voluntary activities, and growing interest in identity issues – can be found in the Netherlands. Salamon's warnings about the unintended consequences of competition between nonprofit and for-profit service providers in the US can also be seen in the Dutch case. However, a major point of contrast is that the concept of a unitary and concrete nonprofit sector does not exist in the Netherlands to the extent that it does in the UK and the US. The Dutch, Dekker argues, are struggling to define the nonprofit sector and the boundaries within which it operates. Dekker describes the nonprofit sector in the Netherlands as 'a category' but not 'an entity', where distinctions between public, private and nonprofit sectors are almost futile. Dekker concludes by challenging the concept of civil society used by allies of the nonprofit sector, arguing that it is too all-embracing and vague to be used in research.

Dekker appreciates Wolch's suggestion of 'decentring' the nonprofit sector and bringing it closer to the idea of civil society as 'an autonomous sphere of voluntary involvement, associational life and public discourse'. However, he rejects her prescription of 'joining the margins' and suggests that Wolch, like Salamon and Deakin, is too focused on defining the nonprofit sector according to its original aims. Dekker argues that it is more relevant to understand the interrelationships between sectors and the specific services they provide, rather than trying to define the boundaries of the nonprofit sector.

Whereas Salamon argues strongly in favour of a public/nonprofit partnership model, almost suggesting a mild version of continental European-style corporatism, the nonprofit sector in countries like Germany is seeking to step away from a governmental embrace increasingly regarded as stifling rather than enabling. This is the tenor Annette Zimmer's chapter on 'Corporatism revisited: the legacy of history and the German nonprofit sector' (Chapter 9). Specifically, she discusses the applicability of Salamon's four-crises framework in the German context, and explores the implication of a mild corporatist model of public/nonprofit relationship to reinvigorate the nonprofit sector.

Zimmer describes Germany as a textbook example of corporatist arrangements, particularly in the fields of healthcare and social services. Whereas American nonprofit organizations are suffering from a crisis of legitimacy caused by marketization, German nonprofit organizations have been confronted with a crisis of legitimacy and identity caused by corporatism since the early 1980s. This particular scenario is, however, not covered by Salamon's analysis, and Zimmer asks therefore whether his corporatist diagnosis applies to the German nonprofit sector.

Like Wolch, Zimmer is sensitive to the implicitly 'corporatist' character of the relationship between the state and the third sector apparently advocated by Salamon. However, focusing on the German case, she argues that crises are manifested in a different form precisely because the third sector has *already* been acting – and is widely understood to have been acting – as a corporatist-style partner with the state. While the ideology prevalent in the US seems to suppress acknowledgement of joint working between the sectors, the principle of subsidiarity, domestically interpreted, until very recently provided a basis for openly endorsing it. However, the crisis of legitimacy in the German case arose as early as the 1980s in social care and healthcare precisely because the inherited arrangements of subsidiarity were seen to be inappropriately privileging the position of traditional providers at the national level (the 'free welfare associations'). Critics (see Zimmer in this volume) charged that this nonprofit 'cartel' of large provider networks operated at the expense of local groups and agencies rooted in the new social movements. Fiscal pressures have subsequently led to quasi-market-style reforms which have now created a more level playing field between these various groups, involving competition for publicly financed, socialized care (rather than direct use of fees and charges, as in the US case). Echoing Wolch's emphasis on the relevance of a spatial dimension in the context of growing population diversity, Zimmer underlines the importance of change-oriented third sector activity at the local level as an alternative to top-down corporatism, noting some of the kinds of developments that are already underway.

Chapters 6 and 7 address the role of foundations and business corporations. 'The role of philanthropic foundations' by Elizabeth T. Boris and Julian Wolpert (Chapter 6) addresses issues of accountability and responsiveness in foundations in light of their significant contributions to social, economic, cultural and political life in America over the past century. Foundations are philanthropic organizations that accommodate donors who have philanthropic agendas. For their services to society, foundations are given tax benefits and have to meet minimal payout requirements in return. The arrangement succeeds, Boris and Wolpert say, so long as foundations pursue an agenda that is more philanthropic than self-serving. The recent growth of foundation resources and greater professionalization of management promises even greater contributions in the future. Yet foundations must balance preservation of their autonomy with the need to be accountable and responsive, a balance that is difficult to measure and assess. Their activities benefit some more than others and occasionally 'offend, neglect, or disappoint' important public constituencies. Boris and Wolpert advocate an increased role for the policy and research community because it has better data resources with which to monitor and assess foundation activities.

'Corporate philanthropy's future' by Dwight F. Burlingame (Chapter 7) reviews the nature of the corporate/nonprofit relationship and trends in corporate philanthropy. Is there a strategic partnership between corporations and the voluntary sector? Burlingame anticipates a fundamental shift in the assessment of the corporate/nonprofit relationship from a traditional comparison of corporate financial performance and corporate social performance towards a 'new' corporate citizenship model that draws on traditional philosophies and incorporates new business practices. The concept of corporate citizenship – the interest of business in maintaining a healthy society and thereby a healthy climate for business – is centuries old. However, it is rapidly becoming a new 'inclusive global term', which defines the role of corporate giving by linking corporate social performance to the quality of management and a range of corporate/stakeholder relationships. Furthermore, Burlingame asserts that public/private distinctions may no longer be viable. The new model of corporate citizenship recognizes that nonprofits have the potential to serve as a bridge between business and government. A strategic corporate/nonprofit partnership can create opportunities for reform that may improve the future prospect of business corporations.

Diana Leat (Chapter 8) discusses the relevance of Elizabeth T. Boris and Julian Wolpert's analysis of the American philanthropic foundations to the British case, particularly the grant-making capacity of the National Lottery Charities Board in Britain. Foundations in Britain are also facing a fiscal crisis, but the level of public scrutiny is not as profound as in the US. As a result, the regulatory framework surrounding philanthropic foundations in Britain is not as strict, and, compared to philanthropic foundations in the US, their British counterparts have much more independence. Several measures in the last few years, however, have put more emphasis on transparency, requiring British foundations to publish annual reports and to make their accounts available to the public, particularly the Charities Act of 1992 and the directory of foundations published by the Directory of Social Change. Leat also discusses the implications of changing boundaries between voluntary and statutory organizations, the New Labour government's emphasis on a partnership funding approach, and the ability of foundations to process grant applications.

Chapter 10 considers the shaping of supra-national policy towards the third sector by focusing on the European institutions. In 'The third sector and the European Union policy process', Jeremy Kendall and Helmut Anheier discuss the emergence of the third, voluntary or nonprofit sector as a recognized actor in the EU policy process. They show how most of the initiatives associated with it have been characterized by inertia, delays and perceived low salience from the perspective of many of the leading actors involved. This chapter represents a first attempt to explore and explain this situation, drawing on Kingdon's 'multiple streams' approach. Five interrelated third sector policy initiatives are discussed: the European Association Statute; Declaration 23 attached to the Maastricht Treaty; a 1997 Communication dealing with the role of associations and foundations in Europe; the third sector's involvement in the Structural Funds; and the third sector's role in overseas development. They conclude that conceptual fault lines exist between the key protagonists, reflecting their contrasting ideologies and interests *vis-à-vis* the third sector, as well as more generic differences in policy style. They also note how outcomes to data have reflected not only these inter-governmental clashes, but also the independent initiative of 'policy entrepreneurs' within and around the EU institutions. In addition, the subfield of overseas development is contrasted with other areas as involving both high salience and the mobilization of coordination and support, a state of affairs tentatively linked to widespread agreement as to the legitimacy of EU action in this domain; the existence of supportive public opinion; the transferability of similar national models to the European stage; and the contribution of policy leadership.

Masayuki Deguchi in 'The distinction between institutionalized and noninstitutionalized NPOs: new policy initiatives and nonprofit organizations in Japan' (Chapter 11) discusses the new role of nonprofit organizations (NPOs) in Japan in the aftermath of the Kobe earthquake in January 1995, and the resulting policy initiative to legalize grassroots NPOs, highlighting the difference between institutionalized (I/NPO) and non-institutionalized (N/NPO) NPOs. The acronym 'NPO' has a much more narrow definition than that used by the International Classification of Nonprofit Organizations or ICNPO (Salamon and Anheier 1997). N/NPOs refer to grassroots organizations which were not afforded legal status before the Law to Promote Specified Nonprofit Activities was enacted in 1998, and which are held in great esteem by the Japanese public, especially since the 1995 earthquake. I/NPOs refers to incorporated organizations which are often quasi-public or quasi-private, such as social welfare institutions and corporate foundations, and which are regarded more sceptically by the public at large. Deguchi uses Salamon's four-crises framework (fiscal, economic, efficiency and legitimacy) to analyse changes in social perceptions of NPOs, highlighting the critical role of public opinion in bringing about changes in policy.

Central and Eastern Europe

Chapters 13 and 14 explore the third sector's policy situation in the so-called 'economies in transition', or countries experiencing post-communist transformation, in Central and Eastern Europe. Generalizations are difficult to sustain because different countries have developed from contrasting pre-transformation circumstances and the transformation process itself has been varied (Anheier and Seibel 1998). Nevertheless, there are two very evident general differences in this region in comparison with the US, UK and (western) Germany. Most obviously, the apparent lack of a recent historical legacy of relationships and mutual recognition on which to draw, coupled with a lack of robust and durable supporting structures, might be expected to lead to a fundamental lack of institutionalization of the third sector concept. This might be so because of the stifling of most independent voluntary initiatives undertaken by the state in communist regimes, but particularly in the east of the region. It could also be expected to limit the inclination and capabilities of individual citizens to autonomously organize for collective gain (Gellner 1994). Second, the financial measures taken by Western countries to support civil society could be expected to raise problems of resource dependency associated with heavy reliance on foreign funding, in a context in which other resources are relatively scarce, and indigenous capacity limited.

Both these expectations are borne out to a certain extent by Éva Kuti's overview of the region (Chapter 14), and by Joanna Regulska's case study of Poland (Chapter 13), which both emphasize the interplay of these restrictive historical legacies with current policy turbulence. It also seems clear that the wholesale importation of Western prescriptions and practices, not tailored to national and subnational contexts, fails to provide an adequate substitute for 'home grown' concepts and expertise. Their accounts parallel findings concerning the limited transferability of Western models for the for-profit sector in Central and Eastern Europe (Hausner *et al.* 1995). At the same time, state policies towards the sector are characterized by unpredictability, contradictions, overt inconsistencies and ambiguities, buffeted and amplified by an often fraught and changeable economic and political environment. While ambivalence and a muddled and piecemeal style of decision-making *vis-à-vis* the sector are far from absent in Western European and American policies towards the sector, particularly at an operational level, at the system level of fiscal and legal provisions, the distinction is clearly a valid one.

At the same time, both authors strongly emphasize differences in the sector's experiences in different countries and locales, and at different levels within the region. Kuti stresses how the chronic problems referred to above are felt most acutely in the least developed and historically under-endowed countries of the East, to the extent that they are at a different 'crossroads' to the Visegrad countries. In the latter case a more mature and locally embedded sector exists, with roots stretching back to well before 1989, in part because of the more tolerant style of socialism practised there. In her account of the Polish case, Regulska contrasts urban and rural experiences at the local level, and the political dynamics at local, national and international levels.

Specifically, Joanna Regulska (Chapter 13) focuses on the development of NGOs in Poland, as a case of the sector's development in the Central and

Eastern European transition economies. It is argued that in this situation, the development and growth of the NGO sector, though shaped, as in the West, by a set of legislative, political, economic, cultural and historical forces, nevertheless is circumscribed by the specific conditions of political transformation. The nature of and the power with which legislative, fiscal or organizational forces condition the development of the sector varies according to the scale at which they operate; and the local, national and international patterns of activity are distinctive in the case of Poland. Moreover, Regulska argues that the position of NGOs is significantly regulated by the state's political ideology, and the formative and evolving character of the latter translates into constant instability of states' actions *vis-à-vis* the nonprofit sector.

In her chapter on Hungary (Chapter 14), Éva Kuti takes an initial step towards providing a better understanding of the complex set of pressing problems that need to be addressed by the Central and Eastern European nonprofit sectors and their supporters in the near future. She gives an overview of the main challenges, and claims that different nonprofit sectors of the region are at different crossroads. Kuti also identifies a general policy crisis, fuelled by the lack of a comprehensive knowledge of the sector and clear political intentions of cooperating with it. In addition, the dependence on foreign funding may result in a sustainability crisis in several CEE countries. In the most developed part of the region, the main elements of the present crisis are the fiscal, economic, effectiveness, identity and legitimacy problems that have something in common with the challenges facing the much more mature nonprofit sectors of the developed world.

Developing countries

The final three chapters on the situation in the South provide assessments of the nonprofit sector in three continents and in political contexts that differ remarkably.

The country included from Latin America – Mexico – contrasts with the other developing countries covered here in that it has experienced no dramatic regime shift ever since the *Partido Revolucionario Institucional* came to power in 1929. In this context, in Chapter 15 José Luis Méndez stresses the historical rootedness and origins of the third sector. The current policy environment is still strongly shaped by this inheritance – most markedly through the compartmentalized treatment of Private Assistance Organizations as opposed to other NGOs, especially with regard to legal treatment. Méndez's analysis of policy towards the third sector in Mexico would suggest that here, as in the South African case, a full blown *general* and *pervasive* crisis has yet to develop. For sure, economic and fiscal problems abound and assume crisis-like proportions because of supply shortfalls in basic services to the poor. Mexico's political elite, however, remains divided on how to respond to this situation, as well as on how to relate to the third sector in the field of under-supply of public services.

As a result, efforts to advance the sector's legal framework and develop fiscal policy towards it have yet to be fully brought to fruition. Instead, a diffuse sense of awareness prevails that the sector has grown dramatically in response to, amongst other influences, natural disasters, political unrest in the southern parts of the country, restructuring of the state, and international funding opportunities. In politically safe fields, the sector is effectively still enjoying a 'honeymoon period' as a novel social actor in comparison to government and politicians, and without those institutions' flawed track records – at least for the time being.

Méndez's account also underpins the extent to which policy is evolving in a 'learning by doing' fashion. The third sector itself, researchers, politicians and policy makers are jointly feeling their way towards the creation of new legislation, partly conditioned by the historical legacy as emphasized above. They also look sideways to the experience of countries in other parts of Latin America, and seek to identify mutually beneficial innovations that respond to the concerns of each party. For example, the third sector appears to have recognized that its calls for extended rights and privileges must be matched by measures to allow the state to achieve accountability goals. For its part, the state has acceded that diversity within the sector calls for tailoring of legal requirements to reflect differences in objectives, size and stage of development.

Ledivina Cariño (Chapter 16) reviews the policy environment and relationship with the state in the Philippines. Unlike the Mexican case, we find a single and obvious regime shift – the replacement of President Marcos in 1986 – when the policy environment for the third sector changed dramatically. The role of NGOs was so pivotal in these events that the new national constitution, just one year later, fully recognized their role as 'guardians of the public interest', and they are even 'glorified', being widely seen as the very embodiment of the 'people power' revolution itself. In this context, Cariño argues that, in general it is possible to characterize this environment positively as 'supportive', 'enabling' and 'facilitating' despite a disappointing subsequent lack of specific legislative follow-through. The language of crisis is conspicuous by its absence, and in connecting with Salamon's four themes, she styles them as 'challenges' instead. She argues that they are defined differently from the American case, and also involve a distinctive response on the part of the Filipino NGOs and government alike, each of which are clearly set out.

One of the most remarkable ways in which the third sector's currently 'enviable' position is institutionalized in the redemocratized Filipino polity is through direct representation in the Congress. This is done on the premise that traditional politicians tended to be unable or unwilling to represent the interests of marginalized members of the population. Moreover, this was seen as one route by which NGOs, for their part, could achieve enhanced legitimacy, since putting the sector on a more democratic footing would serve to move it forward from the status quo, in which many organizations were still effectively operating under self-perpetuating or state-appointed governance. However, the experience of this system's first year of operation in 1998 has been flawed, as 'paper' NGOs were opportunistically created by traditional politicians to compete with those genuinely rooted in deprived communities. It is therefore widely argued that further reforms are required to secure genuine NGO-led community representation.

Habib and Taylor's account in Chapter 17 of the South African scene focuses on anti-apartheid NGOs in particular. These first emerged as a major political and social force *prior* to democratization. Subsequently, NGOs have been active in the transformation process in three respects: effective fusion with the state; operational partnership, but with separate identities retained; and through acting primarily as 'watchdogs'. For its part, the state has moved *relatively* quickly to put in place legislation, new 'corporatist-style' institutions and financial measures in support of NGOs, and appears to have been responsive to NGO concerns along the way.

In this comparatively supportive environment, the tenor of Habib and Taylor's account is that a full blown crisis has not emerged – yet. But they warn that just such a turning point may now be looming, reflecting both a range of operational and implementation problems and pressures. Many of these pressures have parallels with the situation reported in other parts of the world; but the authors stress the impact of one particular macro policy shift: the replacement of the populist, electorally endorsed Reconstruction and Development Programme (RDP) with a Growth, Employment and Redistribution (GEAR) strategy, under pressure from the World Bank and the IMF. In the ensuing neo-liberal economic climate, they argue that NGOs are necessarily poorly positioned to continue to address the needs of the marginalized people they were established to serve, challenging their *raison d'être* and creating fundamental problems of legitimacy.

Conclusion

It is important to keep in mind that the crossroads at which the nonprofit sectors find themselves in the different countries and regions discussed in this volume is not due to any single upward or downward trend in its internal character or external environment, nor to particular events or 'shocks'. On the contrary, the crossroads for the nonprofit sector is brought about by a *combination* of growth in economic size with qualitative repositioning in its political and social contributions, involving 'internal' and 'external' factors. This in turn represents responses to complex combinations of historical and current patterns of social and political continuity and change. All this creates uncertainties and new challenges that are changing the policy position of the third sector in myriad ways which this book only begins to reveal. In this respect, we suggest that the likely changes, and the choices and dilemmas they entail, will be most pronounced in exactly those countries where the sector has experienced the most significant growth over sustained periods of time.

Notes

1 See also the World Bank's web page on 'Nongovernmental organizations and civil society', *http://wbln0018.worldbank.org/essd/essd.nsf/NGOs/home.*
2 For the EU's Phare programme – the main channel for the EU's financial and technical cooperation with the countries of Central and Eastern Europe – see *http://europa.eu.int/comm/enlargement/pas/phare/index.htm.* For the EU's Tacis

programme – one of the key instruments of the EU to develop cooperation with the New Independent States and Mongolia – see *http://www.exin.ru/tacis/tac_en.html.*
3   UIA classifies international organizations as nongovernmental organizations (NGOs) or intergovernmental organizations (IGOs). Numbers for NGOs are used here and include
   (i)   conventional international bodies – federations of international organizations, universal membership organizations, intercontinental membership organizations and regionally oriented membership organizations;
   (ii)   other international bodies – organizations emanating from places or persons or other bodies, organizations of special form and internationally oriented national organizations; and
   (iii) special types – dissolved or apparently inactive organizations, recently reported bodies not yet confirmed, national organizations, religious orders and secular institutes, autonomous conference series, multilateral treaties, intergovernmental agreements and currently inactive nonconventional bodies.

References

Anheier, H. K. and Ben-Ner, A. (1997) 'The shifting boundaries: long-term changes in the size of the forprofit, nonprofit, cooperative and government sectors', *Annals of Public and Cooperative Economics,* 68, 3: 335–54.

Anheier, H. K. and Salamon, L. M. (eds) (1998) *The Nonprofit Sector in the Developing World,* the Johns Hopkins Nonprofit Sector Series, eds Lester M. Salamon and Helmut K. Anheier, Manchester: Manchester University Press.

Anheier, H. K. and Seibel, W. (1998) 'The nonprofit sector and the transformation of eastern Europe: a comparative analysis', in W. Powell and E. Clemens (eds) *Public Goods and Private Action,* New Haven: Yale University Press.

——(2000) *The Nonprofit Sector in Germany,* Manchester: Manchester University Press.

Atingdui, L., Anheier, H. K., Larelya, E. and Sokolowski, W. (1998) 'The nonprofit sector in Ghana', in H. K. Anheier and Lester M. Salamon (eds) *The Nonprofit Sector in the Developing World,* Manchester: Manchester University Press.

Boli, J. and Thomas, G. M. (eds) (1999) *Constructing World Culture: International Nongovernmental Organizations since 1875,* Stanford: Stanford University Press.

Commission of the European Communities (1997) *Promoting the Role of Voluntary Organizations in Europe,* Luxembourg: Office for Official Publications of the European Communities.

Dahrendorf, R. (1990) *Reflections on the Revolution in Europe,* London: Chatto & Windus.

Deakin, N. (2000) 'New initiatives along the third way: testing the parameters of partnership', in H. K. Anheier (ed.) *Third Way – Third Sector,* proceedings of a policy symposium organized by the Centre for Civil Society, Report 1, London: Centre for Civil Society, London School of Economics and Political Science.

Edwards, M. (1999) 'Legitimacy and values in NGOs and voluntary organisations: some sceptical thoughts', in D. Lewis (ed.) *International Perspectives on Voluntary Action: Reshaping the Third Sector,* London: Earthscan.

Fowler, A. (1997) *Striking a Balance: A Guide to Enhancing the Effectiveness of Non-governmental Organisations in International Development,* London: Earthscan.

Gellner, E. (1994) *Conditions of Liberty,* London: Penguin Books.

Hausner, J., Jessop, B. and Nielsen, K. (eds) (1995) *Strategic Choice and Path-dependency in Postsocialism: Institutional Dynamics in the Transformation Process,* Brookfield VT: Edward Elgar.

Hodgkinson, V. and Weitzman, M., with Abrahams, J. A., Crutchfield, E. A. and Stevenson, D. R. (1984–96) *The Nonprofit Almanac: Dimensions of the Independent Sector*, Washington DC: Independent Sector, and San Francisco: Jossey-Bass.

Hood, Christopher (1991) 'A new public management for all seasons?', *Public Administration*, 69, 1: 3–19.

Kandil, A. (1998) 'The nonprofit sector in Egypt', in H. K. Anheier and L. M. Salamon (eds) *The Nonprofit Sector in the Developing World*, Manchester: Manchester University Press.

Kuti, E. (1999) 'Different eastern European countries at different crossroads', *Voluntas*, 10, 1: 51–60.

Landim, L. (1998) 'The nonprofit sector in Brazil', in H. K. Anheier and L. M. Salamon (eds) *The Nonprofit Sector in the Developing World*, Manchester: Manchester University Press.

Lewis, D. (ed.) (1999) *International Perspectives on Voluntary Action: Reshaping the Third Sector*, London: Earthscan.

Linz, J. J. and Stepan, A. (1996) *Problems of Democratic Transition and Consolidation in southern Europe, South America, and Post-communist Europe*, Baltimore: Johns Hopkins University Press.

Lipsky, M. and Smith, S. R. (1993) *Nonprofits for Hire: The Welfare State in the Age of Contracting*, Cambridge MA: Harvard University Press.

Meyer, J., Boli, J., Thomas, G. and Ramirez, F. O. (1997) 'World society and the nation state', *American Journal of Sociology*, 103, 1: 144–81.

Salamon, L. M. and Anheier, H. K. (1996) *The Emerging Nonprofit Sector*, Manchester: Manchester University Press.

Salamon, L. M. and Anheier, H. K. (eds) (1997) *Defining the Nonprofit Sector: A Cross-National Analysis*, Manchester: Manchester University Press.

Salamon, L. M., Anheier, H. K., List, R., Toepler, S., Sokolowski, S. W. and associates (1999) *Global Civil Society: Dimensions of the Nonprofit Sector*, Baltimore: Johns Hopkins University Press.

Smillie, I. (1994) 'Changing partners: Northern NGOs, Northern governments', *Voluntas*, 5, 2: 155–92.

Smith, B. H. (1993) 'Non-governmental organisations in international development: trends and future research priorities', *Voluntas*, 4, 3: 426–44.

UIA (Union of International Associations) (1905–1999/2000) *Yearbook of International Organizations*, 36th edn, vols 3/4, Munich: K. G. Saur.

World Bank (2000a) *Operational Manual: Involving Nongovernmental Organizations in Bank-supported Activities*, Washington DC: World Bank.

——(2000b) *Consultations with Civil Society Organizations: General Guidelines for World Bank Staff*, NGO and Civil Society Unit, Washington DC: World Bank.

2 The nonprofit sector at a crossroads

The case of America

Lester M. Salamon

Despite some encouraging trends, America's nonprofit sector stands in crisis at the present time as a result of an interrelated series of challenges. In the first place, government budget cuts beginning in the early 1980s have eliminated a significant source of nonprofit revenue growth and created a serious fiscal squeeze for considerable numbers of organizations. Although the sector as a whole managed to replace this lost revenue, it has done so largely through fees and charges that have attracted for-profit businesses into traditional fields of nonprofit action, creating a serious economic challenge to the sector. Simultaneously, important questions have been raised about the effectiveness and accountability of nonprofit organizations, and about what some see as the over-professionalization and bureaucratization of the sector. All of this, finally, has undermined public confidence in this sector and prompted questions about the basic legitimacy of the special tax and legal benefits it enjoys. To cope with these challenges, American nonprofits could usefully undergo a process of renewal that revives the sector's basic values, reconnects it to its citizen base, and creates a better public understanding of its functions and role.

Introduction

A global 'associational revolution' appears to be underway around the world at the present time, a striking upsurge of organized private, voluntary activity in virtually every corner of the globe (Salamon 1993; Fisher 1993). While this process is going forward elsewhere, however, the nonprofit sector has entered a period of significant crisis in the United States, the country that, at least since the time of de Tocqueville, has been regarded as the virtual seedbed of nonprofit activity.

How can we explain this paradox? What is happening to the nonprofit sector in the United States at the present time? What future does this portend for the American nonprofit sector and what can be done about it?

The purpose of this chapter is to address these basic questions, to examine the current crisis confronting the American nonprofit sector, to explore the options that exist for dealing with it, and to suggest the implications that flow from this analysis for the nonprofit sector elsewhere. Other chapters in this volume will then assess the extent to which these crises and their implications actually apply.

To do this, the discussion here falls into four sections (the first three draw heavily on Salamon 1997). The first section provides some background on the American nonprofit sector to establish the context against which the current challenges are arising. The second section then identifies four basic challenges that I believe confront America's nonprofit sector at the present time. The third section then outlines several alternative responses to these challenges and indicates the one that this author favours. A concluding section then sketches the implications that this analysis has for our understanding of what is required to preserve a vital nonprofit sector in other countries.

Background: the American nonprofit scene

The nonprofit, or tax-exempt sector is a significant presence in American life, embracing at least 1.6 million formal organizations and several times that number of informal, grassroots groups (Salamon 1999).[1] Quite apart from *member-serving* organizations such as social clubs, professional organizations and business groups, this sector contains some 1.2 million *public-serving* organizations in such fields as health, education, social services, environment and human rights. These latter organizations alone had expenditures of some $525 billion as of 1996, a figure that is the equivalent of more than 7 per cent of the nation's gross national product. Put somewhat differently, the expenditures of the American nonprofit sector exceed the gross national product of all but ten of the world's countries. Well over half of these expenditures are made by large health-care providers, and another 20 per cent by colleges and universities. Indeed, the nonprofit sector accounts for half of the country's hospitals and half of its colleges and universities. In addition, however, it embraces almost all of the country's symphony orchestras, 60 per cent of its social service agencies, and a vast assortment of social and civic organizations.

Embodying, as they do, a critical national value emphasizing individual initiative in the public interest, as well as serving important service delivery, advocacy, and community-building functions, these organizations have long enjoyed a special claim on America's affections. But like all such relationships, this one has been characterized by far more tension and complexity than either party would probably prefer to admit. Complaints about the 'nonprofit sector' even surfaced in town meeting debates over the ratification of the US Constitution, as citizens faulted Harvard College – America's first nonprofit corporation – for shortcomings that sound hauntingly similar to ones being lodged against nonprofit institutions today – elitism, unresponsiveness and lack of public accountability. At the very time that Alexis de Tocqueville was celebrating the penchant for association as one of the defining features of American democracy, in fact, state legislatures throughout the young republic were denying eleemosynary institutions the basic right to incorporate, and forbidding courts from assuming the enforcement power needed to make charitable trusts feasible (Hall 1987: 4–5).

During the late nineteenth century, however, America's deep-seated ambivalence toward nonprofit corporations was replaced by an almost reverential attitude that has come down to us today. Indeed, for more than half a century – from the end of the American Civil War in the mid-1860s until the launching of the New Deal in the early 1930s – support for the nonprofit sector became a central part of the conservative ideology that was used to fend off proposals for expanded government social welfare protections (Lubove 1968). Such protections were not needed, went the argument, because America has a strong tradition of voluntary organizations and private philanthropy that can handle problems much better. In the process, the nonprofit sector became enveloped in a pervasive myth of voluntarism and a resulting set of popular expectations that few merely human institutions could hope to fulfil. Central to this mythology was a belief in the power of purely private, voluntary approaches to solve the problems of poverty and distress, and in the feasibility of relying on private charity alone to sustain the nonprofit sector's work.

So powerful has this mythology been, in fact, that it served to obscure for most Americans the fact that the most dramatic period of US nonprofit growth was actually the one ushered in by the Great Society era of the 1960s, and that the principal engine of this growth was not private giving but the expansion of government support. Yet this outcome is not all that surprising. Given the deep-seated hostility to government involvement in social welfare activity in the United States, the condition for extending such involvement has long been to leave much of the responsibility for delivering the resulting services in private hands, including particularly those of private, nonprofit groups. Such cooperation thus has deep roots in American history (Nielsen 1979: 25–48; Salamon 1987). When the federal government entered the human service field in a massive way in the 1960s, therefore, it was only natural that it would pursue a similar course. The upshot was a wide-ranging partnership between nonprofit organizations and government in a broad assortment of fields. Reflecting this, government support easily surpassed private giving as a source of nonprofit revenue, reaching well over 30 per cent by the late 1970s compared to less than 20 per cent from private giving (Salamon and Abramson 1982; Salamon 1987; Smith and Lipsky 1993).

The current crisis

When conservative political forces gained the ascendance in the early 1980s and launched a series of budget and policy changes that reflected the earlier myth of voluntarism, therefore, the result was to disrupt significantly the prevailing pattern of nonprofit operations. Instead of leading nonprofit organizations back to a hypothesized golden age of purely charitable support, however, the resulting pressures seem to have pushed them towards a more commercial mode. Meanwhile, economic and other forces have been pushing nonprofit institutions in a similar direction, often with less than wholesome results. The consequence is a widespread challenge both to the way nonprofit organizations have actually operated, and to popular conceptions about how they are supposed to behave.

More specifically, America's nonprofit sector confronts a fourfold challenge at the present time. Any single facet of this challenge by itself would pose a serious dilemma for this set of institutions. The fact that they are all hitting at the same time transforms the dilemma into a veritable crisis.

The fiscal crisis

The first aspect of this crisis is fiscal in character. After years of expanding government support, nonprofit organizations have had to adjust to what appears to be a permanent situation of budgetary stringency. This stringency had its origins in the conservative fiscal policies of the Reagan era of the early 1980s. Motivated at least in part by the myth of voluntarism, Reagan set out to strengthen the nation's nonprofit sector through the simple expedient of getting government 'out of its way'. Significant reductions were therefore enacted in federal spending in many of the key fields where nonprofit organizations are active. Overlooked in this process, however, was the extent to which 'getting government out of the nonprofit sector's way' also meant reducing the revenues that nonprofit organizations had available. Although tax reductions were enacted at the same time, at least partly in the hope of offsetting these losses through increased private philanthropic support, the limited scale of private giving compared to the scale of government support made this unlikely. The upshot has been a considerable fiscal squeeze on a large segment of the American nonprofit sector, at least outside of the health field where federal spending continued to rise (Salamon and Abramson 1982; 1984).

Moreover, although federal spending in these fields recovered somewhat in the late 1980s and early 1990s, the election of a highly conservative Congress in 1994 revived the retrenchment process. As of 1998, therefore, the real value of federal spending on programmes of special interest to nonprofit organizations, outside of the health field, still stood some 25 per cent below what it had been in Fiscal Year 1980, almost two decades before. This, in turn, translated into revenue losses for a broad cross-section of nonprofit organizations in such fields as employment and training, community development, international assistance, social services and education. Thus the value of federal support to nonprofit community development and international aid organizations as of 1998 was 46 per cent and 41 per cent respectively below its 1980 level; while for nonprofit organizations in the fields of social services, education, and employment and training it ended up as of FY 1998 still 11 per cent below its level in 1980 (Salamon and Abramson 1998). Indeed, the revenue that nonprofit organizations lost from the federal government over the period 1980 to 1994 alone was equivalent to the total amount of foundation grants they received between 1970 and 1990. In short, while governments elsewhere in the world were actively expanding their reliance on nonprofit organizations to deliver publicly financed services (Ullman 1998; Ranci 1997), the federal government in the United States was moving in the opposite direction, significantly curtailing the substantial partnerships that already existed.

Nor does this process seem likely to abate in the foreseeable future, despite the recent elimination of the national budget deficit. To the contrary, the most recent budget proposals advanced by the Clinton administration in February 1998 would exact further reductions in federal support to nonprofit organizations, at least outside the health field. Under these proposals, federal support to nonprofit organizations outside of health would decline an additional 2 per cent between FY 1998 and FY 2003. This translates into an additional cumulative loss of $13 billion in revenue compared to what would be available if FY 1980 spending levels were to be maintained over this period (Salamon and Abramson 1998). Worse yet, the Congress appears headed for even steeper reductions.

The economic crisis

In the face of this budgetary pressure, nonprofit organizations have either had to reduce their services despite expanding demands, operate more efficiently, or find alternative sources of support. From the evidence at hand, it appears that the sector has mostly pursued the third of these courses.[2] Reflecting this, nonprofit revenue actually grew faster between 1977 and 1996 than the US economy as a whole (96 per cent versus 62 per cent), as Figure 2.1 shows. What is more, this growth was not limited to the hospital and health sector, which has traditionally grown faster than the general economy. Rather, social services and arts and culture organization income grew even faster, and only education organization income lagged behind.

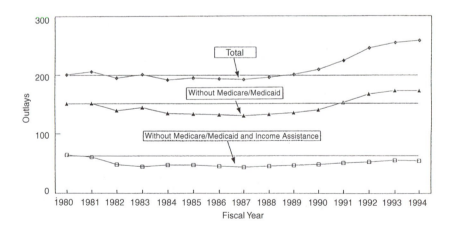

Figure 2.1 Federal spending on programmes of interest to nonprofits, 1980–94 (constant 1980 dollars)

One explanation for this growth was that the budget cuts of the early 1980s barely touched the entitlement programmes such as Medicare and Medicaid, which continued to pump public resources into at least the health and nursing home portion of the nonprofit sector. In addition, state and local governments boosted their own levels of support in a number of fields. As a consequence, despite declines in government support in some areas, government assistance still contributed 40 per cent of the increased revenues that nonprofit organizations captured during the 1980s.

Even more important as a source of nonprofit growth, however, was fee and service-charge revenue. As Figure 2.2 shows, this source alone accounted for 55 per cent of the growth of the nonprofit sector during the 1977–96 period. By contrast, private giving accounted for only 4 per cent, well below the share with which it started. What is more, this pattern was not restricted simply to health and higher education, where fees have historically played a significant role. Rather, social service agencies more than doubled the share of their income coming from fees and charges. In short, faced with the possibility of significant government cutbacks and unable to generate sufficient income from private giving, American nonprofit organizations moved much more massively into the commercial market.

While this 'marketization' (Salamon 1993) has enabled nonprofit organizations to survive the Reagan-era budget cuts and prosper, however, it has also exposed them to a second serious challenge, which I have termed the 'economic crisis'. In a sense, the nonprofit sector has been the victim of its own success. Having created, or newly entered, markets that could yield substantial commercial returns, it is now encountering massive competition from for-profit providers

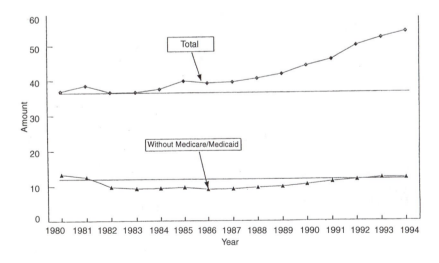

Figure 2.2 Federal support to nonprofits, 1980–94 (constant 1980 dollars)

attracted to these same markets and better able to attract the capital investments that involvement in these markets increasingly requires. In the process, operating margins are being squeezed so severely that it is undermining the ability of the nonprofit providers to subsidize the 'mission-related' activities, such as charity care or research, that pushed them into these markets in the first place. This has, in turn, narrowed the differences between nonprofit and for-profit providers, raising fundamental questions about the justification for the tax advantages that nonprofit organizations enjoy and inducing nonprofits to convert to for-profit status in order to attract the capital required to survive.

In this way, through a series of incremental steps, the basic viability of the nonprofit form appears to be under challenge in a number of fields. While it may be premature to conclude, paraphrasing T. S. Eliot's *The Hollow Men*, that this is the way the nonprofit sector will end, 'not with a bang but a whimper', the fact remains that numerous nonprofit organizations are facing serious challenges of precisely this sort.

The penetration of for-profit firms into traditional areas of nonprofit activity has been most evident in the healthcare field. Between 1980 and 1996, the number of nonprofit hospitals declined by 10 per cent and the number of beds they controlled declined by 15 per cent. During this same period, however, the number of for-profit hospitals increased by 40 per cent and the number of beds they controlled increased by 57 per cent (American Hospital Association 1998; Salamon 1999). This shift reflects a general movement away from reliance on high-cost general hospitals, where nonprofits have traditionally been dominant, toward lower-cost specialty hospitals, where for-profits have had an edge. Also at work has been the growth of pre-paid 'managed care' systems of hospital payment, which has put a special premium on expensive information technologies that nonprofit hospitals have found it difficult to finance (Brown 1996; Hasan 1995; Meyer *et al.* 1996).

While the economic pressures on nonprofit health providers are especially salient, similar pressures are also confronting other types of nonprofit organization, including those providing social services. Nonprofit social service agencies experienced especially robust growth during the 1980s. While the recovery from the Reagan budget cuts played a part in this, so did a massive growth of fee income, as noted above. In fact, fee income accounted for 69 per cent of the income growth that social service agencies achieved during the 1980s, compared to only 9 per cent from private giving (Salamon 1999).

As with the healthcare field, however, nonprofit providers have not been free to pursue these sources of support on their own. To the contrary, intense competition has emerged from for-profit providers. What is more, for-profit providers seem to be gaining the edge in a number of areas. Thus for-profit firms accounted for 80 per cent of the growth in daycare establishments between 1977 and 1992; in the home health field, one of the most explosive in recent years, for-profits essentially accounted for all of the net growth during this period; and even in other social services, where nonprofits retain the edge, for-profits have gained ground during the past decade, accounting for larger shares of the growth than their presence at the beginning of the period would suggest (US Census Bureau 1997; Salamon 1999).

In short, despite recent complaints from small businessmen about 'unfair competition' from nonprofits, the real story of the past two decades is the steady penetration of for-profit firms into domains that were once the near-exclusive preserve of nonprofit providers, threatening the nonprofit sector's continued existence in the process.

The crisis of effectiveness

In addition to a fiscal crisis and an economic crisis, American nonprofits also face a crisis of effectiveness.

Because they do not meet a 'market test', nonprofits are always vulnerable to charges of inefficiency and ineffectiveness. The scope and severity of these charges have grown massively in recent years, however. In fact, the competence of the nonprofit sector has been challenged on at least three different grounds.

First, nonprofit organizations, particularly in the human service field, have been implicated in the general assault on public social programmes that has animated national political debate for more than a decade now. Despite considerable contrary evidence (Schorr 1988), the persistence of poverty, the alarming growth of urban crime, the epidemic of teenage pregnancy and the continuation of welfare dependency have been taken as evidence that these programmes do not work. The resulting open season on government social programmes has caught significant components of the nonprofit sector in the crossfire, particularly since the sector has been involved in administering many of the discredited programmes.

Worse than that, the very motives of the nonprofit agencies have been called into question. Involvement in government programmes 'changes charities' incentives', charges one recent critique, 'giving them reasons to keep caseloads up instead of getting them down by successfully turning around peoples' lives' (Dennis 1996). Nonprofits thus stand accused not only of being ineffective, but also of preferring not to solve the problems they are purportedly addressing.

Second, beyond the political assault on Great Society social programmes lies a more profound line of criticism that takes nonprofit organizations to task for becoming a principal locus for the 'overprofessionalization' of societal problem-solving. This line of argument has a long lineage in American politics, but it has taken on new energy in recent years as critics on both the left and the right have pummelled nonprofit providers for their tendency towards professionalization, and called for a return to the simple virtues of self-help, faith-based charity, or other community-based approaches. According to this line of thinking, the professionalization of social concerns, by redefining basic human needs as 'problems' that only professionals can resolve, has alienated people from the helping relationships they could establish with their neighbours and kin. 'Through the propagation of belief in authoritative expertise', Northwestern University

Professor John McKnight thus notes (1995: 10), 'professionals cut through the social fabric of community and sow clienthood where citizenship once grew'.

Third, complicating matters further is the fact that nonprofit organizations generally lack meaningful bases for demonstrating the value of what they do. Indeed, nonprofit organizations have often resisted demands for greater account-ability on grounds that responding to such demands might interfere with the independence that gives the sector its special character. Instead, nonprofits have tended to point to their not-for-profit status as *ipso facto* evidence of their trust-worthiness and effectiveness.

Increasingly, however, these implicit claims by nonprofit providers have been subjected to serious challenge, as a result not only of a number of recent scandals, but also of growing questions about the basic efficiency and effectiveness of nonprofit agencies. 'Unlike publicly traded companies', management expert Regina Herzlinger (1996: 98) has thus noted, 'the performance of nonprofits and governments is shrouded behind a veil of secrecy that is lifted only when blatant disasters occur'. This is problematic, she argues, because nonprofit organizations generally lack the three basic accountability mechanisms of business: the self-interest of owners, competition, and the ultimate bottom-line measure of profitability.

The legitimacy crisis

All of this, finally, has led to a fourth crisis for the nonprofit sector, a much more serious and profound moral or political crisis, a *crisis of legitimacy* that is ques-tioning the whole concept of the nonprofit sector.

In a sense, the bottom is threatening to fall out of popular support for the charitable sector, leading to a host of embarrassing questions about why this sector should exist and whether there is truly a justification for the special tax and other advantages it enjoys. Ironically, the nonprofit sector's success at adjusting to the realities of postwar, and then post-Reagan, American society may be costing it the support of significant elements of the American public, as a massive mismatch has opened between the actual operation of the American nonprofit sector and popular conceptions of what this sector is supposed to be like, conceptions that the sector itself has helped promote.

In its public persona, the nonprofit sector still holds to a quaint nineteenth-century image of charity and altruism, of small voluntary groups ministering to the needy and downtrodden. In reality, however, the actual operations of the nonprofit sector have become far more complex. For one thing, the financial base of the sector has become far different from what the conventional image would suggest. The sector's self-image stresses private philanthropy as the prin-cipal source of support. In fact, however, fees and service charges are now the principal source of support. Equally important has been the growth of partner-ships between the nonprofit sector and the state. Government support now accounts for 40 per cent of nonprofit revenue in certain fields. The resulting partnerships have much to recommend them, combining as they do the supe-rior flexibility and service delivery capabilities of the nonprofit sector with the superior fundraising and direction-setting capabilities of government. Yet these important partnerships have hardly been fully integrated into prevailing concepts of the sector, and consequently remain somehow suspect. As a result, even the nonprofit sector's involvement in advocacy has been called into question. Having joined with government to respond to public needs, nonprofit organizations are now in the uncomfortable position of appearing to be advocating not on behalf of the clients and communities they serve, but in their own self interest, for the budgets and programmes that support their own operations. This is a point that conservative critics of government spending have pounced upon with great glee.

So, too, with certain other salient features of this sector, such as pay and perquisites that at least some consider inappropriate; a focus that extends well beyond the poor and the disadvantaged; professionalization and bureaucratization, which threatens to undermine the role of volunteers; and representational mechanisms that are often imperfect at best.

The nonprofit sector is thus being hoisted by its own mythology. Having failed to explain adequately to the American people what its role should be in a mature welfare state, the sector has been thrown on the defensive by revelations that it is not operating the way its own mythology would suggest.

This is not to say that these features and developments are bad or unwarranted. What is more, they hardly apply equally to all segments of the sector. But they have become quite widespread and diverge rather sharply from popular conceptions of this sector, and too little effort has gone into bringing popular conceptions into better alignment with reality. As a result, the sector has become vulnerable to any manner of 'cheap shots' and exposés that point to the current realities as an indictment of its current mission. Reflecting this, local governments have been increasingly emboldened to challenge the tax exemptions of nonprofit organizations. Such challenges have surfaced vigorously in Pennsylvania, New York, New Hampshire, Oregon, Maine, Wisconsin and Colorado. A recent study in Pennsylvania found that at least two thirds of Pennsylvania counties are actively seeking taxes or payments in lieu of taxes from nonprofits. In one of the most celebrated cases, an appeals court in Pennsylvania overruled more than 350 years of legal development that had firmly implanted the idea that education is an inherently 'charitable' activity, and ruled that a private, nonprofit college no longer qualified for charitable status under state law because only a small fraction of its students were poor. Although this ruling has since been reversed, it suggests the extent to which support for charitable institutions has eroded. In fact, the Utah Supreme Court upheld a similar challenge to the basic common law concept of 'charity' so far as hospitals are concerned. Instead of treating healthcare as an inherently charitable activity, the Utah Supreme Court established a *quid pro quo* test under which a hospital can lose its exemption from state and local property taxes if it is not supported mostly by donations and gifts, if its patients pay for their care, and if it generates income in excess of operating and long-term maintenance costs (Potter and Longest 1994: 397, 411). Using this standard, most nonprofit hospitals would likely be vulnerable to a loss of tax-exempt status.

More recently, Congressional critics brought the same questioning to one of the other fundamental functions of the voluntary sector – its advocacy and representational function. Under the so-called Istook Amendment, named after its Congressional sponsor, nonprofit organizations receiving federal grants could not use more than 5 per cent of their total revenues, including their private revenues, for a broad range of advocacy activities. This would undercut one of the major rationales for the existence of the nonprofit sector – to give voice to the under-represented and to bring new issues to public attention. Although this amendment ultimately failed, that it came close to passage in the 104th Congress is testimony to the vulnerability of the nonprofit sector today.

Indeed, recent surveys suggest a distressing loss of public confidence in nonprofit institutions. A Gallup survey in 1994, for example, showed that only about one third of the American population felt 'a great deal' or 'quite a lot' of confidence in nonprofit organizations outside of religion or education. This is well above the 15 per cent who expressed this level of confidence in the federal government and the 23 per cent who had 'a great deal' or 'quite a lot' of confidence in state governments. But it was still far behind the 47 per cent confidence levels the federal government enjoyed in 1975, and the 52 per cent and 48 per cent levels that small businesses and the military enjoyed as of 1994 (Hodgkinson and Weitzman 1994; Hart and Teeter 1995: 4).

What to do?

Faced with the challenges identified above, at least three lines of response are evident in the United States' policy debate on the third sector today.

Accentuate the positives

The first of these lines of response, and the dominant one in much of the nonprofit and philanthropic community, essentially questions the severity of the challenges the nonprofit sector faces. Adherents to this perspective point to previous challenges to the philanthropic sector, such as the criticisms that led to the 1969 Tax Act's restrictions on foundations and the Reagan budget cuts of the early 1980s, to suggest that the sector has faced equally serious challenges in the past and survived. What is more, they take comfort in the important countervailing trends that are also part of the current scene, such as continuing vitality in the grassroots base of the sector as evidenced by a blossoming of new grassroots organizations (Garr 1995); growing evidence of civic revival in the United States despite recent worries about the deterioration of the civic infrastructure of American communities (Putnam 1995; Verba and Schlozman 1995; Ladd 1996); an anticipated $10 trillion intergenerational transfer of wealth between the Depression-era generation and the postwar baby boomers over the next forty years, which could yield important new resources for charitable endeavour (Avery and Rendell 1993; Shapiro 1994); and the apparent emergence of a more strategic and long-range form of philanthropic involvement among a number of corporations leading to enduring partnerships with nonprofit organizations (Smith 1994; Logan *et al.* 1997; Nelson 1996). Given these countervailing trends, many in the nonprofit world caution against rocking the boat and attracting attention to the sector when it would do better simply riding out the storm.

While this strategy has much to recommend it, however, it seems unlikely to suffice. For one thing, the evidence of public questioning of the nonprofit sector seems too serious to ignore. For another, the countervailing trends may prove far less effective than they seem. Despite the significant evidence of continued revitalization of the organizational base of the sector, for example, new organizations eventually come up against the same hard realities of institutional survival that confront many of the existing agencies. One of the central conclusions of journalist Robin Garr's journey among 'The grassroots movements that are feeding the hungry, housing the homeless, and putting Americans back to work', for example, is that the success and effectiveness of these grassroots initiatives often comes to depend on their ability to forge partnerships with government, which is precisely what the recent fiscal policies have thrown into question (Garr 1995: 231–2). While the prospect of significant intergenerational wealth transfer and a changing corporate posture towards the voluntary sector offer much needed-relief, moreover, the extent of this relief is open to serious question. After all, charitable giving is not the only potential use of these inheritances, and investment managers have been hard at work devising more profitable alternatives. What is more, the projected inheritances may never materialize, or never materialize to the extent anticipated, if life expectancy continues to expand and medical or nursing care costs absorb more than the anticipated share of the accumulation. Certainly the recent record of bequest giving is hardly encouraging. Far from increasing, the relative scale of bequest giving has been on the decline.[3] Similarly, the reorientation of corporate philanthropy has recently run headlong into the pressures for corporate downsizing. In re-engineering the corporation, many corporate managements are re-engineering the corporate philanthropy function out of existence. In short, for these and other reasons, the pressures on the nation's nonprofit sector are likely to persist.

Accommodation

A second response to the challenges facing the nonprofit sector today has been to accept key segments of the prevailing critique of this sector and push for a full return to a simpler 'golden age' when government was not involved in the helping professions and nonprofit organizations handled these functions on their own, without government support. Central to this strategy is the belief that the current assault on the nonprofit sector, like the one in the early 1980s, is at least partly warranted, that nonprofit organizations have become too dependent on government, that this has undermined the private charitable and volunteer base that has historically been the key to this sector's uniqueness and success, that there are too many nonprofit organizations with too few mechanisms for accountability, and that more competition and improved business methods would improve the sector's performance.

By cutting back on government support, this argument goes, the nonprofit sector would be forced to return to its historic charitable roots, would become more efficient, and would reconnect to the constituencies it is supposed to serve. What is needed, a recent national commission organized by the conservative Bradley Foundation has thus argued, is more effective philanthropy guided by 'civic entrepreneurs'. These are people who 'seek out the organizations that are most effective in revitalizing their communities, focusing laser-like on actual results, not simply money raised, intentions voiced, or services offered' (National Commission on Philanthropy and Civic Renewal 1997: 5).

While there is much to recommend this strategy as well, however, it also has serious limitations. For one thing, the 'golden age' of purely private nonprofit action that is widely used as a basis for opposing government support of the nonprofit sector, has been exceedingly difficult for scholars to locate. In point of fact, collaboration, not conflict or competition, has been the characteristic relationship between the nonprofit sector and government throughout most of American history (Nielsen 1979; Warner 1894; Fetter 1901–2; Whitehead 1973; Salamon 1995). Until the late nineteenth century, nonprofit organizations were thought of as part of the 'public sector' because they contributed to the solution of public problems. Reflecting this, a rich pattern of collaboration existed between nonprofit organizations and government at all levels. The very first nonprofit corporation on American soil, Harvard College, was established, for example, by an act of the General Court of the Massachusetts Bay Colony in the mid-1600s, and the colonial government not only chartered the college but also provided it with £400 in capital and a dedicated tax, the 'college corn', for operating support (Nielsen 1979: 27). What is more, this pattern persisted at the local level throughout the nineteenth century (Warner 1894: 404). Although these relationships may have grown significantly in scope and scale in the 1960s and 1970s, they are thus hardly new.

Not only is the accommodation strategy built on an erroneous view of the past, however, it is also potentially self-defeating. Central to the accommodation response is the belief that private giving and voluntary activity can fill in meaningfully for the reductions in government support that the nonprofit sector is likely to endure as a result of budget cuts. Even if we assume that a significant share of federal spending represents waste, however, the likelihood that this might happen is exceedingly remote. Recent data indicate that the share of household income being devoted to charitable giving has actually been declining – from an average of 1.86 per cent during the 1970s to 1.78 per cent during the 1980s and 1.72 per cent during the early 1990s (Hodgkinson and Weitzman 1994: 88). Reflecting this, giving grew by less than 1 per cent in real terms during the early 1990s (Hodgkinson *et al.* 1996: 88). Similarly, the average contribution per return among upper-income taxpayers has declined steadily from the early 1980s to the early 1990s – from over $200,000 in 1980 to just over $60,000 in 1993 (Hodgkinson *et al.* 1996: 91). Reflecting these trends, far from filling in for government cutbacks, private giving actually lost ground as a source of nonprofit income during the decade that began with the Reagan budget cuts, falling from 15 per cent of total nonprofit revenue in 1982 to 11 per cent in 1992 (Hodgkinson *et al.* 1996: 190). Although there is some evidence that private individual giving may have grown more substantially in 1995 and 1996 in response to improved economic conditions, the difference was still not sufficient to alter the overall picture.

The more likely response, therefore, is that nonprofit organizations will turn even more extensively to fees, service charges and other essentially commercial forms of income to finance their operations. This certainly is the message of the 1980s, as we have seen. But it can be a highly self-defeating course. It seriously blurs the line between nonprofit organizations and for-profit businesses. It thus accentuates the division within the nonprofit sector between essentially 'commercial nonprofits' and 'donative' or public-oriented nonprofits. It also sharpens the divisions between public-benefit nonprofits cooperating with government and organizations focusing more on fee-paying customers.

Renewal

A third possible response to the challenges the nonprofit sector is facing, and the one with which this author is most comfortable, takes its inspiration from the work of John Gardner, a long-standing advocate of the nonprofit sector. In his book *Self-renewal*, Gardner (1981) argues that both individuals and institutions must engage in regular renewal in order to stay vital and alive. Applied to the nonprofit sector at the present time, this strategy sees the current crisis of the nonprofit sector not as an excuse for retreat into some mythical golden age of nonprofit independence or a time for continued drift towards greater commercialization. Instead, it views the sector's predicament as an occasion, and an opportunity, for renewal, for rethinking the nonprofit sector's role and operations, for re-examining the prevailing mythology in the light of contemporary realities, and for achieving a new consensus, a new settlement, regarding the functions of nonprofit organizations, the relationships they have with citizens, with government and with business, and the way they will operate in the years ahead.

Central to such a renewal strategy must be a recognition of the extent to which the evolution of the nonprofit sector in the United States has clearly leaped beyond what popular concepts and values can easily accommodate in a number of ways. Traditional concepts of charity and altruism, of care for the less fortunate, now sit uneasily with the reality of large-scale charitable enterprises headed by well paid professionals and providing assistance to far more than those in greatest financial need. The religious taproots of the charitable sector, with their emphasis on sacrifice and duty, must now make room for new impulses stressing empowerment, self-realization, self-help, and even self-interest. A sector whose mythology celebrates independence must now come to terms with the need for close working relationships with business and government to solve pressing public problems. Finally, traditional notions of arms-length philanthropy, alms-giving and service as the principal vehicles of nonprofit action must be reconciled with new demands for citizen involvement, for active engagement in societal problem-solving, and even for direct means for deciding which public goods are worthy of support. This may require not only new ways of thinking, but also new legal structures. For example, the existing restrictions on the advocacy activity of nonprofit organizations, far from being tightened, as is now being proposed in the US Congress, may need to be significantly relaxed to allow nonprofit organizations to respond to the new citizen demands for involvement that now exist, and that should indeed exist in a robust democracy.

To come to terms with these developments, several steps are needed (Salamon 1997). The first is better monitoring of the changing roles and responsibilities of nonprofit and for-profit institutions in a variety of policy fields to identify more precisely the challenges the sector is facing. Although the information now available on the nonprofit sector in the United States is vastly improved over what it was a decade and a half ago, no regular mechanism exists for monitoring the fiscal health of the sector on a timely basis, or for charting the changing competitive position of nonprofit providers versus for-profit ones across a broad front.

Second, a mechanism is needed through which the basic values and beliefs of this sector can be re-examined in the light of contemporary realities. As Gardner has put it (1981: 115): 'Anyone concerned about the continuous renewal of society must be concerned for the renewal of that society's values and beliefs'. Renewing the nonprofit sector's values and beliefs needs to begin at state and local level, and should involve participants not only from the civil society sector, but from government and business as well.

Third, serious consideration must be given to a variety of concrete proposals that can revitalize the nonprofit sector and reconnect it to its citizen base. These could include the creation of a 'charity tax credit' to replace the current deduction system for stimulating charitable contributions; the deregulation of nonprofit advocacy to stimulate greater nonprofit involvement in civic life; and the increased use of matching grants by government – to tie public funding more directly to citizen desires and provide incentives for nonprofit organizations to preserve their volunteer and charitable bases of support.

Fourth, a significant media campaign is needed to overcome the prevailing misconceptions and educate the public about the role that nonprofit organizations play and the way public problems are actually addressed in the United States. This will require something other than a celebration of nonprofit successes or a recitation of the standard mythology about the importance of voluntarism and the accomplishments of private charity. What should be emphasized instead is the modern reality of nonprofit organizations working collaboratively with government and the business sector to respond to societal needs.

Finally, efforts must be made to restore public trust in both the effectiveness and the honourableness of this sector. This will require strengthening the accountability mechanisms within the nonprofit sector and greater attention to measuring nonprofit effectiveness.

Conclusion and implications

The building of sustainable civil society sectors has been a focus of immense concern in many parts of the world in recent years, from the newly emerging democracies of Central and Eastern Europe to the post-colonial regions of Africa, Asia and Latin America. Taken for granted in these discussions, however, has been the assumption that such a sector is already securely in place in much of the developed world, and certainly in the United States.

What the discussion here has made clear, however, is that the survival and prosperity of nonprofit institutions is not only at issue in the emerging democracies of the East and South; it is also very much in question in the mature market economies of the North and West. Indeed, the very maturation and growth of nonprofit institutions may paradoxically pose challenges to their continued viability and support. Certainly in the United States, where a somewhat naive myth of voluntarism has long enveloped the nonprofit sector, recent years have witnessed a steady broadening of the gap between what nonprofit organizations have had to do to prosper and grow and what popular mythologies have expected them to do to retain public support. The upshot has been a crisis of legitimacy for America's nonprofit sector that has manifested itself in declining public confidence, growing demands for greater accountability, challenges to tax-exempt status, a questioning of the sector's advocacy role, and a growing unease about a whole range of pay and perquisite issues.

Whether the recent American experience is an isolated case, or the harbinger of challenges facing nonprofit institutions in other countries that are not as heavily burdened with America's peculiar myths, is difficult to determine. Indeed, there are those who question how seriously to take the developments outlined here even as they apply to the United States. What the discussion here seems to suggest, however, is that civil society is a rather fragile organism in every society, even one like the United States where commitment to this type of organization is an integral part of national heritage. More than that, the role and character of these organizations can no more be frozen in time than those of other types of institution: they must evolve in response to new circumstances and be re-examined in light of new opportunities and needs.

Those committed to the sustenance of a sphere of independent action outside the market and the state, whether in the United States or elsewhere, can therefore not afford to take the survival of this set of institutions for granted. To the contrary, they would do well to heed John Gardner's reminder that

> The nurturing of values that maintain a society's moral tone – or allow that moral tone to slacken – is going on every day, for good or ill. It is not the dull exercise in ancestral piety that some adults make it seem. ... Men and women who understand this truth and accept its implications will be well fitted to renew the moral order – and to renew their society as well. They will understand that the tasks of renewal are endless. They will understand that their society is not like a machine that is created at some

point in time and then maintained with a minimum of effort; a society is being continuously re-created, for good or ill, by its members. This will strike some as a burdensome responsibility, but it will summon others to greatness.

(Gardner 1981: 127)

It is precisely such greatness that the preservation of a viable private nonprofit sector, even in the developed democracies, apparently continues to require.

Notes

1 Data reported here include religious congregations, which comprise roughly 375,000 organizations.
2 The increased efficiency option, while theoretically available, has limited applicability to many of the fields of nonprofit action, given their labour-intensive, personal-care character.
3 Between 1977 and 1992, the share of all estate tax returns that made provision for charitable bequests declined from 22.1 per cent to 18.6 per cent. During this same period, while the value of estates increased by 74 per cent, the value of the charitable bequests from these estates increased by only 19 per cent. Thus both the share of all estates making provision for charitable bequests and the share of the wealth of these estates going to charitable purposes has declined (Hodgkinson *et al.* 1996: 91).

References

American Hospital Association (1998) *Hospital Statistics 1996*, Chicago: American Hospital Association.

Avery, R. and Rendell, M. (1993) 'Inheritance and wealth', paper prepared for delivery at the American Statistical Association.

Brown, M. (1996) 'Commentary: the commercialization of America's voluntary health care system', *Health Care Management Review*, 21, 3: 13–18.

Dennis, K. (1996) 'Charities on the dole', *Policy Review: The Journal of American Citizenship*, 76: 5.

Fetter, F. (1901–2) 'The subsidizing of private charities', *American Journal of Sociology*, 7, 3: 359–85.

Fisher, J. (1993) *The Road from Rio: Sustainable Development and the Nongovernmental Movement in the Third World*, Connecticut: Praeger.

Gardner, J. (1981) *Self-Renewal: The Individual and the Innovative Society*, revised edn, New York: Norton.

Garr, R. (1995) *Reinvesting in America: The Grassroots Movements that Are Feeding the Hungry, Housing the Homeless, and Putting Americans Back to Work*, Reading MA: Addison-Wesley.

Hall, P. D. (1987) 'A historical overview of the private nonprofit sector', in W. Powell (ed.) *The Nonprofit Sector: A Research Handbook*, New Haven: Yale University Press.

Hart, P. and Teeter, R. (1995) *A National Public Opinion Survey Conducted for the Council for Excellence in Government*, Washington DC: Council for Excellence in Government.

Hasan, M. (1995) 'Let's end the nonprofit charade', *New England Journal of Medicine*, 334, 16: 1055–8.

Herzlinger, R. (1996) 'Can public trust in nonprofits and governments be restored?', *Harvard Business Review*, 74, 2: 97–107.

Hodgkinson, V. and Weitzman, M. (1994) *Giving and Volunteering in the United States*, Washington: Independent Sector.

Hodgkinson, V., Weitzman, M., Abrahams, J., Crutchfield, E. and Stevenson, D. R. (1996) *Nonprofit Almanac 1996–7: Dimensions of the Independent Sector*, San Francisco: Jossey-Bass.

Ladd, E. (1996) 'The data just don't show erosion of America's social capital', *The Public Perspective*, June/July: 5–22.

Logan, D., Roy, D. and Regelbrugge, L. (1997) *Global Corporate Citizenship: Rationale and Strategies*, Washington: Hitachi Foundation.

Lubove, Roy (1968) *The Struggle for Social Security 1900–1935*, Cambridge MA: Harvard University Press.

McKnight, John (1995) *The Careless Society: Community and its Counterfeits*, New York: Basic Books.

Meyer, H., Hudson, T., Cain, J. E., Carr, S. L. and Zacharias, D. (1996) 'Selling…or selling out', *Hospitals and Health Networks*, June, 5: 21–46.

National Commission on Philanthropy and Civic Renewal (1997) *Report of the National Commission on Philanthropy and Civic Renewal*, Washington DC: National Commission on Philanthropy and Civic Renewal.

Nelson, Jane (1996) *Business as Partners in Development: Creating Wealth for Countries, Companies, and Communities*, London: Prince of Wales Business Leaders Forum.

Nielsen, W. (1979) *The Endangered Sector*, New York: Columbia University Press.

Potter, M. and Longest, B. (1994) 'The divergence of federal and state policies on the charitable tax exemption of nonprofit hospitals', *Journal of Health Politics, Policy, and Law*, 19, 2: 393–419.

Putnam, R. (1995) 'Bowling alone: America's declining social capital', *The Journal of Democracy*, 6, 1: 65–78.

Ranci, Constanzo (1997) 'Government policy and future issue', in P. Barbetta (ed.) *The Nonprofit Sector in Italy*, the Johns Hopkins Nonprofit Sector Series, eds Lester M. Salamon and Helmut K. Anheier, Manchester: Manchester University Press.

Salamon, L. M. (1987) 'Partners in public service: the scope and theory of government–nonprofit relations', in W. Powell (ed.) *The Nonprofit Sector: A Research Handbook*, New Haven: Yale University Press.

——(1993) 'The marketization of welfare: changing nonprofit and for-profit roles in the American welfare state', *Social Service Review*, 67, 1: 16–39.

——(1995) *Partners in Public Service: Government Nonprofit Relations in the Modern Welfare State*, Baltimore: Johns Hopkins University Press.

——(1997) *Holding the Center: America's Nonprofit Sector at a Crossroads*, New York: Nathan Cummings Foundation.

——(1999) *America's Nonprofit Sector: A Primer*, 2nd edn, New York: Foundation Center.

Salamon, L. M. and Abramson, A. J. (1982) *The Federal Budget and the Nonprofit Sector*, Washington DC: The Urban Institute.

——(1984) 'Nonprofit organizations: the lost opportunity', in J. L. Palmer and I. Sawhill (eds) *The Reagan Record*, Washington DC: The Urban Institute.

——(1998) *The Federal Budget and the Nonprofit Sector: President Clinton's FY 1999 Budget Proposals*, Washington DC: Report to Independent Sector.

Schorr, L. (1988) *Within Our Reach: Breaking the Cycle of Disadvantage*, New York: Anchor Books.

Shapiro, H. D. (1994) 'The coming inheritance bonanza', *Institutional Investor*, 38, 6: 143–8.

Smith, C. (1994) 'The new corporate philanthropy', *Harvard Business Review*, 72, 3: 105–16.

Smith, S. and Lipsky, M. (1993) *Nonprofits For Hire: The Welfare State in the Age of Contracting*, Cambridge MA: Harvard University Press.

Ullman, C. F. (1998) 'Partners in reform: nonprofit organizations and the welfare state in France', in W. Powell and E. C. Clemens (eds) *Private Action and the Public Good*, New Haven: Yale University Press.

US Census Bureau (1997) *1992 Census of Service Industries*, Washington DC: US Government Printing Office.

Verba, S. and Schlozman, K. (1995) *Voice and Equality: Civic Voluntarism in American Politics*, Cambridge MA: Harvard University Press.

Warner, A. (1894) *American Charities: A Study in Philanthropy and Economics*, New York: Thomas Y. Crowell.

Whitehead, J. (1973) *The Separation of College and State: Columbia, Dartmouth, Harvard, and Yale, 1776–1876*, New Haven: Yale University Press.

3   Putting narrow-mindedness out of countenance

The UK voluntary sector in the new millennium

Nicholas Deakin

Context

The last decade has been one of rapid change in the role of the third sector in the UK, a period 'bookended' by attempts from within the sector to assess the situation in which it now finds itself (Taylor 1990; Independent Commission 1996; 1997).

Essentially, the issue, as these successive inquiries have defined it, is one of finding a means of coping with the new pattern of relationships – both with the state and the market – that has developed over the past decade, without compromising in the process those characteristics that define the distinctive identity of the third sector itself.

But what are these characteristics? The sector (and those who are involved with it) carries a substantial quantity of cultural baggage – some of it inherited from earlier periods, when the third sector discharged many of those functions in civil society which it is now beginning to reclaim. Edwardian debates on the future of social policy are full of resonance for current arguments about the respective roles of state, market and voluntary organizations (Lewis 1995). In the course of that debate, the Webbs – now best remembered as the proponents of the paramount virtues of state action – once defined the role of voluntary organizations as being to act as an 'extension ladder' for the state. That concept still precisely fits the attitude of many politicians and civil servants towards the sector. Similarly, some of the concerns then expressed by many protagonists on the voluntary sector side about compromising the integrity and independence of philanthropic organizations (McBriar 1987) have clear echoes in current debates.

The historical parallels are seductive – and often instructive, too: but pushed to extremes, as they have been recently by some neo-liberal commentators (Whelan 1999) they are misleading. For both the material context and operating style that characterize voluntary action and the values which animate it have been drastically modified over the course of the twentieth century. To take only one obvious example, the brisk wind that blew through the UK voluntary sector in the late 1960s – a heady compound of community activism, second-wave feminism and environmental campaigning – helped focus attention on a different series of objectives: securing citizen participation, establishing proper representation of excluded minorities, and promoting user control. To use Beveridge's distinction, the emphasis in the agenda of this 'new voluntary sector' represents a shift from philanthropy to mutual aid (Beveridge 1948). Yet previous philanthropic concerns – the traditions of charitable donation and the provision of services for the unfortunate – have continued almost unabated, if less prominently displayed. Much of the diversity of the UK third sector, remarked upon by all commentators, is due to the coexistence of these successive layers of different practice and values.

However, in certain crucial respects the environment for voluntary action has altered in ways that fundamentally change the character of the task that it is now called upon to perform. As a result, any analysis that focuses solely on the attitudes and activities in the third sector itself is certain to be incomplete. The changes that have taken place in civil society as a whole and the role of the principal actors within it have helped to define expectations of the third sector and demarcate the space within which it can operate. These changes, which have been occurring at a bewildering pace, have not been confined to those countries in which there have been changes of regime, though these are among the most dramatic examples. They also extend to countries, like the UK, which are habitually thought of as paradigm cases of stability, with an unchanging set of traditional values.

One of the many virtues of the debate on the future of civil society that is now taking place (Putnam 1993; Hirst 1994; Etzioni 1995) is that it requires us to situate the developments that are occurring in the third sector in the context of these broader social and institutional changes. Adopting this perspective also enables us to focus on issues that transcend national boundaries, since many of the issues that are now affecting third sector organizations reflect shifts that are taking place across the entire developed world.

Leviathan becomes chameleon

One obvious example of these developments is the change in the role of the state. It has become a truism universally acknowledged that the days of state intervention to address all the major ills of society are numbered. Daniel Bell's famous dictum that the nation state 'is becoming too small for the big problems of life and too big for the small problems of life' (Wilding 1997) has been echoed both on left and right. It is almost as if the expectation is now that the state, convinced that its historical mission has been discharged, will voluntarily step aside rather than wait to wither away, as Marxist dogma once predicted.

In fact, this is a misperception. What has occurred, at least in Western countries, is not a withering away but a restructuring. The valuable series of studies conducted by the OECD for their PUMA programme (1995) confirms that this is the case in almost all their member countries. The 'enabling' function now defined as the key role for the local and central state requires not a withdrawal but a readjustment both in the nature of activities and the manner in which they are performed (Rhodes 1997). One key example of this change is in the area of regulation. The 'new regulatory state' that has developed to meet the perceived need to exercise control over the expenditure of public money is not, as Christopher Hood has demonstrated (1997), a weaker or a smaller state, but a very different kind of state. The impact of this kind of change has been keenly felt by organizations operating in the space left by the state's withdrawal from frontline functions in service delivery.

It is also a state that is less monolithic and more varied in the manner in which it carries out its functions, some of which are now modelled explicitly on practice in other sectors. Leviathan is no longer a single beast, as Hobbes proposed, but a shoal of smaller creatures – many of them with sharp teeth.

This casts new light on the question of competence. A standard argument for the transfer of functions from state to market or third sector organizations is that bureaucratic inflexibility is endemic to public sector bodies and cripples their capacity to deliver services effectively and responsively. Much of the momentum behind the adoption of privatization as a theory of governance is based on this crude perception. It is true that there is another view – that the state has forfeited its right to play a central role on moral grounds (Duncan and Hobson 1995) – but whatever force this may have in former communist societies (where privatization has also served a quite different function, as an easy source of profit for those politically best placed to benefit from it) it is not convincing as an analysis of developed democracies where a public service tradition in some form still survives.

If government is becoming more efficient – and although the picture will vary from one country to another, the general pattern emerging from the OECD studies suggests that it is – this implies that at least one of the arguments for third sector substitution is losing some of its force. In any event, the state to which the third sector has to relate is certain to be one whose relationships with other players will be of a different character – and in many respects far more demanding of those with whom it engages. This is likely to be as true at local level, where issues around service delivery present themselves in particularly acute form, as it is at national level. The transformation which local government has undergone in the UK is in some respects even more fundamental that that of the civil service nationally. This in turn has fundamentally changed the nature of relations between local authorities and local voluntary and community organizations – typified by the evolving 'contract culture' (Smith and Lipsky 1993; Lewis 1995; Walsh 1995).

Should welfare go to market?

The other potential partner with which the third sector has to deal is the business sector. Attitudes towards business and its role have ridden a switchback over the past decade, at least in the UK. The brash certainties of the 1980s, when business values and businessmen (note gender) were called in to address each and every one of society's problems, have now faded. Partly, this is the result of harsh experience. The collapse of credibility of the Conservative government stemmed in part from the disillusionment brought about by the recession at the end of the decade and the part played in it by the market-friendly policies of successive Conservative chancellors (Lawson 1992). The third sector was among those who suffered the consequences of these market failures, in terms both of its own access to resources and the need to provide an 'ambulance' for the victims (those experiencing loss of jobs and homes).

When George Soros, the principal beneficiary of the British government's ignominious expulsion in 1992 from the European Exchange Rate Mechanism (ERM), expresses doubts about the role of the market, a value shift may be not far behind. As Soros himself put it recently:

> As the market mechanism has extended its sway, the fiction that people act on the basis of a given set of non-market values has become progressively more difficult to maintain. ... Unsure of what they stand for, people increasingly rely on money as the criterion of value. What used to be a medium of exchange has usurped the place of fundamental values, reversing the relationship postulated by economic theory. The cult of success has replaced a belief in principles. Society has lost its anchor.
>
> (Soros 1998)

In a practical sense the perceived limitations of the market (and of some key business figures) has inflicted some damage on the notion of market mechanisms as the means of choice for the delivery of services, just as experience of recession has compromised the 'trickledown' theory of charitable giving as a rent on entrepreneurial success.

Nevertheless, business concepts, like competition, price, contract and customer relations, have permeated the debate about the future of voluntary action. In so doing, they have lost any specific political associations and become generally accepted as legitimate criteria to apply in devising the governance and assessing the performance of third sector organizations (Handy 1988).

If the experience of the past decade signals caution about a dominant role for the market domestically, there is still a major issue about the consequences of the rapidly developing role of global financial markets for developments at the national level and below. It is now frequently asserted that globalization is likely to undermine any attempt to devise new policies and plan for new relationships within individual countries. The scope for new initiatives, it is argued, will be determined by factors outside the control of nation states and their politicians – what amounts to a theory of geo-economics.

However, it is far from clear that this is actually the case, either in practical economic terms (Hirst 1996) or in relation to the domestic policies of nation states. Rather, most of the factors structuring relations in civil society are likely to continue to be determined by the historical, socio-cultural and political dynamic of the experience of individual societies. Nevertheless, it can be predicted that the sharpness of distinctions between them will be softened over time by common experience of structural change, by regional factors (as in the case of the European Union) and ideological shifts, some of which are common to age groups across national boundaries (for example, ecological protest and the trans-European campaign successfully orchestrated by Greenpeace against Shell in the Brent Spar case).

Yet even if the influence of global developments in the financial markets may have been exaggerated, the fact that they are widely credited with possessing a determining role may still be a significant factor. Paul Wilding has referred to a 'Dutch auction' in cuts in welfare expenditure among developed countries triggered off by a perception of punitive interventions in the case of countries not conforming to the market's stereotype of efficient management.

Nevertheless, a detailed analysis in the *Economist* (1997) confirms, with regret – given that organ's deep-seated prejudices on the subject – the view that the nation state is not immediately likely to meet its demise in the face of 'the triumph of international capitalism'.

It follows, then, that the nation state remains an essential feature of the landscape in which the third sector has to operate. At the same time, the impact of the process of transition through which the state is passing will continue to throw up fresh challenges – and provide new opportunities – for the third sector.

The UK case

The increased significance and higher profile of the third sector in the social and political economy of the UK has been ably charted by others (Kendall and Knapp 1996), so only a brief sketch is necessary here.

The rapid extension of activity in the sector has taken a variety of different forms: steady increases in the range of services provided; expansion in campaigning activity; significant levels of community action; a higher profile for charities in national debates; and continued substantial rates of participation in volunteering and informal caring. Triumphalist accounts of the state of the sector stress the richness and variety of this range of activities, and point to the substantial contributions now being made to the economy and to the stock of social capital.

Pessimists prefer to point to the over-stretched nature of much voluntary provision as a result of this expansion of activity, with strong pressure on both human and financial resources, and to the threat that this expansion poses to the values of the sector and its independence.

Following Lester Salamon's account of the situation in the United States (Chapter 2, this volume), we can find in the UK symptoms of all the major 'crises' to which he refers:

• fiscal and economic stresses
• issues around efficiency and accountability
• a potential crisis of legitimacy.

Much of the response to the challenges posed by these developments has been shaped by the changes in other sectors of civil society referred to in the first part of this paper. In particular, one of the most important of these, the rapid transformation of the public sector, has provided a new context for the operation of voluntary and community bodies at both national and local level. The appearance of an intermediate tier of state agencies, as a result of the restructuring of the civil service through the so-called 'Next Steps' programme and the reform of local government – the move towards the so-called 'enabling authority' – are perhaps the most important examples. The Nolan Committee's inquiries into standards in public life is another, which is likely to become more significant as the activities of this committee extend into areas where the voluntary sector now functions.

To help address these and other issues, the leading voluntary sector organizing bodies ('intermediaries') decided in 1995 to set up separate commissions of inquiry into the future of the voluntary sectors in England and Scotland. The decision to establish distinct operations is one reflection of an increasingly important factor – the enhanced emphasis on their separate national identity by the individual nations of the United Kingdom (I return to this point later in the chapter).

Both commissions were explicitly independent, both of government and their sponsoring bodies, and had chairs drawn from outside the voluntary sector – the academic world in one case, journalism in the other. They had virtually identical briefs: in effect, to set an agenda for the voluntary sector for the new millennium.

The English commission reported in July 1996 (*Meeting the Challenge of Change*) and the Scottish commission nine months later, in March 1997 (*Head and Heart*). Alongside these inquiries the Labour Party, then still in opposition, also carried out its own study, under the direction of Alun Michael, of the potential for a changed relationship between government and the voluntary sector in the UK as a whole. This was also published in March 1997, two months before the general election (*Building the Future Together*).

The analysis offered in the three documents is very similar. They all see the activities of voluntary and community bodies as being characterized by great variety – a wide range of industries, types of organization, legal forms and size and sites of operation. Much of the increased activity that has resulted needs no specific encouragement from the state to support it – merely an emphasis on a minimum number of obstacles to growth and freedom of action. But across the sector(s) as a whole, there are three areas that pose problems:

- availability of resources
- appropriateness of legal and fiscal regimes
- potential conflicts of values.

This in turn implies addressing the nature of the relationship with the state and the business sector, the potential for reform of the fiscal and legal environment in which the sector operates and issues around its governance. All these issues were tackled in the recommendations made by the two independent commissions, with the important distinction that the existence of a different legal system in Scotland led to different recommendations for reform in the legal and regulatory framework there.

The character of the government's response to these recommendations was largely conditioned by the stage of the electoral cycle reached at the time of their publication. The English commission, whose report was the subject of full-dress debates in both houses of Parliament, was (in effect) praised with faint damns in a formal response published in November 1996 by the Secretary of State for National Heritage, who was then responsible for the sector; snappily titled *Raising the Voltage* and illustrated with photographs of the Minister releasing balloons. The Scottish Office's response to the Scottish commission, rather more soberly presented and simply titled *The Government's Response*, was published after the Labour victory, on the eve of the triumphant outcome of the Scottish referendum which led to the revival of the Scottish Parliament which has been in abeyance since the Act of Union of 1707.

This more positive response clearly reflects the line laid down in opposition by the Labour Party in *Building the Future Together* and cantering on the concept of 'partnership'. As the preamble to that document puts it:

> In rejecting the old arid split between 'public' and 'private' Labour has recognised the richness and diversity of independent organisations and their potential. ... The need to balance support for voluntary organisations with respect for their independence has been recognised throughout our consultations and must be at the heart of any 'new settlement'.
>
> (Labour Party 1997)

The form that this settlement was to take was expressed as a 'compact' (a proposal originally floated in the English commission report). This would consist of a 'statement of the broad principles that will underpin the way every department and agency of government will work with voluntary organisations' (1997: 3).

'Partnership' is, of course, a highly ambiguous term, with important implications for the future of the sector. There are critics (Robert Whelan, for example) who dislike the whole notion and argue that the independence of the sector is threatened by any relationship with the state that has financial implications. He wants to see the sector revert to its (largely religious) roots and reassert its historical role as an independent force (Whelan 1996). From the opposite end of the spectrum, coalitions of community groups which see the state, both local and central, not as an ally but as an opponent to be challenged, have demonstrated marked unwillingness to be absorbed into the wider 'voluntary sector' in a partnership with their recent enemies. This criticism has much in common with those advanced by an earlier commentator, Barry Knight, in his 'Centris' report on the future of the sector. He would have split the sector into an 'authentic' smaller scale community-based entity and a larger formal, even bureaucratic service-delivering sector, with the concessions attached to charitable status being confined to the first group (Knight 1994).

Similar views have been expressed by those concerned about the implications for the sector's values. The parallel often drawn is with third sector provision of housing through housing associations, now largely funded by the state and (critics would argue) little more than its passive agent – extensions of the statutory sector, with little independent identity or discretion over policy. John Crawley (chief executive of a large association) has referred to partnership as a 'conveniently warm, whimsical and imprecise term like its close cousin "community", covering a multitude of sins', and has criticized the adoption of formal contracting and competitive tendering as the preferred basis for relations between partners, pointing to asymmetries of power and information between them as additional distorting factors (Crawley 1997). Behind these criticisms lie familiar fears about the integrity of the role and objectives of organizations as they adopt new methods of working to cope with the new environment in which they are now functioning – the sociologists' 'isomorphism'.

Where next? Addressing the challenges

Whatever else may be said of the reports of the two commissions (and a rich variety of views have been expressed [Craig 1997; 6 and Leat 1997; Lewis 1999; Kendall 2000]) they manifestly met one of the objectives for which they were established – to crystallize debate and expose key issues. In England, the National Council for Voluntary Organisations took responsibility for follow-up action on the report of the commission.

The most significant of these has been the process of setting in place the compact between the Government as a whole and the voluntary sector in England. This was finally agreed and signed in November 1998 by the Home Secretary for the government and Sir Kenneth Stowe (who had led the consultations on the voluntary sector side) for the English voluntary and community sector. The document follows the broad lines laid down in earlier reports; but it contains the important additional element of systematic review, by means of annual report to Parliament.

The English compact has been followed by an equivalent Scottish document, and now by a sequence of local compacts between local authorities and the local voluntary and community sector. The value of the exercise has lain so far as much in the process under which the compacts have been negotiated, at national and local level, as in the actual content of the documents that have emerged. They have yet to be submitted to the test of an open challenge by either party to the agreement. However, as Ian Hargreaves has commented, the process offers encouragement to the aspirations of the voluntary sector:

> the hoped for destination, from the Third Sector's point of view, is that it emerges as a partner of truly equal significance to the public sector and business, rather than as a partner of last resort.
>
> (Hargreaves 1999)

When the Prime Minister addressed the NCVO's annual conference in January 1999 it was on the compact that he placed particular emphasis; but he added a number of specific references to government policy since coming to power, as it has affected the voluntary sector, for example:

- the New Deal for Communities programme and its explicit emphasis on 'putting the community in the driving seat'
- new government programmes to encourage volunteering, now explicitly branded as 'Millennium Volunteers'
- the creation of a new technological infrastructure to facilitate community action, using advanced information technology
- a shake-up in the organizational arrangements, located in the Home Office once more, but designed to provide more efficient coordination of government policy towards the voluntary sector.

All these programmes and other wider developments under Labour – for example, the new stress on addressing social exclusion – have had important resonance for the voluntary sector. More broadly, the change of approach towards an explicit partnership model and the involvement of many senior figures in the voluntary sector with task forces preparing new policy initiatives, has led to a marked change in the climate of the relationship between the statutory and voluntary sector in the UK. Nevertheless, a number of key issues still remain unresolved.

The wider debate now taking place about the future of the sector stems from a variety of sources. Some of the key issues can be captured under Salamon's main headings:

Fiscal and economic crises

The level of support that can be expected from government in future will turn partly on the character of the relationship that emerges at both central and local levels. The Labour government has already secured close voluntary sector involvement in new programmes in the employment field ('Welfare to Work'); but the extent to which closer involvement will earn more substantial support is still problematic – recent indications are that the most significant impact will be at local level.

The question of support from business is one of the issues under review by a 'post-Deakin' task force. Here, much depends on whether a new relationship can be forged which matches the needs of both parties more closely than some past programmes have done.

The major new source of financial resources for the sector is the National Lottery, first launched in 1995 and phenomenally successful in its first years of operation. Grants to the voluntary and community sector as one of the 'good causes' which the Lottery is intended to benefit are administered by the National Lottery Charities Board (NLCB), which has acquired a good reputation for a balanced approach to the needs of the sector without entirely shaking off the stigma of being a grouping of the great and good practising old-fashioned philanthropy. The future of the Lottery as a whole is under active consideration by the government, and the likelihood is that responsibility for running it will be transferred to a non-profit making body, instead of the current commercial operator. Whatever the outcome, the issue of the use of lottery funds as a substitute for mainstream government expenditure is one that will require especially close attention.

Human resources and the issue of the level and composition of volunteering will also need close scrutiny – there is a real risk of loss of interest and involvement among the younger age group, to whom traditional voluntary action is often profoundly alien.

Efficiency and accountability

One of the key recommendations of the English commission's report was for an urgent review of standards in governance, with a view to promoting codes of good practice for voluntary sector bodies. This work has now taken place, and a report with recommendations has been published by the Joseph Rowntree Foundation (Ashby 1997).

This work has exposed a wider debate around the question of professionalism and professional values, and the extent to which the introduction of techniques of modern management may compromise the original mission of voluntary bodies by substituting alternative goals and a different locus of accountability. That debate continues.

Legitimacy

Diana Leat has a telling image of the way in which the voluntary sector has been regarded in the past by its potential partners – as a fractious adolescent trusted only with strictly defined limits and liable to indulge in bursts of unpredictable and emotional behaviour. In the past, the regulatory framework has sometimes seemed to be modelled on this view of the sector's capacities and maturity.

The regulation of the sector (south of the border) is largely the responsibility of the Charity Commission, which under the present Chief Commissioner has played a very active role in the debate on the sector's future. Strictly speaking, the Commission's jurisdiction only extends to the 180,000 registered charities based in England and Wales, but the Commission has attempted to discharge a broader function, by combining the role of regulator with advice on management for the sector as a whole. One important development has been the relaxation of the previously rigid terms of the Commission's guidance on engaging in campaigning activity, and another that of the status of organizations engaged in urban regeneration. At the end of his term of office, the Chief Charity Commissioner embarked on a systematic review of the Register of Charities with a view to 'shaking out' some of the worst remaining anomalies.

Behind this development of a more active role for the Charity Commission lies a more fundamental question: how far is the concept of charity, in the form in which it has evolved through lengthy processes of scrutiny of individual cases in English common law, still appropriate to modern circumstances?

Should the benefits (tax concessions) and obligations – the duties of charity trustees – attaching to that status continue in their present form? Both commissions recommended the substitution of a simplified form of test for charitable status – essentially, one of 'demonstrable public benefit', a new legal personality for charities, and clearer understanding of the requirements attaching to trustee status. However, these proposals await the outcome of further inquiries now being pursued by the NCVO.

In the interval, the concern Lester Salamon expresses about the incongruity of 'large-scale charitable enterprises which are headed by well-paid professionals and provide assistance to far more than those in greatest financial need' (Salamon 1997: 58) will also continue to be an issue in Britain. Symptomatic of some of the anomalies in the current situation was the discovery that Eton College, which as a educational establishment has the status of an exempt charity but is now required as a result of recent legislation to submit accounts to the Charity Commission, proves to have capital assets that place it among the 600 largest companies in the UK, just below the Body Shop and Hertz UK.

Some themes for the new millennium

By way of conclusion, it might be of interest to offer a number of speculations about the themes that are likely to become especially relevant in the next decade. I have four to suggest:

Privatization under pressure

It has been a noticeable feature of the reviews of developments in Eastern and Central Europe in the decade since the fall of the Berlin Wall in 1989 that enthusiasm for the market model has been distinctly muted. Much of the pain of transition has been put down to an over-enthusiastic reaching out for Western approaches without a full understanding of the implications of a competitive open market of money and skills, especially for those with limited resources (the third sector's traditional clientele). A particular focus of criticism has been the process of privatization and what is perceived as the undue emphasis on profits for business made as a direct result of privatization as against services for consumers.

This critique is part of a more general process of sorting the wheat from the chaff; as John Benington has argued:

> It is noticeable that the Thatcherite model for marketising public services is now being discredited even in terms of commercial business practice. ... Increasingly, modern firms are basing their contracts on close, competitive,

long-term relationships with their suppliers, where the aim is to develop a joint commitment to a common vision and a shared commitment to quality.

(Kramer and Roberts 1997)

This in turn opens up the interesting possibility that business may have some lessons to learn from third sector practice rather than the other way about.

Social democracy without the state?

Although the notion that straightforward imitation of business practice is the way forward for the third sector has now lost some of its force, there is still a substantial legacy from the 1980s in terms of the stress on the virtues of individual enterprise, which has been taken up by parties of the centre left and translates readily into third sector terms. The recent electoral successes of these parties suggests that we may be moving towards a looser and less centralized state which concentrates on facilitating rather than direct delivery of services, and an increasing substitution of networks for formalized institutional links: what is sometimes termed a 'stakeholder' society. All of these are themes which may have substantial implications for future practice. They have found a particular outlet in the vogue for 'social entrepreneurs', who will innovate by manoeuvring imaginatively in the space between the state and the market (Leadbeater 1997).

Towards a federal UK?

More specifically, the future shape of the state is now certain to change substantially in the UK as a result of the Labour Government's commitment to constitutional reform, which has led to the revival of the Scottish Parliament in Edinburgh and the creation of the Welsh Assembly in Cardiff. This development has opened up some important opportunities; there are already signs that a more flexible approach is emerging in the relationship between statutory and voluntary bodies in the new devolved system. An open culture of mutual exchange and learning could provide many benefits.

The other context in which federalism may be a major factor is that of Europe. Although the promised full-dress White Paper on the future of voluntary associations has not yet been forthcoming, the European Union's Communication on 'Promoting the role of voluntary organizations and foundations in Europe', published in June 1997, could open up substantial opportunities for cross-national working.

'New developments in civil society'?

More recently, there has been growing interest in the concept of civil society and the extent to which it provides a balancing third force between the state and the market, and a guarantee of the continued vitality of democratic institutions (Putnam 1993). Much of the current interest in the creation of intermediate institutions in developing and transitional countries is based on this view of the significance of a healthy civil society and the importance of sustaining it through providing the right legal and institutional framework.

Some of the current thinking on the future of civil society and the role of third sector bodies within it has been criticized as being little more than 'soft authoritarianism' in another guise (Phillips 1997). Certainly, the notion that third sector organizations can be called in to redress the failures of state and market (by the exercise of 'tough love') rests on a hopelessly impoverished view of their capacities and objectives. As Benington argues:

> I am under no illusion that civil society is an unproblematic concept or a utopian life-space. Voluntary and community sectors and informal networks are as riven with contradictions and conflicts as are the state and the market. Civil society contains within it a capacity for scapegoating, racism and violence just as it also contains within it a potential for co-operation, care and communal solidarity.
>
> (Benington 1997)

However, it is the diversity and unpredictability of the third sector that Benington portrays in extreme terms which is also one of its main strengths. This is what Ralf Dahrendorf likes to call its 'creative chaos'. To seek to define the role of the sector in purely reactive terms, and limit the space in which it must operate, the tasks it should perform and the style in which it can do so, is to deny the sector's nature. So is the attempt by some New Right critics to define third sector activities as 'non-political' and thereby exclude them from active involvement in the democratic process. This applies especially to the 'pressure groups' that these critics see as the 'typhoid Marys' of their model of democracy (Green 1993).

A broader approach necessarily involves taking risks. As Benington suggests, virtue is not always on the side of the little platoons or villainy the property of large battalions. But if the third sector is to continue to be the yeast in our cultures it must have the freedom to work freely. My title comes from the seventeenth century and the early debates about the respective roles and responsibilities of the individual and society – issues raised by the group that came together in the so-called 'Invisible College'. They argued for 'an endeavour to put narrow mindedness out of countenance by the practice of so extensive a charity that it reaches unto everything called man and nothing less than a universal good-will can content it'.

Three hundred years later, must we be less ambitious?

References

Ashby, J. (1997) *Towards Voluntary Sector Codes of Practice*, York: Joseph Rowntree Foundation.
Benington, J. (1997) 'New paradigms and practices for local government', in S. Kramer and J. Roberts, *The Politics of Attachment*, London: Free Association Books.

Beveridge, W. (1948) *Voluntary Action*, London: George Allen & Unwin.

Craig, G. (1997) Book review of *Meeting the Challenge of Change: Voluntary Action into the 21st Century* (the Deakin Commission Report) (Independent Commission on the Future of the Voluntary Sector in England, London: National Council for Voluntary Organisations, 1996) *Journal of Social Policy*, 26, 1: 111–48.

Crawley, J. (1997) 'A campaign for real partnerships', *Agenda*, 19, December 1996/January 1997.

Deakin, N. (1996) 'The devils in the detail: some reflections on contracting for social care by voluntary organisations', *Social Policy and Administration*, 30, March: 20–38.

Department of National Heritage (1996) *Raising the Voltage: The Government's Response to the Deakin Commission Report*, London: HMSO.

Duncan, A. and Hobson, D. (1995) *Saturn's Children: How the State Devours Liberty, Property and Virtue*, London: Sinclair Stevenson.

Economist (1997) 'The future of the state', special issue, 20 September.

Etzioni, A (1995) *The Spirit of Community*, London: Fontana.

Green, David (1993) *Reinventing Civil Society: The Rediscovery of Welfare Without Politics*, London: IEA Health and Welfare Unit.

Handy, C. (1988) *Understanding Voluntary Organisations*, London: Penguin.

Hargreaves, I. (1999) *NCVO News*, March.

Hirst, P. (1994) *Associative Democracy*, Cambridge: Polity Press.

——(1996) *Globalisation in Question*, Oxford: Blackwell.

Hood, C. (1997) paper presented to conference on 'Future Whitehall', London, 24 September.

Independent Commission on the Future of the Voluntary Sector in England (1996) *Meeting the Challenge of Change* (the Deakin Commission Report) London: National Council for Voluntary Organisations.

Independent Commission on the Future of the Voluntary Sector in Scotland (1997) *Heart and Hand* (the Kemp Commission Report) Edinburgh: Scottish Council for Voluntary Organisations.

Kendall, J. (2000) 'The mainstreaming of the third sector into public policy in England in the late 1990s: whys and wherefores', *Policy & Politics*, 28, 4: 541–62.

Kendall, J. and Knapp, M. (1996) *The Voluntary Sector in the UK*, Manchester: Manchester University Press.

Knight, B. (1994) *Voluntary Action* (the Centris Report), London: Home Office.

Labour Party (1997) *Building the Future Together*, London: Labour Party.

Lawson, N. (1992) *The View from No. 11*, London: Bantam Books.

Leadbeater, C. (1997) *The Rise of the Social Entrepreneur*, London: Demos.

Lewis, J. (1995) *The Voluntary Sector, the State and Society in Britain*, Aldershot: Edward Elgar.

——(1999) 'Reviewing the relationship between the voluntary sector and the state', *Voluntas*, 10, 3: 255–70.

McBriar, A. (1987) *An Edwardian Mixed Doubles: The Bosanquets versus the Webbs*, Oxford: Clarendon Press.

OECD (1995) *Governance in Transition: Public Management Reforms in OECD Countries*, Paris: OECD PUMA Programme.

Phillips, M. (1997) 'Etzioni and his critics', *Prospect*, August: 68–9.

Putnam, R. (1993) *Making Democracy Work: Civic Traditions in Modern Italy*, Princeton: Princeton University Press.

Rhodes, R. A. W. (1997) *Understanding Governance*, Buckingham: Open University Press.

Salamon, L. M. (1997) *Holding the Center*, New York: The Nathan Cummings Foundation.

Scottish Office (1997) *The Government's Response to the Report of the Commission on the Future of the Voluntary Sector in Scotland*, Edinburgh: Scottish Office.

Smith, S. R. and Lipsky, M. (1993) *Non-profits for Hire: The Voluntary Sector in the Age of Contracting*, Cambridge MA: Harvard University Press.

Soros, G. (1998) *The Crisis of Global Capitalism*, London: Little, Brown.

Taylor, M. (1990) *Report on the Future of the Voluntary Sector in England*, London: NCVO.

Walsh, K. (1995) *Public Service and the Market Mechanisms*, Basingstoke: Macmillan.

Whelan, R. (1996) *The Corruption of Charity: From Moral Renewal to Contract Culture*, London: IEA Health and Welfare Unit.

——(1999) *Involuntary Action*, London: IEA Health and Welfare Unit.

Wilding, P. (1997) 'Globalisation, regionalisation and social policy', *Social Policy and Administration*, 31, 4: 410–28.

6, Perri and Leat, D. (1997) 'Inventing the British voluntary sector by committee: from Wolfenden to Deakin', *Non-profit Studies*, 1, 2: 33–46.

4 Decentring America's nonprofit sector

Reflections on Salamon's crises analysis

Jennifer Wolch

Introduction

Lester Salamon (Chapter 2 in this volume) highlights bright spots on the nonprofit horizon, notably continued grassroots energies, growing intergenerational wealth transfers, and new corporate philanthropy paradigms. Nevertheless, he argues that the US nonprofit sector faces crises of fiscal integrity, economic role, organizational effectiveness and public legitimacy. Sectoral renewal is needed if the nonprofit sector is to 'hold the centre' and maintain its historically significant role in American society. Such renewal involves a re-examination of the sector's core values, and an embracing of a 'partnership model' of state, capital and voluntary sector relations in which the role of nonprofits is recast as the central, equilibrating 'civil society sector'. Salamon proposes concrete actions, including tax code changes, loosening constraints on advocacy, the establishment of a Civil Society Commissions, and public education programmes.

Many of these conclusions are incontrovertible. The sector stands at a significant crossroads in the US and elsewhere, and efforts at renewal make sense. However, drawing on analyses of the nonprofit sector as 'shadow state' (Wolch 1990) as well as recent US evidence on dynamics of globalization, localization of the welfare state, and cultural politics of difference, I advance a contrasting view. Rather than helping nonprofits 'hold the centre' through 'partnership' models, under conditions of economic globalization, social fragmentation and localization of public responsibilities, we need to 'decentre' the US nonprofit sector – away from dominant institutions, powerful groups and privileged places. Only by decentring can we challenge entrenched myths about sectoral independence and philanthropic values, and enable voluntary organizations to address the profound problems that confront so many societies today.

Economic globalization and the fiscal/economic crisis of the nonprofit sector

In the partnership model, the nonprofit or 'civil society sector' stands at the equilibrating centre of corporatist relations between state and capital. Ironically, however, the sector's fiscal and economic crises highlight risks of just such a corporatist arrangement. Optimally, all partners have equivalent power, problem solving together despite differences. But in practice nonprofit organizations are often junior partners (Kramer 1994; Smith and Lipsky 1993; Fabricant and Burghardt 1992). Thus when government defunds social programmes delivered by voluntary organization 'partners', crises ensue, revealing the sector's vulnerability as contract or shadow state partner. David was just lucky; Goliath usually wins.

These are the oft-rehearsed weaknesses of 'partnership'. Moreover, the 1980s nation-state restructuring linked to the adoption of market models of organization, make it varied, flexible, and efficient – and thus a potentially more exacting partner for nonprofits. But weaknesses of partnership loom even larger in light of economic globalization, which involves integration of financial and currency markets, and production, trade and capital formation networks worldwide, along with the rise of supra-national policy making bodies that partly govern economic, environmental and social policy (Drucker 1997; Webber 1997; Gibson-Graham 1996; Waters 1995; Dicken 1992; Leyshon 1992). The partnership model assumes relative state autonomy, but globalization undermines national autonomy, as certain powers and authorities are not only ceded to international agencies and governance bodies, but to multinational corporations. In world regions where globalization has followed massive nation-state realignment (e.g. the former Soviet Union), state autonomy may be so compromised that many 'service delivery' functions have been abandoned to mafia-like organizations (so-called 'gangster nations'; Koss 1996; Handelman 1995; Guillermoprieto 1994).

Globalization has important implications for a partnership model, limiting nation-state ability to create rules of the game. International agreements such as the General Agreement on Tariffs and Trade (GATT), the North American Free Trade Act (NAFTA) and the World Trade Organization (WTO) delimit nation-state powers to regulate, tax and spend if policies are deemed 'barriers to trade' (Mander and Goldsmith 1996). Multilateral initiatives in other issue areas also bypass nation-states or involve supra-state institutions in decisions that affect internal political affairs and development priorities. Such forms of global governance have spawned new transnational nonprofits as well as local sites of resistance and oppositional associations.

Internationalization has also triggered internal shifts in national economic, social and environmental policy to maintain competitive advantages and enter new markets. Such internal policy shifts are not dictated by globalization, but rather arise out of social relations and political cultures in specific nation-states. The central and local state therefore continue to be of utmost importance in shaping voluntary sector contexts, underscoring the importance of place-specific historical, political and socio-cultural factors. Nonetheless, policy changes linked to globalization will increasingly shape the nonprofit sector's ability to enter into stable partnerships with the state. Reductions in social spending in many Western countries are an example. Prompted in part by concerns about global competitiveness, so-called welfare reforms may trigger a 'race to the bottom' as countries worried about welfare magnet effects and a looming labour-surplus population seek to inoculate themselves from the social fallout of global competition (Peck 1996).

Partnership also relies upon the proper conduct of business enterprises, and Salamon points to the new, salutary style of corporate philanthropy as evidence that firms may be trustworthy partners. But this rosy picture of corporate responsibility is unlikely to spread beyond large-scale organizations interested in, and able to afford such public relations (Wolch and Geiger 1985). Globalization has accelerated capital mobility, weakening corporate commitments to local communities and regions (Hurd *et al.* 1998; Heyring 1997; Galaskiewicz 1985). Moreover, competitive pressures in many sectors have led to vertical disintegration and outsourcing, flexible specialization, reliance on low-wage contingent labour, and plant closures (Storper and Walker 1989; Lash and Urry 1987; Gibson-Graham 1996). This is a world in which community-oriented philanthropy in the pursuit of enlightened self-interest is no longer as compelling as ensuring short-term returns to stockholders and gaining market share.

To summarize, in an era in which indigence may rise dramatically, largely due to state and corporate responses to globalization, how can the partnership model work? Moreover, should nonprofits help legitimize the emerging distribution of power and resources by softening impacts rather than challenging the processes producing such outcomes? Oppositional tactics by nonprofits will be increasingly vital to the redress of social ills and disadvantage. Yet will such opposition, if forthcoming, be tolerated? In the US, heightened political activity is intolerable; the recent serious consideration in Congress of the Istook Amendment, referred to by Salamon in his chapter, implies that bounds of acceptable opposition have already been breached, and could narrow dramatically in future.

Instead of collaborating to 'hold the centre', might a better strategy be to advance to the margins, and transform the sector into a space of resistance? Take, for example, the case of US welfare reform and its implications for the many nonprofit 'partners' providing services to poor people. Welfare reform rhetoric blamed public assistance programmes and clients for their economic marginality, and argued that the private sector would shoulder 'the burden' of employing welfare recipients. But what exactly is this burden that the private sector will bear? The real burden is on nonprofit agencies suddenly faced with rising demands for service, altered patterns of public funding, and mandates to monitor clients and enforce sanctions which include benefit terminations and evictions, on behalf on their partner the state (Salamon 1997; Wolpert 1997; Thomason 1997). Moreover, the risk of scapegoating nonprofit organizations is high, since reform was sold in part by asserting that with proper incentives, charitable giving and the voluntary sector would fill in the gaps (Gillespie and Schellhas 1994; Wolch and Sommer 1997). Rather than stand quiescent as the social safety net is dismantled, nonprofits could become the most critical site of resistance to pauperization in the name of 'ending welfare as we know it'.

Social fragmentation and the search for nonprofit sector legitimacy

Salamon recognizes the crisis of legitimacy facing the US nonprofit sector, rooted in contradictions between what nonprofits must do to survive, and how the public thinks they should behave, based on nineteenth-century conceptions of alms-giving, charity and altruism. The public must abandon such outmoded ideas, but nonprofit organizations must themselves 'make room for new impulses stressing empowerment, self-realization, self-help and even self-interest' (Salamon, this volume).

But the challenge is greater than Salamon intimates. Rapid social change has redefined the very nature of individual subjectivity, making 'citizen participation' a far more challenging proposition. Struggles around the rights of people of colour, women, Native Americans, immigrants, and gay and lesbian people, have stimulated new and varied conceptions of personal identity (Hooks 1990; Ferguson *et al.* 1990; Sandoval 1991). Simultaneously, transnational population flows associated with globalization, geopolitical shifts, economic crises and the communications revolution have increased place-specific diversity and awareness of interpersonal difference (Castells 1997). Individual subjectivity is shaped by multiple facets which include class, race, gender, sexual orientation, disability, place of birth and/or residence, immigration status, position as a (post)colonial subject, etc. (Woodward 1997; Canclini 1996). Since intersubjective identity shapes one's standpoint or perspective, growing population diversity has increased social fragmentation, especially in those major cities where diversity is a defining condition and urban populations may lack majority ethnic groups.

Such fragmentation is catalysing new forms of political practice and notions of citizenship that may impinge upon voluntary sector/state relations and the partnership model. Traditional party, interest group, and issue-based politics have been overshadowed by new political practices, in particular identity politics, which can penetrate (and even overpower) conventional types of political engagement. Identity politics has emerged as different aspects of identity have become discursively constructed as politically meaningful in new contexts (especially globalization; Painter 1995). These discursive constructions can serve to contest the legitimacy of certain identities (such as homosexuality or immigrant status) perceived as threatening to dominant values (heterosexism and 'family values' or national identity and security). Identity politics may also work to resist various forms of oppression (such as gay- or immigrant-bashing), through conscious attempts to revalue older identities (such as the gay community's reappropriation of 'queer' identity), by creation of valued new identities ('people of colour'), or by contesting dominant identity constructions (recasting immigrants as taxpayers and good citizens).

Identity politics challenges conventional notions of citizenship central to the partnership model. Citizenship is typically defined as 'a political identity of entitlements and responsibilities that is (potentially) equally shared in a liberal democratic society' (Brown 1997: 5). Conventional debates assume a unitary citizen-subject operating in a public sphere, but once we admit difference into the equation, this definition of 'citizen' (often implicitly white, male, thin, middle-class, and heterosexual) becomes problematic. Rather, 'the citizen' is recast as a social production, in flux, and open to multiple influences (Mouffe 1995). Citizenship practice, moreover, is not restricted to voting or campaigning, but involves an increasingly broad range of activities as the state devolves responsibilities to domestic, for-profit and nonprofit sectors (Staeheli 1994).

These perspectives on subjectivity, politics and citizenship suggest the need for decentring the nonprofit sector in another way – to allow for a radical openness to alternative standpoints, and active incorporation of different, marginalized voices from the periphery into a nonprofit sector traditionally dominated by society's mainstream groups. This is not easy, it cannot happen fast, and it will change the character of nonprofit enterprises. For example, Eric Mann, a Los Angeles labour activist, decided that instead of fighting the erosion of labour power on factory floors (which were closing down around him) he would establish a nonprofit labour/community strategy centre, addressing not only labour-related issues but community issues. His vision was of a multi-ethnic, multi-class, multilingual organization to strengthen the labour movement. But after many heated discussions about what the organization should do, voices from the periphery altered the course of the enterprise. The centre first challenged the regional air-quality agency to fight environmental racism. Then they organized a bus riders union to contest the disproportionate allocation of transportation funds to high-cost, low-ridership subways instead of buses, eventually winning a class-action discrimination lawsuit against the regional transportation agency – hardly endearing to potential corporatist partners! The centre's news comes in English, Spanish and Korean; events are multilingual. Thus decentring the organization – away from Mann's own white, male, class-oriented perspective, and towards participant concerns – recast the centre's orientation and process, and altered environmental and transportation politics in Los Angeles.

Decentring the third sector requires intellectual and moral flexibility, and a capacity for ambiguity and inconsistency; a mutual willingness to grapple with problems of unequal power and authority rooted in race, class and gender relations; and recognition of the disabling aspects of professional care-giving for clients. It may also involve surrendering cherished goals in favour of what others with a very different standpoint perceive as more crucial. Moreover, rebuilding support for nonprofit action through decentring the sector will involve redistribution of nonprofit resources across social groups, as opposed to self-sustaining loops in which donors support the provision of nonprofit services which they then consume. Finally, decentring is relatively inefficient and typically involves ongoing conflict resolution. This poses problems, since nonprofits are increasingly required by funders – especially government partners – to meet conventional and increasingly 'marketized' standards of accountability, as Salamon highlights (also Smith and Lipsky 1993; Kramer 1994; Gibelman and Demone 1998). But retreating to the centre in the face of such challenges relegates the nonprofit sector to irrelevance. The middle class is shrinking; the concerns of women multiply as they enter the labour market in ever greater numbers; and at least in the US, a majority will soon be people of colour, many of them immigrants who have faced death squads but have never read Alexis de Tocqueville.

Localization and the limits of nonprofit effectiveness

As Salamon makes clear, the nonprofit sector's effectiveness is increasingly contested. Such charges are in part spillovers from more general claims about government failure especially potent during the Reagan-Thatcher era. Here, nonprofits in partnership with the state become tarred with the same brush. Effectiveness is also questioned on the basis of the sector's perceived excessive professionalization and lack of accountability (Smith and Lipsky 1993; Leat 1990; Wolch 1990). But effectiveness may also be compromised by rapid devolution and localization of responsibility for social problems. Localization makes partnership even more problematic for nonprofit partners. Partly this relates to conflict management functions of the local state; the local arena is where the most volatile conflicts over resource allocation and distribution typically erupt, and where the most intense negotiations over how to handle dissent are conducted (Clark and Dear 1984; Cockburn 1977). As they are increasingly caught in this web, and dependent upon it for resources, nonprofit partners may be asked to solve problems but be unable to do so, adding to perceptions of sectoral ineffectiveness.

Constraints on nonprofit effectiveness in the context of localization arise from two features of the American landscape. One is geographic unevenness in nonprofit sector development (Wolpert and Reiner 1985; Wolpert 1988; Wolch 1990). Spatial patterns of nonprofits do not necessarily reflect the distribution of problems or service needs, but rather varying levels of local wealth; local traditions of generosity, government initiative and corporate philanthropy; and inherent limitations on redistribution in local economies vulnerable to pressures of global competition (Peck and Tickell 1994). Unevenness applies not only between regions but within urban areas also, with the poorest neighbourhoods having the weakest nonprofit fabric and resource levels (Wolch and Geiger 1983; Bielefeld *et al.* 1997).

Second, as higher tiers of government increasingly leave locals to cope with globalization, demographic change and withdrawal of safety-net programmes, place-specific and place-based politics loom larger for nonprofit organizations (Kodras 1997). In reasonably progressive places, this may not be so bad. But the situation is far less benign in the 'revanchist' (or vengeful) city, whose well-off residents and local politicians resist downward redistribution, work to reverse past social justice gains, and criminalize a growing labour surplus population no longer supported by the welfare state (Smith 1996). Should the nonprofit sector participate in such revanchism? Should nonprofit groups enter partnerships with local corporate and public sectors to silence the most disenfranchised by creating networks of homeless shelters, recovery houses and jails through which they can be recycled, or co-opt protest by promising to bring capital back to the inner city while refusing to spend the resources necessary to do so? Even where local politics are not so venal, devolution and localization with reduced resources may make local governmental and corporate actors unstable partners for nonprofit organizations, and tightly constrain their effectiveness.

A compelling example of these dynamics unfolded in Los Angeles after the 1992 civil unrest. Following withdrawal of federal Great Society programmes from poor neighbourhoods, and state and local service cuts after tax limitation measures of the late 1970s, local officials and their growth machine allies built a glittering postmodern downtown for international capital instead of investing in their internal peripheries (Davis 1990). These neighbourhoods had few nonprofit resources, which were instead concentrated in more affluent suburbs (Wolch and Geiger 1983). Combined with long-term private sector disinvestment, rapid immigration-driven demographic change and deep-seated ethnic tensions, these areas came to exist in a state of social and economic emergency (Wolch and Dear 1993). When the Rodney King verdicts touched off the worst civilian uprisings in US history, there was no federal allocation of funds to help the decimated areas and population. The city immunized itself from charges of neglect by conjuring up a nonprofit partner. Called 'Rebuild LA', this agency was charged with fixing the mess by calling on major corporate partners to locate their large-scale operations in the hardest-hit neighbourhoods. All hopes focused on this unfortunate organization, but the effort was doomed and the agency shut down after five years – after being universally castigated for lack of effectiveness. Thus a nonprofit organization was created to take political heat off the city, and became a scapegoat as, inevitably, it failed to meet public expectations.

Localization concentrates the problems of a partnership model arising from economic globalization and loss of state relative autonomy, social diversity and fragmented subjectivities, funnelling them into a limited area and burdening local actors with relatively limited capacities to resolve them. This context only reinforces the need for nonprofits to become sites of resistance if necessary, and for incorporating a greater range of subjects and standpoints. But since geographic unevenness of the sector also contributes to the crisis of effectiveness, it may be vital to literally decentre the sector, away from downtown corporations, foundations and major nonprofit agencies, and away from affluent suburbs which are now centres of power in an age of 'edge cities'. This is a tricky proposition; it is unlikely that communities of South Central LA would welcome hordes of rich do-gooders from Beverly Hills trying to set up nonprofit agencies. Instead, localization may argue for the creation of cross-town coalitions whose purpose is resource redistribution linked to programmes of mutual learning. These programmes could be designed to build nonprofit capacity in poor communities, provide alternative understandings of urban disadvantage among participants from more affluent communities, and keep the 'centre' responsive to the social problems and needs of the periphery.

Concluding remarks

Salamon's perspectives on the current dilemmas of the US nonprofit sector, and strategies for overcoming these problems, are grounded in long-term and intensive study of the so-called third sector. Many of his conclusions are incontrovertible: the sector faces fiscal, economic, accountability and legitimacy crises. However, I have argued that his favoured strategy of sectoral 'renewal' via a partnership with state and capital is unlikely to resolve such crises, at least in the US. Indeed, because of the rapidly changing context of nonprofit initiative – marked by globalization, social fragmentation and localization – a partnership approach could intensify these problems.

In a world characterized by social difference, resource contrasts and uneven development, it is risky to generalize from US experience alone. Other regions of the world differ sharply in nonprofit sector size, role and relation to welfare states (which are themselves heterogeneous). Moreover, the impact of large-scale dynamics such as economic globalization varies widely across nation-states, as do state policy responses. But a partnership model in which nonprofits might 'hold the centre' of an expanding welfare state system seems even less applicable to many other places, where civil society is undeveloped, state power is unfettered by democratic process, welfare protections are minimal, or the economy faces globalization without buffer. In such places – and there are many – Salamon's strategy of renewal and his suggested course of concrete action are unlikely to work. Indeed, it may be even more necessary to abandon 'the centre', which so often stands without a fig leaf to hide its corruption. Neither 'civil society' commissions, nor charity credit cards, nor a corporate Good Housekeeping Seal of Approval are apt to have much effect on the underlying dilemmas facing nonprofit sectors in such locales.

The rhetoric of social change and betterment, so pervasive in the nonprofit world, masks a reality in which the sector is increasingly expected to uphold dominant norms and values, protect existing resource distributions, and shield the state from attacks on legitimacy. Is this the centre we would hold? Locations at the margin are crucial standpoints for struggle, and thus for altering the terms of public debate and the concrete management of economic and social life. Decentring the nonprofit sector and joining the margins may therefore stand as an alternative – and ultimately more viable – strategy for the weaving of a new, more humane and inclusive social contract.

References

Bielefeld, W., Murdoch, J. C. and Waddell, P. (1997) 'The influence of demographics and distance on nonprofit location', *Nonprofit and Voluntary Sector Quarterly*, 26: 207–25.
Brown, M. (1997) *RePlacing Citizenship*, New York: Guilford Press.
Canclini, N. G. (1996) *Cultural Hybrids*, Minneapolis: University of Minnesota Press.
Castells, S. M. (1997) *The Power of Identity*, Cambridge MA: Blackwell.
Clark, G. L. and Dear, M. J. (1984) *State Apparatus: Structures and Language of Legitimacy*, London: Allen & Unwin.
Cockburn, C. (1977) *The Local State*, London: Pluto Press.

Davis, M. (1990) *City of Quartz: Excavating the Future in Los Angeles*, London: Verso.

Dicken, P. (1992) *Global Shift: The Internationalization of Economic Activity*, New York: Guilford.

Drucker, P. F. (1997) 'The global economy and the nation-state', *Foreign Affairs*, 76, 159–71.

Fabricant, Michael B. and Burghardt, Steve (1992) *The Welfare State Crisis and the Transformation of Social Service Work*, Armonk NY: M. E. Sharpe.

Ferguson, R., Gever, M., Minh-ha, T. T. and West, C. (eds) (1990) *Out There: Marginalization and Contemporary Culture*, Cambridge MA: MIT Press.

Galaskiewicz, J. (1985) *Social Organization of an Urban Grants Economy*, Orlando: Academic Press.

Gibelman, M. and Demone, H. W. Jr (eds) (1998) *The Privatization of Human Services*, New York: Springer.

Gibson-Graham, J. K. (1996) *The End of Capitalism (As We Know It)*, Oxford and Cambridge MA: Blackwell.

Gillespie, E. and Schellhas, B. (eds) (1994) *Contract with America*, New York: Times Books.

Guillermoprieto, A. (1994) *The Heart that Bleeds: Latin America Now*, New York: Knopf.

Handelman, S. (1995) *Comrade Criminal: Russia's New Mafia*, New Haven: Yale University Press.

Heyring, C. H. (1997) 'Civic elites and corporate delocalization: an alternative explanation for declining civic engagement', *American Behavioral Scientist*, 40: 657–68.

Hooks, B. (1990) *Yearning: Race, Gender, and Cultural Politics*, Boston MA: South End Press.

Hurd, H., Mason, C. and Pinch, S. (1998) 'The geography of corporate philanthropy in the United Kingdom', *Environment and Planning C: Government and Policy*, 16, 1: 3–24.

Kodras, J. E. (1997) 'Restructuring the state: devolution, privatization, and the geographic redistribution of power and capacity in governance', in L. A. Staeheli, J. E. Kodras and C. Flint (eds) *State Devolution in America: Implications for a Diverse Society*, Urban Affairs Annual Reviews, Thousand Oaks: Sage.

Koss, M. (1996) 'Gangster nations', *Los Angeles Weekly*, December 6–12: 22–8, 30–3.

Kramer, R. (1994) 'Voluntary agencies and the contract culture: dream or nightmare?', *Social Service Review*, 68, 1: 33–60.

Lash, S. and Urry, J. (1987) *The End of Organized Capitalism*, Madison: University of Wisconsin Press.

Leat, D. (1990) 'Voluntary organizations and accountability: theory and practice', in H. K. Anheier and W. Seibel (eds) *The Third Sector: Comparative Studies of Nonprofit Organizations*, Berlin and New York: de Gruyter.

Leyshon, A. (1992) 'The transformation of regulatory order: regulating the global economy and environment', *Geoforum*, 23, 249–67.

Mander, J. and Goldsmith, E. (eds) (1996) *The Case Against the Global Economy*, San Francisco: Sierra Club Books.

Mouffe, C. (1995) 'Post-Marxism: democracy and identity', *Environment and Planning D: Society & Space*, 13, 3: 259–65.

Painter, J. (1995) *Politics, Geography and 'Political Geography': A Critical Perspective*, London: Edward Arnold.

Peck, J. (1996) *Work-Place: The Social Regulation of Labor Markets*, New York: Guilford.

Peck, J. and Tickell, A. (1994) 'Searching for a new institutional fix: the after-Fordist crisis and the global-local disorder', in A. Amin (ed.) *Post-Fordism: A Reader*, Oxford: Blackwell.

Salamon, L. M. (1997) *Holding the Center: American's Nonprofit Sector at a Crossroads*, New York: Nathan Cummings Foundation.

Sandoval, C. (1991) 'US Third World feminism: the theory and methodology of oppositional consciousness in the postmodern world', *Gender*, 10: 1–24.

Smith, N. (1996) *The New Urban Frontier: Gentrification and the Revanchist City*, London: Routledge.

Smith, S. R. and Lipsky, M. (1993) *Nonprofits for Hire: The Welfare State in the Age of Contracting*, Cambridge MA: Harvard University Press.

Staeheli, L. (1994) 'Restructuring citizenship in Pueblo, Colorado', *Environment & Planning A*, 26, 6: 849–71.

Storper, M. and Walker, R. (1989) *The Capitalist Imperative: Territory, Technology and Industrial Growth*, New York: Blackwell.

Thomason, R. E. (1997) 'Heeding the cry: as welfare rolls decline, church charities are answering more pleas from area's poor', *Washington Post*, 23 August.

Waters, M. (1995) *Globalization*, London: Routledge.

Webber, M. (1997) 'Globalization: states, markets and Australia's industrial policy', unpublished manuscript, Department of Geography, University of Melbourne.

Wolch, J. R. (1990) *The Shadow State: Government and Voluntary Sector in Transition*, New York: The Foundation Center.

Wolch, J. R. and Dear, M. (1993) *Malign Neglect: Homelessness in an American City*, San Francisco: Jossey-Bass.

Wolch, J. R. and Geiger, R. K. (1983) 'The urban distribution of voluntary resources: an exploratory analysis', *Environment & Planning A*, 15: 1067–82.

——(1985) 'Corporate philanthropy: implications for urban research and public policy', *Environment & Planning C: Government and Policy*, 3: 349–69.

Wolch, J. R. and Sommer, H. (1997) *Los Angeles in an Era of Welfare Reform: Implications for Poor People and Community Well-being*, Los Angeles: Southern California Inter-University Consortium on Homelessness and Poverty.

Wolpert, J. (1988) 'The geography of generosity: metropolitan disparities in donations and support for amenities', *Annals, Association of American Geographers*, 78: 665–79.

——(1997) 'How federal cutbacks affect the charitable sector', in L. A. Staeheli, J. E. Kodras and C. Flint (eds) *State Devolution in America: Implications for a Diverse Society*, Urban Affairs Annual Reviews, 48, Thousand Oaks: Sage.

Wolpert, J. and Reiner, T. A. (1985) 'The not-for-profit sector in stable and growing regions', *Urban Affairs Quarterly*, 60: 487–510.

Woodward, K. (ed.) (1997) *Identity and Difference: Culture, Media and Identities*, London: Sage.

5 What crises, what challenges?

When nonprofitness makes no difference

Paul Dekker

Introduction

The previous chapters have supplied rich and thought-provoking accounts of major developments and challenges facing the nonprofit sector in the United States and the United Kingdom. As a continental European one would expect highly similar descriptions and analyses for both nations. The Britons and their cousins across the Atlantic are often found together in the same cell of typologies of economic systems and national policy styles: Reaganomics looked like Thatcherism, and the search for a third way by the next generation political leaders had something in common, too.

Indeed, some similarities can be found in the chapters by Salamon (Chapter 2) and by Deakin (Chapter 3) regarding government policy in the recent past and its impact on the nonprofit, third or voluntary sector. However, these similarities are overshadowed by very different assessments of the present situation and prospects for the sector. Against the background of a depressing combination and accumulation of well documented financial, economic, effectiveness and legitimacy crises in the US, the UK voluntary sector makes for a refreshing contrast, with only a few stress points and a great deal of willingness to address the challenges.

This different approach may have been partly caused by the positive shift in the political mood in the UK following the last general election,[1] but most of it seems to reflect real differences, especially the fact that the American nonprofit sector has deteriorated significantly. The UK may be closer to continental Europe than people in Europe sometimes think. And the US may be more distant: the cutbacks in federal spending that Salamon mentions are unimaginable in Western Europe. Other differences are evidently a consequence of focusing on different kinds of organizations: large sectors of public-serving and public-benefit organizations in the US case, and a more diffuse set of more-or-less voluntary and independent, service delivering as well as community developing, old and new organizations and initiatives in the UK.

Inspired by the British and American scenarios, I want to offer some reflections on the Dutch case. I start with the lack of the concept of a nonprofit sector in the Netherlands; then I offer a brief description of the structure of the sector as we constructed it for the Johns Hopkins Comparative Nonprofit Sector project; and finally I deal with ideas for 'revitalizing' the sector with visions of civil society.

The historical nonexistence of the Dutch nonprofit sector

Salamon's and Deakin's chapters outline a number of trends and problems which can also be recognized in the Netherlands. To mention but a few in Deakin's analysis of the UK: the evolving 'contract culture' in relations between government and nonprofit organizations; the risk of loss of voluntary involvement among the younger age groups; the growing importance of lotteries as a financial resource; and the growing interest in identity issues, especially the pleas to backtrack to the (religious) roots of the sector. Salamon's diagnosis of crises is more concrete, but similar national phenomena are harder to identify because of huge differences both of scale and of financial and administrative arrangements. For the Netherlands, some of the developments described by Salamon foreshadow what may happen in our country if we do not put the brake on recent administrative innovations and reject a number of proposals for further modernization of the welfare state. His warnings about the unintended consequences of narrowing differences between the nonprofit and for-profit providers are highly relevant for Dutch policy debates.

There can be no doubt that Salamon's and Deakin's accounts contain many relevant experiences and discussions for Dutch policymakers and their critics. However, a barrier to recognition of the relevance of the American and British trends and ideas, and to turning these into fruitful initiatives in our country, is the vocabulary of a single nonprofit, voluntary, independent or third sector. A unitary conception of the sector has no appeal and little concrete meaning in the Netherlands. The nonprofit sector is a category, but not an entity. One can construct it statistically (see below), but it does not exist as an object of government policy or subject of public debate. One might speak of a common culture of nonprofit organizations: someone who works in the nonprofit sector probably has more meetings and is more wordy than someone in the business community, and suffers less from hierarchy and more from insecurity than someone in the civil service. There are unions for the civil service and nonprofit organizations, and it is possible to write books about management in nonprofit organizations and to organize expensive conferences on the same subject. But talking about a nonprofit sector will almost immediately lead to questions about what is included and what is not, and most ordinary people would be quite astonished if the answer were that government agencies are not included, but unions and other interest groups are, as well as political parties and even churches. For economists, the nonprofit sector does include government. However, they normally talk about the collective sector as a financial category (taxes and social premiums are the source of expenditures including transfer payments) and about the quaternary sector if they talk about employment (categories of the standard industrial classification that are wholly or largely financed from the public purse). These sectors too both include the government. Closer to the international understanding of the nonprofit sector is the subsidized and premium-receiving sector which comprises organizations that receive government subsidies or funding from social security premiums.

All this is the vocabulary of economists, statisticians and bookkeepers. Historically, the economic framing of nonprofits has been outshone by concepts with stronger ideological and administrative connotations. When nonprofit organizations are discussed in politics or by the general public, two terms are used: 'societal midfield' and 'private initiative' (Burger *et al.* 1997). The 'societal midfield' stands for a wide variety of organizations situated between the individual citizen and the state. It encompasses organizations that provide services to the public (sometimes including independent government agencies, such as public universities), interest groups, and hobby and sports clubs and other voluntary associations. Traditionally, the term has been applied in particular to the pillars of denominational organizations in the Netherlands, with the exception of the political parties. Today the term focuses strongly on interest and advocacy organizations and on the vertical mediating functions of other organizations between the state and (groups of) citizens. Organizations in the societal midfield typically represent group interests and ideologies at government level, and they may support the implementation and acceptance of government policies in society.

'Private initiative' refers to groups of citizens rallying together in voluntary associations in pursuit of issues that supersede individual interests. Again, the term has traditionally been applied in particular to the pillars of denominational organizations in the Netherlands. Today the term is also used to depict – and to advocate – new forms of engagement by citizens in organizing initiatives in their own neighbourhood, for people who need help, and for mutual support. A typical societal midfield organization is a labour union; a typical private initiative is a home-help organization where volunteers predominate.

If people talk about a school as a private initiative, they are referring to the historical background of the non-state school; if they talk about the same school as an organization of the societal midfield, they are probably talking about noneducational functions of the school, such as the expression of some regional or denominational identity, the offering of opportunities to meet other people and discuss neighbourhood problems, etc. The term 'civil society', not translated, has become popular in the Netherlands because many people identify the societal midfield with the traditional denominational organizations and as the power base of the Christian Democrats. However, at the moment – several years after the defeat of the Christian Democratic party in the 1994 elections and the formation of a coalition government of right- and left-wing liberals and social democrats – the 'midfield' terminology seems to be experiencing a comeback, often with attributes such as 'new' and 'modern'.

Some of the trends and problems Salamon and Deakin discuss take on a different context in discussions about the societal midfield and the private initiative. Other such trends and problems play hardly any role in these discussions. In public opinion and political discourse there is no manifest overall concept of a nonprofit sector in which Lester Salamon's crises can accumulate. Of course, there are the financial problems of the welfare state, and some facilities and charities are more successful than others in finding financial alternatives to funding from taxes, and thus preventing an economic crisis. But this is not a problem specific to nonprofit organizations. A public 'public library', owned by the local authority, might be more successful in its request for voluntary contributions from parents than a nonprofit 'public library' that functions under the same financial regime (many clients probably do not even know whether their local library is public or private). Of course, there is a crisis – or at least severe and persistent problems – of effectiveness in the healthcare sector. But that is because we have an ageing population, more but expensive medical capabilities, and restrictions on raising the productivity of the care and cure of people. And of course, some people see a crisis of legitimacy in the educational sector: it is not self-evident that there should be a majority of denominational schools in one of the most secularized countries in the world.[2] There is no need to discuss these issues further here. The point is that few people in the Netherlands feel the need to connect the budgetary problems of the state and social security system to effectiveness problems (or at the moment, manpower shortages) in healthcare and to the denominational mismatches in the education sector in order to construct a comprehensive crisis of the nonprofit sector.

The present state of the Dutch sector and some disturbing trends

According to the Johns Hopkins Comparative Nonprofit Sector Project (CNP), the Dutch have the relatively biggest sector of twenty-two countries (Salamon and Anheier 1999: 6). According to the most recent figures for 1995 (Burger and Dekker 2001: 37) nonprofit employment (full-time equivalent) accounts for 12.3 per cent of the entire economy (12.9 per cent of nonagricultural employment; this figure is 7.8 per cent for the USA and 6.2 per cent for the UK). Following the CNP categorization, the most important source of income for the Dutch nonprofit sector is 'public payments' (58.4 per cent),[3] followed by 'private earnings' (38.1 per cent) and with only a small portion left for 'private giving' (3.4 per cent).

Table 5.1 shows distributions of employment, expenditures and revenues over fields in the nonprofit sector. The largest field is health, with 41 per cent of employment, 28 per cent of operating expenditures and 46 per cent of public (and third party) payments (almost all of this is insurance money).

Four areas of the welfare state are separated by a line from the rest of 'the sector'. The big four account for 90 per cent of paid employment, have 84 per cent of the operating expenditures, and receive 95 per cent of the tax and insurance money spent in the nonprofit sector. The biggest of the other areas is culture and recreation, but this is a borderline case: 'culture' (libraries, museums,

Table 5.1 Employment, operating expenditures and sources of revenue of the Dutch nonprofit sector in 1995 (%)

ICNPO groups	Employment[a]		Operating expenditures	Revenues		
				Public payment	Private giving	Private earning
Health	42.1	(5.0)	27.6	45.7	6.1	2.3
Education and research	27.1	(3.3)	20.0	31.3	6.1	4.2
Social services	18.9	(2.3)	13.4	15.1	10.9	10.9
Development and housing	2.5	(0.3)	23.2	208	0.0	56.6
Culture and recreation	4.0	(0.5)	6.5	2.8	14.2	10.4
Business/professional associations	1.9	(0.2)	2.3	0.0	6.9	5.5
Religion	1.1	(0.1)	0.9	0.0	21.4	0.4
Environment	0.9	(0.1)	1.5	0.6	7.2	2.4
International	0.6	(0.1)	2.1	1.6	21.9	1.1
Law, advocacy, politics	0.6	(0.1)	1.3	0.1	4.2	3.0
Philanthropy and voluntarism promotion	0.4	(0.1)	1.3	0.0	1.1	3.2
Entire nonprofit sector	100	(12.1)	100	100	100	100

Source: Burger and Dekker 2001: 38ff.

Note: [a] Full-time equivalent (fte) employment: percentages of the nonprofit sector (and of the entire economy between brackets).

theatres), with a lot of paid employment and public money, can be said to belong to the welfare state part of the sector as well, but 'recreation' (sports, social clubs) strongly depends on membership fees and voluntary work. This area and the other ICNPO-groups below the line form the less-welfare-state-dependent 'civil society' element of the Dutch nonprofit sector.[4] This division of nonprofit areas, which is similar to the situation in Germany (cf. Zimmer, Chapter 9 in this volume), contributes to the absence of a unitary understanding of the nonprofit sector.

As regards the welfare state element of the sector, it is becoming harder to draw a line between nonprofits and other organizations. In most areas it is still possible to distinguish nonprofit organizations that are rooted in the old private initiative, from the independent public bodies, PGOs (Para-Government Organizations) and Quangos (Quasi-Autonomous Non-Government Organizations) that have been established by government in recent decades. But if reorganization and privatization continue in the directions set out in the 1980s and 1990s – with further mergers and loss of identity of the old private initiative, increasing independence of public agencies, and unifying professionalization, marketing and management trends – the result will be large clusters of service delivery organizations, for which making a distinction between public, profit and nonprofit elements becomes futile.

Two examples of these trends must suffice here (for more examples see Dekker 2001). Elementary schools are the first instance. Since 1920, the Dutch constitution has prescribed a dual system of public and private nonprofit education. In the classrooms most differences between both kinds of schools have already faded away through secularization and converging professional standards, but in the 1990s a kind of amalgamation in governance began. Many municipalities are trying to increase the administrative autonomy of public schools. Since 1996 they have been able to opt for becoming independent bodies with a board of parents, or for full privatization in a foundation. Since 1998 even partnership schools, which offer both public and private education, have been allowed. There is still some debate about this legal innovation, and there are still many bureaucratic obstacles, but the growth of semi-public autonomous schools seems to be a clear trend.

The second example is domiciliary care. It began with private initiatives, and until the 1980s home nursing services were organized in 'cross associations', often several in each municipality in accordance with the local strength of the Catholic, Protestant and neutral pillar (Burger *et al.* 1997). These small cross associations have been merged with other facilities into large regional organizations (130 in the entire country) that no longer have any membership accountability, but behave as ('social') enterprises, basically paid for by social security money. Their managers want to be paid and want to operate like real managers in business; commercial employment services for nurses and additional commercial services for the clients are introduced as subsidiary companies, and so forth. At the moment there are many criticisms of the work of the home care organizations, and attempts are made to restrict them to the core business of care, but in the long run it seems unlikely that the introduction of full commercial enterprises to the home care market can (or should) be avoided.

In both examples, an ambiguity of public/nonprofit and nonprofit/for-profit institutional clusters has developed. The minor problem is whether the organizations for domiciliary care still qualify – or whether the privatized public schools already qualify – for nonprofit status in the Johns Hopkins Comparative Nonprofit Sector Project or any other research undertaking. The real challenge is to discover the dynamics of the new organizations and their interrelationships, and to develop policy and management tools to get the best out of these postmodern private initiatives for the public good. From this perspective, 'sectors' of specific services and client groups deserve more attention than 'sectors' of organizations with similar institutional economic features.

(How) should we defend the nonprofit sector?

The likelihood of diminishing boundaries around the nonprofit sector is also discussed by Salamon (in particular the for-profit/nonprofit distinction) and Deakin (more about crossing government/voluntary boundaries). The present situation gives rise to the strategic question of how to defend as much independent nonprofit territory as possible. I am not optimistic about the outcome of the present debate, and I am definitely not impressed by the way some allies of the nonprofit sector have embraced the 'civil society' concept to give their interests a more sympathetic and appealing label. The concept might make sense as a framework to discuss the present state of membership organizations and voluntary action, the contribution of advocacy groups to democratic governance, the importance of associational life for the reproduction of social capital, etc. But the concept is quite vague and needs a good deal of clarification and specification before it can be used in research. More importantly, it is potentially relevant mainly for the smaller, economically marginal organizations of the nonprofit sector in modern Western countries (in the case of the Netherlands, the non-welfare-state-dependent groups below the line in Table 5.1).

To me it seems a pure swindle to redefine established service delivering nonprofits as core institutions of civil society, as is a popular pursuit among allies of the nonprofit sector nowadays. In his chapter, Salamon proves himself to be a strong supporter of a revitalization of the nonprofit sector into a 'sustainable civil society'. However, it is not very clear what this might be, beyond something very sympathetic and all-embracing: it includes the modern reality of nonprofit organizations working collaboratively with government and business to respond to societal needs as well as representing a sphere of independent action outside the market and the state. I do not think this 'civil society' choice for the best of all worlds is a very helpful guide for the renewal of nonprofits. Wolch's alternative strategy (Chapter 4 in this volume) of 'decentring' the sector comes closer to the original idea of civil society as an autonomous sphere of voluntary involvement, associational life and public discourse. As far as it is a plea for a more critical attitude towards vested interests and a stronger focus on deprived groups in nonprofits, I sympathize with Wolch's reflections, but I do not think that her 'joining the margins' strategy offers a viable route for service delivering enterprises.

In my view Salamon and Wolch, and on a more abstract level Deakin too, remain much too focused on the nonprofit sector and its original aims: here and nowhere else should the great dreams of voluntary involvement, citizenship and solidarity come true. It might be better to recognize that major nonprofits have become part of huge semi-state and semi-commercial provision networks, *and* to generalize original nonprofit aims so they can apply to other organizations as well. Strategies to civilize service delivering institutions and make them more democratic, more responsive to client groups or more supportive of local communities, should no longer be restricted to nonprofits. To come back to the example of elementary schools in the Netherlands: one may regret that nonprofit schools have been bureaucratized, but is it not good that public schools are now adopting the nonprofit legacy of autonomy and parent participation? The question of whether nonprofits should universally aspire to the qualities of good institutions, public or private; or of starting new nonprofit 'private initiatives' of clients and patients as countervailing powers to the bureaucratic/commercial services, are ones that can only be answered by the different areas of the service delivery industry. They can certainly not be answered in the intellectual prison of 'nonprofit sector research'.

Notes

1 Another aspect of the difference might be caused by a overly pessimistic worldview of the American author. Salamon's account of public attitudes towards nonprofit organizations is too gloomy to the extent that he seeks to persuade the reader of a *specific* decline in confidence in this kind of institution. There is a well documented *overall* decline in the trust of Americans – in other people, in government and in all kinds of institutions (cf. contributions to Warren 1999).

2 Accommodation and core activities of the Dutch nonprofit schools are 100 per cent state-financed; generally small parental fees are used to fund extra facilities. Nowadays only a minority of the Dutch consider that they belong to a Christian church, but the vast majority of nonprofit schools are still Catholic or Protestant. In 1900 about 66 per cent of the pupils of elementary schools attended a public facility; in 1970 this figure was 27 per cent (and 43 per cent attended a Catholic school, 28 per cent a Protestant school and 3 per cent another nonprofit school), and in 1995 32 per cent (and 34 per cent Catholic, 28 per cent Protestant and 7 per cent other nonprofit).

3 'Public payments' are very dominant, but they are not all genuinely public (31.6 per cent is government, and 26.8 per cent is health insurance, including payments from private insurances) and the percentage is lower than in some other European countries and lower than can be expected from the positive statistical relationship with size of the sector for twenty-two countries.

4 International activities is another group receiving substantial public payments (1.6 per cent of all public payments for the nonprofit sector, but 45 per cent of the revenues of nonprofit international activities). This is so because a large part of public development aid is spend through NGOs, like NOVIB, that cannot ignore the government priorities in this field, but are much less regulated than for instance hospitals or schools.

References

Burger, A., Dekker, P., van der Ploeg, T. J. and van Veen, W. J. M. (1997) *Defining the Nonprofit Sector: The Netherlands*, working paper of the Johns Hopkins Comparative Nonprofit Sector Project, Baltimore: Johns Hopkins University Press.

Burger, A. and Dekker, P. (with T. J. van der Ploeg and W. J. M. van Veen) (2001) *The Nonprofit Sector in the Netherlands*, SCP Working Document 70, The Hague: SCP.

Dekker, P. (1998) 'Nonprofit sector, civil society and volunteering: some evidence and questions from the Netherlands and the rest of western Europe', *Third Sector Quarterly*, 4, 2: 125–43.

——(2001) 'Nonprofit-organisationen in den Niederlanden: entsäult, verpoldert und was jetzt?', in A. Zimmer and E. Priller (eds) *Der Dritte Sektor im Gesellschaftlichen Wandel*, Berlin: Sigma.

Hupe, P. L. and Meijs, L. C. P. M. (2000) *Hybrid Governance: The Impact of the Nonprofit Sector in the Netherlands*, SCP Working Document 65, The Hague: SCP.

Salamon, L. M. and Anheier, H. K. (eds) (1999) *The Emerging Sector Revisited: A Summary; Revised Estimates*, Baltimore: Johns Hopkins University Press.

Warren, M. (ed.) (1999) *Democracy and Trust*, Cambridge: Cambridge University Press.

6 The role of philanthropic foundations

Lessons from America's experience with private foundations

Elizabeth T. Boris and Julian Wolpert

Foundations are philanthropic organizations that accommodate donors who have agendas for society's betterment. Society's representatives in government reward the contribution of wealth with tax benefits and minimal regulation of its targeting. The accommodation is stable so long as foundations pursue an agenda that is more philanthropic than self-serving, and find a niche of good works that achieves some recognition. Foundation contributions in the past century to social, economic, cultural and political life in America have been very significant, but difficult to measure and assess. The recent growth of foundation resources and greater professionalization of management promise even greater contributions in the future. Yet foundations must balance preservation of their autonomy with the need to be accountable and responsive. Their activities benefit some more than others, and occasionally offend, neglect or disappoint important public constituencies. The policy and research community has the responsibility and better data resources now to monitor and assess foundation activities; this scrutiny may help them to 'be all that they can be'.

Introduction

After years of relative neglect by journalists and policy makers, America's foundations are increasingly newsworthy. The media have stories about tax breaks for foundation donors and accusations of self-dealing, foundations awash in more money than they can spend, slush funds for political campaigns, conspiracies to de-fund the Left, and get-out-the-vote campaigns to defeat the Right. These stories all contain some elements of truth, but much of the revelations apply to only a small minority of America's 40,000 foundations. Serious analysts note difficulties in making generalizations about foundation structure and programme activities because they are independently managed, largely autonomous and highly diverse. Nevertheless, they share in common custodianship over large resources of wealth that are enhanced by tax benefits but removed from public control. Analysts can not establish rigorously that American society benefits more from foundation custody of these resources than if government or individual citizens controlled them. But an accommodation has been reached that acknowledges the contributions of foundations as well as the obstacles to changing the status quo so long as benevolent acts greatly exceed the occurrences of egregious abuse or offence to power brokers.

The current crises facing America's nonprofit service providers have been nicely classified by Lester Salamon into four categories: fiscal, economic, effectiveness and legitimacy (Salamon 1997). How well do these categories apply to the nation's private philanthropic foundations? The term 'challenge' seems more appropriate than 'crisis' because the foundations have the upper hand as grantmakers rather than the petitioners. Foundations' assets have been growing so rapidly that for many the primary *fiscal* and *economic* challenges are how to distribute additional funds knowledgeably and carefully without surrendering autonomy over their priorities. The *effectiveness* challenge is a real enigma for foundations who themselves know little about the outcomes or impacts of their grants, and seem to prefer little visibility in major arenas of American life. The *legitimacy* of foundations is less of a problem now than in the past because of the regulatory framework set up in the Tax Reform Act of 1969 as well as self-regulation. Effective foundation lobbying and public education has neutralized much of the harshest criticism in the policy community within and outside government.

The lessons from analysing policy concerns about American private foundations are well summarized by Viola's remark in *Twelfth Night*: 'What is yours to bestow is not yours to reserve'. The sizable recent accumulation of wealth and scrutiny about how it is spent are burdens as well as challenges for foundations more than for the private sector or other forms of charitable giving. The major lesson from the evolution of America's foundations is the importance of foundation accountability in establishing a satisfactory accommodation with society. The understanding has been achieved, however, by their caution in questioning the status quo in America's institutions, and their even greater reluctance to claim a leadership role on controversial issues.

The coverage in this paper is limited primarily to current policy issues and challenges relating to private independent philanthropic foundations, not corporate, community or operating foundations. The analysis concerns the social, political and economic roles private foundations are currently playing in the US, and the key issues shaping the place and contributions of foundations in the future. The analysis starts with a brief description of source materials on foundation behaviour, an analysis of foundation origins and development, basic information on their niche in American philanthropy, and foundation policies and activities of concern to government. We then examine in broad strokes the implications of current regulatory policy affecting foundations, remaining policy issues, and the manner in which they are being resolved.

Source materials on foundation behaviour

The development of theory about private philanthropy and, more specifically, the behaviour of private foundations and their impacts are still at very preliminary stages. Some generalizations are possible in explaining why and how foundations come into existence, how their assets grow with the economy, and how they respond to government policies and regulations. Most inadequate is our understanding of how foundations select and target programme areas for their grant activities, and the impacts of their individual and aggregate efforts on American political, social and economic life.

Information and accountability

Thanks to the efforts of America's larger and more professionally managed foundations, to the Foundation Center, and to required annual reports to the IRS, a great deal of information is readily available about foundation assets and the uses to which the funds have been devoted. Open access to this information is an initial step towards accountability that benefits the public as well as the foundations themselves (McIlnay 1995). Readily available information allows society and government to observe how wisely, effectively and generously foundations spend their entrusted funds. The public can also assess how the foundations' privileged tax status, command over resources and targeting decisions do justice to civic needs and the opportunities for having beneficial impacts. Open access allows society to notice also how concentrated foundation resources are and how they have grown in recent years, raising its expectations about the good that could be accomplished.

Improved data about foundations are important to policy analysts as well, although very little empirical analysis of the vast data resource has been carried out thus far. Policy analysts must assess which elements of foundation development and activity are best left untouched by government, and which attributes and practices require remediation through public intervention and regulation.

An objective analysis of the political, economic and social role foundations play in contemporary American society would be a formidable task. The larger and more professional foundations do provide information about their philanthropic agendas, management, assets and allocations in annual reports and through survey responses to the Council on Foundations, a membership organization, and to the Foundation Center, an organization created to serve as a clearing house of essential data to assist grant applicants, the foundations themselves and the public at large (see Boris 1991; Council on Foundations 1996; Renz *et al.* 1999; Salamon and Voytek 1989; Trotter 1990). The data tell us a great deal about the management and grant activities of the largest foundations (from which the analyst can only attribute goals and priorities and roughly assess distributional effects), but virtually nothing about outcomes and impacts. The view of impacts is sketchy because of the inherent problems of isolating and measuring the instrumental role of grant activities and then aggregating their distinctive effects into some composite of foundation impacts. While foundations are conducting more evaluations than in the past, and scholarly analyses are more evident, the vast majority of foundations do not track the impact of their grants (for examples of evaluations see Council on Foundations

1993; Weissert and Knott 1995). Additionally, the vast majority of foundation grants are channelled through nonprofit intermediaries who themselves rarely carry out rigorous evaluation studies of performance and impacts.

Sources for modelling the behaviour of foundations

Can the behaviour of foundations be abstracted and modelled to yield meaningful insights for policy makers? A rational actor model with a single objective function would clearly be inadequate to capture the variety of foundation activities and practices. Rich descriptions of foundation behaviour are needed instead which give attention to: organizational and bureaucratic factors; the role of key donor and management gate-keepers; and the activities of government, peer foundations and other key players in the philanthropic arena (for examples see Diaz 1996; Magat 1998; Odendahl *et al.* 1985; Gibbons 1998).

Much of what is known about the role and impact of foundations in the past comes from the voluminous literature of historical case studies about the older and larger foundations and their founders that have traced the effects of selective grant activity on educational, cultural, social, humanitarian and scientific institutions. Yet most of the activities that are described occurred at a time when foundations were the principal agents in initiating new highly ambitious ventures (see for example Lagemann's 1992 account of the Carnegie Foundation; Karl 1987; Karl and Katz 1987). Foundations are more inclined now to provide incremental and supplementary assistance in programme areas that have been well established and are supported principally through other revenue sources.

The more contemporary case studies supplement the highly subjective and often self-congratulatory statements one finds in foundation annual reports, press releases and sessions of professional organizations of grant-makers. Valuable insights about foundation influence and impact can also be pieced together, but with some caution, from social, political and policy critics of foundations (see for example Freund 1996; Colwell 1993; Lord and Seymour 1997; Rudy 1970; Stefancic and Delgado 1996; Covington 1997). However, before turning to the specific policy issues, it is important first to outline some of the critical parameters of foundation origins, structure and behaviour that have sparked government interest and arguments for intervention.

The invention of foundations

Philanthropic foundations are marvellous societal inventions for capturing wealth in large chunks that can be directed into civic betterment. Foundations are especially useful in tapping civic-minded donors who have accumulated more wealth than they can or want to spend on consumption, reinvestment, or passing on to heirs. Donors and societies both benefit from the trade-offs that emerge from this partnership. The concentration of assets in the hands of foundations enables them to undertake ambitious projects, initiate and sustain charitable institutions and their services, finance the construction of buildings, provide educational opportunities through scholarships and fellowships, create a service infrastructure, and support diverse societal perspectives as well as unpopular causes. Foundations can also perpetuate philanthropic dynasties and enhance the reputations of their founders.

The origin of the foundation species

The societal conditions that appear to foster the growth of large fortunes, which in turn encourage the emergence of foundations, are

- a growing economy that favours individual enterprise
- tax laws (or their absence) that enable wealth to accumulate in private hands
- estate taxes that limit inter-generational transfers of wealth
- donors with a philanthropic agenda that is perceived as complementary to government's efforts
- a society that tolerates or promotes discretion by affluent donors or their agents for targeting activities that promote the common good.

A developmental framework for foundations that has been abstracted from numerous case study descriptions would posit an initial stage of total donor autonomy over disposition of accumulated wealth during a period of limited government and minimal taxation of income, wealth or inheritance. Society may be anxious to attract additional large donors to philanthropic efforts because government has a limited social agenda or until political forces can be mobilized to tax off more of the wealth. Foundations that form at this stage of the cycle are relatively unregulated. The outcomes of their early activities are mixed relative to the donor's own and society's expectations. Some philanthropic efforts are welcomed and others condemned. The lessons lead to further experimentation about the foundations' missions, comparative advantages and niche. Early donors are likely to be motivated by philanthropic concerns, but in later decades their ranks are joined by others more motivated by tax advantages, as those become more valuable. The early lessons provide insights for new government-sponsored programmes where foundation activities have pioneered, as well as policy remediation efforts to correct foundation practices that were seen as abusive.

The trade-offs

The donors who establish foundations are willing to surrender some very limited degree of autonomy in determining how and at what pace the wealth can be put to best use, in return for the tax privileges. In the trade-off, society, represented by governmental institutions, determines the price of giving by donors through its income and estate tax laws, and exercises some limited measure of control over the operations of the foundation, once established, through regulations, audits and courts.

If society's agenda for civic, social and cultural progress coincides with that of donors, then the donors spend their assets through the foundations that are established as government would have preferred had the wealth been taxed. In this happy state, government is inclined to reduce the price of giving and loosen its regulatory discretion. How much better it is to tax and regulate less and still have private wealth be dedicated to the public interest.

When prevailing values and preferences of society and those of donors are significantly at variance, however, then government may want to restrict the establishment and activities of foundations through taxation and regulations. Potential donors and governments can be expected to bargain with the carrots and sticks available to them until some accommodation is reached in the trade-offs involved in this private/public partnership relationship. One can expect a good deal of experimentation and probing until the partners have reached a satisfactory accommodation and some short-run equilibrium in the relationship is established.

Conflict of values

However, societies are generally diverse and rarely represented by unitary notions of the public interest or common good. One can argue that the preferences of those who have accumulated enormous wealth are certain to be different from those of the general populace and that conflicts are therefore inevitable. Wealthy individuals in a relatively unregulated free enterprise system with a weak governmental structure could try to impose their ideology, agenda and priorities on society through the foundations they control. Financial success is often accompanied by paternalism and arrogance. Some donors establish foundations because they feel that government (or the average voter) is seriously flawed or deficient and successful entrepreneurs like themselves are better equipped to exercise control over how the funds are spent for the public good. Many have also felt that existing charities were run inefficiently by 'feelgood' social workers. Early foundation donors recognized that planning of societal institutions was essential, but were alarmed by the growth of state-sponsored planning in European countries.

On the other hand, wealthy potential donors may not define their philanthropic preferences along narrow ideologic and class lines. Many are motivated by religious, political and stewardship values (Odendahl *et al.* 1985). They may in fact prefer that their wealth be dedicated to humanitarian and civic purposes that match broad societal goals or even be used in a compensatory or redistributive fashion. They may also be willing, after identifying a set of broad philanthropic objectives, to surrender control over management to an independent board of trustees and a professional staff.

The professionalization stage

Professionalization of management often leads to an entirely new foundation agenda. The original donors have often been anxious to see the fruits of their philanthropy in their own lifetimes, and to be quite open about their agenda for the nation or community. The Sears philanthropist Julius Rosenwald maintained 'the generation that contributed to making of a millionaire should also be the one to profit from his generosity' (cited in Rudy 1970). On the other hand, current donors and professional managers may measure their achievements by the growth and preservation of foundation assets and their stature as grant-makers.

Foundation decision-making

The critical decision-making issues for the individual foundation arise when they are initially established. Most foundations construct broad general mission statements and grant-making policies in their early stage of development and make only modest incremental changes over time. The original donors of the largest foundations set targeting objectives and operating procedures that are generally maintained by their governing boards and professional staff. Fundamental shifts in programme emphasis or style do not usually occur unless and until the locus of executive control has passed to professional managers who are given discretion for instituting change. Foundations generally do not have specific and clearly articulated programme or performance objectives that can be easily modelled. The policy decisions for the individual foundation include:

1   finding and establishing its niche in the charitable sector relative to perceptions of societal needs, opportunity to have an instrumental effect, and identification of appropriate and fiscally responsible nonprofit organizations to perform the agreed-upon service or tasks;
2   determining its governance and management structure, including the role of donors and professionals, board composition and its inclusiveness, disclosure policy, investment policy, expected lifespan and spending rate;
3   deciding its programme targeting priorities by sector, agenda, international or national or regional scope;
4   developing its grants policies concerning applicant-initiated or targeted grants, seed grants, grants for operating revenue, one time or long-term funding, monitoring and evaluation of grants and their impacts;
5   determining its values and orientation, for example, support for social change, interest in challenging societal institutions and public policy and interest in being an independent voice for community betterment and progressive change; and
6   deciding on its links with other grant-makers, funding forums, nonprofit service providers, corporations, government and the general community.

Of course, many smaller foundations never arrive at these levels of decision-making. They do local good works cheque by cheque. Even in larger foundations, many of these decisions evolve over time, especially if the foundation starts small and receives gifts that cause it to grow substantially.

Foundation responsiveness

Some of these initial policy decisions are altered over time in response to changing perceptions of how the foundation can be most responsive to emerging societal needs and opportunities for effective involvement. The foundations retain complete autonomy in most policy areas. They are free to develop programme areas and target their grants as they choose, as long as the activities fall within the governmental definition of charitable purposes – educational, religious, scientific, literary, relief of poverty, and other public benefit activities. They can theoretically be as responsive or unresponsive to society's priorities as they choose. The larger foundations, however, are sensitive to their reputation for achieving some good in areas recognized as important among society's leaders and the foundations they see as peers. Their grants policies, annual reports and public pronouncements typically reflect these sensitivities.

Yet foundations perceive themselves as innovators and initiators of programme activity, and often reject the new roles proposed for them, i.e. simply compensating for government cutbacks or bailing out nonprofits when their revenues from other sources are jeopardized. Salamon (1997) has shown very convincingly that foundation resources, even if retargeted strategically and spent at an accelerated level, could not compensate for federal cutbacks. Furthermore, to abdicate the discretion foundations now have to decide how their resources can best be used to enhance the quality and variety of American life could rob society of a badly needed independent voice.

Questions for foundations

A host of important issues currently concerns the larger and professionally staffed foundations, as reflected by discussions in their annual reports and sessions at professional meetings:

1 How to retain independent discretion about programme activities and yet be responsive to national and community needs.
2 How to fulfil the leadership role associated with command over significant philanthropic resources.
3 How to allocate the foundation's resources between responsiveness to current as opposed to anticipated future priorities.
4 How to become more knowledgeable about effective intervention strategies.

5   How to avoid the arrogance and bureaucratic problems that can come from an insulated community and a donor-recipient relationship characterized by grantees viewed as petitioners.
6   Who has the greater moral legitimacy, wisdom and ability to set priorities in targeting foundation funds – the foundation donors, professional staff, nonprofit service providers, or service users themselves? How is the responsibility best shared?
7   How to communicate more and be less 'gun-shy' about lobbying, advocacy, and support of risky service programmes and controversial issues.
8   How to communicate more and be more accountable and less self-serving in describing foundation achievements.
9   How to be more critical of abusive practices that are observed in the foundation community.
10 How to demand better performance from grant recipients, especially the nonprofit service providers.
11 How to determine the outcomes and impacts of their grants through effective evaluation practices.

External criticism

Foundations generally maintain a low profile, and their functions and accomplishments are not well understood by the general public. The consequence is often public under- or over-expectation, or more generally a lack of awareness of their role in supporting programmes and activities. Other shortcomings that have been cited recently are:

*   atomization in the foundation community that precludes concerted action
*   difficulty in exercising leadership in the wider community
*   persistence of a considerable gulf between the best run and the least capable foundation funding programmes
*   a communication gap between funders, fundees and policy makers
*   insufficient early alerting of the policy community about the warning signs and service needs for emerging crises.

Foundation efforts appear to be most effective and most appreciated when applied to programmes in their own host communities (which is the arena of most foundations).

Other critics, like Pablo Eisenberg (1996) have commented that

foundations have little concern for standards, performance, innovation and change. Their bureaucratic management has no clear vision and stifles intellectual ferment. There is failure of leadership and no vision in the big foundations and in the Council on Foundations. They have made collegiality into an art form and are not appropriately critical of one another. They need greater diversity by social class among their staff and board members.

Self-improvement and self-regulation

Foundations are currently experiencing growing professionalization of their staffs, somewhat greater penetration into riskier programme areas (such as family planning, drug policy, healthcare provision, etc.), more emphasis on field reviews of grant evaluations, and greater communication with nonprofit service providers on issues of mutual concern.

This highly simplified description of the framework of private foundations, the evolution of their partnership with government, and their current niche in American philanthropy was intended to identify the major issues that are pertinent to foundation decision-making and public policy. Many of society's concerns about their activities and practices may be remedied through their growing professionalization, pursuit of inclusiveness on boards and staff, and their greater openness and accountability (see for example Abramson and Spann 1998). Yet other concerns persist that are apparently not self-correcting. Some of the issues are structural and relate to foundations as a whole; others concern abuses that have been highly publicized but apply only to a few violators.

The structural problems concern the interrelated issues of the growth and concentration of foundation assets, the independence and autonomy from public control that these resources have made possible, and the limitations of self-regulation within the foundation community.

The current foundation niche in American philanthropy

The United States now has more than 44,000 grantmaking foundations (of which 39,200 are private independent, 2,000 are corporate, 2,500 are operating and 400 are community) with total assets of $330 billion ($282 billion for the private independent foundations). Their grants to nonprofit organizations totalled $16 billion in 1997 ($12.4 billion for private independent foundations). Grants for all foundations equalled 4.8 per cent of their assets (Table 6.1) (Renz *et al.* 1999). The focus is reserved here for the private independent foundations and excludes corporate foundations, community foundations and operating foundations. (We refer to independent foundations generically as private foundations, although technically both corporate and operating foundations are also private foundations.) Independent foundations represent 89 per cent of foundations, over 85 per cent of assets and 77 per cent of grants.

Concentration of foundation resources

The resources of private foundations, as in the nonprofit sector as a whole, are highly concentrated among a small number of very large foundations. The top

Table 6.1 1997 aggregate fiscal data by foundation type (thousands of dollars)

Foundation type	Number of foundations	%	Assets	%	Gifts received	%	Qualifying distributions[a]	%	Total grants[b]	%	PRIs/ loans	%
Independent	39,248	88.9	282,618,485	85.7	11,012,655	69.6	13,591,237	74.4	12,375,399	77.4	117,702	80.2
Corporate	2,029	4.6	10,886,570	3.3	1,872,479	11.8	2,181,679	11.9	2,066,454	12.9	13,018	8.9
Community	403	0.9	19,699,826	6.0	2,223,753	14.0	1,242,913	6.8	1,192,301	7.4	12,585	8.6
Operating	2,466	5.6	16,705,416	5.1	724,068	4.6	1,254,215	6.9	351,277	2.2	3,515	2.4
Total	44,146	100	329,910,297	100	15,832,955	100	18,270,044	100	15,985,431	100	146,820	100

Source: Renz, Mandler and Treiber 1999

Notes:

[a] Qualifying distributions is the amount used in calculating the required 5 per cent payout; includes total giving, as well as reasonable administrative expenses, set-asides, PRIs, operating programme expenses, and amount paid to acquire assets used directly for charitable purposes.

[b] Includes grants, scholarships, and employee matching gifts.

Table 6.2   Analysis of independent foundations by assets, 1997*

Asset range	Number of foundations	%	Assets	%	Grants	%
$250 million +	139	0.4	149,686	53.0	5,029	40.6
$50 to $250 million	493	1.3	49,952	17.7	2,129	17.2
$10 to $50 million	2,043	5.2	42,672	15.1	2,184	17.6
$1 to $10 million	10,686	27.2	33,405	11.8	2,024	16.4
Under $1 million	25,887	66.0	6,904	2.4	1,009	8.2
Total	39,248	100	282,618	100	12,375	100

Source: Renz, Mandler and Treiber 1999
Note: * Dollar amounts in millions; due to rounding, figures may not add up.

139 (0.4 per cent) of independent foundations (with $250 million or more in assets) account for about 53 per cent of total foundation assets, and the top 632 (1.7 per cent) foundations (with $50 million or more in assets) account for over 70 per cent. The 2,291 largest private foundations, i.e. those with assets of at least $10 million, have combined assets of more than $248 billion (85 per cent of total foundation assets) (Table 6.2). Only the largest foundations are professionally managed. About 2,000 of the largest 12,500 independent foundations (16 per cent) report employing staff. Independent foundations are less likely to employ staff than corporate or community foundations. Only at asset levels of $25 million or more do more than half of foundations report paid staff (Renz *et al.* 1999). The unstaffed foundations are generally managed by donors, their families and descendants, trustee boards and by legal advisors.

The foundation share of nonprofit revenues

The data also tell us that the independent foundation share of total US contributions, an estimated 8 per cent (i.e. $133.5 billion) in 1997 is dwarfed by individual giving (77 per cent) – and the independent foundation share of total nonprofit revenues ($621.4 billion) averages about 1.7 per cent (2.2 per cent for all foundations) (AAFRC 1998). Foundations must search for opportunities to be instrumental in a service arena in which federal, state and local government as well as individual and corporate donors have very prominent roles, and where many nonprofit recipients of grants also earn fees from their services, have grants and contracts and derive income from their endowments. Still, the $12 billion-plus of 1997 private foundation grants is critically important, especially in higher education and the arts.

Targeting of foundation grants

Foundations contribute to a comprehensive and diverse array of nonprofit institutions. In 1997, more than 80 per cent of foundation grant dollars tracked by the Foundation Center have been awarded in five broad areas: education (24 per cent); health (17 per cent); arts and culture (13 per cent); human services (15 per cent); and public and societal benefit (12 per cent) (Table 6.3). During this period, over 90 per cent of grant dollars was awarded to nonprofits for five purposes: programme support (43 per cent); capital support (24 per cent) (especially for higher education); general support (13 per cent); student aid (6 per cent) and research (6 per cent). The larger foundations generally support very diverse programme areas with hundreds of large and small grants. By way of illustration, the Ford Foundation, with assets that exceed $9.6 billion, distributed more than $390 million annually in programmes relating to urban, rural and community development, welfare issues, youth, environment, agriculture, AIDS, etc. A recent Ford grant to the National Housing Institute, for example, led to a report on *What Community Groups Can Do and Government Should Do to Save Affordable Housing*. The Kellogg Foundation used the income from its assets of $5.4 billion to provide $308 million in grants to international, national and local programmes in youth development, higher education, health, and rural and community development. The Annenberg Foundation has made substantial grants to improve instruction in elementary schools. The Mellon Foundation is more specialized in higher education and cultural programmes. The Surdna Foundation, with assets of $528 million, collaborates closely with other foundations and with grantees on programmes to prevent irreversible damage to the environment. At the regional level, the Fund for New Jersey uses the income from its $50 million assets to provide small grants to dozens of New Jersey organizations that try to remedy social, economic and environmental problems in the state.

Table 6.3 Percentage of foundation grants by major area of funding, 1931–97

Year	1997	1996	1995	1993	1991	1987	1977	1966	1957	1931
Arts/culture	13	12	12	15	14	15	13	17	4	3
Education	24	25	25	24	25	18	25	42	53	26
Health	17	16	17	18	17	18	24	10	16	32
Human services	15	17	17	15	14	27	21	13	10	14
Public/social benefit	12	12	12	11	10					
Science/ technology	5	4	5	4	6					
Social science	3	3	2	3	3	21	15	12	14	23
Environment	5	5	5	5	5					
International	4	3	4	4	4					
Religion	2	2	2	2	2	2	2	5	3	1
Other	0	0	0	0	0	0		2		1

Sources: Renz, Mandler and Treiber 1999; Margo 1992: table 7.5: 221

Critics of targeting decisions

How can the various grant programmes and their political, social and economic roles be interpreted? One way is through the assessments of critics of foundations. Criticism of foundation practices has come from both conservative and liberal sources. Foundations are either 'tools of reaction' or they are 'endangering our existing capitalistic structure'. Some analysts and critics suggest a biased political slant is observable in grants that support causes such as social engineering, incrementalism rather than fundamental societal change, change agents, civil liberties, citizen participation and engagement, building civil infrastructure, voting rights, and population planning.

Conservatives have attacked the big foundations for violating the values and intentions of the original donors with their grants; for being trendy and politically correct; for their involvement in issues such as family planning, abortion rights, gender preferences, voter registration and welfare rights. They accuse foundations and their recipient nonprofit agencies of improper advocacy, lobbying and political involvement.

The liberal National Committee for Responsive Philanthropy (NCRP) proposed in the late 1980s that foundations be publicly challenged by evaluating and rating their performance through studies of board composition and risk-taking in grantmaking, and publicly rewarded for good performance in assisting the economically and politically disenfranchised. NCRP's recent analysis of twelve 'right-wing' foundations shows that they are making large grants to think tanks, advocacy groups, and colleges for conservative projects on free-market economics and ways to limit government (Covington 1997). These foundations are said to support groups attempting to influence national policy and the next generation of politicians and voters. The conservative foundations maintain that they are only reacting to the so-called liberal bias of the large foundations.

Distributional effects

Margo's 1992 analysis of the distributional effects of foundation grants showed a pre-World War II pattern that emphasized the health, education and scientific research categories with little attention devoted to the arts, social welfare or religion (Margo 1992). A shift towards the education and arts categories occurred by the late 1950s and into the 1960s, and the share of grants declined in health, welfare and scientific research – then grants for education declined while those for health rose somewhat. Margo concludes that the distribution of grant dollars has varied in response to social trends and government activity, has probably been regressive in its targeting, and has bypassed certain population groups (especially minorities). The data record since the late 1980s shows consistent emphasis on higher education and somewhat more progressive tendencies especially among the very large and the regionally focused foundations (Table 6.3) (see also Ylvisaker 1987).

The composite effects

This basic information tells us that private foundations are now very numerous, have very considerable assets especially among a few very large foundations, and as a group donate, through grants and other charitable activities, about 5 per cent of their assets each year, and target with their donations nonprofits in most areas of civic and public life. Foundations are highly diverse and relatively autonomous in their programme activity, and are only loosely organized into a growing number of programme-related networks as well as regional associations. Critics can point to general tendencies towards encouragement of modest incremental changes in American society and selective biases in grant activity by specific foundations, but the aggregate picture shows a balance between responsiveness (with some lag) to society's prevailing social agenda mixed with sporadic attempts to advance public discourse on a range of controversial issues. Foundations want to be effective, but not so effective that they are accused of undue influence.

Do foundations have a powerful influence on contemporary American life and the public policy agenda? The answer would have to be that despite exhortations from their association, the Council on Foundations, most foundations do not try very hard to be influential in the policy arena (except on issues pertaining to their own regulation and tax privileges).

The US currently has a maturely developed and relatively stable partnership between foundations and government. The incentive structures, rules, comparative advantages, divisions of responsibility and practices are well established and function quite adequately in many respects for the benefit of American society. Private foundations, along with community and corporate foundations, command substantial resources and contribute substantially (and could contribute even more) in diverse ways to our civil society.

Policy issues for government

Why should society and government be interested in learning more about foundation operations and governance, and in developing policies to regulate their establishment and activities? Conflict with government about foundation activities and practices arises currently (in contrast to the past) only in very limited areas, including revenue losses from foundation tax privileges; accountability, disclosure and openness in operations; investment policies; political partisanship and lobbying; and payout rates. The policy concerns involve controversial foundation practices under current laws and regulations that some feel may justify review and possible new legislation, as well as areas of possible abuse of existing regulations or public trust.

Government may be interested in reviewing, for example, the annual pace of foundations' grants relative to the growth of their investment income and assets, and the sufficiency of current information reporting requirements. The potential abuses that merit monitoring include lobbying for partisan political candidates, use of foundation resources for private gain, excessive administrative expenditures, and potential fraud in investment practices.

The 1969 Tax Reform Act and its aftermath

The formation of foundations, the size of their assets and the amount of grants paid out are affected by both tax and regulatory policy and the state of the economy. The most significant recent legislation affecting foundations, the 1969 Tax Reform Act, resulted in increased regulation and taxation of private foundations. Foundations became subject to an excise tax on all income or an annually adjusted percentage of net income. Foundations were also prohibited from 'self-dealing' with each other and with donors, restricted from ownership and control of private business, limited from activities that influence legislation or political campaigns, and required to keep records on grants to individuals and non-tax-exempt organizations.

The 4 per cent excise tax on investment income (intended to cover IRS' regulatory costs) was reduced during the 1980s and currently stands at 1 or 2 per cent depending on grantmaking levels. The all income or fluctuating percentage payout rate was reduced to 5 per cent. A provision adopted in the late 1980s which limited administrative expenses that could be counted towards the minimum payout was dropped. Foundations must have qualifying distributions that equal 5 per cent of their three-year average of assets each year, or face payment of excise taxes. The rules allow for carryover of excess distributions to succeeding years, and permit newly formed foundations to phase in their required payout.

Margo shows how the number of new foundations and the real value of their assets declined in the 1970s after passage of the Tax Reform Act of 1969, but later rebounded and then accelerated after legislation permitting deductions of appreciated stock gifts to foundations at their full market value (Margo 1992). His analysis also shows grant rates of more than 7 per cent in the early 1980s before declining to less than 6 per cent by the late 1980s. Current grant rates (excluding loans, operating programmes, programme-related investments and other distributions that count toward the mandated payout) are 4.7 per cent, but there is great variation by size of foundation. In 1997, grants as a percentage of independent foundation assets ranged from almost 5 per cent for the 25,887 foundations with less than $1 million in assets to 3.4 per cent for the 139 largest foundations. Larger foundations tend to have a higher proportion of non-grants activities, as well as staff expenses that count towards the required payout.

The formation of new foundations and gifts to foundations provided strong growth in resources in 1997. Almost 300 independent foundations received gifts of $5 million or more, and nearly 150 received gifts of $10 million or more. Total 1997 gifts to independent foundations reached $11 billion. Older foundations without living donors are not generally recipients of new gifts. Gifts to smaller foundations are often used for grants, but some are added to endowments.

Among the largest independent foundations (with $1 million or more in assets or $100,000 in grants) assets have shown variable real growth, ranging from exceptional growth of 37.6 per cent the year before the 1986 tax reform took effect, to -3.9 per cent in 1990. Weak growth from 1990–4 was followed by growth rates of 11.5 per cent in 1995, 14.6 per cent in 1996, and 22.6 per cent in 1997 (Table 6.4 overleaf).

The 1969 Tax Reform Act also increased foundations' annual reporting requirements to the IRS – i.e. forms 990-PF and 990-AR (later eliminated) – and specified that the forms be made available for public inspection. The IRS enforces the regulations through review of the 990-PF forms that are filed, and through audits. States, sometimes through the office of their attorney general or charity officials, may also regulate foundations, but usually do not.

Issues government now neglects

Government does not seem concerned at present with a host of issues regarding foundations that it either does not regard as problematic or has chosen to put aside for the moment. These include the growing number of large individual fortunes which can potentially be attracted to philanthropic purposes through establishment and gifts to foundations; the assets flowing into foundations that may be too little or too much relative to the growth of wealth in our society and the taxes foregone as a result of current foundation tax privileges; the potential hazards of concentrated foundation assets in few hands; and the targeting of foundation grants relative to societal needs and priorities.

Some of the issues of concern to government are likely to be remedied by the foundations themselves; other issues are structural or pertain to a minority of organizations and may require revised legislation or greater enforcement of existing laws. Many critics of foundations from both conservative and liberal perspectives contend that individual foundations have been major players in setting the public agenda and influencing policy. A number of critics urge more extensive governmental restraints on foundations to limit their role. An equal number of critics decry the lack of policy interest by most foundations.

The issue of payout rates

Additional donor contributions to foundations, sounder investment policies, and booming stock prices have built up foundation assets much faster than the 5 per cent mandatory spending rate that most of the largest foundations seem to view as a ceiling rather than a threshold. The endowments of private foundations (with over $1 million in assets) grew by $54.1 billion (22.6 per cent in constant dollars) from 1996 to 1997, but their grants only rose from $9.5 billion to $11.4 billion, 17.2 per cent in constant dollars, between 1996 and 1997. Gifts to private foundations by their donors included the

Table 6.4 Growth of larger independent foundation grants and assets, 1975–97*

Year	Number of foundations	% Change	Grant dollars (in billions)				Asset dollars (in billions)			
			Current dollars		Constant dollars[a]		Current dollars		Constant dollars[a]	
			Amount	% Change	Amount	% Change	Amount	% Change	Amount	% Change
1975	2,284		1.47		1.47		25.56		25.56	
1977	2,470	8.1	1.63	10.9	1.45	1.6	28.75	12.5	25.52	0.1
1979	2,618	6.0	1.91	17.2	1.42	2.2	33.83	17.7	25.07	1.8
1981	3,208	22.5	2.58	35.1	1.53	7.9	41.53	22.8	24.58	2.0
1983	3,466	8.0	2.90	12.4	1.57	2.6	52.71	26.9	28.47	15.8
1985	4,100	18.3	3.72	28.3	1.93	23.0	75.66	43.5	39.18	37.6
1987	5,383	31.3	4.62	24.2	2.31	19.9	90.41	19.5	45.21	15.4
1989	6,147	14.2	5.24	13.4	2.48	7.4	109.65	21.3	51.93	14.9
1990	7,277	18.4	6.06	15.6	2.63	5.9	114.97	4.9	49.88	3.9
1991	7,489	2.9	6.54	7.9	2.58	1.7	132.91	15.6	52.50	5.2
1992	7,905	5.6	7.20	10.1	2.76	6.9	141.85	6.7	54.39	3.6
1993	8,403	6.3	7.94	10.3	2.96	7.1	151.66	6.9	56.47	3.8
1994	9,255	10.1	7.80	1.8	2.83	4.2	156.91	3.5	56.96	0.9
1995	9,685	4.7	8.61	10.4	3.04	7.3	179.95	14.7	63.53	11.5
1996	10,456	8.0	9.48	10.1	3.25	6.9	212.29	18.0	72.79	14.6
1997	12,458	19.1	11.38	20.0	3.81	17.2	266.34	25.5	89.22	22.6

Source: Renz, Mandler and Treiber 1999

Notes:
* Includes independent foundations with assets of at least $1 million or making grants of at least $100,000 in the year reported. In 1997, larger independent foundations held 94 per cent of assets and awarded 92 per cent of grants of all independent foundations.

[a] Constant 1997 dollars based on year average Consumer Price Index, all urban consumers, US Department of Labor, Bureau of Labor Statistics, as of March 1999.

$5.8 billion bequest of David Packard to his foundation, the $1.2 billion of start-up assets for the California Endowment, and the $1.2 billion to the Doris Duke Charitable Foundation, part of a total of $27.2 billion in foundation gifts for 1996 and 1997. While foundation gifts represent a significant percentage of foundation grants in some years, they are highly variable. However, assets and gifts have continued to grow a great deal faster than grants in the past two years.

Foundations cannot predict the growth of their assets, so most adopt a long-term payout strategy to sustain steady growth levels in their grants. Corporate and community foundations, as well as the smaller private foundations, with substantial flow-through revenues have much higher payout rates than the largest private foundations. The issue of payout rates is of fundamental importance because the tax deduction for the donor's gift (and thus the revenue loss for government) is generally taken immediately, while the foundation's grants are extended over a very long period. One could argue that foundation resources are enhanced mainly in boom periods and thus can be held in reserve for periods of greatest need, but one might question, as some do, whether it is desirable in view of the current growth of assets, to recommend higher payouts for the largest foundations. To make that determination, a more refined analysis would include the size of foundations relative to the growth in the nonprofit sector and the overall US economy. Still, the National Network of Grantmakers, an association of progressive funders, is recommending a higher payout for foundations (Triano 1998).

Why then do foundations not spend more? Why don't foundations plan for a limited life and spend their assets down? Smaller foundations do spend at rates much higher than 5 per cent, many larger ones have increased their spending rate recently, and a few have spent their assets completely and gone out of existence. In isolated cases, some may conceal inflated administrative costs in their programme budgets, with the result that yields to grant recipients are considerably less than 5 per cent. Others engage in operating programmes, enhanced communications, evaluation, technical assistance, and other activities that make them more accessible and visible. Attempts by Congress to impose higher spending thresholds have been met by strenuous, influential and effective lobbying. Based on research commissioned by the Council on Foundations, the 5 per cent payout was shown to permit foundations to exist in perpetuity given the variability of investment returns over the past fifty years (Trotter 1990). Foundations that depend on their endowments alone for revenue, tend to heed that research. The hope remains that foundations, with further prompting by their critics, will at some time in the future make better use of both their resources and their independence.

Summary and discussion

America's private foundations contribute in significant (but not easily measurable) ways to the nation's social, political and economic life. Though dwarfed by individual giving, foundation grants are strategically targeted, for the most part by professional staff, to have an instrumental role in arenas of public and civic life that are important to a significant segment of society but considered to be 'underfunded' by government, the private market and other charitable efforts. Foundations are independent organizations with virtual autonomy over their funding decisions, but they have organized collective efforts to provide information about their governance and grant activities and to lobby for preservation of their autonomy and prerogatives. Some foundations are more venturesome than others in targeting controversial and sensitive subjects for their intervention. The largest tend to make grants at the minimum level required by law, and a few support activities with very questionable potential benefits.

The activities of foundations that have attracted public concern, strong criticism and demands for additional government control, have led to greater efforts at self-regulation but also greater reluctance to become advocates or show leadership on controversial issues at the national or community level. Much as some critics deplore the recent activities of right-wing foundations to redefine America's social agenda, these foundations are pursuing a number of purposeful and well orchestrated objectives with a single-mindedness worthy of emulation. In contrast, the inventory of most foundation programmes and activities contains a multitude of individual good works, often at the local level, that lack clear direction and realizable goals. The full potential of foundation resources and their capacity for 'making a difference' is yet to be achieved.

References

AAFRC (1998) *Giving USA: The Annual Report on Philanthropy for the Year 1997*, New York: AAFRC.

Abramson, A. J. and Spann, J. (1998) *Foundations: Exploring their Unique Roles and Impacts on Society*, Washington DC: Aspen Institute.

Boris, E. (1987) 'Creation and growth: a survey of private foundations', in T. Odendahl (ed.) *America's Wealthy and the Future of Foundations*, New York: Foundation Center.

——(1991) 'Administrative expenses of private foundations: results of a multi-year study', working paper for 'Leadership and Management 1991 Spring Research Forum', Washington DC: Independent Sector.

——(1992) *Philanthropic Foundations in the United States: An Introduction* (revised 1998) Washington DC: Council on Foundations.

Colwell, M. A. (1993) *Private Foundations and Public Policy*, New York: Garland.

Council on Foundations (1993) *Evaluation for Foundations: Concepts, Cases, Guidelines and Resources*, Washington DC: Council on Foundations.

——(1996) *Foundation Management Report*, Washington DC: Council on Foundations.

Covington, S. (1997) *Moving a Public Policy Agenda: The Strategic Philanthropy of Conservative Foundations*, Washington DC: National Committee for Responsive Philanthropy.

Diaz, W. A. (1996) 'The behavior of foundations in an organizational frame: a case study', *Nonprofit Voluntary Sector Quarterly*, 25, 4: 453–69.

Edie, J. (1987) *Congress and Private Foundations: A Historical Analysis*, Washington DC: Council on Foundations.

Eisenberg, P. (1996) 'Philanthropy under fire', speech delivered at a meeting of Northern California Grantmakers, San Francisco.

Freund, G. (1996) *Narcissism and Philanthropy: Ideas and Talent Denied*, New York: Viking.

Gibbons, M. (1998) 'Who funded AIDS?: the role of funders concerned about AIDS, grantmakers as advocates and activists', working paper, Washington DC: Nonprofit Sector Research Fund, Aspen Institute.

Karl, B. D. (1987) 'Philanthropic institutions', *Science*, 236: 984–5.

Karl, B. D. and Katz, S. N. (1987) 'Foundations and ruling class elites', *Daedalus*, 116, winter: 1–40.

Lagemann, E. C. (1992) *The Politics of Knowledge: The Carnegie Corporation, Philanthropy, and Public Policy*, Chicago: University of Chicago Press.

Lord, M. E. and Seymour II, E. (eds) (1997) *Foundations in International Affairs*, Washington DC: Access.

Magat, R. (1994) 'Organized labor and philanthropic foundations: partners or strangers?', *Nonprofit and Voluntary Sector Quarterly*, 23, 4: 353–70.

——(1998) *Unlikely Partners: Philanthropic Foundations and the Labor Movement*, Ithaca: Cornell University Press.

Margo, R. A. (1992) 'The distributional impact of foundations: a historical perspective', in C. Clotfelter (ed.) *Who Benefits from the Nonprofit Sector?*, Chicago: University of Chicago Press.

McIlnay, D. P. (1995) 'The privilege of privacy: twenty-five years in the public accountability record of foundations', *Nonprofit and Voluntary Sector Quarterly*, 24, 2: 117–41.

Odendahl, T. (1987) 'Wealthy donors and their charitable attitudes', in T. Odendahl (ed.) *America's Wealthy and the Future of Foundations*, New York: Foundation Center.

Odendahl, T., Boris, E. and Daniels Kaplan, A. (1985) *Working in Foundations: Career Patterns of Women and Men*, New York: Foundation Center.

Renz, L. (ed.) (1997) *The Foundation Directory*, New York: Foundation Center.

Renz, L., Mandler, C. and Treiber, R. (1999) *Foundation Giving*, New York: Foundation Center.

Reynolds, A. (1997) *Death, Taxes and the Independent Sector*, Washington DC: Philanthropy Roundtable.

Rudy, W. H. (1970) *The Foundations: Their Use and Abuse*, Washington DC: Public Affairs Press.

Salamon, L. M. (1997) *Holding the Center: America's Nonprofit Sector at a Crossroads*, New York: Nathan Cummings Foundation.

Salamon, L. M. and Voytek, K. P. (1989) *Managing Foundation Assests: An Analysis of Foundation Investment and Payout Procedures and Performance*, New York: Foundation Center.

Schulman, B. (1996) 'Foundations for a movement: how the right wing subsidizes its press', *Responsive Philanthropy*, summer: 6–7.

Simon, J. E. (1987) 'Tax treatment of nonprofit organizations', in W. W. Powell (ed.) *The Nonprofit Sector*, New Haven: Yale University Press.

Smith, J. A. (1989) 'The evolving role of foundations', in V. A. Hodgkinson and R. W. Lyman (eds) *The Future of the Nonprofit Sector*, San Francisco: Jossey-Bass.

Stefancic, J. and Delgado, R. (1996) *No Mercy: How Conservative Think Tanks and Foundations Changed America's Social Agenda*, Philadelphia: Temple University Press.

Triano, C. (1998) *Private Foundations and Public Charities: Is It Time to Increase Payout?*, San Diego CA: National Network of Grantmakers.

Trotter, D. W. (1990) *Payout Policies and Investing Planning for Foundations*, Washington DC: Council on Foundations.

Weissert, C. S. and Knott, J. H. (1995) 'Foundations' impact on policy making: results from a pilot study', *Health Affairs*, 14, 4: 275–86.

Ylvisaker, P. N. (1987) 'Foundations and nonprofit organizations', in W. W. Powell (ed.) *The Nonprofit Sector*, New Haven: Yale University Press.

7 Corporate philanthropy's future

Dwight F. Burlingame

The last twenty years has witnessed a major increase in the number of nonprofits (NPOs) or nongovernmental organizations (NGOs), as well as an increase in study and research on them. The increase in the number of such organizations has been referred to by Lester Salamon (1994) as a global associational revolution. (In the press release for the September 1997 meeting of CIVICUS, a 'World alliance for citizen participation', the increase in democracy and growth of civil society around the world is given as the reason for such growth in NPOs and NGOs.) 'Hungary has experienced a 600 percent increase in the number of nonprofits since 1990. In Brazil, an estimated 200,000 nonprofit organizations are functioning; in Egypt, some 20,000; and in Thailand, close to 11,000' (CIVICUS 1997). Researchers have often focused on the relationship between NPOs and the government. The neglected relationship between such organizations and business will become increasingly more important in the next decade. How corporations interact with private voluntary organizations in obtaining mutually desired goals will be the focus of much of the corporate giving debate in the twenty-first century.

Corporate social responsibility (CSR), or those actions by which companies meet the expectations of society in any particular time (Sethi 1979) has been the general term in use for most of the last forty years. Various other terms that have been used to express this concept include corporate social performance, corporate community involvement, corporate community investment, corporate philanthropy, and most recently corporate citizenship. Corporate citizenship is well on the road to becoming the inclusive global term, and is usually meant to convey 'a multi-faceted concept which brings together the self-interest of business and its stakeholders with the interest of society more generally' (Logan *et al.* 1997: iii).

Corporate philanthropy, on the other hand, is understood to be a narrower term restricted to the charitable giving that a company may do to meet part of its felt citizenship responsibilities. This paper will focus primarily on corporate giving, volunteering programmes and cause-related activities as the major interactions between businesses and nonprofits. However, the future may well see major shifts in how we have traditionally thought of the corporate/nonprofit relationship.

Some history

Corporate philanthropy is a relatively new arrival to the global community. F. Emerson Andrews in his *Corporation Giving* study of 1952 had difficulty finding much evidence of corporate philanthropy in the United States. Corporate citizenship, however, has been around in various forms and to different degrees for several centuries. Some of the most ancient are in the Chinese tradition (J. Smith 1987; Lum 1985; Twitchett 1959). Even Adam Smith in his work of 1776, *An Inquiry into the Nature and Causes of the Wealth of Nations*, appropriately notes that one appeals to business interests through their own self-interest. In other words, the interest in maintaining a healthy society is present in business culture because it helps create a climate of success for business.

In the United States, corporate philanthropy has developed along the lines of the legal history of the corporation. In the nineteenth century owners gave some of their profits to their personal causes. With the growth of corporations in the early twentieth century, the question became one of how much of the company's profits could be used to benefit the community without causing a shareholder revolt (Karl 1991). Because corporate managers in publicly held companies were to act in the interests of the owners, only donations that were of direct benefit to the firm were considered legitimate. Examples of early donations that fit this guideline were those given to YMCAs for house workers. From 1921 until 1953 companies could only give to causes that directly benefited the company. In the 1953 *Smith v. Barlow* case in New Jersey, the state supreme court ruled that A. P. Smith Manufacturing Company did not violate the law in donating $1,500 to Princeton University. This case in essence overturned the principle of direct corporate benefit, and from it the rationale of public responsibility of business was established in the United States.

The relationship between corporate profits and corporate social responsibility or performance has become an active field of research ever since Milton Friedman's (1970: 70) famous claim in 1962 that the 'social responsibility of business is to make a profit for the shareholders', more commonly paraphrased as 'the business of business is business'. The debate continues as we enter the twenty-first century with a renewed emphasis on competitiveness in a global context.

During the last thirty-plus years, researchers and practitioners have explored the empirical relationship between corporate financial performance (CFP) and corporate social performance (CSP) with conflicting results (for reviews of the research in this field see Burlingame 1994; Wood and Jones 1996; Griffin and Mahon 1997).

A number of data sets have been used in trying to measure corporate social performance. The most frequently used measures include the *Fortune* survey, the KLD Index, the TRI and generosity index. The *Fortune* survey encompasses a reputation ranking based on an opinion poll of executives, financial analysts and outside directors. Many researchers believe it to be problematic because it is a perception survey as opposed to one which measures 'what a company is actually doing and what its actual impacts are' (Wood and Jones 1996: 53).

The KLD Index, which was developed by Kinder, Lydenberg, Domini & Co. Inc. (1993) is a composite index of corporate performance based on eight dimensions of social performance. The firm produces a rating based upon social screens which include employee relations, nuclear power involvement, environment, product, treatment of women and minorities, military contracting, community relations, and South Africa involvement.

This index offers an improvement over the purely perceptual *Fortune* survey, but it still contains limitations, such as the crudeness of the numerical rating – all screens carry equal importance without any theoretical basis for believing such should be the case – and there is no explanation of why the categories chosen are used instead of others that might have been chosen.

A third source which has been used is the Toxics Release Inventory (TRI) which tabulates environmental discharges by companies. The fourth measure is a 'generosity index' of corporate philanthropy, which is often obtained from the *Corporate 500 Directory of Corporate Philanthropy*.

In examining the usefulness of the above indices, Griffin and Mahon (1997) conclude that

> The focus of future research should be on one industry to increase the internal validity of the findings rather than a broad-based survey of multiple firms in various industries. ... to focus on a few, key CSP and CFP research measures to increase internal validity rather than generalizability.
>
> (25)

After reviewing the current state of research in the field, Young and Burlingame (1996) identified four models to categorize why businesses engage in giving and volunteering. The four paradigms are derived from alternative ways of thinking about how companies actually work. They are 'the neoclassical or corporate productivity model; the political model; the ethical or altruistic model; and the stakeholder model' (Young and Burlingame 1996: 159).

The neoclassical/corporate productivity model takes as its frame of reference that the business of business is to make money, and corporate giving enhances the financial bottom line. Product gifts of companies to nonprofits; investments in improving employee morale; and improving public images through cause-related marketing or investing in future company employees or in technological research in universities, are all examples of 'enlightened self-interest' which is focused on the long-run profitability of the corporation.

The political model takes as its reference point maintaining corporate power and autonomy by building relationships and coalitions with NPOs or NGOs as an alternative to the growth of government. The works of Neil Mitchell (1989) and Jerome Himmelstein (1999) have explored this conception in some detail.

The ethical/altruistic model   is based on the premise that corporations are given certain powers by society and thus have a social responsibility to do what is right for society. It allows management discretion to make gifts that will maintain the business as a responsible partner in addressing societal problems directly without being tied to the bottom-line mentality.

The stakeholder model   posits that a firm is a complex entity with many constituent groups – managers, shareholders, customers, suppliers, community groups, and so on, which hold certain claims on the company. The company therefore is drawn in many different directions – political, financial and social. How these groups interact to determine corporate policy is not exactly clear. The development of the use of stakeholder theory is most associated with Freeman (1984). Wood (1991) and more recently Clarkson (1995) have been credited with the development of the application of stakeholder theory to corporate performance (for a review of the empirical research on corporate social performance see Wood and Jones 1995).

In a recent study, Waddock and Graves (1997) provide further understanding of how the stakeholder theory of CSP can be used in identifying 'quality management'. Departing from the traditional way of empirically testing the hypothesized relationship between CSP and financial performance, Waddock and Graves recognize the historical methodological problems related to the measurement of CSP and strike out new ground by changing the research question from 'Is financial performance related to social performance?' to 'Is corporate social performance related to quality of management?'. This formulation of the research question 'shifts attention away from discretionary activities (e.g. philanthropy, volunteer activities, school/business partnerships) toward a range of critical stakeholder relationships as the defining characteristic of CSP, including relationships with employees, customers, communities, and the environment, as well as shareholders or owners' (Waddock and Graves 1997: 253). Quality of management and quality of stakeholder relationship are thus positively related, and financial performance is used as only part of the stakeholder construct since it in essence becomes part of CSP.

Buchholtz *et al.* (1999) developed and tested a model on the relationship between corporate philanthropy and the firm's resources 'mediated by managerial discretion and managerial values' (1999: 167). From 1986 to 1998, business pre-tax profits in the United States increased significantly, yet giving as a percentage of profits fell. Why did this happen? Buchholtz *et al.* offer organizational slack as a partial answer which is mediated by managerial discretion and to a lesser degree by managerial values (1999: 182).

By using two databases – one which assesses corporate social performance (the KLD Index) and one that measures perceptions of quality of management (*Fortune*'s 'Most admired' data set), Waddock and Graves test the correlation between the data sets and conclude that there is 'strong support' for shifting the research away from financial performance and CSP to 'a more fundamental question about the relationship between overall quality of management and a company's treatment of primary stakeholders, including owners' (Waddock and Graves 1997: 270).

The above research seems consistent with a new emphasis in business on corporate citizenship which focuses giving on a cluster of issues related to the firm's business interest.

Corporate citizenship

In many ways, the above four conceptions reviewed by Burlingame and Young (1996) are operant today and find expression in the notion of 'global corporate citizenship'. Logan *et al.* (1997) argue that corporations have a vested interest in 'strategic social investment' because investment in civic, social, physical infrastructure and the natural environment are 'necessary prerequisites for successful business' (Logan *et al.* 1997: 16). Thus corporate citizenship becomes relevant to every department within the company and every constituent external to the company. Philanthropic initiatives help advance the business interest by strategic relationships with the human resources, governmental affairs, research and development, and marketing divisions of the company.

The current move to corporate citizenship and to the 'new' corporate philanthropy has been elegantly argued by Craig Smith (1994; 1997). This new paradigm encourages corporations to support and play leadership roles in movements for social change while also advancing business goals. 'Like citizens in the classical sense, corporate citizens search for ways to align self-interest with the larger good of society' (C. Smith 1994: 107).

It is supported in practice by the idea that 'competing on price and corporate citizenship is a smarter strategy than competing on price alone' (C. Smith 1994: 110). Enlightened self-interest may explain why a large percentage of America's largest corporations engage in some form of philanthropy.

The new model of corporate citizenship of the late twentieth century demands a new look at why investment in corporate philanthropy appears to be the right thing to do. Continued high rates of giving by companies in the current economic crisis in Thailand may illustrate how business might perceive the reason for corporate philanthropic involvement in social issues. That is, giving is a way to create reforms which make for future positive climates for business, rather than a form of repaying the community because of successful economic ventures. Another way that this idea has been expressed is that nonprofits are vital in a system of free enterprise to serve as a bridge between business and government.

The level of giving by American companies in 1998 increased significantly to $8.97 billion – a 9.3 per cent increase over 1997 (AAFRC 1999). However, the corporate contribution as a percentage of pre-tax net income has declined from a high of 2.1 per cent to an estimated 1.24 per cent in 1995 (Johnson 1997). Companies are increasing their giving at a rate which is less than their increase in profits. Why? The answer to this question no doubt has many facets. However, it is reasonable to assume that part of the answer can be attributed to the following:

1   A decline in the support for traditional corporate philanthropy by the CEO and other senior company leaders. In a recent article, Charles Heying (1997: 657) argues that destabilization of communities results when corporate ownership is 'disconnected from place'. Using longitudinal data from elite networks in Atlanta as well as supportive evidence from other authors (among them Gronbjerg *et al.* 1996; Adams 1991; Sampson 1988), Heying notes that delocalization has caused a decline in the elite leadership which in turn has negatively affected the philanthropic giving of companies.
2   A decline in business organizations encouraging companies to give more. The decline of 2 per cent giving clubs promoted by local chambers of commerce, and of companies participating in providing information on their giving to organizations that set standards, such as the Conference Board and Council For Aid to Education, have led the way for companies to set their own internal criteria regarding their giving polices.
3   Increased global competitiveness which in the short term argues for cost cutting of functions perceived not to be vital. The giving budget has been one area offering an easy target for reductions. 'The number of full-time staff members assigned to the corporate giving function has dropped by an estimated 80 per cent in the past six years' (C. Smith 1997: 3).
4   A change in the way giving is carried out by companies. One need only note that the US giving figures do not include corporate volunteer labour, which has been estimated at $200 billion (Corporate Giving Report 1997). In addition, income to nonprofits from corporations via cause-related marketing, sponsorships and research departments are also excluded. Reliable estimates of their value are not available to this author, but many argue that in the United States they exceed the total of all giving by companies, i.e. $9 billion.

However, in the new vision for corporate citizenship, measuring a company's success would not be done by measuring a certain percentage of net income that is given to charity, but rather by using tools and techniques that answer such questions as:

> Will the activity increase company revenues or reduce costs? Will the activity have a positive impact on customers? Is the activity important to employees or company–employee relations goals? Will the activity improve the image or reputation of the company with keystakeholders? What will the ultimate impact of the initiative be on the company if successful?
>
> (Council on Foundations 1996: 2)

A similar project to provide a method for evaluating corporate contributions to the community is reported in the London Benchmarking Report (Logan 1997). Grand Metropolitan (1997) utilized the London Benchmarking Group's template for reporting their community involvement. The four areas used to report community investment were charity, social investment, management costs and commercial initiatives. Charity includes donations, social sponsorships, consultancies, in-kind giving, employee-matched giving, employee volunteering and facilitating giving such as United Way drives at company locations. Social investment includes grants, in-kind contributions, in-house training, consultancies and supplier development. Management costs are the charity and social investment costs (overheads of the company to support its social investment activities). Commercial initiatives include sponsorship, cause-related marketing, strategic contributions and staff training (that is, community assignments which are part of developing management within the company). Keeping with the trend it is interesting to note that in the case of the Grand Metropolitan corporation, product donations represented 21 per cent of all of the above social investments (Grand Metropolitan 1997). Similar methods of measurement are underway in Australia, and also in Europe where members of the European Foundation Centre have developed a network of intermediary organizations to assist in the evaluation of corporate philanthropy and social responsibility.

Globally, will the future development of the corporate philanthropy function in developing capitalistic economics focus on creating a space for nonprofits to function separately from governments, which in turn will provide a 'buffer' between business and government? Craig Smith (personal communications 1997–99) has observed that conditions are right for a new philanthropic movement in Asia. The trends he identifies as setting the stage for this movement include:

1   Overseas Chinese corporations becoming advisors to Asian government officials and significant donations flowing into these countries.
2   Asian governments condoning nonprofits or quasi-governmental organizations as a way in which to allow private wealth to be utilized to assist the public good in ways governments are unable to do.
3   Western governments and companies providing expertise and technology for various reform efforts in Asia.
4   US involvement by universities and private foundations serving a technical assistance role to Asian governments. The once-dismissed organizations from China and elsewhere are now returning to the region as advisors for innovation and local development.

These changes feed the associational revolution identified by Salamon (1994) and others. An important observation from this author's perspective is that the old paradigms of corporate versus government, private versus public and other either/or analogies appear no longer viable. What is emerging is a corporate citizenship model which views business with responsibilities within the context of traditional philosophies, including Asian ones.

Barnet Baron (1996) appropriately re-emphasizes that despite Western ignorance, there exists a long history of Chinese philanthropy and charitable giving. However, he notes that the two outstanding characteristics of a Chinese firm

are '(a) the centrality of the family and personal relationships in business relationships in business organization, financing, and decision-making, and (b) a
pervasive sense of personal and financial insecurity' (Baron 1996: 8). He therefore cautions against imagining a new set of global business practices and
norms that will replace culturally and historically determined practices. This
appears to be somewhat at odds with the arguments made by Logan *et al.*
(1997: 179) that for global corporate citizenship to address community problem
solving, it must be based upon 'a strategy for collaboration among the sectors of
society that is rooted in reciprocal relations rather than extractive actions'.

Perhaps for many overseas Chinese business leaders, an historical moment
may be now, which will allow for many of the historical insecurities tied to the
merchant class to be dropped. Business philanthropy may provide the face-
saving way to interact with government through NGOs. In other words, a civil
society space is created in which all sectors collaborate to address social issues.

Can the corporate contributions function be 'empowered' in the twenty-first
century by using the strategy of corporate citizenship, which defines the role of
corporate contributions by linking giving objectives to internal strategies? Or
should the strategy try to reinforce the traditional way of thinking about corporate giving as corporate social responsibility, and to build on narrower notions
of giving? A noteworthy empirical question in this regard, is whether or not
corporate leader involvement in community translates into corporate advancement in today's global economy. According to a recent study conducted by
James Austin of Harvard Business School, reported on by Ross (1997), 82 per
cent of the 316 CEOs of *Fortune 500* companies served on nonprofit boards, and
many thought it was important for their career advancement as well as important in serving the community.

Business/education interaction

The current trend for increased volunteerism on the part of business to demonstrate their citizenship and to give expertise and time to social issues is evident
around the globe. In addition, more and more examples of planned community
volunteer experiences and service learning experiences for business students are
evident as ways in which to develop long-term relations between educational
institutions and the business community. Further, such experiences serve to
educate future leaders of business in the role that service plays in collectively
addressing social issues. Can these relationships be enhanced by an understanding of what a corporate citizenship perspective could bring to their
development and thereby contribute to the overall goals of the company? The
increased development of nonprofit management courses across the United
States provides another sign of increased opportunities for stressing multiple
perspectives of the social responsibility of business in society. In addition, more
and more managers are moving between nonprofits and for-profits. As students
from business schools and students from liberal arts interact, social policy issues
are more likely to be the focus of active discourse and learning.

One future test of academic research in the corporate philanthropy field will be the success by which a theoretical framework develops that will help companies predict the effects of their decisions on social issues as well as their economic well-being. Most past research has focused on the stakeholder conflicts that arise out of bottom-line questions or other ethical conflicts that arise, either between employee and employer or between business action and various external constituents.

Perhaps part of the reason we have not observed a great deal of interest in corporate philanthropy research issues among the business faculty reflects the lack of a unified way of understanding the role of philanthropy within and among the business components of the company. Therefore the subject has been generally dismissed as not part of the 'real stuff' of corporate policymaking. C. Smith (1994); Schwartz and Gibb (1999) and others have begun to set the stage for an understanding of corporate citizenship which could address the marginalization of the study of business and society within business schools.

Included within this understanding is the recognition that the globalization age is causing a move beyond just a 'business ethics' approach to corporate social responsibility, to a 'public expectations' of business approach based upon geopolitical, demographic and economic considerations globally.

Conclusion

Once it is recognized that corporate philanthropy is indeed at a crossroads and it cannot be generalized to one model, progress can be made in understanding the mixed motives that in fact serve various public interests. There is no single motive for corporate citizenship, and it would appear that the social good that results from corporate action should be the focus of evaluation of corporate citizenship, rather than an attempt to assess motives. If one agrees that the main function of corporations is to provide efficient means for capital for shareholders as well as stakeholders, it would appear that Joel Schwartz is correct in arguing that, 'the central contention of strategic philanthropy (in effect also the central contention of Adam Smith) is largely valid: corporations can benefit themselves insofar as they benefit society, including the poor' (Schwartz and Gibb 1999: 146).

As corporations grow larger and more global, and as government provision of services declines, the business sector is called upon to make a greater contribution to societal human needs and to commit to sustainable development through good community health as well as economic health. We will witness in the twenty-first century the success or failure of business to cross the divide between introverted 'pure' capitalism and capitalism informed by social need.

References

AAFRC (1999) *Giving USA*, New York: AAFRC Trust.
Adams, C. T. (1991) 'Philadelphia: the slide toward municipal bankruptcy', in H. V. Savitch and J. C. Thomas (eds) *Big City Politics in Transition*, Newbury Park: Sage.
Andrews, F. E. (1952) *Corporation Giving*, New York: Russell Sage.

Baron, B. (1996) 'Chinese philanthropy and the east Asian regional context', in J. J. Deeney (ed.) *Chinese Philanthropy*, Occasional Paper 4: 3–11, Hong Kong: The Hong Kong-America Center.

Buchholtz, A. K., Amason, A. C. and Rutherford, M. A. (1999) 'Beyond resources: the mediating effect of top management discretion and values on corporate philanthropy', *Business and Society*, 38, 2: 167–87.

Burlingame, D. F. (1994) 'Empirical research on corporate social responsibility: what does it tell us?', *Nonprofit Management and Leadership*, 4, 4: 473–80.

Burlingame, D. F. and Young, D. R. (eds) (1996) *Corporate Philanthropy at the Crossroads*, Bloomington: Indiana University Press.

CIVICUS Secretariat (1997) press release, 12 August, Washington DC.

Clarkson, M. B. E. (1995) 'A stakeholder framework for analyzing and evaluating corporate social performance', *Academy of Management Review*, 20, 1: 92–117.

Council on Foundations (1996) *Measuring the Value of Corporate Citizenship*, Washington DC: Council on Foundations.

Frederick, C. (1998) 'Cultures, corporations, communities, chaos, complexity: a naturological view of the corporate social role', *Business and Society*, 37, 4: 358–89.

Freeman, R. E. (1984) *Strategic Management: A Stakeholder Approach*, New York: Basic Books.

Friedman, M. (1970) [1962] 'The social responsibility of business is to increase profits', *New York Times Magazine*, 13 September, 122–6.

Grand Metropolitan (1997) *Report on Corporate Citizenship*, London: Grand Metropolitan.

Griffin, J. J. and Mahon, J. F. (1997) 'The corporate social performance and corporate financial performance debate: twenty-five years of incomparable research', *Business and Society*, 36, March: 5–31.

Gronbjerg, K., Harmon, L., Olkkonen, A. and Raza, A. (1996) 'The united way system at the crossroads: community planning and allocation', *Nonprofit and Voluntary Sector Quarterly*, 25: 428–52.

Heying, C. H. (1997) 'Civic elites and corporate delocalization: an alternative explanation for declining civic engagement', *American Behavioral Scientist*, 40, 5: 657–68.

Himmelstein, J. L. (1999) *Looking Good and Doing Good: Corporate Philanthropy and Corporate Power*, Bloomington: Indiana University Press.

Hsiao, H. M. (1993) 'Chinese corporate philanthropy in east and southeast Asia: a typology', in K. Jung (ed.) *Evolving Patterns of Asia Pacific Philanthropy*, Seoul: Yonsei University Press.

Johnson, D. C. (1997) 'The changing face of corporate giving', *Advancing Philanthropy*, spring: 35–7.

Karl, B. D. (1991) 'The evolution of corporate grantmaking in America', in Shannon, J. P. (ed.) *The Corporate Contributions Handbook*, San Francisco: Jossey-Bass.

Kinder, P. D., Lydenberg, S. D. and Domini, A. L. (1993) *Investing for Good: Making Money While Being Socially Responsible*, New York: Harper Business.

Kulik, T. (1999) *The Expanding Parameters of Global Corporate Citizenship*, New York: Conference Board.

Logan, D. (1997) *Companies in Communities: Getting the Measure*, London: Benchmarking Group.

Logan, D., Roy, D. and Regelbrugge, L. (1997) *Global Corporate Citizenship: Rationale and Strategies*, Washington DC: Hitachi Foundation.

Lum, R. D. (1985) 'Philanthropy and public welfare in late imperial China', unpublished dissertation, Cambridge MA: Harvard University.

Mitchell, N. J. (1989) *The Generous Corporation: A Political Analysis of Economic Power*, New Haven: Yale University Press.

Ross, J. A. (1997) 'Community service: more rewarding than you think', *Harvard Business Review*, 74, 4: 14.

Salamon, L. M. (1994) 'The rise of the nonprofit sector', *Foreign Affairs*, 73, 4, 109–22.

Sampson, R. J. (1988) 'Local friendship ties and community attachment in mass society: a multilevel systemic model', *Sociological Review*, 53, 5: 766–79.

Schwartz, J. (1997) 'Corporate philanthropy today: from A. P. Smith to Adam Smith', in J. W. Barry and B. V. Manno (eds) *Getting Better, Giving Smarter: Working Papers of the National Commission on Philanthropy and Civic Renewal*, Washington DC: National Commission on Philanthropy and Civic Renewal.

Schwartz, P. and Gibb, B. (1999) *When Good Companies Do Bad Things: Responsibility and Risk in an Age of Globalization*, New York: Wiley.

Sethi, S. P. (1979) 'A conceptual framework for environmental analysis of social issues and evaluation of business response patterns', *Academy of Management Review*, 4, 1: 63–74.

Smith C. (1994) 'The new corporate philanthropy', *Harvard Business Review*, 72, May/June: 105–16.

——(1997) 'The promotion of corporate citizenship', *Essays on Philanthropy*, 26, Indianapolis: Indiana University Center on Philanthropy.

——Personal conversation, September 10, 1997, Indianapolis: Indiana University Center on Philanthropy.

Smith, J. F. H. (1987) 'Benevolent societies: the reshaping of charity during the late Ming and early Ch'ing', *Journal of Asian Studies*, 46, May: 309–37.

——(1994) 'Chinese philanthropy in its historical context', paper presented at a symposium on Philanthropy and Cultural Context, 3–4 November, Rockefeller Archive Center, Tarrytown, New York.

Twitchett, D. (1959) 'The Fan clan's charitable estate, 1050–1760', in D. Nivison and A. Wright (eds) *Confucianism in Action*, Stanford: Stanford University Press.

Waddock, S. A. and Graves, S. B. (1997) 'Quality of management and quality of stakeholder relations', *Business and Society*, 36, 3: 250–79.

Weeden, C. (1998) *Corporate Social Investing*, San Francisco: Berrett-Koehler.

Wood, D. J. (1991) 'Corporate social performance revisited', *Academy of Management Journal*, 57, 4: 691–718.

Wood, D. J. and Jones, R. E. (1995) 'Stakeholder mismatching: a theoretical problem in empirical research on corporate social performance', *The International Journal of Organizational Analysis*, 3, 3: 229–67.

——(1996) 'Research in corporate social performance: what have we learned?', in D. F. Burlingame and D. R. Young (eds) *Corporate Philanthropy at the Crossroads*, Bloomington: Indiana University Press.

Young, D. R. and Burlingame, D. F. (1996) 'Paradigm lost', in D. F. Burlingame and D. R. Young (eds) *Corporate Philanthropy at the Crossroads*, Bloomington: Indiana University Press.

8 On 'The role of philanthropic foundations: lessons from America's experience with private foundations'

Diana Leat

Background

Discussing the relevance of Elizabeth T. Boris and Julian Wolpert's chapter on lessons from American experience with private foundations (Chapter 6 in this volume) to the role of philanthropic foundations in Britain requires first some brief comments on differences in the historical political environment in which foundations in Britain operate.

The first, and striking, environmental difference is that there has never been the level of political and public attention paid to British foundations as that which has pertained in the United States (Simon 1996). Indeed, if you asked the person in the street, or even the average Member of Parliament, to name more than a handful of philanthropic foundations they would probably be hard put to do so. Interestingly, in the last five years there has been a growing debate concerning the perceived democratic deficit created by the growth of quangos, spending increasing sums of public money and accountable to none (Jenkins 1995). But there has been little or no reading across to the parallels with philanthropic foundations. In part, this lack of interest in philanthropic foundations may be explained in terms of the very much smaller resources which British foundations command.

There are around 8,800 charitable grantmaking foundations currently distributing around £1.25 billion per annum in grants to other bodies. In addition, the National Lottery Charities Board alone gave £680 million to nearly 12,000 projects between 1995 and 1997; and the total figure given is further swelled by the contribution (around £280 million in total) of a dozen large operating charities which give grants in the course of their work, giving an overall total of around £1.9 billion (Pharoah and Siederer 1997).

Another reason why foundations in general attract relatively little political attention may be the widespread trust enjoyed by all things 'charitable' in Britain, although this appears to be changing as the British public increasingly perceive (correctly or incorrectly) high costs and unnecessary duplication in the voluntary sector (Henley Centre 1997; see also Hems and Passey 1996).

The lack of attention paid to philanthropic foundations has various consequences of which the regulatory framework is one. Compared with the US, the regulatory framework in Britain is characterized by a very light touch (Chesterman 1979; Siederer 1996). There is, for example, no equivalent of the payout requirement applied in the US. British foundations have traditionally assiduously, and assertively, guarded their independence and privacy, and in this some might argue that they have been indirectly assisted by the lack of resources available to the Charity Commission (the main regulatory agency in England and Wales).

Recent charity legislation has placed more emphasis on regulation of fundraising and fundraising charities, and has had relatively few direct implications for endowed grantmaking foundations. The main requirements of the Charities Act 1992 of particular relevance to foundations included the duty to publish an annual report (something relatively few foundations had previously done and to which some foundations objected for different reasons) and a statutory duty to keep accounts in the form specified in regulations to be based on the SORP 2. The accounting rules required grantmaking foundations to list the grants they have given to organizations but not to individuals, thus meeting one objection from foundations. Even more radically, perhaps, foundations were required to make their accounts available to any member of the public who asks for them and pays a reasonable fee, and both annual reports and accounts were to be available for inspection at the Charity Commission.

The Act also required an annual return to the Charity Commission from all foundations, and those which broke the new and more stringent accounting rules were likely to be specially marked. In addition, the 1992 Act gave the Charity Commission statutory powers to demand information from charities and to hold formal enquiries, as well as legal authority to exchange information with other government bodies, including the Inland Revenue. However, it is not entirely clear how infringements of the requirements of the Act will be monitored.

Interestingly, probably the more powerful force for greater transparency in foundations' activities comes from a less formal force. In recent years the Directory of Social Change, a voluntary organization specializing in training and publications, has published a directory of foundations which unlike the rival and older publication from Charities Aid Foundation (see for example Villemur 1991) has included analysis of and commentary on foundations' policies and practices (Fitzherbert *et al.* various years: Fitzherbert, Addison and Rahman 1999).

The DSC publication has, over the last ten years, drawn attention to individually named foundations which pay out only a very small percentage of their annual income, those which do not file returns to the Charity Commission, those which seem to preach one message and practise another, and those which simply refuse to provide any information at all. Although initially viewed by some foundations as an outrageous violation of their privacy, and despite being the subject of legal threats, the publication appears to have had some remarkable effects in increasing the flow of information from foundations and, in at least one case of a very wealthy foundation, leading to a significant overhaul of policy and practices.

In the coming years the requirements of SORP 2 (a statement of recommended accounting practice for charities) should lead to more and better data from foundations regarding the level and distribution of their grantmaking. Thus the combination of the effects of the Directory of Social Change publication and requirements for SORP 2 should shed some light in the generally gloomy world of foundation activity, but transparency is still a contested goal within many British foundations (ACF 1997a).

National Lottery Charities Board: ripples in the pond?

The closest we have come in recent years to public discussion of the role of foundations is the flurries of attention paid to the activities of the National Lottery Boards, and in particular in this context, the National Lottery Charities Board (NLCB). Under the National Lottery etc. Act 1993 five distributing boards were created, giving to the arts, sport, heritage, charities and the millennium, collectively and generally referred to as 'the good causes'.

The effects of the creation of these distributing boards on foundations varies depending in large part on the particular policies and practices of the individual boards in grantmaking. But one general effect of the creation of the five boards has been to dwarf the contribution of foundations and to radically alter the ecology and the balance of power in charitable grantmaking. Foundations, once accused of being able to upset the priorities of government by creating new responsibilities but not following through, suddenly find themselves being given a taste of their own medicine. There's a new and very rich gang on the block, which is changing the rules of the game without consulting the old players.

One area in which existing foundations have felt the wind of change blown in by the National Lottery especially fiercely is the arts. Unlike the distributing board for the arts, the National Lottery Charities Board does not require its grant recipients to raise matched funding and it can make funds available for revenue costs, and not simply for capital. But its effect on foundations working in the broad field of social welfare has nevertheless been seen as immense (Fitzherbert *et al.* 1996).

In 1996/7 NLCB made grants exceeding £300 million to charities and other good causes (Unwin and Westland 1997). By 1998 NLCB (September 1998) the Board had distributed £782 million in grants in five main programme categories:

*   poverty (19 per cent)
*   youth issues and low income (19 per cent)
*   health, disability and care (19 per cent)
*   new opportunities and choices and voluntary sector development (19 per cent)
*   improving living environments and voluntary sector development (16 per cent).

In addition, NLCB has given £13 million in small grants (2 per cent) and £50 million (6 per cent) in international grants.

The very size of NLCB's grantmaking capacity is sufficient for its weight to be felt, dwarfing the contribution of other foundations. Its more tangible effects on other foundations are said to be that it has led to an increasing number of applications to other foundations for grants to assist in applying for NLCB funds, and that its large grants have raised expectations and aspirations among voluntary organizations which have then been reflected in applications to other foundations. Some foundations argue that NLCB has effectively encouraged some small organizations to grow too far too fast, and that other foundations are then asked to fund the associated support and infrastructure costs.

Given its constitution, it would be somewhat odd to describe NLCB as a 'private foundation' (not, incidentally, a term that would be recognized in Britain anyway), but it acts in ways which are almost indistinguishable from other foundations giving money to charities. The money received by NLCB is not public in the sense that it does not count within public expenditure totals, even though it is raised from the public in a form of purchase tax. As noted above, the Board was appointed by government with the chief intention of operating independently and there have been no additional policy constraints placed on the Board. In whatever way we choose to categorize NLCB, it has raised issues which have important implications for the future of all foundations.

The sheer size of the funds distributed by NLCB has raised the profile of grantmaking to charities, and to some extent has drawn mainstream charitable foundations into the public policy arena. Traditionally, British foundations have argued that they are independent of public policy, neither affecting it nor being influenced by it, and some have displayed a remarkable lack of awareness of the wider policy context in which they operate (Leat 1992; 1993). NLCB has changed this, in that few foundations can afford to ignore the implications of the existence and practices of this big fish which has dived in their quiet pond and sent ripples to all shores. Three ripples are worth highlighting.

Raising the profile of foundations

The grants awarded by NLCB have been subject to a relatively high degree of media attention, especially from the tabloid press which has highlighted some of the more controversial grants and recipient organizations (e.g. refugee projects, and a project to provide AIDS/HIV education to rent boys). This has raised questions about the proper scope of charities and the use of 'charitable' monies.

Questions about the power of foundations

Perhaps more significantly, local authorities are beginning to ask questions about the power of unelected bodies to put sometimes substantial funds into an area with no consultation about local government policies and priorities (Unwin and Westland 1997). Furthermore, because NLCB funding is likely to be short-term, local authorities, and others, are not unreasonably concerned about the longer-term sustainability of projects, the lack of exit strategies, and subsequent political implications when NLCB funding ends. Such fears may have been heightened by a statement in 1999 by a senior member of staff at NLCB that the Board is not, and does not intend to become, a source of long-term funding for voluntary organizations (reported in *Third Sector*, 22 July 1999, issue 165).

Pressures for change in processes

Finally, because of the scale of NLCB operations and its public accountability, it has set new standards in application, assessment and reporting procedures. NLCB's concern to ensure consistency, fairness and transparency in its grant-making is in marked contrast to the approaches of some other charitable foundations, and has raised a number of hitherto rarely discussed issues in the foundation world (Leat 1998).

The use of charitable monies, relationships with local government policies and priorities, the effects of short-term funding, consistency, fairness and trans-parency in grantmaking are all issues which could be raised in relation to foundations in general. At present public attention to these issues is confined largely to NLCB, but the parallels seem too close for the link not to be made sooner or later. It is perhaps significant that in recent years the Association of Charitable Foundations has published guides to 'fairness in funding', funding gay and lesbian groups and ethnic minority groups.

Inadequate knowledge

Boris and Wolpert highlight the inadequacy of our 'understanding of how foun-dations select and target programme areas for their grant activities and the impacts of their individual and aggregate efforts'. The same point could well be made in Britain. Despite a significant increase in research into the voluntary sector more generally, there is a real dearth of work on grantmaking foundations (Leat 1992). In part this may well reflect the still widespread view that raising money is more difficult than spending it. It may also be related to the fact that it remains difficult to obtain funding for research into foundations, not least because no foundation views research into foundation activities as among its priorities, and other funders argue that foundations should pay for such work themselves.

Apart from basic data on the scale and shape of the foundation world, we also need more research into foundations' perceptions of their roles, as well as into organizations and the way in which they work. We need to move away from generalization about 'foundations' to identification of different types of founda-tion and key variables. Size is clearly one variable, but, as I have argued elsewhere, foundations also vary in their dominant cultures of grantmaking, in their structures, in the role of donors and composition and role of their board (Leat 1992; 1996). Other variables worth exploring are sources of moral legitimacy, public profile, credibility, relationship to elites and sensitivity to criticism, among others. (For discussion of some of these issues in the UK context see, for example, Bulmer 1999. But because Bulmer adopts a particular narrow definition of foundations this discussion is of limited relevance to the wider world of UK foundations.) These factors are all likely to make a difference to the way in which foundations work, and are distinctions which would be one ingredient in Boris and Wolpert's 'rich descriptions' of foundation behaviour.

Rich descriptions

Such descriptions would also explore not merely the ways in which foundations select priorities and policy for grantmaking, but also the way in which they recognize the 'good application' and the 'good project'. What processes are involved, what assumptions are made and where do these come from? What implications do foundations' assumptions regarding the 'good' organization and project have for the shape and contours of the voluntary sector? For example, are foundation criteria forcing voluntary organizations into a common organizational structure and common management practices which, arguably, have little empirically demonstrable evidence to support their effectiveness?

My own recent research is concerned with application and pre-grant enquiry and selection processes and assumptions. The work also raises a number of wider issues to do with the knowledge base and knowledge dependence of foundations. Some foundations appear to be income rich, or at least independent, and knowledge poor/dependent, in ways which are difficult to deal with within existing cultures and structure. Where does knowledge for 'good' grantmaking come from, what form does it take and how can new knowledge for grantmaking be generated? The study suggests that knowledge for grantmaking is largely tacit, and for that reason moves only stickily between individuals and foundations. Furthermore, explicit knowledge seems typically to flow in a vertical line, rather than forming a productive loop. At present, it seems that even if foundations require monitoring and evaluation of projects funded, the knowledge derived is rarely fed back into (subsequent) pre-grant application and selection processes (Leat 1998).

Rich descriptions of foundations' behaviour would also include attention to the rhetoric of foundations. The prevailing British foundation rhetoric includes words such as 'sustainability', 'risk' and 'additionality'. What do these mean? How are they applied and recognized? What role do they play in the drama/performance of grantmaking? Do their meanings and roles differ between and within, different types of foundation?

One example highlights some of the subtleties in the meaning and role of the term 'risk' in the performance of grantmaking by one foundation. The regional advisory committee of a foundation with a high public profile recently considered a grant application for a project working with young male prostitutes. The regional committee decided to recommend a grant. The head office rejected the recommendation on the grounds that the project was too 'risky'. The regional committee interpreted this as head office being autocratic, conservative and over-concerned with public reaction, and demanded a meeting with the National Director. The National Director visited the committee and explained that the project had been rejected not because of the risk of adverse public reaction, but because the apparently weak management of the project created risks for the staff who would be working alone, at night, in potentially dangerous situations.

Key current issues for foundations

Boris and Wolpert's list of remaining open questions for foundations are probably all relevant to the larger and professionally staffed foundations in Britain. But some may be questions that it might be fruitful to discuss rather than ones which, in reality, keep foundation executives and board members awake at night.

Five issues which are of day-to-day concern to foundations in Britain are additionality; sustainability; the effects of the entry of NLCB and more recently the New Opportunities Fund, now and in future; the implications of the changing boundaries and relationship between voluntary and statutory organizations; and the effects on foundations' incomes of changes in fiscal policy which, in theory, had nothing to do with foundations.

Additionality

Additionality is a major issue for foundations, both at a philosophical and practical level, as the old definition of their role as 'doing what the state doesn't do' becomes increasingly untenable as a guiding principle. The state no longer does a whole range of things it used to, but foundations are generally reluctant to fund a project merely because the state no longer does. They resist this on the grounds that to do so would open the floodgates, allowing hard pressed local and central government to opt out of past, current and future provision without responsibility or political pain. In addition, filling in for the state is resisted on practical grounds – foundations simply do not have the funds consistently to fund what is or was provided by the state. Some foundation board members cling to the notion that statutory responsibilities are clearly defined (when in fact, or course, most are hedged with qualifications about efficient and effective use of resources) and choose between projects on the basis of their own perceptions of what those responsibilities are, were, or ought to be. But many appear to find it difficult to maintain their policy when the reality that, irrespective of their stand, those in need will go without becomes apparent.

The tension for foundations is obvious: on the one hand their mission is to assist those in need (or some variant of this) and those served by grant applicants are assumed to be in need, but on the other hand, they believe that it is not in the long-term interests of those in need to give grants which not only cannot be sustained but may further undermine statutory provision. A further complication in Britain may be foundations' perceptions of public nervousness about erosion of the welfare state – a political project, particularly during the Thatcher years, many foundation members had, or came to have, moral qualms about.

Sustainability

Sustainability is another growing concern among larger foundations. In part this arises because the old notion of grantmaking as 'priming the pump' is no longer tenable when there is clearly little water left in the well. Now foundations are increasingly asking 'Where will future funding for this project come from, and if that is unclear is there any point in the foundation putting money into this project?'. Some foundations are trying to deal with the problem of sustainability by being more selective in their choice of applicants, giving money only to those who do not stand a reasonable chance of becoming self-sufficient or obtaining funding from other sources. However, this approach tends to rule out the least attractive, socially and financially skilled applicants. Some deal with sustainability by giving longer-term grants on the grounds that this will give projects more time to demonstrate their worth and secure other funding. The problem with this approach is that foundations may quickly find their entire programme silted up with ongoing commitments. Another approach is to have exit strategies in place from the start and to demand from applicants assurances regarding plans for future funding. But some foundation staff privately admit that such strategies can be little more than heroic hopes which serve to make everyone feel happier and more responsible (Unwin and Westland 1997).

The National Lottery Boards and New Opportunities Fund

The immediate and medium-term effects of the entry of the NLCB, and the other lottery boards, is another concern for British foundations. This has been discussed above, but may have more general effects in encouraging foundations to see themselves as part of a complex ecology of funding, rather than as totally individual independent operators, in which one foundation's grant is another foundation's application/problem a year or so later (Leat 1993).

The Lottery Act 1998, introduced by the Blair government, created significant developments in relation to the National Lottery distributions. The National Lottery Act 1998 has the effect of:

- relaxing many of the restrictions on Lottery funding in the arts and heritage fields, and should correspondingly reduce the pressure felt by other foundations giving (inter alia) in these fields
- requiring NLCB (and other distributing bodies) to plan strategically, to consult each other and other funders, and to focus on people rather than buildings
- permitting NLCB to solicit applications, to delegate decision-making and to take a more flexible approach to partnership funding

- creating two new distributing bodies: the New Opportunities Fund to fund initiatives in education, health and the environment and a National Endowment for Science, Technology and the Arts.

Of these new provisions, the creation of NOF has been the most controversial and has become more so with the news that NOF will receive the whole of the Millennium Commission's share of the Lottery Distribution Fund from 2001. With £400 million per year this will make NOF the largest Lottery grantmaker.

Three NOF initiatives are already in place: Healthy Living Centres, out-of-school education and childcare, and IT training for teachers and librarians. Three further initiatives were announced at the Labour Party Conference in autumn 1998: cancer treatment, prevention and care; use of green spaces; and life-long learning.

Changing boundaries between sectors

The changing boundaries and relationships between voluntary and statutory organizations is of concern to foundations for various reasons. At a practical level it is becoming more and more difficult to distinguish clearly a voluntary organization application from a 'disguised' statutory application. In the past, applications from or on behalf of statutory organizations were regarded by some foundations as dirty tricks to be instantly rejected. Now, however, there is a growing range of organizations with 'mixed' parentage from which applications cannot be so easily dismissed. Even more difficult to detect are applications from voluntary organizations working on contract to the local authority for funds which would directly or indirectly subsidize the contract price paid by the statutory purchaser. More generally, some foundations are recognizing that the old clear maps in which organizations clearly belonged in one sector or another are fading. Joint working, strategic alliances, networks and partnerships are now the preferred way of arranging service provision and funding.

The Blair government's emphasis on 'third way' policies and 'joined up' policy making and provision reflects and reinforces these trends, further undermining old sectoral, as well as organizational, divisions. The plethora of policy initiatives and funding packages emanating from the New Labour government have in common a 'partnership' approach in which voluntary and statutory funding sources are increasingly interdependent. In this context it becomes difficult for foundations to distinguish to whom they are really giving and, as important for some, who is defining priorities and setting the agenda.

Changes in fiscal policy

In July 1997 in its first budget the new government abolished Advance Corporation Tax Credit. This was a measure which was not intended to have any effect on charitable giving, rather it was designed to encourage reinvestment by businesses. But abolishing the credit obviously had an effect on tax-exempt investors, and some foundations forecast that their investment income would drop by 10 per cent or more (ACF 1997). Anticipating this change, the Association of Charitable Foundations made representations in advance to the Chancellor of the Exchequer, pointing out that charities would be caught in a net not primarily designed to affect them and arguing that charities would be adversely affected by the rumoured change. This secured a transitional arrangement for charities which meant that the abolition of the tax credit was delayed for two years and then phased in over a further five years, giving time for charities to re-order their investments.

By the autumn of 1997, however, a growing number of UK multinationals were starting to pay foreign income dividends (FIDs) which, unlike traditional dividends, do not allow tax-exempt investors to reclaim tax. Companies paying FIDs included many of the 'blue-chip' investments favoured by foundations. The practice of paying FIDs had come about as an indirect result of the abolition of Advance Corporation Tax Credit. Companies had previously been reluctant to pay FIDs because their biggest shareholders, the pension funds, could reclaim tax on traditional dividends. When this ability to reclaim tax on traditional dividends was abolished in the July budget there was nothing to stop companies switching to FIDs.

The effect on foundations (and charities in general) was to undermine the transitional arrangement negotiated by ACF and to significantly reduce many foundations' investment income. For example, the Wellcome Trust estimated that Glaxo Wellcome's decision to pay an FID instead of a traditional dividend would reduce the trust's income by £5 million.

Policy issues for government

As noted above, government has appeared to be relatively disinterested in charitable foundations, as compared with the United States. The Thatcher administrations saw charities as a means of supplementing, if not replacing, various aspects of statutory provision and, particularly at certain stages, believed that charitable funds could be used for this purpose. But specific policies related to foundations were less clear. Despite a pre-election disposition towards the voluntary sector, the present government's policy is little clearer, and the emphasis on not increasing public expenditure, combined with strong preferences for partnerships and alliances, may suggest little change.

As noted above, the Labour government introduced NOF, in effect diverting a portion of funds from the National Lottery to purposes which some would regard as statutory responsibilities. What effect this will have on attitudes to and behaviour of other foundations is as yet unclear. One possibility is that it will have very little effect. The principle of additionality is already full of holes and, arguably, all that government is doing is slipping through an existing hole rather than vandalizing a sound structure. On the other hand, it could be argued that the government's move is likely to backfire, encouraging foundations to cease funding in these areas. But, as discussed above, the most pressing policy issue is likely to be demands from local government (prompted by their growing concern over the activities of the NLCB) for closer scrutiny of the freedom of foundations, and demands for consultation. Such pressure seems likely to increase as the effects of the termination of early NLCB grants become more apparent. These effects will include not only loss of services, but also loss of jobs funded by NLCB grants. Demands for local government to pick up the tab may be difficult to resist without political damage.

Boris and Wolpert suggest that American foundations do not try very hard to be influential in the policy arena. The same observation might be made in Britain – with three provisos. First, although foundations do not typically try to be influential in the policy arena, their funding interventions can unwittingly create friction, especially in local arenas.

Second, a few British foundations do try to influence policy via both research and demonstration projects. One notable example is the Joseph Rowntree Foundation. Interestingly, its success in influencing policy is almost certainly not due solely to the quality of the work it funds, but also to its developed dissemination practices.

Third, the growing strength of the relatively recently formed Association of Charitable Foundations (ACF 1992) appears to be changing the way in which foundations respond in the policy arena. ACF has increasingly developed lobbying activities to defend the interests of foundations when legislation affecting especially their income is being discussed in Parliament. To date ACF's attempts at political influence have been largely restricted to relatively narrow matters of foundation interest. It remains to be seen whether it will adopt a similar role in relation to substantive policy matters impinging on particular groups of beneficiaries.

Working in a new terrain without a destination or a map?

Charitable foundations in the UK are facing unprecedented challenges, and it is not yet clear which paths they will take in dealing with these.

As I have argued above, the entry of the NLCB, and now NOF, on the grant-making scene has brought to the fore important questions about the roles, capacities and freedom of foundations. Many foundations would undoubtedly argue that it is not their role to pick up 'commitments' created by the Lottery givers: that they do not have the financial capacity to do so; and that, in any case, they will not have their priorities and agendas dictated by anybody.

At the same time, foundations are facing challenges from low interest rates and other fiscal changes (discussed above) to their income. Furthermore, as the boundaries between the statutory, voluntary and commercial sectors become less clear, and partnership is the policy of the day, old formulations of roles as 'doing what the state doesn't do', 'pump-priming', 'innovation' and so on, are becoming increasingly problematic.

At present many UK foundations seem to be working in a dramatically altered terrain in which they have yet to find a destination, let alone a map.

References

ACF (Association of Charitable Foundations) (1992) *The First Three Years 1989–92*, London: ACF.

——(1997a) *Promoting the Effectiveness of UK Grant-making Trusts, Annual Review 1996–7*, London: ACF.

——(1997b) *Trust and Foundation News*, June/July.

——(1998) *Trust and Foundation News*, December/January.

Bulmer, M. (1999) 'The history of foundations in the United Kingdom and the United States: philanthropic foundations in industrial society', in H. K. Anheier and S. Toepler (eds) *Private Funds, Public Purpose: Philanthropic Foundations in International Perceptive*, London: Kluwer Academic/Plenum Publishers.

Chesterman, M. (1979) *Charities, Trusts and Social Welfare*, London: Weidenfeld and Nicolson.

Fitzherbert, L., Addison, D. and Rahman, F. (1999) *A Guide to the Major Trusts 1999/2000*, London: Directory of Social Change.

Fitzherbert, L. and Forrester, S. (1991) *A Guide to the Major Trusts*, London: Directory of Social Change.

Fitzherbert, L., Forrester, S. and Grau, J. (1997) *A Guide to the Major Trusts 1997–8*, London: Directory of Social Change.

Fitzherbert, L., Giussani, C. and Hunt, H. (eds) (1996) *The National Lottery Yearbook 1996*, London: Directory of Social Change.

Hems, L. and Passey, A. (1996) *The Voluntary Sector Statistical Almanac 1996*, London: NVCO.

Henley Centre (1997) *Planning for Social Change 1996–7*, London: Henley Centre.

Jenkins, S. (1995) *Accountable to None*, London: Hamish Hamilton.

Leat, D. (1992) *Trusts in Transition: The Policy and Practice of Grant-giving Trusts*, York: Joseph Rowntree Foundation.

——(1993) 'Increased demands on charitable foundations: understanding the ecology of funding', in S. Saxon Harrold and J. Kendall (eds) *Researching the Voluntary Sector*, 1st edn, Tonbridge: Charities Aid Foundation.

——(1996) 'British foundations: the organisation and management of grant-making', *Voluntas*, 6, 3: 317–29.

——(1998) *Faith, Hope and Information: Assessing a Grant Application*, York: Joseph Rowntree Foundation.

Pharoah, C. and Siederer, N. (1997) 'Number, income and assets: new estimates', in C. Pharoah and M. Smerdom (eds) *Dimensions of the Voluntary Sector, 1997*, West Malling: Charities Aid Foundation.

Siederer, N. (1996) 'Giving in trust: the role of the grantmaking trust', in C. Hanvey and T. Philpot (eds) *Sweet Charity*, London: Routledge.

Simon, J. G. (1996) 'The regulation of American foundations: looking backward at the Tax Reform Act of 1969', *Voluntas*, 6, 3: 243–54.

——(1997) 'Independent funding: the role of the charitable trust', *Trust and Foundation News*, June/July.

Unwin, J. and Westland, P. (1997) *Local Funding: The Impact of the National Lottery Charities Board*, London: Association of Charitable Foundations.

Villemur, A. (ed.) (1991) *Directory of Grant Making Trusts 1991*, Tonbridge: Charities Aid Foundat

9 Corporatism revisited

The legacy of history and the German nonprofit sector

Annette Zimmer

Introduction

The United States is generally regarded as a very efficient problem solver by providing the right answers to various difficulties all over the world. However, in his analysis, Lester Salamon (Chapter 2 in this volume) departs from this opinion. Instead of arguing in favour of a truly American solution for present-day difficulties in the American nonprofit sector, his 'corporatist' prescription of intensified 'partnership' in order to overcome the legitimacy crisis the sector faces has a decidedly European flavour.

The corporatist version of public/private partnership, which Salamon describes in more detail in his chapter, departs significantly from the model of 'third-party government' (Salamon 1990), because the cooperation between government and the nonprofit sector is extended to the process of policy formulation and is no longer restricted to service provision. Moreover, Salamon implies that 'corporatism' might provide a quite reasonable solution and way forward to preserving vital nonprofit sectors in other countries.

This chapter uses Germany as a national example to discuss the implications of Salamon's crisis diagnosis and his proposed corporatist model of public/nonprofit relationships to safeguard the vitality of the nonprofit sector. For this kind of analysis, Germany provides an interesting test case because the country serves as a textbook example for political scientists studying the conservative or Christian-Democratic form of corporatism (Esping-Andersen 1990; Anheier and Seibel 1993; van Kersbergen 1994). In Germany, the areas of healthcare and social services are traditionally modelled according to Salamon's corporatist version that guarantees nonprofit organizations a remarkable share of the healthcare and social services market, while at the same time the German nonprofit organizations enjoy a prominent position in the process of policy formulation (Alber 1992). However, the effectiveness of this corporatist arrangement is increasingly disputed in Germany (Heinze 1998).

This gives way to the question of whether the corporatist model of the public/nonprofit relationship does indeed correspond to the needs of post-modern societies. In order to answer this question, it is necessary to first provide a profile of Germany's nonprofit sector. Subsequently, the subject of whether and to what extent Salamon's crisis diagnosis applies to the social-policy-related fields of the German nonprofit sector will be discussed.

A profile of the German nonprofit sector

Size, composition and government support

Like its American counterpart, the German nonprofit sector shows a remarkable mix of member-serving as well as public-serving organizations (Zimmer 1996). Since the mid-1970s, the German nonprofit sector has been growing continuously; recent surveys show increases in membership as well as in volunteering, particularly in the leisure-related fields of nonprofit activity (Priller and Zimmer 1998). Whereas member-serving organizations – such as sports clubs, choral societies or theatre groups – are primarily active in the fields of leisure activities, organizations serving the public dominate in healthcare and social services.

According to the results of the Johns Hopkins Comparative Nonprofit Sector Project Germany, in 1995, the German nonprofit sector involved $84 billion total operating expenditures, or about 4.0 per cent of GDP, and its share of the total labour force amounted to 5.0 per cent. With respect to its internal composition, the sector is dominated by nonprofits active in the fields of healthcare and social services. About 61 per cent of the operating expenditures of the sector is taken up by the combined total of those nonprofit organizations which are engaged in these two areas. Furthermore, the labour force in these two fields is highly professionalized. About 67 per cent of the sector's total workforce is employed in healthcare and social services. In terms of revenues, nonprofit organizations active in healthcare and social services are predominantly financed by cost-reimbursements from insurance funds, as well as by public subsidies. In 1995, these two areas of nonprofit activity received more than 78 per cent of public subsidies supporting the sector. Indeed, government support of nonprofit organizations active in the social-policy-related areas is guaranteed by law, and even local governments are obliged to subsidize nonprofit organizations active in healthcare or social service activities in Germany (Zimmer 1996: 132–45).

From a narrow economic point of view, nonprofit activities in the areas of sports, culture and recreation are of less importance with regard to the number of employees and the volume of expenditure. While these areas of activity attract only 5.8 per cent of the NPO labour force, in Germany more than 40 per cent of NPO volunteers are active in leisure-related voluntary organizations such as sports clubs. With respect to operating expenditure, the combined share of the nonprofit organizations active in leisure-related fields amounts to only 9 per cent, which is relatively low compared to the 61 per cent of the public-serving nonprofit organizations. In these fields, the main source of revenues is membership dues; however, to a certain extent, member-serving nonprofit organizations are also supported by public subsidies in Germany. In the case of sports clubs, for instance, local governments provide the training facilities such as tennis courts or swimming pools. Furthermore, on a strictly voluntary basis, local governments also provide financial support to member-serving organizations (Zimmer 1996).

In sum, the German nonprofit sector is divided into two dinstictive parts. Due to a very specific form of private/public partnership, those nonprofit organizations active in the fields of healthcare and social services are semi-public professionalized entities, and to a remarkable extent are integrated into the system of the German welfare state, whereas nonprofits which are engaged in leisure-related activities such as sports, show a greater degree of 'civicness' in the sense of member and volunteer participation.

The challenges, which Lester Salamon has identified as those confronting the nonprofit sector in the United States, primarily apply to German nonprofit organizations active in the fields of healthcare and social services, because like their US counterparts, they form a privately organized part of the German welfare state. In contrast to the United States, corporatism has always been the cornerstone of the relationship between government and nonprofit organizations in Germany. This very specific form of corporatism, animated by the principle of subsidiarity, until recently guaranteed nonprofit organizations active in healthcare and social services unique status (Anheier and Seibel 1993: 18f; Salamon and Anheier 1998: 242).

The legacy of history: corporatism and the principle of subsidiarity

It has been argued that the nonprofit sector in Germany stands out for its high degree of corporatism (Anheier and Seibel 1993: 29). According to the political science literature, corporatism represents the incorporation of societal actors into the policy process, typically by means of non-parliamentary consultation. As a style of policy making, corporatism involves the process of bargaining, consultation and close cooperation between the state and a limited number of private corporate actors which are predominantly associations (Reutter 1991).

In Germany, almost every nonprofit organization is a member of an umbrella or peak association like, for example, the powerful Welfare Associations or the German Sports Association. With branches at every level of government, the associations of the German nonprofit sector are vertically integrated and modelled in accordance with the administrative set-up of the country. The representatives of these associations work closely together in issue specific networks with the representatives of the political parties, trade unions and the professionals of the various administrative units of the German government, thus expressing a high degree of corporatism. In other words, the German nonprofit sector serves as an interface between state and civil society, as well as between the different levels of government. According to the analysis of the political scientist Peter Katzenstein, the very decentralized state of the Federal Republic of Germany is thus largely balanced by a highly centralized society consisting of umbrella and peak associations which are directly involved in the process of policy formulation as well as of implementation (Katzenstein 1987: 15).

Nevertheless, each nonprofit organization operating at the local level enjoys a remarkable degree of self-determination, because the associations are only loosely coupled systems. There is no top-down enforcement of rules and regulations, but integration and coordination is achieved by means of persuasion and discussion. Until recently, the authority of the associations had not been brought into question by the membership organizations, because the German nonprofit sector has until recently been structured along specific norms and values expressing a significant degree of pillarization (Zimmer 1998a: 105–8).

Germany's society used to be firmly divided along ideological and religious lines, of which the Social Democratic, Catholic and Protestant camps were the most important. In the leisure-related areas of nonprofit activity, these factions were not re-established after the Second World War. In the case of sports, for instance, instead of rebuilding the various sports associations linked to the different ideological camps, one all-encompassing umbrella organization – the German Sports Association – was set up in the 1950s. In contrast, in the social-policy-related fields of nonprofit activity, the German Welfare Associations were re-established along the traditional ideological lines. The German Welfare Associations are therefore quite unique and represent an organizational 'repository' of previous societal conflicts, of which the most important was the struggle between the modern German state and the church (Anheier 1990: 314; Schmid 1996).

The two largest Welfare Associations are Caritas, which is closely affiliated with the Catholic church in Germany, and Diakonie, which represents the Protestant equivalent of Caritas. Their origins date back to the German Empire, but they were set up as peak associations in the early years of the Weimar Republic, when the state's centralized welfare bureaucracy was established (Sachße 1996). Accepting the two church-related Welfare Associations as privately organized counterparts and partners in social policy making and implementation, the welfare bureaucracy, and therefore the state, bridged the religious division between Protestants and Catholics in the field of social policy in Germany. This corporatist arrangement was re-established in the early years of the Federal Republic. Moreover, after re-unification this corporatist arrangement was extended to the territory of the former Democratic Republic, although society in the new *Länder* (states) is considered to be very secular in its orientation (Anheier *et al.* 1996).

By the early 1960s, the nonprofit organizations affiliated with the Welfare Associations were already transformed into functional equivalents of public sector institutions (Zimmer 1998b). The guiding rule for this transformation was expressed by the principle of subsidiarity. Originally the principle was designed to protect individual citizens against possible state dominance by fascists or communists (Sachße 1998: 370f). In the 1960s, under the patronage of the German Christian-Democratic government, the principle was institutionalized and strictly interpreted in favour of the Welfare Associations. In the areas of healthcare and social services, those nonprofit organizations affiliated with the Welfare Associations were granted a privileged position by law, particularly compared to commercial competitors. In these two areas of welfare state policy, government was obliged to cooperate exclusively with the Welfare Association and to provide it substantial financial support, while at the same time the independence and self-determination of the local service-delivering nonprofit organizations was guaranteed. The result of this peculiar interpretation of the principle of subsidiarity was that the nonprofit organizations affiliated with Welfare Associations became a significant element in the growing healthcare and social service fields in Germany. In these two areas a protected market came into existence, where those nonprofit organizations affiliated with the Welfare Associations enjoyed a highly privileged status, while commercial organizations as well as nonprofit competitors which did not belong to the Welfare Associations were kept out of the market.

This specific interpretation of the principle of subsidiarity was exclusively put into practice in the social-policy-related fields of healthcare and social services, thus protecting the Welfare Associations from commercial as well as from nonprofit competition. Due to their privileged position, the Welfare Associations developed into the largest segment of the German nonprofit sector (Zimmer 1999). At the same time, they became an integral part of public administration, thus changing from 'value-based communities' into service provision enterprises (Sachße 1996: 169; Rauschenbach *et al.* 1995).

As a result of this development, the Welfare Associations faced a deep crisis of legitimacy in the early 1980s. They were accused of having lost their ties to their local constituencies and having turned into huge bureaucracies (Bauer 1995). Moreover, the Associations were sharply criticized by self-help groups and local initiatives, which were at that time closely connected to the new social movements in Germany (Roth and Rucht 1991). According to the self-help, women's rights, and gay and lesbian movements, the Welfare Associations were unresponsive to the needs of a heterogeneous postmodern society, and were interested only in securing their dominant position in the market of healthcare and social service provision.

Unfortunately, Salamon does not cover the scenario of a crisis of legitimacy caused by corporatism in his analysis. As Esping-Andersen (1990) has shown, corporatist arrangements tend to stabilize the societal status quo, expressing a high degree of conservatism and being particularly unfavourable towards the needs of new actors such as social movements. If the 'logic of influence' exercised by the representatives of the associations in the process of policy planning and implementation is no longer supported by the 'logic of membership' (Streeck 1987) the corporatist arrangement is seriously endangered. To put it differently: Germany's corporatist model of public/nonprofit partnership is no longer in accordance with the needs of its postmodern society. This is the crisis of legitimacy which the German nonprofit sector has been facing since the early 1980s.

Nevertheless, some of Salamon's observations do apply to the actual situation of Germany's nonprofit sector, because in the United States, as well as in other parts of the highly industrialized Western world, the nonprofit sector is deeply affected by the consequences of the so-called crisis of the welfare state.

Welfare state policy and the nonprofit sector in Germany

In his diagnosis, Salamon identifies the following four challenges which face the nonprofit sector in the United States at the moment: a fiscal crisis, an economic crisis, a crisis of effectiveness and a crisis of legitimacy. The fiscal crisis, which resulted in the reduction of government subsidies to nonprofit organizations, can be characterized as a result of mainstream neo-liberalism and its specific approach of new public management which tries to replace 'big government' by the establishment of competitive environments, or at the very least quasi-markets. Salamon's account of the economic crisis primarily deals with the actions and strategies carried out by nonprofit organizations in the United States which are designed to keep their position in the market of healthcare and social services, while they have to cope with the various shifts of social and welfare state policy. These efforts of the American nonprofit organizations were to a degree successful. However, according to Salamon's analysis the current crisis of legitimacy of the nonprofit sector in the United States represents a price that nonprofit organizations have had to pay for their strategy of 'marketization'.

Since the transition of the welfare state is a worldwide phenomenon, the fiscal crisis as well as the crisis of effectiveness has influenced the American and the German nonprofit sector alike. However, marketization in Salamon's sense as a significant increase of revenues from fees and charges does not apply to German nonprofit organizations, because compared to their American counterparts, they are operating in a very different legal and political environment (Anheier and Seibel 1993). It is this different environment that we now turn to.

From social democracy to neo-liberalism

During the postwar period, government was charged with the responsibility of ensuring the well-being of its citizens. Similar to the development in the United States (Salamon 1990), the extension of the welfare state in the 1960s and 1970s resulted in the remarkable growth of the German nonprofit sector. Due to the very specific interpretation of the principle of subsidiarity, the Welfare Associations in particular gained, as mentioned earlier, a very prominent position in the healthcare and social service market (Anheier 1990).

In the mid-1970s, the emergence of neo-liberalism and its 'free-market' approach with the emphasis on consumer choice replaced concerns for equality and egalitarianism. Now the welfare state was no longer perceived as a problem solver. Neo-liberals, even in the field of social policy, advocated the replacement of government with the flexible corporate arrangements of the market (Zimmer 1999). During the Reagan administration a competitive environment was established in the areas of healthcare and social services that forced providers to engage in stiff competition for contracts and pre-paid insurance plans, resulting in 'marketization' in the United States.

In Germany, however, the policy shift did not lead to 'marketization' of the sector, but resulted in the liberalization of the principle of subsidiarity, thus undermining corporatism and the cartel-like position of the Welfare Associations. Besides growing criticism that focused on their bureaucratic structures, since the late 1970s the Associations had had to face the emergence of competition in the form of self-help groups. Although the Associations forcefully tried to protect their privileges (Bauer 1995), the self-help groups were nevertheless gradually integrated into the system of service provision, particularly at local level. The establishment of a self-help fund by the city government of Berlin, followed by other municipalities, was particularly groundbreaking (Zimmer 1998c). Furthermore, the non-partisan Welfare Association, Deutscher Paritätischer Wohlfahrtsverband, began to accept self-help groups as members, and thus developed into the umbrella organization of the new initiatives and organizations affiliated with the new social movements. With respect to membership, it has subsequently developed into the fastest growing Welfare Association (Merchel 1989).

In the early 1990s the principle of subsidiarity was finally de-institutionalized. Major changes in social and healthcare legislation were introduced, which resulted in a deregulation of the healthcare and social service market, as well as in the market of out-patient care and care for the elderly (Backhaus-Maul and Olk 1994; Backhaus-Maul 1998). The Welfare Associations lost their privileged position because, particularly in youth welfare services, out-patient care and care for the elderly, less well established nonprofits, as well as commercial providers, were accepted on equal footing with the Associations and therefore eligible for insurance allowances as well as government grants. Furthermore, in accordance with the market approach, government and insurance funds moved away from statutory grants and lump sum reimbursement for medical and social services, by introducing schemes of cost-reimbursement at predetermined rates. In contrast to the former regulations, these schemes do not include compensation for losses.

These changes were introduced because the ongoing fiscal crisis of the state has also spread to the quasi-public social insurance system. There are several reasons for today's budget constraints at every level of government in Germany. First, the costs of re-unification put a heavy burden on public finances. Second, government income from corporate taxation has fallen, reflecting the impact of globalization processes. Finally, the insurance system is strongly affected by Germany's high rates of unemployment (Kühl 1996). The German welfare state is based on compulsory social insurance financed by contributions from employers and employees (the Bismarckian model). While insurance funds are confronted with rising costs because of the socio-democratic changes and developments in medical technology, income from contributions is decreasing (Berthold and Schmid 1997). Whereas a radical change in the funding system of the German welfare state has never been on the political agenda, in accordance with the neo-liberal approach, starting in the late 1980s social policy experts have been advocating liberalization of the healthcare and social service market in Germany (Berthold and Fehn 1997). In the meantime, German insurance funds are working on equal footing with commercial providers, public entities and nonprofit organizations.

Due to these shifts of social policy, for the first time in their history the Welfare Associations now have to face commercial competition, primarily in the new and growing market of out-patient care, and more specifically in care for the elderly, which was opened up by the introduction of care insurance in 1994 (Landenberger 1995). Moreover, the Associations are having to adjust to the fact that they no longer operate in a protected market where they enjoy a cartel-like position. In order to compete successfully with commercial providers, the Associations and their affiliated organizations are being forced to prove their accountability. In order to improve their management and accounting systems, the Associations have increasingly become more business-like, introducing management and marketing techniques and replacing social workers with business managers (Zimmer 1998d).

Whereas in the 1980s the Associations faced a crisis of legitimacy because they were unresponsive to the specific needs of postmodern German society, today they are suffering from a crisis of identity because they have turned into a social service industry, putting a high emphasis on efficiency. Similar to US nonprofits, the German Welfare Associations increasingly face the problem of lack of funds to finance their 'mission-related' activities. As a result of the introduction of cost-reimbursement on predetermined rates, the institutional or legal form of the service provider no longer matters. Public entities and insurance funds reimburse the service provision of nonprofit organizations and commercial enterprises on equal terms. The actions and strategies the Welfare Associations are taking to cope with this problem are basically twofold: First, they have started to separate their lobbying activities from service provision. Whereas local nonprofit organizations are focusing on provision of services, the associations at the various levels of government are intensifying their lobbying efforts in order to draw attention to the needs of specific constituencies and marginalized groups such as unemployed people, single parents, people with disabilities or immigrants (Pabst 1996). Some local nonprofits engaged in service provision, particularly hospitals, have already changed their legal form to businesses, because the *Verein*, as the most common legal form for German nonprofits, does not really suit effective management (Zimmer 1996). Second, nonprofit organizations active at local level are trying to preserve a specific organizational culture and identity which remains in accordance with their ideological or religious roots. In practical terms, they are trying to achieve this by integrating volunteers into their day-to-day operations (Deutscher Caritasverband 1995). Whereas in the past a premium was put on professionalization, volunteerism is emphasized today.

Welfare pluralism and the growing importance of the local level

Currently, there are numerous studies, articles and books which deal with the so-called *Bürgerkultur* or civic culture in Germany. This new wave of civic activity has to be seen in connection with the very recent trend of welfare state politics which is expressed by the approach of welfare pluralism as a rather vague and highly normative concept (Evers and Olk 1996). In accordance with neo-liberalism, welfare pluralism argues in favour of a competitive environment consisting of a mix of commercial, nonprofit and public service providers (Evers 1995). At the same time, however, the approach advocates the integration of volunteers, self-help groups and family members into a flexible system of health-care and social service provision, that is therefore not exclusively left to the market. Although welfare pluralism has not yet developed into a clear-cut strategy of social policy, there is no doubt that this new approach represents a further de-institutionalization of the principle of subsidiarity, as well as the waning of traditional corporatism in Germany.

According to Streeck and Schmitter (1985), negotiation among a limited and fixed number of Associations, which are privileged and therefore licensed by the state, is at the core of corporatist arrangements (Streeck and Schmitter 1985: 124). The Welfare Association's unique position in the market of healthcare and partic-ularly social services has already been modified by integrating commercial providers and also those nonprofit organizations which are not affiliated with the Associations. Under the logic of welfare pluralism, the transformation, and more specifically the de-institutionalization, of German corporatism will be acceler-ated. Informal units, such as neighbourhood initiatives, will increasingly be accepted as healthcare and social services providers, particularly at local level. At the same time, the representatives of these informal groups will gradually be inte-grated into the process of social policy planning. Therefore, in the long run, welfare pluralism coupled with volunteerism will give way to a significant change in the power structure and set-up of the German nonprofit sector. Whereas the associations which are guided by the 'logic of influence' are losing their impor-tance, the 'logic of membership', and therefore the influence of local constituencies, will increase.

Conclusion: towards new forms of public/private partnerships

Although in Germany, those nonprofit organizations working in healthcare and social services are being confronted with a crisis of legitimacy and identity, the situation of the German nonprofit sector is nevertheless very different from its counterpart in the United States. To put it in a nutshell: the legacy of corpo-ratism is at the core of the current problems of the German nonprofit sector. The unique version of corporatism which in the areas of healthcare and social services is expressed by the principle of subsidiarity has faced criticism since the early 1980s. German nonprofits, particularly those organizations which are affiliated with the Welfare Associations, must decide whether to continue to act in the spirit of corporatism and semi-public service provision or to define a new role.

However, the corporatism option is increasingly open to question. The umbrella and peak associations, which are such a typical feature of the German nonprofit sector, are losing their integrative functions. A case in point is the area of sports and recreation, where the umbrella organizations – such as the German Sports Associations – are no longer accepted by their membership organizations. Since the mid-1970s, more and more people have been getting involved in club life and associational activities at the local level. By now, even volunteering is on the increase in Germany (Priller and Zimmer 1998). This represents a very positive and promising development. There is an augmentation of civic activity at local level, whereas peak associations and umbrella organizations are losing both civil support and legitimacy.

New forms of public/private partnerships are being primarily tested at the local level. In the city of Münster, for instance, the local administration and public healthcare organizations, as well as nonprofit organizations active in healthcare and social services, have just started to set up a so-called 'community health centre' or *Gesundheitshaus*. The centre will be located in the city centre; it will serve as host for two public entities – the Department of Health (*Gesundheitsamt*) and the Service Centre for care for older people (*Info-Pflege*) – as well as for a variety of nonprofit organizations. Among these will be two sports clubs, which are engaged in health prevention activities for children and the elderly; the service and counselling centre for self-help groups, which provides information and support to the self-help groups in the region; and finally the counselling centre for cancer patients, which as a nonprofit organization receives substantial financial support from local government. The landlord of the centre will be the local government, which will rent office space to the above-mentioned organizations and groups, as well as to nonprofit organizations or individuals wishing to use the facilities of the house only for a day or a couple of hours.

Finally, a very unique form of public/private partnership has come into existence, particularly in the field of sports and leisure at local level. Elected representatives of local sports and leisure clubs, along with cultural nonprofit organizations, are forming so-called 'intermediary committees'. These operate as functional equivalents to their local government counterparts. The committees are responsible for the distribution of public funds and for the setting of priorities in their specific areas, such as sports or cultural policy. In other words, without interference from local politicians or administrators, the committee members are responsible for policy and politics (Zimmer 1998c). There are two reasons why local politicians and administrators are deliberately handing over power by standing aside for intermediary committees. First, reflecting the fiscal crisis in Germany, politicians and administrators lack the resources to continue a redistributive policy. Second, confronted with the heterogeneity of modern German society, they want to avoid taking risky decisions which might not be in accordance with the preferences of the average voter and therefore might pose a threat to their re-election.

Thus it is increasingly local nonprofit organizations which are confronted with a situation where they, instead of government, have to act. This development puts a heavy burden on the sector. Although this new trend is in accordance with postmodern society, which is highly individualized, at the same time there is a vital need for a new role and more specifically for a new identity for the nonprofit sector. In this context, the corporatist approach of 'holding the centre', preferred by Lester Salamon, is definitely not appropriate for safeguarding the vitality and spontaneity of the sector. At least in Germany, the third sector cannot go back to corporatism, but must define a new role of nonprofit activism which is rooted in the tradition of social movements and societal change.

References

Alber, J. (1992) *Das Gesundheitswesen der Bundesrepublik Deutschland: Entwicklung, Struktur und Funktionsweise*, Frankfurt: Campus.

Anheier, H. K. (1990) 'The third sector in West Germany', in H. K. Anheier and W. Seibel (eds) *The Third Sector: Comparative Studies of Nonprofit Organizations*, Berlin and New York: de Gruyter.

Anheier, H. K., Priller, E. and Zimmer, A. (1996) 'Civic society in transition: the East German nonprofit sector six years after unification', Working Paper 13, Baltimore: Johns Hopkins University Center for Civil Society Studies.

Anheier, H. K. and Seibel, W. (1993) 'Defining the nonprofit sector: Germany', Working Paper 6, Baltimore: Johns Hopkins University Institute for Policy Studies.

Backhaus-Maul, H. (1998) 'Etablierte und Außenseiter. Freie Wohlfahrtspflege im Deutschen Sozialversicherungsstaat', *Forschungsjournal Neue Soziale Bewegungen*, 11, 2: 38–50.

Backhaus-Maul, H. and Olk, Th. (1994) 'Von Subsidiarität zum "outcontracting": zum Wandel der Beziehungen von Staat und Wohlfahrtsverbänden in der Sozialpolitik', in W. Streeck (ed.) *Staat und Verbände*, Opladen: Westdeutscher Verlag.

Bauer, R. (1995) 'Nonprofit-Organisationen und NPO-Forschung in der Bundesrepublik Deutschland', in R. Schauer, H. Anheier and E.-B. Blümle (eds) *Nonprofit-Organisationen: Dritte Kraft Zwischen Markt und Staat, Universitätsverlag*, Linz: Rudolf Trauner.

Berthold, N. and Fehn, R. (1997) 'Reforming the welfare state: the German case', in H. Giersch (ed.) *Reforming the Welfare State*, Berlin: de Gruyter.

Berthold, N. and Schmid, C. (1997) 'Krise der Arbeitsgesellschaft und Privatisierung der Sozialpolitik', *Aus Politik und Zeitgeschichte*, B 48–9, 97: 3–11.

Deutscher Caritasverband (1995) 'Ehrenamtliche Tätigkeit in der Caritas: Bestandsaufnahme, Perspektiven, Positionen', *Caritas*, 96, 7/8: 309–29.

Esping-Andersen, G. (1990) *The Three Worlds of Welfare Capitalism*, Cambridge: Polity Press.

Evers, A. (1995) 'Part of the welfare mix: the third sector as an intermediate area', *Voluntas*, 6, 2: 159–82.

Evers, A. and Olk, Th. (eds) (1996) *Wohlfahrtspluralismus: vom Wohlfahrtsstaat zur Wohlfahrtsgesellschaft*, Opladen: Leske & Budrich.

Heinze, R. (1998) *Die Blockierte Gesellschaft*, Opladen: Westdeutscher Verlag.

Katzenstein, P. (1987) *Policy and Politics in West Germany: The Growth of a Semisovereign State*, Philadelphia: Temple Press.

van Kersbergen, K. (1994) *Social Capitalism: A Study of Christian Democracy and the Welfare State*, London: Routledge.

Kühl, J. (1996) 'Warum schaffen zwei Millionen Betriebe und Verwaltungen nicht genügend gute Arbeitsplätze für alle?', *Aus Politik und Zeitgeschichte*, B 3–4, 96: 26–39.

Landenberger, M. (1995) 'Pflegeversicherung – Modell für sozialstaatlichen Wandel', *Gegenwartskunde*, 1: 19–31.

Merchel, J. (1989) *Der Deutsche Paritätische Wohlfahrtsverband: Seine Funktion im korporatistisch geführten System sozialer Arbeit*, Weinheim: Deutscher Studienverlag.

Pabst, St. (1996) *Sozialanwälte: Wohlfahrtsverbände zwischen Interessen und Ideen*, Augsburg: Maro-Verlag.

Priller, E. and Zimmer, A. (1998) 'Bowling alone or bowling together? Membership and volunteering in Germany', paper presented at the Third International Conference of the Society for Third-Sector Research, 8–11 July, Geneva, Switzerland.

Rauschenbach, Th., Sachße, Ch. and Olk, Th. (eds) (1995) *Von der Wertegemeinschaft zum Dienstleistungsunternehmen*, Frankfurt am Main: Suhrkamp.

Reutter, W. (1991) *Korporatismustheorien*, Frankfurt: Lang.

Roth, R. and Rucht, D. (eds) (1991) *Neue soziale Bewegungen in der Bundesrepublik*, 2nd edn, Bonn: Bundeszentrale für Politische Bildung.

Sachße, Ch. (1996) 'Public and private in German social welfare, the 1890s to the 1920s', in M. Katz and Ch. Sachße (eds) *The Mixed Economy of Social Welfare: Public-Private Relations in England, Germany and the United States, the 1870s to the 1930s*, Baden-Baden: Nomos.

Sachße, Ch. (1998) 'Entwicklung und Perspektiven des Subsidiaritätsprinzips', in R. Graf Strachwitz (ed.) *Dritte Sektor – Dritte Kraft*, Düsseldorf: Raabe-Verlag.

Salamon, L. (1990) 'The nonprofit sector and government: the American experience in theory and practice', in H. K. Anheier and W. Seibel (eds) *The Third Sector: Comparative Studies of Nonprofit Organizations*, Berlin and New York: De Gruyter.

Salamon, L. and Anheier, H. K. (1998) 'Der Nonprofit-sektor: ein theoretischer Versuch', in H. K. Anheier, W. Seibel, E. Priller and A. Zimmer (eds) *Der Dritte Sektor in Deutschland*, Berlin: Sigma.

Schmid, J. (1996) *Wohlfahrtsverbände in Modernen Wohlfahrtsstaaten*, Opladen: Leske & Budrich.

Streeck, W. (1987) 'Vielfalt und Interdependenz', *Kölner Zeitschrift für Soziologie und Sozialpsychologie*, 39, 3: 452–70.

Streeck, W. and Schmitter, Ph. (1985) 'Community, market, state – and associations', *European Sociological Review*, 1, 2: 119–38.

Zimmer, A. (1996) *Vereine: Basiselemt der Demokratie*, Opladen: Leske & Budrich.

——(1998a) 'Der Verein in Gesellschaft und Politik', in R. Graf Strachwitz (ed.) *Dritte Sektor – Dritte Kraft*, Düsseldorf: Raabe-Verlag.

——(1998b) 'Public-private partnerships: Staat und Nonprofit-sektor in Deutschland', in H. K. Anheier, W. Seibel, E. Priller and A. Zimmer (eds) *Der Dritte Sektor in Deutschland*, Berlin: Sigma.

——(1998c) 'Vereine und lokale Politik', in R. Roth and H. Wollmann (eds) *Kommunalpolitik*, Bonn: Bundeszentrale für Politische Bildung.

——(1998d) 'Modernisierung des Staates und der Nonprofit-sektor', in D. Grunow and H. Wollmann (eds) *Lokale Verwaltungsreform in Aktion: Fortschritte und Fallstricke*, Basel: Birkhäuser-Verlag.

——(1999) 'Welfare pluralism and healthcare: the case of Germany', in J. Kovács (ed.) *The Politics of Welfare Reform: East and West. Between Governmental Policy and Civic Initiative*, London and New York: Routledge.

10 The third sector and the European Union policy process

An initial evaluation

Jeremy Kendall and Helmut K. Anheier

Introduction

Third sector organizations[1] have entered relatively late on the EU scene. At the beginning, and in accordance with the spirit of the Treaty of Rome,[2] the third sector remained excluded from the list of EEC/EC competencies, and it was not until the mid-1980s that the third sector *per se* received first mentions in official documents (with the key exception of overseas development agencies). In particular, a resolution, commonly known as the Fontaine Report,[3] became influential in putting the possibility of EU policy making on the third sector on the agenda. The Report enthusiastically endorsed an important – though largely unspecified – role for the 'nonprofit' sector in helping create the new Europe. In its closing paragraph, the Report calls on the Commission to see the 'nonprofit' sector as an important ally in building the new Europe:

> Europe needs inspiration to take a further step towards its destiny as a Community. Nonprofit organizations are an opportunity to be taken in this respect. Inertia must be overcome and this opportunity must be boldly seized.

In the 1990s, several initiatives were launched under the auspices of DG XXIII, a department in the Commission newly charged with attending to the third sector as part of its *économie sociale* brief,[4] and/or were jointly developed by other EU institutions. However, none of these initiatives have progressed smoothly, instead being characterized by precisely the inertia which Fontaine feared. As we shall portray, they have tended to involve varying combinations of political stalemate, seriously delay and downgrading, or have remained little more than declarations of political will attached to the EU's Treaties.

Why has this been the case? To understand the fate of recent policy initiatives and their ambivalent outcomes, it is useful to consider the position of the third sector in the context of EU policy making in general. Our major working hypothesis at the highest level of generality is that what appears as a relatively subdued, underperforming, or cautious policy style can only be understood by explicating the constellation of interests, values and ideas among the parties involved in the context of European policy making more generally. That is, focusing on the third sector not in isolation, but as a competitor for agenda and policy space with other topics. A subsidiary hypothesis is that while ultimately some form of general evaluation is helpful, we also expect considerable variation between particular issues and policy subfields, reflecting the complexity and diversity of EU institutions and the third sector alike.

Four propositions

To help guide our analysis we use four largely contradictory propositions to conceptually mark out the possible range of EU policy making in this field. These propositions include two dimensions: first, the importance or *salience* key actors attach to a particular policy. The second dimension refers to the *overall style* that characterizes the policy making process. This would include taking into account particular patterns of essentially political bargaining – such as cooperation, conflict and compromise – as well as the scope that institutional constraints allow for persuasion, argument and the exchange of ideas.

Proposition 1: low salience and muddling-through

EU policies on the third sector remain relatively uncoordinated and are generally regarded as a matter of low importance beyond the occasional lip-service being paid to their social and economic contributions. This reflects lack of interest, will or commitment among the actors that shape the Commission's agenda.

Proposition 2: low salience but effective coordination

While EU policies concerning the third sector remain a matter of low salience in day-to-day 'high' politics, low visibility efforts are nevertheless being made to move the EU's interest in the sector forward. Cognizant of the political sensitivities involved, and aware that the European-wide policy infrastructure for these organizations *qua* a third sector remains underdeveloped, EU policy initiatives are proceeding, but are cautious and low-key.

Proposition 3: high salience and politicking

EU policies are becoming ever more important relative to member states' national and local policies because of the increasingly high stakes that are involved in both political and economic terms. Policy making is characterized by active 'strategizing' among key players, and includes a broad range of tactics like preventive stalling, deal-making and bullying. No broad-based consensus seems to emerge among the major parties involved.

Proposition 4: high salience and effective coordination

EU policies reflect a relatively well coordinated attempt by EU institutions to provide an enabling policy environment, with the third sector emerging as a widely recognized and high-visibility actor in both policy design and policy implementation.

In the balance of this chapter, we will first look at the policy making process in the EU as it relates to the third sector at the highest level of generality: can we trace the recognition of a 'third sector' by EU institutions? We also set our description in the context of a framework which seems reasonably well equipped to handle the phenomena and complexities at stake, suggesting both the range of *participants* with whom we should be concerned, and the nature of the *policy process* itself.

Armed with the four propositions spelt out above, and our model of participants and policy process as reference points, we then explore five particular 'case study' policy initiatives in more detail. The chapter concludes with an overall assessment of EU initiatives in this field, and tentatively uses the framework introduced in the first section to explore some of the underlying issues involved.

The complexities of European policy and the third sector; and an organizing framework

It is now well understood that EU policy making is an extremely complex, unstable and unpredictable activity in general, particularly concerning issues that cut across traditional bureaucratic divides (Richardson 1996a: 4; 1996b: 3–4; McCormick 1996: 204). But when one turns to consider the policy process and the third sector in particular, there appear to be at least two further difficulties. First, within any particular member state, it is clear that this sector is incredibly diverse, heterogeneous and populated by organizations with hugely varied goals, structures and motivations (cf. Salamon and Anheier 1997). How can an overarching policy be possible towards such a 'loose and baggy monster' (Kendall and Knapp 1995; 1996)?

Second, across member states there is a lack of shared understanding as to what the concept actually means, and what it might embrace. This has been reflected in a not inconsiderable degree of diversity and confusion in the usage and vocabulary at the level of the Community's institutions.[5]

Do these multiple complications mean that it is impossible or fruitless to talk of European Union policy or policies towards 'the third sector'? We would argue no, for three main reasons. First, it is now well understood that individual member states have, in various ways, historically and currently, treated organizations that fall between the market and the state differently from those institutions. At the very least, some or all of these tend to benefit from both legal privileges and tax breaks of various kinds because of their sectoral identity, even if a unified 'sector' is implicit rather than explicit, and many national, regional and local government funding programmes support these agencies. Whether this is piecemeal, *de facto*, *ad hoc* and organically developed, or systematized, coherent and 'rationalist', explicit or implicit policies covering a wide range of third sector organizations exist. If it is accepted that sector-specific policies of one form or another, do, therefore, operate at the member state level, then logically there is the possibility that an equivalent or near-equivalent institutional terrain can form a policy focus for European Union institutions.

Second, the institutions of the European Union have *already* begun to develop positions, take decisions and undertake actions which have as their focus some recognizable 'sector'. Box 10.1 fleshes this out with a (non-exhaustive) chronology of some of the most obvious indications of such institutional recognition and

---

Box 10.1   Some significant events in development of EU 'policy' towards the third sector

1976   NGO/EU liaison committee set up by mutual agreement between DGVIII and European international development and relief organizations.

1984   Resolution of European Union on the 'role and administration of association and the laws governing them' provides the impetus for the production of the Fontaine Report (published in 1987).

1985   Economic and Social Committee (ECOSOC) initiates conference making first European attempt to compile statistical inventory of the *économie sociale*.

1989   'Social economy' unit established at DGXXIII.

1992   Commission publishes first draft Regulation for European Statute for Associations.

1992   Declaration 23 attached to the Treaty of Maastricht calls for 'co-operation between the European Community and [social welfare] charitable associations and foundations'.

1996   Draft ESA regulation referred to COREPER working group and features on Council of Ministers' agenda.

1996   DGV promotes idea of 'civil dialogue' with NGOs at Social Policy Forum in run-up to Amsterdam Treaty.

1997   Declaration 38 attached to the Amsterdam Treaty singles out 'voluntary service activities' which are 'recognise[d for their] the important contribution by voluntary service activities to developing social solidarity'.

1997   DGXXIII and DGV jointly launch Communication, 'Promoting the role of voluntary organizations and foundations in Europe'.

1998   ECOSOC, COR and two European Parliament committees table draft reports in response to the Communication.

1999   Forward Studies Unit (reporting directly to the President of the European Commission) invites 'national experts' and Commission bureaucrats to seminar on 'Economics of the Third Sector'.

---

acknowledgement. This provides *prima facie* evidence that, at least since the mid-1980s (and somewhat earlier in the case of international development organizations), the EU has departed from the *de facto* pure 'leave it to member states' option.

Finally, there is a new spate of evidence that has recently emerged concerning the pervasiveness of the voluntary sector across the European Union in economic terms (most recently, see Salamon *et al.* 1999). It is also clear that the social and political role of these organizations at European level is gaining higher visibility. Over 100 third sector networks and federations now operate, many with offices in Brussels (Harvey 1995: 93). And focusing on the sector's advocacy role, the European Citizen's Action Service has recently argued that somewhere between 5 per cent and 10 per cent of the lobbying activity undertaken at the Commission level is for public purposes rather than by private businesses (ECAS n.d.: 28). The European Commission itself has issued a Communication calling for 'open and structured dialogue' with 'interest groups', although admittedly not distinguishing between those representing business interests, subnational state interests and third sector interests (Commission of the European Communities 1992a).

Effectively, then, with one exception the European Union appears to have moved from a 'do nothing' policy for some thirty years between the 1957 Treaty of Rome and around the time of the 1986 Single European Act, towards a surge of explicit recognition of the sector *per se* during the course of the past decade. We observe a wide array of participants: the Commission; the European Parliament and some of its Committees; national politicians (at the Council of Ministers and during Treaty renegotiations), and national civil servants (through participation in a COREPER working group); 'national experts' (for example, those invited to the Forward Studies Unit seminar); institutionally recognized interested parties (through ECOSOC and COR); and the third sector itself (as a sponsor of research, and participant in public hearings and fora).

How are we to structure and analyse such a complex process? To make our account manageable, in the remainder of the paper we focus in two ways. First, operationally, we consider only a small number of policies, initiatives or events. We will attend to:

- the European Association Statute (EAS)
- Declaration 23, attached to the Maastricht Treaty
- the 1997 Communication
- the third sector as an actor in the allocation of the Structural Funds
- the third sector as an actor in overseas development policy.

This particular combination was chosen for four reasons. First, these represent important topics in the discourse of discussions of the third sector amongst practitioners and analysts alike, at least in the first four instances. Second, coverage of overseas development policy and the Structural Funds mean we include the two single most important sources of financial support from the EU for the third sector. Third, and relatedly, the 'cases' each represent slightly different aspects of the policy process, ranging from agenda setting and 'symbolic' policy making (the 1997 Communication and Declaration 23), through (potentially at least) legal decision-making via regulation (EAS), to policy implementation (overseas development policy and the Structural Funds), and so potentially shed light on different aspects of the process. Fourth, these choices are pragmatic: in many cases, we were acquainted with some of the most important actors, and thus were in a position to secure access to valuable primary information.[6]

Second, we find it useful to deploy Kingdon's 'multiple streams' approach (1995) in an attempt to make some initial sense of, and impose some structure upon, what seems a chaotic set of events and outcomes.[7] In summary, this framework, in the first place, recognises that various *participants* – which would include, in our terms, the various actors and institutional players discussed above, plus, importantly, the general public and the media – can all potentially be sources of, or indirectly affect, policy agenda items and alternative policy proposals, or 'solutions' to conditions which powerful actors sense are 'problems' and therefore merit a policy response.

Second, the policy process is portrayed as involving three 'largely independent … streams': problems, politics and policies. The *problems stream* helps us grasp how and why states of affairs come to be considered problematic, and is said to involve such factors as the availability of systematic indicators, focusing events including crises and disasters, and feedback from the operations of current programmes. The *policy stream* is treated as analogous to biological natural selection: ideas float between communities of specialists, and those proposals which meet certain criteria – including technical feasibility and budgetary workability – are the ones that survive. Finally, the *politics stream* is affected by swings in the national mood, turnover of elected officials and pressure from interest groups. According to Kingdon, the all-important *coupling* of these streams:

> Is most likely when *policy windows* – opportunities for pushing pet proposals or conceptions of problems – are open … windows are opened either by the appearance of compelling problems or by happenings in the political stream [while] … alternatives are generated by the policy stream. *Policy entrepreneurs*, people who are willing to invest their resources in pushing their pet proposals … are responsible not only for prompting important people to pay attention, but also for coupling solutions to problems and for coupling both problems and solutions to politics.
>
> (Kingdon 1995: 20; emphases added)

The contrasting development of five third sector relevant policy initiatives

Before we examine the five initiatives separately, we will tentatively sketch out the features of what appear to be the shared roots of at least two of them, the European Association Statute and the Communication.[8] The origins are almost certainly to be found outside the European institutions themselves, and principally from a group of low-visibility French actors who were later to form CEDAG, the Comité Européen des Associations d'intérêt Général. This now operates as a pan-European umbrella group with some financial support from DGXXIII. In the early 1980s, these individuals appear to have lobbied French MEPs in particular and the wider socialist and Christian Democrat groups of which they were part, for some form of EC acknowledgement and recognition of the role of 'associations'.

Although the precise nature of their original goals and motives is unclear, their efforts are closely related to the European Parliament resolution of 1984, and the resulting Fontaine Report tabled in 1986 and published in 1987. The Report argued that a legal basis for Commission action in this field could be found, entitling it (through Article 7 of the Treaty of Rome) to intervene at member state level to prevent associations' 'discrimination on the grounds of nationality', and (under Articles 100 and 235 of the Treaty of Rome, and Article 100A and other articles of the Single European Act) to facilitate transnational activity in this field. A wide ranging array of provisions was proposed to promote the cross-border operations of associations, including (6–7):

- the automatic recognition in other member states of associations recognized in their home country
- the creation of an European Association Statute for those organizations wishing to operate across Europe who found existing legislative alternatives inappropriate
- the setting up of an 'European fund for the development of associations'
- a 'better representation' of the association sector at the level of Community institutions.

The report also made a general suggestion that 'greater funds be made available, in the service of the community, to nonprofit making associations which perform a service in the common interest by increasing their power to accept donations from individuals' (7).

The European Association Statute (EAS)

One of the most tangible and specific proposals contained in the Fontaine Report was the suggestion that a legal instrument be created to enable third sector bodies to operate with greater ease transnationally. Several years later, a draft legislation was officially submitted to the Council by the Commission (Commission of the European Communities 1992b), and revised and resubmitted the following year (Commission of the European Communities 1993). Importantly, the EAS became part of a package which included equivalent regulations for cooperatives and mutuals, together with accompanying directives on worker participation. These are voluminous documents, spelling out in great details proposals for internal decision-making in the proposed EA. Overall, however, little progress was made, and the EAS, together with the other parts of the package, remained stalled in the absence of decisive action.

Gjems-Onstad (1995) has outlined some of the factors that shaped this regulation's limited progress between 1992 and 1995. He suggests that 'it is obscure whether anybody, either outside or inside the official bureaucracy of Brussels, much cared about what happens to the proposals' (1995: 4) with the notable exceptions of CEDAG and presumably its allies in the European Parliament. Significantly, he refers to official statements from the German government questioning the need for EU action in this regard.

At the same time, in Britain an insider told us that the knowledge that there was activity at the European level 'raised all kinds of vague fears about "Was the Commission going to come along with great big boots and spoil our nice back yard?" '. As it became clearer that the main issue in hand was the particular proposal for a transnational legal structure, British opinion in both the home civil service and amongst national experts working in the Commission began to coalesce in two ways: first, in sympathy with the German view that European action was unnecessary, since transnational third sector organizations could reasonably well operate simultaneously under national laws in each member state; and second, that an adapted version of an alternative structure, the European Economic Interest Grouping, would form a better starting point for a tailored legal instrument. Moreover, anecdotal evidence on attitudes towards the Statute within the Council of Ministers[9] suggests that the UK government began to use the idea of 'subsidiarity' as a rationale for opposing the measure from 1992 onwards (Gjems-Onstad 1995: 4).

At the level of the associations themselves, three active positions were discernible. The French associations favoured the EAS because it offered them a chance to overcome the limitations of existing legislation in France, in particular the restrictions on property ownership and the centralized system of public governance of third sector organizations (Archambault 1996). Second, the German free welfare associations (see below) appear to have been against the measure, on the grounds that it might in some way challenge their privileged position regarding the collection of 'church tax', although how this might have been the case is obscure and the issue was rarely discussed. Finally, by 1996, the Italian third sector had been actively supportive enough to secure, under the Italian presidency, the convening of an expert working group at the Council (COREPER). This examined the draft regulation, meeting four times during the course of that year, and as a result the regulation featured explicitly on the agenda of a Council of Ministers meeting for the first time.

However, the policy making style remained cautious, and the significance of this mention on the Council agenda should not be overestimated. In fact, reference to the existence of the expert working group was confined to a rather bland paragraph that 'under the Italian presidency there has been work on a regulation for associations and further work will be conducted in the future'.[10]

While the EAS had technically made it onto the Council of Ministers' agenda, it still faced major barriers. The matter was particularly complicated by different national positions concerning the Directive for workers' participation that accompanies this and the other two *économie sociale* statutes (as well as the proposed regulation for European (for-profit) companies). Broadly speaking, these positions reflected fundamental disagreements concerning the scope and purpose of 'social' Europe. The UK government under Thatcher and Major had been hostile to this Directive – again, referring to the principal of subsidiarity as grounds for opposition – while the German government saw it as not going far enough in extending workers' rights as part of their broader vision of a federal-style Europe.

Although the deadlock around the workers' participation Directive now appears to have been resolved, the most widely held view appears to be that this will not in itself open the way for the EAS to come to legal fruition in the immediate future: more obstacles are being set up for the Statute, this time by members of the third sector community itself in at least one member state: Germany. In a recent official policy statement, arguing on the basis of nineteenth-century civil law, the Association of Free Welfare Organizations in Bonn issued the opinion that the free welfare associations, which dominate the third sector in Germany (Anheier and Seibel 1998), are voluntary, *ideal* associations, and inherently cannot be 'economic' firms or entities at all. The very coupling of matters economic with matters social under the banner *économie sociale*, and the joint packaging therein of the association statute with statutes for cooperatives and mutuals, has come to be perceived as threatening to this part of the German third sector.

Relatedly, its opposition has also been motivated by concerns about the implications of the workers' participation Directive. Rightly or wrongly, it has been interpreted as implying an increase in the likelihood that trade unions or their equivalents could play a legally sanctioned role in large third sector hospitals, social service providers and educational institutions. This would be a new development given the current exemption of many of these establishments from unionization under existing German law.[11]

We can attempt to summarize some of this complexity using our descriptive propositions and Kingdon's model. First, given its rather obscure packaging and the lack of agreement that a 'problem' existed, in many ways it is quite surprising that it managed to even get as far as a draft legal instrument, let alone to take the particular form of the EAS. There were initially certainly no obvious 'focusing events' in terms of the crises or indicators which Kingdon argued are so important in prompting interest from policy makers. Most activity proceeded relatively independently in the 'policy stream', as first Commission civil servants, and subsequently national experts, quietly sought to take the matter forward. In this phase, even actors against the EAS in principal were not much bothered to concern themselves with it, as its chances of success seemed remote.

However, a shift can be detected around the mid-1990s, as one particular set of stakeholders – the German free welfare associations – began to formulate a position which was *proactively* hostile. The resolution of the log-jam over the workers' participation Directive seems to have acted in part as a 'focusing event' for these organizations' leadership. Particularly as the regulation's French and

Italian supporters upgrade their efforts to support the measure in response, a 'politicking' scenario seems to be emerging.

The 1997 Communication

To understand the genesis and development of the Communication, it is important first of all to understand how the 'social economy' unit which spawned it is situated within the Commission, and the political and cultural pressures that led to its establishment in the first place.

The 'social economy' unit, dealing with overarching responsibility for associations, cooperatives and mutuals, was added to DGXXIII's portfolio in 1989 to sit alongside its existing ambit of enterprise policy and small and medium businesses (SMEs), distributive trades and tourism. Overall, DGXXIII is one of the Commission's smallest departments, and is one of the few to share its Commissioner with another DG: Its Greek socialist Commissioner, Christos Papoutsis, an economist, also works at the Euratom supply agency and also heads the department concerned with energy (DGXVIII). Moreover, there is no evidence that he has a substantive personal or other interest in the third sector.[12] Within DGXXIII, the social economy unit accounts for only a tiny proportion of its activities.[13] It is only a slight exaggeration to state that the social economy unit is the smallest part of a DG located at the margins of EU politics and operations, headed by a commissioner with little opportunity or inclination to attend to the third sector.

The 'official' language of DGXXIII's Work Programme in the early 1990s concentrates heavily on mutuals and cooperatives rather than associations, referring extremely vaguely to a rationale in terms of protecting the sector's 'specificities' in the face of economic integration.[14] One senior insider indicated to us that there was, in fact, no guidance other than to 'keep an eye on' the EAS. In addition, it was suggested that a White Paper should be drafted – but with little or no instructions as to what it could or should contain.[15] A first draft of the White Paper was produced by DGXXIII in late 1994. Asked to comment on the response to the drafting process within the Commission, a DGXXIII insider argued:

> When it was being drafted, we couldn't get anyone's attention, nobody cared less, DGV couldn't have cared less … so when the thing was finally put around nobody had anything to say about it … [We] had no weight in the Commission. … and there was general apathy on the part of other *Cabinets*. So the thing would be on the agenda, and nothing would be done to push it, and then it would fall off as something more urgent came along.

In fact, it was an abbreviated and slightly redrafted version of the same document which was to appear as a Communication some three years later in June 1997. Box 10.2 sets out its key elements. A Communication carried less official weight than a *Livre Blanc* (which is usually a first step to major policy action). Why was the idea of a *Livre Blanc* abandoned in favour of the 'weaker' Communication, and why the long delay?

The main official reason for the delay was to take account of the expanding EU membership in the document. But two other factors seem much more important. First, the continued indifference and apathy of most actors in the Commission. Second, the delay was partly due to the emergence of DGV (social policy and employment) in a newly proactive mode, expressing far greater interest in the idea of a 'third sector' than previously, and now insisting on having an input into the drafting process where beforehand it had indicated no such interest. In fact, the Communication was in the end launched as a joint initiative by both DGV and DGXXIII.

Two reasons for DGV's apparent change of attitude and new found role as promoter of 'civil dialogue' with the third sector seem particularly important.

Box 10.2   The 1997 Communication 'Promoting the role of voluntary organizations and foundations in Europe'

This document (Commission of the European Communities 1997) contains fifteen pages of main text, together with three annexes (sixty-seven pages). The main text includes:

Primary aims: to illustrate the growing importance of the sector within the EU, to show what problems and challenges these organizations are facing and to open up a dialogue ... to improve their capacity to meet future needs and maximize their contribution to European integration. (p. 5)

Three pages describe the voluntary sector's economic scope and scale, and political and social importance.

Two pages describe 'the sector and the European institutions working together'. This section notes the existence of contacts between a number of DGs and the voluntary sector prior to 1992, but states that these 'took place on a completely *ad hoc* basis ... it was not until the [Maastricht] Treaty that the importance of links with this sector was first formally expressed with the creation of declaration 23' (p. 11).

Three pages describe 'problems and challenges facing the sector', ranging across a number of issues primarily relating to financial resources.

A four-page Conclusion is divided into suggestions at three levels. First, at member state level the Commission urges member states, *inter alia*, to develop data. Second, the section 'Voluntary sector and foundations level' is just two paragraphs urging diversification and encouragement of 'relevant' training. Third, at European Community level, it is proposed that 'civic dialogue' be progressed in part through the operation of the new 'consultative committee' for 'social economy' organizations.

First, we noted above the 'mushrooming' of lobbying activity by the third sector, and this has been particularly noticeable in the social policy arena. Having culti-vated these groups and networks since the mid-1970s, this arm of the Commission was helping to lay foundations from which a European third sector could emerge around 'social policy' in the Brussels of the late 1990s.

This helps explain why DGV should have been interested in recent years, but is less obviously a reason for the abrupt change of heart we have described. The catalyst here appears to have come primarily from inside the Commission, through the European statecraft of a new Commissioner from Ireland, Padraig Flynn – in Kingdon's terms, effectively a 'policy entrepreneur'. Flynn had come to DGV in 1993 at a time when the Commission's involvement in 'social policy' was an extremely sensitive issue – most obviously because of the UK's hostility to aspects of the Social Charter, although other countries also expressed deep concerns less vocally. The ambitious new Commissioner was proactively on the lookout for 'new ideas' which could command support across the EU in social domains, and thus keep the momentum going at a difficult time.[16] The partic-ular situation meant that this Commissioner faced considerable incentives to focus on the third sector, a state of affairs which could be sharply contrasted with that prevailing at DGXXIII.

Why was 'civil dialogue' the 'big idea', rather than any other possible orga-nizing concepts that could potentially have been promoted? We cannot provide a full answer here, but it is worth noting the vagueness and generality of this idea and the associated rhetoric of 'closeness to the citizen' through promotion of the third sector. As such, it fitted with existing thinking about European citizenship (Comité des Sages 1996), while at the same time being unlikely to be regarded as an obvious encroachment on member states' control over social policy. This was crucial, because social policy is one of the most crucial instruments by which countries foster their populations' allegiance (van Kersbergen 1997).

From the early 1990s, spurred by the scale of the first European Social Policy Forum in 1996, which attracted over 1,000 NGOs (a second followed in 1998), Flynn was increasingly joining forces to strongly promote the idea of civil dialogue with the third sector with key members of the European Parliament's Committee of Social and Employment Affairs, including British MEP Simon Hughes and Italian MEP Fiorella Ghilardotti. Our interviewees inside and outside the Commission also mentioned the personal interest in the third sector taken by Howell Jones, British Deputy Director of DGV.[17] Other signs of interest have come in the form of opinions from ECOSOC and COR. Perhaps most significant has been the involvement of the Secretariat-General – the 'nerve centre' and 'gatekeeper' of the Commission, with formal responsibility for coordinating the work of the various DGs (Christiansen 1996: 85). With the Communication finally coming to fruition, for the first time the Secretariat-General has the third sector *per se* on its agenda.

Yet despite an apparent upsurge in interest in some quarters of both the Commission and the European Parliament for the time being, we still seem to have a 'muddling', low-salience scenario: scraping onto the agenda, but still very far down it! There are no signs yet that the Secretariat-General's involvement has spurred interest in the Commission beyond that described above (attendance at follow-up meetings to progress the Communication's recommendations has been poor) and at the Parliament only a handful of MEPs are active in the inter-group that deals with third sector issues. Moreover, there are few or no signs of an animated reaction or commitment to the Communication's proposals from *national* politicians, civil servants or third sector organizations.

In sum, we might suggest that the biggest actual and potential splash made by the Communication is its possible impact in the problem stream. However, developments in this stream alone are not enough to produce major policy change, and it does not seem that a 'policy window', to use Kingdon's termi-nology, can be said to have been opened.

Declaration 23

If the proposed European Statute and the founding of the social economy unit at DGXXIII can be understood as essentially French in origin, then the attach-ment of Declaration 23 to the 1992 Treaty of Maastricht (see Box 10.1) was also, at least initially, the outcome of pressure from a single, but different member state: Germany. As a Declaration, this is annexed to the Treaty and is not part of it, and therefore does not actually constitute part of the corpus of European law. Nonetheless, as an expression of political will, it puts 'coopera-tion' firmly on the agenda, and serves as an important reference point for future policy making in this field.

The proposal was instigated and lobbied for with considerable vigour by actors seeking to defend the privileged position of the German free welfare asso-ciations (Evers 1996). As with these organizations' response to the ESA, described above, this reaction reflects their perception that the economic element of European integration with its attendant free market logic has threatened, threatens now, or could potentially threaten, their special status.

What is distinctive about this particular initiative is the fact that key politicians (including Helmut Kohl, the then incumbent Christian Democrat Chancellor), trade unions and churches had already been willing and able to ally themselves with the free welfare associations, in the context of domestic politics, as a reac-tion against market-like reforms in the German healthcare system, led by the Health Ministry and the Free Democrats. As part of their anti-commercial, yet expansive strategy, the free welfare associations had secured special treatment in Germany's 1990 Unity Treaty under the heading of youth welfare, where their role was explicitly framed in terms of the dominant domestic interpretation of the concept of subsidiarity.[18]

As it turned out, the Unity Treaty was then to lead directly, though in unex-pected ways, to the existence of Declaration 23 for two reasons. First, parts of the initial wording for this Declaration were lifted straight from the Unity Treaty. Second, the German negotiators perceived that since the UK and France had been present at the negotiating of the Unity Treaty and accepted the privileging of the free welfare associations within it, it was thought that it would have been hard for them to argue against a similar clause in the context of Maastricht and the general emphasis on subsidiarity in it. In the event, the UK was neutral to the Declaration, and France positive. With both French and German support, an interviewee advised us, 'the rest were politically easy'.

For those parts of the third sector that found it difficult to identify with DGXXIII and the idea of 'social economy', Declaration 23 represented a victory. As one of our interviewees remarked: 'The beauty of it all was that it happened without DGXXIII being involved, perhaps not even knowing about it. This is our policy, not theirs'. In other words, the Commission and Europe's third sector are increasingly meeting each other on contested territory.

To conclude, whereas the Communication and the EAS have seemed plagued with inertia, delays and ambiguity, the situation that produced Declaration 23 and its reverberations provides an example of high-stake *Realpolitik* among an unlikely coalition of actors – that is, a proposition 3 outcome *without* a long and drawn-out prelude. Driven by unforeseen events in the 'political stream', a window of opportunity arose in an entirely unanticipated way – and German policy entrepreneurs, by a combination of luck and judgement, were there to take advantage.

The European Social Fund (ESF)

While the interest of DGXXIII and DGV in the third sector that we have described above has been backed by relatively small quantities of finance in support of low-visibility programmes, the two cases with which we complete this section – the ESF and overseas development allocations – are high-profile and represent massive financial commitments. Around one third of the EU's total budget is accounted for by the Structural Funds (see Heinelt and Smith 1996), of which the ESF is a major element. In fact, the third sector receives just a tiny fraction of the total – probably less than 1 per cent. However, an apparently small proportion converts to a relatively significant slice for the recipients (concentrated in a small minority of member states, as we describe below) when other European funding opportunities are so limited.

The nature of the third sector's involvement in the ESF can only be understood by first of all being clear on how the 'problem stream' that constitutes the EU's response to joblessness and attempts to foster 'social cohesion' has been constructed. While using the growing Structural Fund budget to address the increasingly pervasive problem of unemployment came to be an important priority during the 1980s, the policy response was still framed in terms of providing support for key (private, for-profit) industrial fields, and regional policy. Even with the more general pursuit of 'economic and social cohesion' explicitly on the agenda from the late 1980s onwards – not a concept inherently tied to geographical regions – this approach continued to dominate. This emphasis reflects both the reality of explicit power struggles at the level of high politics – the 'the intergovernmental logic of compensation and package deals' (in which member states with net beneficiary regions have incentives to strongly defend these rules and procedures) – and, more subtly but nevertheless decisively, the way in which the key indicators and information which influences decision-making privileges regional perspectives, and keeps others off the agenda (McAleavey and De Rynck 1997).

However, McAleavey and De Rynck argue that despite this institutionalized regional/industrial bias, actors in and around the EU seeking to promote a new dimension – a geographical but *sub*regional, local (essentially urban) agenda for EU action – have achieved some success. They describe a range of low-visibility adjustments to existing regulations, and programme elaborations – that is, in the 'policy stream'; and the extent to which the Dutch presidency of the EU (in 1997), taking the lead from a Communication on the matter, effectively incorporated the issue into the 'political stream' by having it discussed at an informal ministerial meeting. In addition, they note the greater mobilization of local actors in Brussels, and the constitution of umbrella groups and official bodies with an urban orientation.

This adoption of an urban dimension to the unemployment/social cohesion agenda is relevant here because there are a number of ongoing developments which can similarly be portrayed as providing opportunities for increased involvement – for the third sector. First, the third sector-specific programme to foster 'civil dialogue', described in the previous section above, could be seen as a (currently very small-scale) example of an adjacent programme elaboration. A second parallel is the new situation created by the departure from traditional regional and industrial logic of the Structural Funds, which has occurred from 1988 onwards with the introduction of the 'Community Initiatives' (now accounting for around 4 per cent of the ESF budget), and in particular the Human Resource Initiatives allocated as transnational programmes. While this is not a third sector-specific programme, it is aimed at improving the job prospects of a number of its important constituencies, including a range of socially excluded people. Third sector intermediaries in the UK and elsewhere, as well as the client group-specific transnational networks whose growth we highlighted in the previous section, proactively have certainly raised awareness of the availability of these programmes to their members (see Davison 1997).

However, in two fundamental ways, the third sector sympathizers' situation has been very different from that faced by the promoters of an urban dimension. Most obviously, critical mass has not been secured in the political stream equivalent to persuading a country with Commission presidency to thematize a link between the third sector and social cohesion/combating unemployment at the European level. Second, the third sector's identity has thus far *not* been institutionalized in the sense of being recognized as a distinctive category of stakeholder in its own right. The involvement of the third sector in the programme that *has* materialized at member state level has been the outcome of national level conditions and negotiations. As it turned out, left to the discretion of individual member states, this involvement has ranged from none at all – in most cases – to relatively significant involvement (from the perspective of third sector recipients, if not from that of the programme as a whole). In particular, a recent survey of seven member states found that the third sector was involved in the programme (as programme deliverer, or through representation on monitoring, administration or evaluation committees) in just three countries: the UK, Ireland and Germany (EAPN 1998; see also Harvey 1996).

It is possible however, that the situation may change. First, as they currently stand, the draft new regulations (to come into force in 2000) being developed in negotiations between member states and the Commission for the programme as a whole still make no explicit mention of the third sector as a 'partner'.[19] However, the regulations are not yet settled, and an insider advised us that it is possible that a strong intervention on behalf of the third sector, even at this late stage, could result in different and less ambiguous language being incorporated in the regulations.[20]

Second, an innovation in the draft new regulations does involve top-slicing support *specifically for 'non-governmental organizations'*. The current draft of Article 4.3 relating to the ESF requires that 'at least 1 per cent of Fund appropriations B shall be available [for] ... Global Grants, for the distribution by intermediary bodies of small grants with special access for non-governmental organizations' (Coyne 1998). This 'social risk capital' proposal, as it has informally become known, if adopted, would be the first time that member states were required by European law to support the third sector. One of our interviewees revealed that the idea behind the initiative was the outcome of both internal dialogue within DGV (between the section dealing with the Structural Funds and the section dealing with civil dialogue, discussed above), and seminars on the topic of 'social exclusion' conducted jointly with a small number of foundations active at the European level.

To conclude our penultimate case, we can see that, at the present time, it fits what we described in the first section as a proposition 3 scenario. For now, the third sector's involvement in this massive programme has been a matter of low salience, far removed from the political stream, with most discussions conducted amongst small groups of low-visibility actors. At the level of a handful of member states, some third sector representatives have secured involvement by direct negotiations with national authorities, but this has been relatively limited to date.

Third sector organizations in overseas development policy

Our final case involves a policy field at some remove from all those discussed thus far. While we have seen that a number of actors have been involved across two or in some instances even three of those cases, policy in this area in many ways represents a completely different world; and the place within it of the third sector is utterly unlike its positioning in the initiatives that we have described.

This field turns out to be unique in the extent to which it involves a history of institutionalized joint working between DGVIII and the third sector, a relationship which also extends to closeness to DG1a, and more recently to DG1b and ECHO,[21] as well as to the relevant European Parliament committees (those dealing with Development and Foreign Affairs). Part of this relationship involves the flow of sector-specific funding[22] which completely dwarfs equivalent flows elsewhere: between 1976, when the Liaison Committee was established, and the end of 1994, co-financing of projects initiated by third sector development agencies had totalled over 1 billion ECU, mostly in support of activities undertaken in sub-Saharan Africa and Latin America.[23] Through the Liaison Committee, with its elaborate structure of national platforms involving 800 European third sector agencies, an ongoing dialogue is maintained concerning the content, design and delivery of overseas development policy.

While finance was just one aspect of the relationship, it has, however, been a crucially important one in setting the tone. Indeed, the origins of the Liaison Committee itself were tied up with the creation of the first DGVIII funding scheme for the third sector. One of our interviewees explained that this was modelled on similar schemes operating at member state level, and involved MEPs, Commission officials and third sector leaders who

> jointly had the idea that the European public was willing to support NGO action in the South. Wouldn't it be good if the Commission could show its backing for that by providing a co-funding scheme? And it started with a little budget line of 2 MECU, and now it's 200 MECU!

We were assured in interviews that at least as far as the Liaison Committee's directors were concerned, at the broadest level, the relationship that had evolved was one of genuine partnership, in a positive dialogic sense, as well as in financial decision-making. Unlike the structural funds, for example, not only was the third sector legally recognized as a 'partner', but the expression was felt to have real meaning.

The Communication described in Box 10.2 above had referred in passing to the existence of the Liaison Committee and some of the major development funding programmes. Asked to reflect on the relevance of this exercise for his policy field, one leading Committee insider remarked:

> In a sense we have developed a fairly good relationship with DGVIII over the years, structured, well established – it's got its ups and downs obviously – and the level of the relationship of other sectors to the other DGs with which they deal is really quite far behind us. … There's a feeling of 'we're all right, Jack', although perhaps that's a bit short-sighted.

Three institutional developments are perhaps symptomatic of the established style and close coordination that characterizes this relationship. First, prompted by the Commission, the Liaison Committee through the so-called 'Elewijt process' developed a set of jointly agreed principles concerning values, structures, approach, the relationship of the development third sector to civil society in Europe, professionalism, and accountability to various key constituencies. Second, as part of the Elewijt process, the harmonization of budget control procedures – crucially, involving a first draft of 'what we would like to see' being produced by the Committee itself, rather than by Commission officials. Third, each 'partner' in the relationship has a reasonably clear view as to the legitimacy, purpose and rationale of their mutual links, as set out in recent document summarized in Box 10.3 below.[24]

The case of overseas development agencies therefore represents an extremely sharp contrast with cases one to four. To summarize in the language of our first section above, it shares with the Structural Funds the existence of established

---

Box 10.3   Rationales underpinning the relationship between the EU and third sector development organizations

Why does the Community support the activities of development NGOs?

- A response to the European public's commitment: co-financing is the Community's response to the European public's commitment in the non-governmental sphere. The Community wishes to support the upsurge of solidarity felt by the European public towards the most underprivileged populations in the Third World
- … the ECUs invested by the European public [through making donations to third sector agencies] have generated additional funding [over and above the Commission's co-financing]
- The NGOs supplement the Community's range of action … enabling it to respond directly to the needs of marginalized populations
- [Their] flexibility [resulting from] agencies' small size and committed personnel
- [Their] professionalism … while motivated by a moral commitment rather than profit or a purely technical approach

Why do NGOs want a partnership with the Community?

- Expanding projects: the first reason is obviously financial
- Listening constructively: in the Commission the NGOs have, in its co-financing officers, contacts who will listen to them in a spirit of pluralism
- Innovation: both parties share an interest in innovative local projects and awareness-raising projects; the Commission recognizes the fundamental influence NGOs have on European public opinion with regard to development problems
- Joint working: both parties recognize the value of projects involving two or more NGOs
- Influence: NGOs recognize the opportunities they have to influence and shape Community policy through the close relationships that become established.

---

coordination mechanisms, although because of the nature of the activities involved, this does not directly involve member states.[25] But it differs significantly in the extent to which the third sector *per se* is fully institutionalized in the full range of policy activities: framing and design; monitoring; eligibility for funding and implementation; and even evaluation.

From the perspective of the third sector, there is a comparatively mature 'policy stream' in which it is fully integrated. This appears to have been considerably facilitated by the existence of models at the national level, which could be readily transferable to the European arena. We also seem to discern a clear, mutual understanding of the 'problems' that the relationship is seeking to tackle. Finally, for the first time, we find a situation in which the political stream, including at the level of high politics, is unambiguously supportive. Not only is the third sector able to apply pressure from within to push its views and protect its position, but we find integrated into the discourse frequent references to the European equivalent of 'national mood'. A recent scandal concerning ECHO's lack of financial controls during its first three years as revealed by a internal audit has prompted concerns in the Parliament and Commission, and generated threats to freeze spending.[26] Moreover, ECHO has had major organizational and communicative problems (Mowjee 1998; 1999), and there is now evidence to suggest that aspects of day-to-day implementation between the EU and development NGOs more generally are 'operationally dire' (Fowler 2000). Nevertheless, the actors seem to believe that public opinion strongly supports their joint efforts – not only because any recent 'irregularities' are claimed to have been relatively limited, but because the Commission views most of these organizations' success in raising funds from the public as clear evidence of the latter's support for their activities.

Policies, issues and fault lines

At the most general level, our account of the development of these five initiatives appears to lend support to the notion that EU policy making towards the third sector exhibits *in extremis* some of the features which characterize the European policy process in general, to which we drew attention at the start of the first section. In general, there is considerable evidence that fluidity, ambiguity, unpredictability, instability and complexity all seem to be appropriate descriptions of the developments at stake.

However, there do appear to be some patterns in the chain of events, which we have sought to draw out using our propositions (see Table 10.1) and the notion that analysis of policy can be structured using the idea that developments in three streams – problems, policy and politics – need to be taken simultaneously into account.

In the balance of this part, we summarize what we see as some of the key issues and 'fault lines' that seem to drive European policy making towards the nonprofit sector. We focus first on what appear to be some of the differences between different groups of participants, which to some extent cut across cases

Table 10.1   Policies and propositions

	Muddling through/politicking	Significant coordination and support
Low salience	*Proposition 1:* • Path to communication • EAS (early 1990s)	*Proposition 2:* • European Social Fund
High salience	*Proposition 3:* • Declaration 23 • EAS (late 1990s)	*Proposition 4:* • Role of third sector in overseas development policy

one to four, and especially cases one to three. We then seek to contrast these cases with case five, where the clearest distinction can be drawn.

Conceptual cleavages

One of the consistent issues in EU third sector politics is the fault line between active players as far as organizing concepts and terminology are concerned. France and Germany emerge as the most active protagonists on the European stage. We can contrast the francophone idea of *économie sociale*, which deliberately draws together the 'economic' and the 'social', with the German position which seeks to emphasize and reinforce a sharp distinction between them, and locates the third sector firmly in the 'social' pigeon-hole. As participants are keenly aware, the path chosen can potentially have major implications for how the third sector is ultimately treated in European law. The concepts also have their ideological baggage, which also animates the debate. While *économie sociale* tends to connect the third sector to socialist traditions and 'economistic' reasoning, the *subsidiarity* argument as applied to the third sector in the German context has a corporatist, anti-market flavour and seeks to protect special ideologies and interests.

Imported national scripts

Certainly at the beginning of the processes we have examined, when the issues at stake were fuzzy and obscure, we found some evidence that national participants were falling back on 'typical' policy stances, as already refined in other contexts. For example, we found a British style combining a minimalist attitude to the EU, with a pragmatic approach based on questioning the functional utility of proposed measures, and a concern with things European to the extent that they involve new resources for the sector.

In contrast, French, Italian and German stakeholders, and to a lesser extent their Italian and Irish counterparts, while of course also interested in Europe for financial reasons, have been relatively more active in considering how the third sector, ideologically and philosophically, fits in with their (different) pro-European ambitions. For example, the French focus on the *économie sociale* is congruent with their overall emphasis on economic integration, while the

German concern with non-economic matters dovetails with their traditional emphasis on the political aspect of European integration. These generalizations are a limited – but important – part of the story in understanding national positions in discussions on the future of the EU, including recent Treaty negotiations (Nugent 1994: ch. 3).

National level and European level influence

In the European policy literature, one of the most discussed issues is the relative importance of member states and supranational European institutions in determining the content and direction of policy. At its crudest, the battle lines are pitched between those who argue that in the final analysis, all substantive policy outcomes are simply the outcome of political bargaining between member states, and the EU agencies enter the field as relatively passive instruments of implementation; at the other extreme, some have argued that the European institutions have established their own identities and constituencies and are able to heavily influence all aspects of the policy process, but particularly agenda-setting.

Our analysis of the case of policy towards the third sector would seem to provide support for an intermediate position, as spelt out at the highest level of generality, for example, by Pollak (1996). It is certainly true that lack of interest in the third sector at the Council of Ministers has played an important role in slowing down the process of initiating some form of policy towards the sector at the European level, and its failure to get on the agenda of any countries holding the presidency thus far has been a missed opportunity.

On the other hand, despite this lack of endorsement, we have found the beginnings of third sector-specific policy entrepreneurship within the Commission, and in the European Parliament, as these actors have creatively exploited very narrow openings to begin to place the third sector higher on the European agenda. Thus far, these efforts have involved such activities as transnational network creation and mobilization; the formation of new, albeit for now small, sector-specific budget lines; and attempts to 'bend' existing structures and regulations so as to provide a place for the third sector where previously one did not exist. While the third sector policy window may not have fully opened, it seems that if and when it does, the low-visibility groundwork of European officials is unlikely not to have a major impact on the shape which third sector policy assumes.

Understanding the uniqueness of overseas development policy

One of the most striking findings of this study has been the extent to which the third sector's experience in the realm of development policy is utterly different from all other cases that we have examined. An exploration of why this may be the case would require a separate paper in itself, but it is relatively easy to point to four *prima facie* differences.

First, unlike the other initiatives which fall within or close to the terrain of social policy where the division of labour between member states and the European institutions is an extremely fraught and contested issue, there is a marked degree of agreement that Community level policies are both efficient and legitimate in the field of overseas development.

Second and relatedly, policy here involves engagement with what appears to be a genuinely 'European' mood in favour of joint action between the EU institutions, member states, and (by implication at least, because of the signals provided by co-financing achievements) the third sector – a state of affairs creating support and recognition in the political stream which cannot be said to exist in the case of social policy in general, let alone the specific role of the third sector within it.

Third, the institutional arrangements for the delivery of social policy, and support for the third sector within it, vary enormously between member states, while in contrast, national overseas development policies may have exhibited many more features in common. Therefore, selecting a model to transpose to the European level proved to be a relatively straightforward task, and has not been stymied by member states' rivalry to see 'their' approach adopted at European level.

Finally, we have seen that as early as the 1970s, a critical mass of entrepreneurship within and between this sector *and* the European institutions appears to have existed. Collective action was made easier by the existence within the third sector of a small number of high-profile, and (in the eyes of their constituents) legitimate organizations with whom it was relatively easy for the European institutions to do business. Such a leadership across the third sector as a whole, or embracing its 'social policy' component, cannot be said to exist at present. It is too early to say at this point whether there is the capacity or will within the third sector for it to do so.

Notes

1 In this paper we use 'third sector' as convenient shorthand unless citing or demonstrating other people's usage. We have in mind all organizations which are formal, non-profit-distributing, self-governing and significantly voluntary (Kendall and Knapp 1995; Salamon and Anheier 1997) save trade unions and employers' associations. As 'social partners' involved in an institutionalized 'social dialogue' with the EU's institutions, the latter represent a special and particular case which is beyond the scope of this paper.

2 For example, in dealing with freedom of trade, the Treaty of Rome in Article 58(2) appears to exclude what we refer to here as third sector organizations from the right of establishment across member states when it defines companies and firms as entities 'constituted under civil or commercial law, including cooperative societies, and other legal persons governed by public or private law, *save for those which are non-profit-making*' (see 6 1995).

3 The Report was written by Mrs N. Fontaine, who served as the rapporteur of the European Parliament's Committee of Legal Affairs and Citizens' Rights between June 1985 and November 1986. The report was tabled in December 1986 and published in 1987.

4 Many other Directorate-Generals have some degree of engagement with the third sector, but the four most significant are probably DGVIII (Development), DGV (Social Policy and Employment), DGXI (Environment), and DGXXII (Youth). In contrast to DGXXIII, these DGs do not have an explicit institutional mandate under EU law for attending to third sector issues broader than that suggested by their substantive 'industry' or policy field.

5 Terminology has varied both between different components of the Community, and even within them, 'private, non-profit institutions serving households' (EUROSTAT), 'NGOs' (DGVIII), 'non-profit sector' (Economic and Social Committee), 'non-profit associations' (European Parliament) and 'voluntary organizations' (DGV), and 'voluntary organizations and foundations' and 'third sector' (Forward Studies Unit) are examples of terminology which are all used in European discourse focusing purely or primarily on (a version of) the third sector; while 'third system', 'social economy' or *économie sociale* and most recently CMAFs, i.e. cooperatives, mutuals, associations and foundations, are now used to refer to the sector within a broader universe. To add to the confusion, these terms and groupings are often used without, or with only partial, explanation or qualification.

6 Evidence was gathered through three main routes. First, face-to-face and telephone interviews, typically lasting 1–1.5 hours, with fifteen key stakeholders across the five areas (with most involved in some capacity in two or more of our cases); second, conventional desk-based research gathering literature and documentation from a wide variety of official and unofficial sources; and third, conducting internet searches, for example to retrieve biographical details of, and copies of speeches made by, Commissioners, MEPs and senior civil servants who were not available for interview. A fuller account of each case reviewed here is included in Kendall and Anheier 1998.

7 We should be wary of transposing an approach developed to analyse the particular context of the US in the 1970s to a different time, a different place and a different set of institutions. However, its relevance for approaching the analysis of European policy in the 1990s has been argued by prominent scholars in the field (Peters 1996; Richardson 1996a); moreover, it is not clear what alternative models would be more suitable.

8 Kingdon (1995: 77) asserts that to make sense of the policy process, 'the critical thing is not to understand where the seed comes from, but what makes the seed fertile', and notes that attempts to trace origins of policies can come up against the problem of infinite regress. We would qualify this observation by emphasizing that some acknowledgement of origins is important, because these can impose a durable imprint over time. This may be particularly important in the case of the ESA: a knowledgeable insider discussing this remarked 'To an extraordinary degree, what the Commission does, and particularly what it produces by way of draft legislation, is heavily conditional upon who does the first draft. The ESA is … basically French'.

9 In describing the position of the Council of Ministers, we have to rely purely on 'insider' accounts and anecdote. As McCormick remarks, 'despite its powers, the Council is less well-known and more poorly understood than either the Commission or the Parliament. Its deliberations are secretive, there has been surprisingly little scholarly study of its structures and processes'(1996: 124).

10 This statement was buried in documentation circulated to the Council in advance alongside many others, covering a wide variety of issues. As such, according to EU rules of procedure, the agenda was automatically approved as a matter of procedure without any debate or discussion.

11 Under this regime, these facilities are regarded as *Tendenzbetriebe*, organizations governed by ideological (religious, social, political) concerns; as such they are treated as if they were not characterized by the capital/labour conflict, which would be the case for 'economic' enterprises. As a result, there are no unions in Catholic or Protestant third sector organizations in Germany, although some form of employee participation exists.

12 This claim is based upon information retrieved on the internet, and anecdotal information: it did not prove possible to speak to the Commissioner directly to refute or verify the claim.

13 The Unit represents 5 per cent of its budget, and employs a total of twelve staff. This is less than a tenth of one per cent of the Commission's total staffing of around 20,000.

14 'Social Europe' is deemed outside the 'scope of analysis' in one of the documents which provides the legal basis for the unit (European Commission 1989).

15 Separate White Papers were also planned for cooperatives and mutuals, but these apparently never came to fruition in any shape or form.

16 The frustrations leading Flynn to search for a 'third course' soon after the start of his term of office are vividly illustrated in a joint hearing on the social charter held in Brussels in 1995 (Flynn 1995). Predictably, he refers to the 'distinctly unhelpful role' of the UK (which was involved in negotiations, but at that time had 'opted out'). But more interestingly, he also refers to 'huge differences of view between the [traditional social partners], with the employers' organizations becoming increasingly critical of the nature and scope of European legislation, while the unions grew increasingly frustrated with why there was inadequate progress'. He also talks of the difficulties of drafting legislation acceptable to member states:

> the reality is that many member states were not interested in having truly European legislation; the price of having social legislation adopted by the council tended to be an end product which was complex and overlain with exemptions, derogation and special treatment for sectors and for particular member states.

17 Their interest in and DGV's enthusiasm for the third sector continued in the negotiations leading up to the Treaty of Amsterdam, at which DGV actively lobbied alongside NGOs for the inclusion of a reference to them within the body of the Treaty (Flynn 1997a; 1997b). These lobbying efforts failed: neither of the Declarations concerning the third sector (see Box 10.1) have been incorporated into the body of the Treaty as DGV and some transnational nonprofit lobbyists had sought (ECAS 1997).

18 In the context of German welfare service delivery, subsidiarity is interpreted to mean that while state funding is often appropriate, traditional, particularly church-linked nonprofit providers are necessarily best placed to actually supply these services.

19 Instead, alongside the incorporation of references to mandatory involvement by the economic and social partners (trade unions and employers) in each member state, the more vague expression 'other competent bodies' is used.

20 There would, however, be intense opposition from individual member states, who generally wish to keep the regulations as general as possible to maximize their own room for manoeuvre at the national level.

21 These are the Directorate-Generals handling external relations with Africa, the Caribbean and the Pacific, Central and Eastern Europe, Latin America and most Asian countries; and the European Community Humanitarian Office established in 1992 to 'respond more efficiently to humanitarian crises and [having] at the heart of its approach an emphasis on the need for a better relationship with NGOs' (Cox *et al.* 1997: 36).

22 These funds are only available under existing regulations to 'autonomous, non-profit making NGOs established in a member state of the European Community' (DGVIII 1988: 3).

23 In addition, a significant but unknown proportion of the huge range of projects initiated and designed by the Commission itself rather than NGOs has actually been delivered by NGOs under contract (Cox *et al.* 1997: 38–9).

24 Little is known in concrete terms about 'European' attitudes towards NGOs *per se*, but there is some data available on public opinion *vis-à-vis* the legitimacy of national versus EU decision-making in different 'industries'. In particular, a Eurobarometer poll in 1993 sought to ascertain the views of a representative sample of people from nine member states on whether decisions 'should be taken by the EU or national governments'. The form of activity in which EU action was preferred over national government to the greatest extent was 'cooperation with the third world', which 74 per cent saw as a 'matter for the EU'; at the other extreme, only 31 per cent saw 'health and social security' as a matter for the EU. The interpretation offered in an official leaflet is that 'people preferred joint European decision-making in all areas where the problems transcend national borders (notably cooperation with developing countries)' (DGX 1996: 12).

25 Of course, in addition, member states have separate bilateral arrangements for joint working with third sector development agencies based in their countries: in 1995, in total (across and through all sectors), the EU disbursed $7.1 billion of aid, but individual member states allocated some $33.3 billion (Cox *et al.* 1997: 1).

26 See the report 'EU blunder lost aid fund millions', *Sunday Times*, 4 October 1998.

References

Anheier, H. K. and Seibel, W. (1998) *The Nonprofit Sector in Germany*, Manchester: Manchester University Press.

Archambault, E. (1996) *The Nonprofit Sector in France*, Manchester: Manchester University Press.

Christiansen, T. (1996) 'A maturing bureaucracy? The role of the Commission in the policy process', in J. J. Richardson (ed.) *European Union: Power and Policy Making*, London: Routledge.

Comité des Sages (1996) *For a Europe of Civic and Social Rights: Report of the Comité des Sages Chaired by Maria de Lourdes Pintasilgo*, Brussels: Office for Official Publications of the European Communities.

Commission of the European Communities (1989) *Businesses in the 'Économie Sociale' Sector: Europe's Frontier-free Market*, Communication from the Commission to the Council, SEC(89) 2187 final, 18 December, Brussels.

——(1992a) *An Open and Structured Dialogue between the Commission and Interest Groups*, SEC(92), 2272 final, Brussels.

——(1992b) Proposal for a Council Regulation (EEC) on the Statute for a European Association; Proposal for a Council Directive supplementing the Statute for a European Association with regard to the involvement of employees; Proposal for a Council Regulation (EEC) on the Statute for a European cooperative society; Proposal for a Council Directive supplementing the Statute for a European cooperative society with regard to the involvement of employees; Proposal for a Council Regulation (EEC) on the Statute for a European mutual society; Proposal for a Council Directive supplementing the Statute for a European mutual society with regard to the involvement of employees. See *Official Journal of the European Communities*, 92/C 99/01 to 92/C99/06.

——(1993) Amended proposal for a Council Regulation (EEC) on the Statute for a European Association; Amended proposal for a Council Directive supplementing the Statute for a European Association with regard to the involvement of employees; Amended proposal for a Council Regulation (EEC) on the Statute for a European cooperative society; Amended proposal for a Council Directive supplementing the Statute for a European cooperative society with regard to the involvement of employees; Amended proposal for a Council Regulation (EEC) on the Statute for a European mutual society; Amended proposal for a Council Directive supplementing the Statute for a European mutual society with regard to the involvement of employees, COM(93) 252 final – SYN 386 to 391, Brussels, 6 July. See *Official Journal of the European Communities*, 93/C 236/01 to 93/C 236/06.

——(1997) *Promoting the Role of Voluntary Organizations in Europe*, Luxembourg: Office for Official Publications of the European Communities.

Cox, A. and Koning, A., with Hewitt, A., Howell, J. and Marr, A. (1997) *Understanding European Community Aid: Aid Policies, Management and Distribution Explained*, Brussels: Overseas Development Institute, London and European Commission.

Coyne, D. (1998) 'The European Social Fund and Agenda 2000', presentation at NCVO conference, April, London, National Council for Voluntary Organisations.

Davison, A. (1997) *Grants from Europe: How To Get Money and Influence Policy*, London: NCVO Publications.

DGVIII (Directorate-General for Development) (1988) 'General conditions for the cofinancing of projects undertaken in developing countries by non-governmental organisations (NGOs)' (Budgetary item B7–6000) VIII/764/87/EN, Brussels: European Commission Directorate-General for Development.

——(1995) 'Partners in development: The European Union and NGOs', Brussels: DGVIII (Development) NGO co-financing – Decentralized Cooperation Unit.

DGX (Directorate-General for Information, Communication, Culture and Audiovisual) (1996) 'Europe … questions and answers: how does the European Union work?', Brussels: Directorate-General for Information, Communication, Culture and Audiovisual Publication Unit.

EAPN (1998) *Social Inclusion: A Priority Task for the New Structural Funds*, Brussels: European Anti-Poverty Network.

ECAS [n.d.] 'European citizenship: giving substance to citizen's Europe in a revised Treaty', memorandum from the ECAS hotline, Brussels: European Citizens' Action Service.

——(1997) 'The Treaty of ambiguity', *The European Citizen*, Newsflash special edition.

European Parliament (1987) 'Report drawn up on behalf of the committee of legal affairs and citizen's rights on non-profit making associations in the European Community', European Parliament Working Documents, Series A, Document A 2-196-86, PE 107.283/Fin., Brussels: European Parliament.

Evers, A. (1996) 'Freie Wohlfahrtspflege und Europaeische Integration: der "Dritte Sektor" im geeinten Europa', *Zeitschrift fuer Sozialreform*, 3, 43: 208–26.

Flynn, P. (1995) Text of speech by Padraig Flynn made at joint hearing on the Social Charter, 22 May, Brussels, retrieved from the internet.

——(1997a) Summary of text of speech by Padraig Flynn delivered at European conference 'For a Europe of Civil and Social Rights', 4 June, Brussels, retrieved from the internet.

——(1997b) Summary of text of speech by Padraig Flynn delivered at conference 'Foundations in Partnership: The Example of Social Inclusion in Europe', 19 June, the Hague, retrieved from the internet.

Fowler, Alan (2000) personal communication, 24 June.

Gjems-Onstad, O. (1995) 'The proposed European Association: a symbol in need of friends?', *Voluntas*, 6, 3: 3–22.

Harvey, B. (1995) *Networking in Europe: A Guide to European Voluntary Organisations*, London: NCVO.

——(1996) *Equality and the Structural Funds*, Belfast: Community Workers Cooperative and the Northern Ireland Council for Voluntary Action.

Heinelt, H. and Smith, R. (1996) *Policy Networks and European Structural Funds*, Aldershot: Avebury.

Kendall, J. K. and Anheier, H. K. (1998) 'The third sector and the European Union policy process: an initial evaluation', paper presented at the third ISTR conference, Geneva, 8–11 July.

Kendall, J. K. and Knapp, M. (1995) 'A loose and baggy monster: boundaries, definitions and typologies', in J. D. Smith and R. Hedley (eds) *An Introduction to the Voluntary Sector*, London and New York: Routledge.

——(1996) *The Voluntary Sector in the United Kingdom*, Manchester: Manchester University Press.

van Kersbergen, K. (1997) 'Double allegiance in European integration: publics, nation-states and social policy', EUI Working Paper RSC no. 97/15, Florence: European University Institute.

Kingdon, J. W. (1995) *Agendas, Alternatives and Public Policies*, New York: HarperCollins.

Kleinman, M. and Piachaud, D. (1993) 'European social policy: conceptions and choices', *Journal of European Social Policy*, 3, 1: 1–19.

McAleavey, P. and De Rynck, S. (1997) 'Regional or local? The EU's future partners in cohesion policy', EUI Working Paper RSC no. 97/55, Florence: European University Institute.

McCormick, J. (1996) *The European Union: Politics and Policies*, Boulder and Oxford: Westview.

Mowjee, T. (1998) 'The European Community Humanitarian Office (ECHO): 1992–1999 and beyond', *Disasters*, 22, 3: 250–67.

——(1999) 'It takes two to tango: factors shaping donor/NGO relationships', paper presented at the International Research Symposium on Public Management III, Aston Business School, Birmingham, March.

Nugent, N. (1994) *The Government and Politics of the European Union*, Basingstoke: Macmillan.

Peters, G. (1996) 'Agenda-setting in the European Union', in J. Richardson (ed.) *European Union: Power and Policy Making*, London and New York: Routledge.

Pollak, M. A. (1996) 'The new instititutionalism and EC governance: the promise and limits of institutional analysis', *Governance: An International Journal of Policy and Administration*, 9, 4: 429–58.

Richardson, J. (1996a) *European Union: Power and Policy Making*, London and New York: Routledge.

——(1996b) 'Policy making in the EU: interests, ideas and garbage cans of primeval soup', in J. Richardson (ed.) *European Union: Power and Policy Making*, London and New York: Routledge.

Salamon, L. and Anheier, H. K. (1997) *Defining the Nonprofit Sector: A Cross-National Analysis*, Manchester: Manchester University Press.

Salamon, L., Anheier, H. K. and associates (1999) *The Emerging Sector Revisited: A Summary*, Baltimore: Johns Hopkins University Press.

6, Perri (1995) 'The voluntary and nonprofit sectors in continental Europe', in J. Davis Smith and R. Hedley (eds) *An Introduction to the Voluntary Sector*, London and New York: Routledge.

11 The distinction between institutionalized and noninstitutionalized NPOs

New policy initiatives and nonprofit organizations in Japan

Masayuki Deguchi

Introduction

This chapter discusses the trends and policies of nonprofit organizations in the wake of the Kobe earthquake of 17 January 1995. Although this earthquake was a major disaster that claimed the lives of more than 6,000 people, in its aftermath many people volunteered their time and energy to assist the victims, which led to a clear recognition of the role of nonprofit organizations in Japanese society (Homma and Deguchi 1996).

In fact the Japanese term 'NPO' has become a frequent topic of discussion and appeared often in newspapers after the earthquake. Discussion and research into Japanese nonprofit organizations in the aftermath of the Kobe earthquake is of major significance, but in doing so it should be noted that the acronym 'NPO' that is used for nonprofit organizations in Japan has a much narrower meaning than that used by the International Classification of Nonprofit Organizations (ICNPO).

'NPO' had been used to mean grassroots organizations that were not incorporated as a legal entity until the new Law to Promote Specified Nonprofit Activities was enacted in 1998.[1] The Japanese mass media had invented a new Japanese acronym, 'NPO', for these non-institutionalized organizations. There was a large body of public opinion which felt that these organizations should have legal status, and that social systems be organized to assist them. As a result of this, a new law was enacted and referred to as the NPO law. Many such organizations, however, have not yet achieved legal status. In this chapter, therefore, the term 'N/NPO' includes non-institutional NPOs prior to the law of 1998. In other words, N/NPO refers to both a new NPO which has legal status under the new law, and a non-institutional NPO which is still without legal status. This is the general usage of the term 'NPO' in Japan.

On the other hand, there is not so much discussion of these issues *vis-à-vis* institutionalized nonprofit organizations (I/NPO), which include medical institutions, social welfare institutions, foundations and other incorporated bodies which are active under laws other than that of 1998. Rather, since the Kobe earthquake, public opinion has been a two-edged sword, with praise for N/NPOs going hand-in-hand with criticism of I/NPOs. In this chapter I shall use the term 'nonprofit organizations' to indicate the entire spectrum of nonprofit organizations according to ICNPO's definitions, and at all other times I will differentiate by using the terms N/NPO and I/NPO.

Three peak periods in the public estimation of N/NPOs

Before discussing Japanese nonprofit organizations' policies after the Kobe earthquake, it is useful to summarize the changes in public perceptions of N/NPOs in the postwar years. This is because changes in social awareness of N/NPOs are of major importance both in understanding the several crises that I will discuss later, and in considering the course of Japanese policies.

In Japan, where government policies play an extremely large role, 28 per cent of the I/NPOs (*zaidan-hojin* and *shadan-hojin*) are, in fact, quasi-NGOs (quangos) (Hayashi and Iriyama 1997: 61), and in the general public's mind these two are fairly indistinguishable. In Japanese, the term 'third sector' ('Daisan sector') means government initiated organizations (Maeda 1993: 41). When thinking of 'nonprofit organizations', Japanese people are more conscious of the private sector nature of N/NPOs.

When concentrating mainly on N/NPOs, we can discern at least three peaks in the public's awareness of N/NPOs in the postwar period. The first peak came in the 1970s. After World War II, the Japanese government and business sectors joined hands in an effort to catch up with the countries of Europe and the US. In the 1960s, the doubling-income policy of Prime Minister Ikeda resulted in Japan achieving growth rates of over 10 per cent per annum.

However, from the beginning of the 1970s, the darker side of this high growth rate began to make itself felt, at the same time as the Japanese were enjoying more and more prosperity. One example was the deepening problem of pollution, at a number of levels. In addition, after the oil shock in 1973, many instances surfaced of Japanese corporations trying to deceive consumers by hoarding goods or arranging secret cartels. In the 1970s housewives' organizations, consumer groups and other grassroots organizations began to take active steps to expose the deceitful nature of these corporate activities (Keizaidoyukai 1972; MITI 1977).[2] These groups, which were neither government organizations nor business corporations, were very vocal, and this brought them to the attention of the mass media. Many Japanese had no reservations about the existence of these organizations, and they played a major role in encouraging a revision of the economy-first attitude. One concrete outcome has been that corporations have developed a strong awareness of their own social responsibility (Morimoto 1994). Corporate foundations were set up in greater numbers from the 1970s. Corporate foundations in the 1960s numbered sixty-six, whereas they had increased to ninety-four by the 1970s (Amemiya 1992; Imada 1993). In addition, Amemiya states that in the early 1970s the public was very critical of the profit-making attitudes of corporations, and many people saw the corporate foundations set up at that time as existing to return the corporate profits to society. This significance and public image is not the positive one that is current today.

(Amemiya 1992: 9)

The position of most community groups, however, was very prejudiced against profit-making companies, claiming they did bad things without any thought for others. This movement was recognized as being an anti-establishment movement with a socialist ideological background (Deguchi 1995).

The second peak came in the last half of the 1980s and the early 1990s, which is known in Japan as the era of the Bubble Economy. During this period the actions of the supply side or corporate philanthropy stimulated the activities of the NPOs. The acceptance of a higher-valued yen in the 1985 Plaza Accord was a clear turning point, and Japanese economic strength increased immensely, on a global scale when calculated on a dollar basis. Against the background of a strong yen and weak dollar, corporations began to invest directly in the US and other countries,[3] and interest in corporate citizenship grew within companies (Bob and SRI International 1990; Deguchi 1995; Imada 1993; Keidanren 1996; Matsuoka 1992). In 1990, the Federation of Economic Organizations (Keidanren), taking its cue from US corporations, suggested that its members set up the One Percent Club, and devote one per cent of their pre-tax profits to society.[4] The Association for Corporate Support of the Arts (Kigyo Mesena Kyogikai), whose membership was mainly larger corporations, was formed in the same year.[5] This association was the result of efforts to actively encourage corporate support of cultural activities. From around 1990, corporations also began to set up in-house philanthropy sections, under such names as the Corporate Philanthropy Department, the Corporate Culture Department or the Community Department (Deguchi 1993; Keidanren 1994; Hayashi and Imada 1999). This corporate response stimulated the activities of N/NPOs. In the 1970s N/NPOs had positioned themselves in a clearly antagonistic stance to corporations, but during the N/NPO peak in 1990, corporations sought to deepen their partnership with N/NPOs (Deguchi 1996).

The third peak came in 1995. The Kobe earthquake of 17 January triggered a boom in N/NPO activities throughout Japan.[6] Volunteer activities, especially those organized by N/NPOs, grew enormously, and donations for post-earthquake relief funds were collected actively. The mass media created terms such as 'the first year of true volunteerism' and 'the volunteer revolution' to describe this phenomenon, and took a cheerleader role in encouraging these activities (Tachiki 1997; Sotooka 1996; Iwasaki *et al.* 1999).

What is the situation for Japanese NPOs today, in the wake of the Kobe earthquake? How have NPO policies changed? This chapter loosely deploys

Salamon's framework (Chapter 2) to examine the changes in policy and social context affecting NPOs: the concepts of fiscal crisis, economic crisis, crisis of efficiency and crisis of legitimacy.

The fiscal crisis

Between the second and third peak, as defined above, the 'Bubble Economy' collapsed, and the Japanese fiscal situation deteriorated rapidly due to the drop in tax revenues and the economic stimulus packages which involved an increase in public investment. In 1995, the central government and the local governments posted a combined deficit equal to 6.8 per cent of GDP. Even if the deficit amount equal to the surplus in the social security fund is cancelled out, the general government deficit stood at 4.0 per cent. According to the Economic White Paper, the long-term government debt to the end of 1996 was 445 trillion yen, or 88 per cent of GDP (Figure 11.1).

What effect has this government fiscal crisis had on subsidies and other funds made available to NPOs? We will examine both the Hashimoto administration (1996–8) and the Obuchi administration. The two administrations are clearly contrasting. Hashimoto had tried to face and overcome the fiscal crisis. For example, measures taken to meet the crisis included raising the consumer tax to 5 per cent from April 1997, and the Medical Care Reforms and Health Act which came into force in June 1997, and which raised the insured member's medical bill payments from 10 per cent to 20 per cent.[7]

It is, however, amazing that despite the proportions of this fiscal crisis, the lack of political leadership in Japan has meant that the government has not taken any drastic measures to cut government spending. The budgets of each ministry are fiercely protected by the bureaucrats and Diet members with specific interests, and it is almost impossible to cut these as they are seen as vested rights.

Moreover, the Liberal Democratic Party (LDP) lost seats in the 1998 election. The new, Obuchi administration was formed. Obuchi's policy looked very

Table 11.1   The ratio of fiscal surplus to GDP (%)

Year	1990	1991	1992	1993	1994	1995
Total	3.5	3.4	0.1	-1.4	-3.0	-4.0
Central government	0.3	-0.2	-2.1	-2.8	-3.7	-4.2
Local government	-0.3	-0.1	-1.1	-1.6	-2.0	-2.7
Social security fund	3.5	3.7	3.4	3.1	2.7	2.8

Source: Economic White Paper 1997

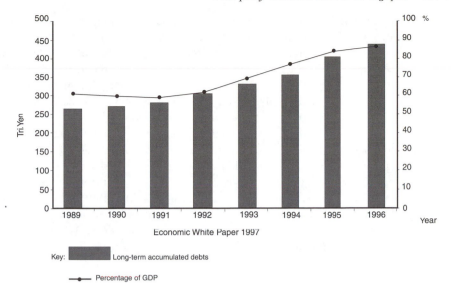

Figure 11.1 Central and local governments' long-term accumulated debts in Japan
Source: Economic White Paper 1997

manifest. Obuchi has used Keynesian strategy to expand government spending and encourage the economy. As the result of this, NPOs have been free from fiscal crisis. Subsidies to NPOs (especially I/NPOs) will not be reduced in the near future.

The economic crisis

The Japanese economy experienced a long economic recession after the collapse of the 'Bubble Economy'. When debating the effects of this economic crisis on the nonprofit sector, one has to first take into consideration trends in donations, and second, the influence of low-interest rate policies.[8]

Most donations given in Japan originate from corporations (Yamauchi 1997). Corporate donations increased rapidly in the second half of the 1980s – designated in this chapter as the second peak period of interest in NPOs. In 1987 the total value of donations was 355.9 billion yen, an increase of 16.2 per cent on the previous year. This trend continued with large increases of 10.6 per cent in 1988 and 7.2 per cent in 1989. By 1990, the increase was 30.0 per cent over the previous year, giving a total of 549.1 billion yen. In 1991 this increase fell suddenly to a mere 2.6 per cent, or 563.4 billion yen, and following that the totals started to shrink rapidly, falling to 453 billion yen by 1995 (Kokuzeicho 1997).[9] However, it should be noted that according to the report by the National Tax Administration Agency, these donations include political donations as well as donations to NPOs.

The situation regarding personal donations by Japanese individuals is virtually unknown. As the tax system is very strict about tax rebates for donations, the figures in tax statistics represent only a small percentage of philanthropic giving in Japan. An investigation of the trends in tax statistics shows that giving by individuals dropped after 1992, in the same way as corporate giving, but increased in 1995 to reach a total of 41.9 billion yen (Kokuzeicho 1998). The Kobe earthquake clearly affected the 1995 aggregates, but as a total of more than 170 billion yen was collected after the earthquake, and in view of the fact that a very considerable percentage of this was given by individual donors, it is clear that a major proportion of these donations did not receive any tax deduction.

The second factor in the current economic crisis has been the low-interest policy maintained by the government. The collapse of the 'Bubble Economy' ushered in an era of low interest rates, and currently the long-term rate is between 2 and 3 per cent, while the short-term interest rate is 0.5 per cent. Japanese foundations do not have to meet the minimum payout requirement that is a condition for private foundations in the US. On the other hand, they are not permitted to dip into their endowment funds (known as 'basic assets') which are obliged to be registered with the competent agencies. As a result, the operations of these foundations are directly affected by the low interest rates. In this respect, Japanese grantmaking foundations are facing their greatest crisis of the postwar period. Fortunately, most of Japan's major grantmaking foundations are corporate foundations, and although corporate performance is weak, they are still able to carry on their activities one way or the other, with donations from their parent company. Thus the economic crisis in the wake of the collapse of the Bubble Economy has created a major crisis among donors to NPOs. As the second peak of interest in NPOs occurred on the supply side, the backlash has had a major effect on NPOs.

The crisis of efficiency

A symbolic crisis of efficiency occurred in 1995, the year of the Kobe earthquake, which corresponded to the third peak in interest in NPOs. This crisis took place not only within nonprofit organizations but also within the government. The Kobe earthquake occurred on 17 January. It was centred on the city of Kobe, and also affected the areas of Hyogo Prefecture and Osaka. The earthquake registered a magnitude of 7.2 on the Richter scale, and wreaked great havoc: 6,308 killed, 93,775 houses completely destroyed and 106,972 houses partially destroyed. Japan is a country of frequent earthquakes and each local government has drawn up its own anti-disaster plan. Hyogo was no exception. The earthquake victims were evacuated to the elementary and junior high schools and other designated evacuation sites as soon as the earthquake was over. In the days following the earthquake 320,000 people gathered in the 1,232 evacuation sites. Temporary housing was erected for those who had lost their homes and, by October 1997 a total of 47,251 dwellings had been erected (Asahi Shimbun 1996). All of this work was undertaken entirely by the government.

The government's response to the earthquake has continually been at the centre of a vortex of criticism. The request for assistance from the military for primary rescue operations was delayed, and no fire-fighting activities were able to be put in place in response to the conflagrations engulfing the earthquake area. Many people expressed apprehensions about the government's lack of a risk-management organization, due to the time lag in the Prime Minister's response to the earthquake. Kobe City and other local governments also called for volunteers, but although they registered over 14,000 people, the governments were unable to designate any tasks to them.[10] Furthermore, relief supplies sent to the area were just left piled up on the ground, an action which earned the scorn of local residents.[11]

Each I/NPO had registered each special mission with the government. On the other hand, immediately following the earthquake television and radio stations were quick to praise the activities of N/NPOs. The overall number of volunteers in Hyogo Prefecture alone was estimated to exceed 1,400,000. In addition, from the day following of the earthquake, donations were quickly collected by twenty organizations including the Japanese Red Cross Society, the Kyodo Donations Association (modelled on the United Way in the US), the government and the mass media, and the total mounted rapidly to more than 170 billion yen. If this is calculated in dollars at the rate of $1 = 80 yen at that time, then this figure comes to a gigantic $2 billion. This is where the issue of efficiency came to bear. For example, on the day after the earthquake, the executives of one corporation discussed to which organization they should choose to make a donation. They had a choice of the Asahi Shimbun, Kobe City, Kyodo Donations Association or the Japanese Red Cross Society. In the end, they chose to donate 300 million yen to the Japanese Red Cross Society, from humanitarian concerns. However, in a surprising turn of events, all the donations collected by the Japanese Red Cross Society, the Kyodo Bokinkai (Japan's Community Chest), the local governments and the mass communications organizations were given a blanket name of 'Gienkin Charitable Giving' and collected under the umbrella of just one distribution committee. Thus the deliberations of the company mentioned above were rendered completely irrelevant. After the donations were collected, the distribution committee decided on three policies to govern their distribution. First, the money would be distributed uniformly. Second, it would be distributed to every person who had suffered damage or who had lost a family member. Third, all the money, including any interest earned, would be distributed. As a result, at the first distribution, 100,000 yen was given for each person killed, 100,000 yen for each house destroyed completely, and 50,000 yen for each house partially destroyed. In other words, not one yen was used to support the activities of the Japanese Red Cross Society, neither did any money from these donations get passed along via the Kyodo Bokimkai Association to the volunteer organizations (Deguchi 1996).

Furthermore, a certificate of earthquake damage issued by the local city office was necessary to receive the disbursements of the relief funds that each earthquake victim was eligible to collect. The disbursements were conducted by the city offices. In order to receive the certificate, however, the earthquake victims had to queue up outside the city offices for many long hours in the February cold. Also, although fundraising activities commenced quickly, the day after the earthquake, the first distribution of these funds was not made until 6 February. Six months after the earthquake, a total of more than 100 billion yen of the original 170 billion yen remained completely untouched[12] (Asahi Shimbun 1996; Deguchi 1996).

The 'Gienkin' money was neither used for I/NPOs nor N/NPOs. This was because the principle that all the money was to be distributed only to earthquake victims had been established. I/NPOs such as the Japanese Red Cross Society and the Kyodo Donations Committee had, of course, participated in the collection of these donations, but their methods and approaches were identical in every respect to the government bureaucracy. It is common in Japan for I/NPOs to become set into uniform responses[13] and adopt the action patterns typical of government bureaucracies.

On the other hand, N/NPOs were very flexible in their activities and approach.[14] A number of N/NPOs were organized following the earthquake and these included the Citizens' Association to Support Earthquake Victims,[15] the Higashi-nada Community Assistance Network,[16] the Kobe Genkimura,[17] the Local NGO Liaison Council,[18] the Nishinomiya Volunteers Network,[19] the Earthquake Relief Activities Records Office, and the Multicultural Coexistence Centre. None of these were incorporated. The Hanshin Awaji Community Fund, which was set up by the Nihon Foundation to use assets of 800 million yen in three years, is not a legal corporation either. Assessing this situation, Homma states that non-institutionalized volunteer organizations were active after the Kobe earthquake, while institutionalized organizations were not.[20] This situation was recognized early on by the government. As early as February 1995, internal government sources were expressing the need for N/NPO support to be encoded in law. There are differing opinions, however, as to the efficiency of N/NPOs. The successful groups were those held together by a strong leadership, and were, without question, very flexible in their organization. As these groups were unable to use the relief donations, they experienced economic limitations. Above all, however, there was a conspicuous lack of personnel, which made it impossible for these groups to move beyond an 'amateur' level. Furthermore, many organizations were very lax in their financial accounting procedures, as they had commenced activities in the emergency situation which followed the earthquake.

The crisis of legitimacy

With regard to legitimacy, two vectors moving in diverging directions came into play in the third peak after the Kobe earthquake. The division between N/NPOs and I/NPOs remained valid in this area also. The I/NPOs continued to be the focus of a variety of scandals. In 1996 the Aya Group's Shakai-Fukushi Hojin (a social welfare corporation) gave bribes to leading officials in the Ministry of Health and Welfare in return for a large subsidy.[21] This money was used in the construction of old peoples' facilities, and the work was undertaken by a construction company which was managed by the director of Shakai-Fukushi.[22] Another instance which came to light was that of the Yasuda Memorial Hospital, which submitted inflated figures on the number of doctors and nurses in its employ, enabling it to dishonestly receive subsidies for twenty or more years.[23] The biggest scandal to rock the whole of Japan, however, was the crimes committed by the Aum Supreme Truth cult, which was registered as a religious organization. This cult organization manufactured salin gas which they used randomly to kill many people. The reaction to these incidents was a movement to strengthen the supervisory responsibilities of the ministries and agencies responsible for supervising all I/NPOs. The Religious Corporation Act was amended at the end of 1995 to strengthen its regulations. In January 1996, the Regulations Liberalization Committee of the Liberal Democratic Party's Administrative Reform Department, and the government parties' administrative reform team began a review of the administration of *koeki-hojin* (incorporated foundations and associations, that is to say, I/NPOs for the purposes of this chapter), and in July the 'Initiatives for the management of *koeki-hojin*', which strengthens existing regulations, was published.

Following this, the cabinet adopted the 'Supervisory standards for the establishment and supervision of *koeki-hojin*' in September 1996. These standards set rules for limits on business income activities, guidelines on the length of terms for directors (two years), forbade the holding of shares, set limits on the amount of funds retained internally, and set up frameworks for autonomous release of information. The above events led to a trend towards the strengthening of the supervisory role of the government departments with jurisdiction over these organizations.

On the other hand, the activities of the volunteer organizations in the wake of the Kobe earthquake led to calls for reforms to the legal system so as to provide more support for N/NPO activities. Only ten days after the Kobe earthquake, on 27 January, Chief Cabinet Secretary Igarashi told the House of Representatives Budget Committee that a team would be brought together from all the related ministries and agencies to seriously study the legal measures required to encourage volunteer activities, including granting of legal entity status and favourable tax measures. This statement was a clear expression of the incipient trend of protecting and nurturing N/NPOs, and was in opposition to the way in which I/NPOs were regulated.[24]

Where do these new policies lead?

In view of the above, some discrepancies may be discernible in the current NPO system. The Japanese legal system for incorporation is based on the Civil Code which was established in 1887.[25] Corporations are divided into profit-making corporations and *koeki-hojin* (nonprofit and for public benefit). Originally there was no concept of a nonprofit corporation. Furthermore, the establishment of *koeki-hojin* is subject to 'permission' from the relevant authorities.[26] An organization can only be incorporated if the authorities recognize the public benefit accruing from its activities. Thus there had been no path to incorporation for groups that were at the same time both nonprofit and non-public-benefit organizations until the new law was passed. To circumvent this situation, special laws such as the Labour Union Act and the Religious Corporations Act were enacted so that a variety of organizations were able to become incorporated. Currently, there are over 100 special laws relating to the incorporation of organizations.[27] The reality is, however, that it is almost impossible for grassroots organizations to become incorporated under the civil code. The authorities will not permit their establishment if they do not have a considerable financial basis, on the grounds that even if these organizations are involved in activities which benefit the public, there is no guarantee that they will be able to continue their activities (London 1991). Although lack of incorporation does not hinder N/NPOs in their volunteer activities, they face the administrative problem of having to use the names of individuals when having a telephone line installed, buying a car or renting an office. According to a 1996 survey of N/NPOs by the Economic Planning Agency, 12 per cent of N/NPOs indicated that they had on occasion felt the need for incorporation. The multiple reasons for this felt need for incorporation were given as 'Incorporation would improve our public credibility' (65 per cent); 'It would be easier to qualify for donations and public subsidies' (47 per cent); 'It would convince others that we are not a profitmaking concern' (45 per cent); and 'We would qualify for favourable tax treatment' (10.6 per cent).[28] In drafting the NPO bill, the policy makers were without a doubt aiming for the development of N/NPOs. However, there is some room for doubt as to whether the NPO Law will be of any real use in encouraging the growth of N/NPOs. The reason is that this bill has been drafted as a special law within the current Civil Code. It was thought that, although the bill had great discrepancies with the Civil Code, which is the general law in this case, the possibility of achieving an amendment to the Civil Code was remote and would take a long time. As a result, the Law was drawn up without addressing the issue of the legal technicalities encountered in the drafting process.

In terms of democracy in Japan, the drafting of this Law followed a very unique process. First, there was a strong insistence that this Law be brought as a private member's bill.[29] Second, the Law's sponsors were mainly young Diet members who had only experienced one or two elections (Kumashiro 1998).[30] Third, the drafting process was carried out in conjunction with frequent discussions with citizens' groups and open forum meetings (Amemiya and Hotta 1998).[31] These three points have a very deep significance in the light of the usual democratic processes in Japan. A further two points are, fourth, that the draft was submitted without resolving the legal problems inherent in it, and, fifth, that it was drafted at a time when the cold wind of public distrust of I/NPOs, as exemplified by the Aum incidents, were blowing (Deguchi 1999). These were the reasons why the bill followed a very tortuous course to submission.

Let us now take a look at the Law to Promote Specified Nonprofit Activities.[32] In order to align it with the general statutes of the Civil Code, the bill provides for twelve categories of NPO activity. Only those organizations whose activities correspond with these categories are to be given the legal status of 'specified nonprofit corporation' (SNC). The twelve categories are listed below:

- activities to promote health, medical care and welfare
- activities to promote social education
- activities to promote community development
- activities to promote culture, the arts and sports
- activities to protect the environment
- disaster-relief activities
- activities to ensure community safety
- activities to protect human rights and promote peace
- international cooperation activities
- activities to promote the creation of a gender-equal society
- activities to promote the sound nurturing of youth
- liaison, advisory, or support activities related to the operation or activities of organizations performing any of the activities listed above.

These are not examples of specific activities, but a limited list of categories. Each organization must correspond to one of these twelve categories if it is to be a candidate for incorporation. The prefecture government which has jurisdiction is responsible for deciding whether or not an organization fits one of these categories.[33] A dichotomy will, no doubt, arise between existing N/NPOs according to whether their activities fit these categories or not. Furthermore, the focus is simply on obtaining corporate status, and SNCs are not accorded any favourable treatment within the tax system.[34] So this bill resembles a dead-end street. Unfortunately, as I have explained several times in this chapter, a distinction of the roles of N/NPOs and I/NPOs has emerged in recent years, and this has led to a consensus among the Japanese that a new system is needed for N/NPOs.[35] The emphasis of the resulting bill, however, is on feasibility, so that instead of approaching the issue with the view to improving the legal environment of the nonprofit sector, it has been reduced to simply enabling N/NPOs to obtain corporate status. This bill will do nothing more than further emphasize the distinction between N/NPOs and I/NPOs. It is commendable, however, that the drafting of this law was guided by the idea that N/NPO activities should not, as far as possible, be limited by the supervisory authorities. Turning now from the discussion of N/NPOs, I/NPOs are currently facing a trend towards the strengthening of regulations at a time characterized by the bleak outlook for a reform of the I/NPO system. There exists two schema of NPOs in Japan: I/NPO and N/NPO. Yet, nobody can indicate in Japan in which direction the NPO sector – as defined by the ICNPO – will go.

Notes

1 Currently in Japan, the term 'NPO' is still unclear, but it is usually defined as both specified nonprofit corporations (see below) and unincorporated grassroots organizations.
2 These developments have, without doubt, been influenced by the US consumer movement and its leaders such as Ralph Nader.
3 In 1985 Japanese corporations had 250 factories in the US, but by 1990, an interval of only five years, this number had jumped to 1,600 (Keidanren 1996: 16).
4 In 1996 the One Percent Club of the Keidanren had 992 members (Keidanren 1996).
5 Currently there are 173 corporate members (Kigyo Mesena Kyogikai 1997).
6 According to a *Mainichi Shimbun* survey, 86 per cent of adults throughout Japan had either been involved in volunteer work or had given a donation (*Mainichi Shimbun*, 28 March 1995).
7 The Nursing Care Insurance Act is still being deliberated, and has been carried over to the next Diet session.
8 The impact of marketization on NPOs is also relevant to this debate, but sufficient data to discuss this informedly is not available.
9 According to the latest data, corporate giving has experienced an upturn, although the economy has yet to experience the same.
10 *Yomiuri Shimbun*, evening edition, 26 January 1995.
11 *Mainichi Shimbun*, 22 January 1995.
12 Donations are still being received. The total received as of the end of August 1997 was 178.66 billion yen. 4.8 billion yen still remains undistributed.
13 Uniform responses are often referred to as 'fairness'.
14 For example, the Dentsu Institute for Human Studies edition entitled *What are NPOs?* (Nihon Keizai Shimbun).
15 Inaugurated on 19 January as an organization functioning as a Disaster Volunteers' Centre. The basic routine was for volunteers to go to the disaster area only during the day, and return to Osaka at night so as not to add to the burdens of the disaster area.
16 A centre which provides support aimed at developing volunteer organizations has been set up. These changes have been made in response the need to support elderly people, and other elements of voluntary activity.
17 This group concentrates on distributing rice in the temporary housing areas, and installing emergency alarm systems called bell boxes. It also functioned as a volunteer centre after the oil spill that occurred when the Russian tanker *Nahtoka* ran aground on a reef in 1996.
18 The Kobe Residents Rescue Liaison Committee was set up mainly through the efforts of the PHD Association which is headquartered in Kobe. Its name was later changed to the Kobe Earthquake Local NGO Liaison Committee, and the committee set up a communications network between volunteer organizations in the disaster area.
19 This organization provided support for the departments in the City Office, and distributed daily necessities and post office parcels to the community associations. It also provided support for the distribution of materials for the temporary housing, and conducted surveys of the situation of the temporary housing. Its other activities included keeping in close contact with the Federal Emergency Management Agency (FEMA) in the US and it took over the functions of the Nishinomiya Volunteer Network so that this could be actively phased out. It now provides initiatives on the swift establishment of rescue operations in the case of a future disaster, as well as planning for local anti-disaster measures. It is also linked to NVNAD (Nippon Volunteer Network for Assisting in Disasters), which is the first private sector disaster rescue coordinating organization in Japan.
20 Deguchi 1996: 3.

21 *Asahi Shimbun* 7 December 1996.
22 *Asahi Shimbun* 4 December 1996.
23 *Mainichi Shimbun* 14 April 1995.
24 These circumstances were almost all ignored by the mass media. A detailed report is given in the Prime Ministers' Secretariat Management Office Rules, 'Standards for the establishment and management of charitable organizations' (Association of Charitable Organizations, 1997).
25 Tanaka (1980) gives the details.
26 According to Tanaka (1980), legal experts interpret the 'permission system' to mean that the government has discretionary powers.
27 Takako Amemiya (1997) 'Bill to promote citizens' activities', *Association of Charitable Organizations*, 1997, 26 (21).
28 The Economic Planning Agency conducted a random survey of 10,000 organizations from a pool of 85,786 N/NPOs throughout Japan. A total of 4,152 valid responses were received, and of these one third listed their annual expenses as less than 100,000 yen (Economic Planning Agency 1996).
29 Private members' bills are rare in Japan. In almost all cases, bills are drafted by the bureaucracy.
30 Ranking within Japanese political parties is determined by the number of times a politician has been elected. Diet members who have only been elected once or twice have almost no influence or say.
31 An organization called C's, which is based in Tokyo, played a pivotal role.
32 The Law in English is presented on the following website: *http://www.epa.go.jp/98/c/19980319c-npo-e.html*.
33 In a reaction to the discretionary powers of the Civil Code, the term 'certification' has been used when inaugurating organizations, as this term does not have as great a nuance of discretionary power as does 'permission'. However, the number of categories of activity remains limited to twelve, and somebody has to decide whether an organizations' activities correspond to one of these twelve categories. It was confirmed during the Diet deliberations that a wide interpretation would be made in the application of this law.
34 However, a supplementary resolution stated that the favourable tax status would be reviewed within two years.
35 In the election of October 1996, every major political party made an official promise to pass the NPO bill.

References

Amemiya, T. (1992) 'Kigyo zaidan no genzyo' ('Situation of corporate foundations'), in K. Koeki-Hojin (ed.) *Nihon-No Kigyo Zaidan* (*Corporate Foundations in Japan*) Tokyo: Koeki-Hojin Kyokai (Association of Charitable Organizations).

——(1997) 'Shimin katsudo sokushin hoan' ('Bill to promote citizens' activities') Koeki-Hojin, 26, 21. Tokyo: Koeki Hojin Kyokai.

Amemiya, T. and Hotta, T. (eds) (1998) *NPO Ho Konmentaaru* (*NPO Law Commentary*) Tokyo: Gyosei.

Asahi Shimbun (ed.) (1996) *Hanshin Awaji Daishinsai-Shi* (*The Great Kobe Earthquake*) Tokyo: Asahi Shimbunsya.

Bob, D. and SRI International (1990) *Japanese Companies in American Communities*, New York: Japan Society.

Citizens' Association to Support Earthquake Victims (ed.) (1996) *Shinsai Borantea: Hanshin Awaji Daishinsai Hisaiti No Hitobito Wo Oensuru Simin No Kai Zenkiroku* (*Volunteers After the*

Quake: All Records of the Citizens Association to Support Earthquake Victims) Osaka: Kaisai Magazine Center.

Deguchi, M. (1993) *Firansoropi: Kigyo to Hito No Syakaikoken (Philanthropy: Corporate and individual Social Contributions*) Tokyo: Maruzen.

——(1995) 'Suito kappuru: kigyou to NPO no atarasiikannkei' ('Sweet couple: a new relation between N/NPO and companies') *ESP*, September: 69–73. Tokyo: Keizaikikaku Kyokai.

——(1999) 'Tokutei hieiri katsudou sokushinho no hikarito kage' ('Light and shadow of the law to promote specified nonprofit activities') Yokosuka: Seisaku Kenkyu Yokosuka, 1.

Dentsu Soken (ed.) (1996) *NPO Toha Nanika (What is NPO?*) Tokyo: Nihonkeizai Shimbunsya.

Economic Planning Agency (1996) *Shimin Katsudo Report: Shimin Katsudo Kihon Tyosa (Citizen's Activities Report: Fundamental Survey of the Citizen's Organizations*) Tokyo: Okurasyo Insatsukyoku.

Hayashi, C. and Iriyama, A. (1997) *Koeki-Hojin No Jitsuzo (The Reality of Koeki-Hojin*) Tokyo: Daiyamondo-Sha.

Hayashi, Y. and Imada, M. (eds) (1999) *Firansoropi: no Shiso (Thoughts on Philanthropy*) Tokyo: Nihon-Keizai Hyoronsya.

Homma, M. and Deguchi, M. (eds) (1996) *Volunteer Kakumei (Volunteer Revolution*) Tokyo: Toyo Keizai Shimposya.

Imada, M. (1993) 'Corporate Philanthropy in Japan', in Shimada (ed.) *Kaikasuru Philanthropy (Blooming Philanthropy*) Tokyo: TBS-Britanica.

Iwasaki, N., Ukai, K., Urano, M., Tsuji, K., Nitagai, K., Noda, T. and Yamamoto, T. (eds) (1999) *Hanshin Awaji Daishinsai No Syakaigaku (The Sociology of the Great Hanshin-Awaji Earthquake*) vol. 1, Kyoto: Showado.

Keidanren (Federation of Economic Organizations) (1994) *Kigyo No Syakaikoken Handobukku (Handbook of Corporate Philanthropies*) Tokyo: Nihonkogyo-Shimbun.

——(1996) *Syakai Koken Hakusyo (White Paper on Corporate Philanthropy*) Tokyo: Nihon Kogyo Shimbun.

Keizaidoyukai (Japanese Committee for Economic Development) (1972) *Corporate Social Resonsibilities*, Tokyo: CED.

Kigyo Mesena Kyogikai (ed.) (1997) *Mesena Hakusyo 1996 (White Paper on Corporate Support to the Arts*) Tokyo: Daiyamondosya.

Kokuzeicho (National Tax Administration) (1997) *Heisei 8 nenbun Zeimu tokei Kara Mita Houzinn Kigyou No Zittai (Situation of incorporated Business from the Statistical Tax Data, Fiscal Year 1996*) Tokyo: Okurasyo Insatsukyoku.

——(1998) *Heisei 8 nenbun Shinkoku Syotokuzei No Zittai (Situation of Declared income Tax, Fiscal Year 1996*) Tokyo: Okurasyo Insatsukyoku.

Kumashiro, A. (ed.) (1998) *Nihon No NPO Ho (Japan's NPO Law*) Tokyo: Gyosei.

London, N. (1991) *Japanese Corporate Philanthropy*, Oxford: Oxford University Press.

Maeda, S. (1993) 'Daisan sector to saad sector' ('Daisan sector and the third sector') in T. Imamura (ed.) *Daisan Sector No Kenkyu (Study of the Daisan Sector*) Tokyo: Chuohoki, 41.

Matsuoka, N. (1992) *Kigyo-Shimin No Jidai (Age of Corporate Citizenship*) Tokyo: Nihonkeizaishimbunsya.

MITI (Ministry of International Trade and Industry) (ed.) (1977) *Situation and Problems of Business Behavior*, Tokyo: Tyushosangyou tyousakai.

Morimoto, M. (1994) *Kigyo Syakai Sekinin No Keieigakuteki Kennkyu (The Management Study of Corporate Social Responsibilities*) Tokyo: Hakuto Shobo.

Naikaku Souridaijin Kanbo Kanrishitsu (ed.) (1997) *Koeki-Hojin Setsuritsu Unei No Kizyun* (*Standard Policy Guidance to Koeki-Hojin*) Tokyo: Koeki-Hojin Kyokai.

Salamon, L. M. (1994) 'The rise of the nonprofit sector', *Foreign Affairs*, 73, 3: 111–24.

——(1995) *Partners in Public Service: Government-Nonprofit Relations in the Modern Welfare State*, Baltimore: Johns Hopkins University Press.

Salamon, L. M. and Anheier H. K. (eds) (1997) *Defining the Nonprofit Sector*, Manchester: Manchester University Press.

Sorifu (Prime Minister's Office) (1999) *Heisei 10 nenndo Koekihojin Hakusho* (*Koeki-Hojin White Paper 1998*) Tokyo: Okurasyo Insatsukyoku.

Sotooka, H. (1996) *Jishin to Shakai* (*Earthquake and Society*), Tokyo: Misuzu Shobo.

Tachiki, S. (ed.) (1997) *Volunteers and Civil Society: Citizen Makes Publicness* (in Japanese) Kyoto: Koyo Shobo.

Tanaka, M. (1980) *Koeki-Hojin to Koeki-Shintaku* (*Koeki-Hojin and Public Trust*) Tokyo: Keiso Shobo.

Yamamoto, T. (ed.) (1998) *The Nonprofit Sector in Japan*, Manchester: Manchester University Press.

Yamaoka Yoshinori (1998) 'NPO ho sekou to kongo no shiminkatudou' ('Enacting NPO law and citizens' activities in the future') *Koeki-Hojin*, 27: 2–7, Tokyo: Koeki-Hojin Kyokai.

Yamauchi, N. (1997) *The Nonprofit Economy* (in Japanese) Tokyo: Nihon Hyoronsya.

——(1999) *NPO Nyumon* (*The First Step for NPOs*) Tokyo: Nihon-Keizaishimbun.

12 The American third sector at the end of the twentieth century

Public and private revisited

Eleanor L. Brilliant

Warnings about crises in the American nonprofit sector come with some degree of frequency. Advocates for the sector worry about the vulnerability of voluntary institutions to changing political views and economic conditions (Salamon, Chapter 2, this volume). The idea of crisis seems endemic to the historic development of the voluntary sector in the United States, although the sector contains such vital organizations of daily life as churches, schools, museums and hospitals. Even before the voluntary, nonprofit sector gained a new sense of identity in the mid-1970s, the Peterson Commission, a citizen's group established by John D. Rockefeller in 1969, reported that charitable organizations in the United States would shortly be facing a financial crisis:[1] the Commission also reported that foundations were already in trouble, at least in part due to their own failings.

In the years after the Peterson Commission Report was published, voluntary organizations generally flourished. However, during the economic stagflation of the mid-1970s, there were financial problems in the charitable world, and particularly in some parts of it, such as the United Way system (Brilliant 1990: 51–71). In addition, in the aftermath of the turbulent 1960s, the value of most formal institutions was challenged, and serious questions were raised about the relationship between the three major elements of the American political economy – business, government and voluntary organizations. Indeed, at the very time that the notion of a third sector was being articulated (Levitt 1973; Nielsen 1972), parallel attention was given to the blurring of distinctions between the three sectors in the United States (Brilliant 1973; Pifer 1970; Smith and Hague 1971).

In this essay I will consider current problems in the American nonprofit sector as part of a continuing pattern of disquieting issues facing the sector over the past two decades. I analyse these problems with particular regard to:

1 trends in the size and value of the 'third' sector
2 changes in public/private relationships

3   the concept of civil society
4   problems of accountability and abuse.

And I conclude by addressing the question: Where should we go from here?

Health of the sector: trends, data and unknowns

It is thirty years since the Tax Reform Act of 1969 (Pub. 1. nos. 91–172) imposed tighter restrictions on many tax-exempt organizations, particularly foundations, and also required more encompassing mandatory annual reporting requirements. However, despite proclamations of disaster at the time, the period since the passage of the Act has generally been marked by continued growth in the American third sector, in the number of organizations as well as in the financial value of assets and expenditures. Weisbrod has documented rapid growth in the number of nonprofits between 1967 and 1984, in addition to an earlier spurt in 1964, when applications for tax-exempt status doubled in response to a favourable situation and government funding of new and emerging groups (Weisbrod 1988: 64–5).

Hodgkinson *et al.* (1996: 3) also report two recent periods marked by extensive growth (1977–82 and 1987–92). Over one million tax-exempt organizations are currently on the Exempt Organizations Master File of the IRS. The IRS Master File lists twenty-nine different categories of tax-exempt organizations and encompasses trade associations, labour unions and benevolent societies; by far the largest group is the 501 (c) (3) category of charitable organizations.[2]

Additionally, there is a substantial number of other organizations that are not required to register with the IRS, including an estimated 300,000 churches and religious congregations (Salamon 1999), and possibly millions of small, informal grassroots organizations that are even more difficult to pinpoint (Smith 1997). According to Independent Sector, operating expenditures of American nonprofit organizations represented about 7.9 per cent of the gross domestic product (GDP) in 1993, an increase from 6.0 per cent in 1983 (Hodgkinson *et al.* 1996: 48). With some noted fluctuations, after a low of 1.1 per cent in 1987, contributions hovered around 2 per cent of the total GDP in the past decade; personal giving represented 1.9 per cent of personal income in 1998 (AAFRC 1997; 1999);[3] from 1992 to 1997, assets of public charities reportedly increased by over one third, to the total of around $1 trillion (NCCS 1999). Within aggregate numbers there are of course significant differences, including shifts in the source of contributions as well as in their destination. Overall giving seems to directly reflect socio-economic conditions; for example, in the face of corporate downsizing and economic uncertainty, corporate giving declined in real dollar value (taking account of inflation) from the late 1980s into the early 1990s; from 1992 to 1996 corporate giving increased slightly in inflation-adjusted dollars, but remained relatively stagnant, at about 1.3 per cent of pre-tax income (AAFRC 1997: 21, 199–207). Along with a rising stock market and general prosperity, from 1997 to 1998 corporate contributions reportedly increased by 9.3 per cent (or about 7.7 per cent in inflation-adjusted numbers), but remained at only 1.01 per cent of pre-tax income (AAFRC 1999: 10).

Considerable progress has been made in developing an accurate and significant database for the nonprofit sector. The work of Independent Sector and other academic centres or 'think tanks' has contributed to this process. Nonetheless, researchers in the field recognize that difficulty persists in the collection of precise data as well as in the technological capability for analysing massive amounts of non-uniform data. As a result of efforts of the National Center for Charitable Statistics, and in cooperation with the IRS, accuracy in data collection and analysis may improve. Still, difficulties are likely to continue in the foreseeable future, because of limited resources and fundamental impediments in comprehending the nature of a sector which is dispersed, diverse, and committed to maintaining independence from central regulation (David Horton Smith, cited in AAFRC 1997: 58). Moreover, the much-cited Master File is accumulative, and evidently includes vast numbers of inactive or defunct organizations (Salamon 1999: 40, n1). Thus even leading scholars are often forced to make important policy analyses with data that are out of date or actually best estimates.

In addition, however, I would argue that while we must refine our techniques for data collection and analysis, we also need to reassess some fundamental assumptions that affect our present evaluation of that data. For example, it is generally assumed that individual contributions, including bequests (which together are reported as accounting for close to 90 per cent of charitable contributions since the mid-1960s) are particularly important for a 'healthy' third sector (AAFRC 1997: 31). Similarly, it is strongly held that more is always better in regard to the head count of entities or the amount of money spent in the sector (whether in the aggregate or in organizational subsectors). Indeed, currently much attention is being given to the potential philanthropic share of an estimated $10 trillion in intergenerational transfers which is expected to occur in the next decade (Avery and Rendall 1993; Shapiro, cited in Salamon 1997: 51–2).

The issue of size was subject to considerable discussion in the 1970s when it was argued that 'small is beautiful'. This issue once again has saliency at a time when big corporations and for-profit entities are struggling with contrary pressures of mergers and consolidation together with the decentralization of activity. As already suggested, a great number of voluntary organizations are small; but in 1993 the top 6 per cent (9,901 organizations) controlled 80 per cent of total assets and 85 per cent of total expenses for the independent sector (Hodgkinson *et al.* 1996: 15). Indeed, the image of large organizations dominates the reality, as well as our perception, of the nonprofit field.

Despite overall growth of the nonprofit sector in the early 1990s, there were some signs of decline in the growth rate of the 'independent sector' in those years. As delineated, the independent sector represents more than two thirds of the total tax-exempt entities registered with the IRS; it includes organizations in the 501 (c) (3) 'charitable' category of the Internal Revenue Code, as well as 501(4) social welfare and action groups under the IRS Code. According to the

Nonprofit Almanac 1996–1997, the share of national income generated by the independent sector declined from 6.5 per cent in 1992 to an estimated 6.3 per cent in 1994, including volunteer time (Hodgkinson *et al.* 1996: 3–4).

Using another measure, the IRS Master File of exempt organizations indicates continued but slow increases overall in the numbers of tax-exempt entities in the 1990s, with a slightly accelerated growth rate after 1992, when 1,085,206 entities were registered. By 1994 1,138,598 entities were in the IRS Master File; in 1996 the number had risen to 1,188,510. In 1997 the number grew to 1,232, 214. Moreover, there was a significant increase in the number of organizations registered in the charitable classification, which between 1995 and 1997 went from 626,226 entities to 692,524 listed entities. In addition there has been a small increase in the related 501 (c) (4) category, which after several years of declining numbers, grew almost imperceptibly from 139,451 entities (1995) to 139,512 (1996), and was at 141,776 by 1997 (IRS 1997). But the question remains: What do these changes really mean?

To put this question another way: Should we assume that an increase in the growth rate of either the number of government organizations or the amount of government expenditures is necessarily a good thing? Or that a decline in the share of the GDP of government or business activities is necessarily bad? In considering the meaning of changes in any of the sectors, including the nonprofit sector, we need to develop an overall perspective on rates of growth and their direction in light of the overall political economy, including all three sectors. I will return to this issue below.

Changing public and private relationships

In the years since John D. Rockefeller created the Peterson Commission (1969–70) and the Filer Commission (1973–7), to consider problems of philanthropy in the USA, a veritable industry has developed around analysis of public and private relationships. When this issue was initially formulated by Eli Ginsberg and others in the 1960s, the delineation between not-for-profit and for-profit entities in the private sector was not a primary focus of attention (Ginsberg *et al.* 1965; Phelps 1965; Reagan 1963). Subsequently the distinction was given much greater importance, although certainly no consensus has ever developed concerning the ideal arrangement among the three sectors. Over the years, however, a number of different conceptualizations of the relationship between organizations in the nonprofit sector and government have been advanced. Accordingly, relationships between the two sectors have been characterized as: parallel bars of a ladder (Kahn 1977); producing a shadow state (Wolch 1990); structuring a primary role for government with in effect, subsidiarity of voluntary organizations (Anheier 1992); a conflict model (Piven and Cloward 1977; Staples 1984); or conversely a partnership relationship between the nonprofit sector and the government (Salamon 1995); and more specifically, a contract relationship between the sectors (Wedel *et al.* 1979). The partnership concept as argued by Salamon

and others possibly enjoys more respectability than most of the others, particularly that of the conflict model, and in fact the notion of partnership was
espoused by John D. Rockefeller III in the 1970s.

It would be easy to dismiss the search for a more unified understanding of a
normative effective relationship between the sectors in the United States as a
fool's search for a magic elixir. Perhaps we could argue that attempts to categorize this relationship should be abandoned. But doing so would be unwise,
because the delineation of appropriate relations among the sectors has real
consequences for praxis, and profoundly affects social policy in this country. For
example, relationships among the sectors determines payments to cover delivery
of a variety of critical services; indeed, federal payments for health services
through Medicaid and Medicare have provided significant sources of public
revenues for the voluntary sector, and the 1995 proposed congressional cuts in
these entitlement programmes represented the largest amounts of projected cuts
in funds to the sector (Salamon 1997: 16–21). In addition, the involvement of
business in providing jobs for welfare recipients is now a core aspect of welfare
policy. Perhaps even more fundamentally, interaction among the sectors has real
significance in shaping the dialogue between citizens and their institutions in a
democratic society.

Ultimately, the critical difference between 'public' and 'private' is not limited
to the making of sectoral distinctions but is essentially philosophical, with even
moral implications concerning the concepts themselves and their shifting boundaries. Indeed, one can define the distinction by contrasting the concept of public
interest with that of private property (an old Lockean issue) as well as with reference to Hansmann and Weisbrod's delineation of market failure as justification
for nonprofit or governmental spheres of activity (Hansmann 1987; Schultz
1977; Weisbrod 1988). But the term 'public' is still more problematic for advocates of the American nonprofit sector. This is at least partly because its meaning
affects discussions about the basic rights of charitable nonprofit organizations.
These organizations are presumed by law to operate for the public good and also
have traditionally been permitted to be particular or exclusionary (e.g. in regard
to race, sex or religion), while at the same time they have enjoyed various tax
exemptions – from local and state property taxes, from income taxes, and for
their donors, a charitable deduction from income.

The interpretation of public and private rights and responsibilities has been
an ongoing issue for judicial debate, and has impacted the charitable sector
increasingly since the 1960s. In this regard a landmark case was decided by the
Supreme Court in 1983. In *Bob Jones University v. United States*, the IRS argued
successfully to remove the tax-deductibility privilege of Bob Jones University
because of its racially discriminatory admissions policies (Hopkins 1992: 82–6).
The Court decided against the university on the basis of the tenet that in order
to maintain tax deductibility, private educational institutions had to operate in
the public interest and could not 'violate established public policy' (nondiscrimi-
nation). Thus the point was made emphatically that private charity could not be
considered immune from the strictures of public policy.

As we know, belief in the value of voluntary activity is embedded, not only in de Tocqueville's pieties about the role of voluntary associations in America (recently reinvoked by Presidents Bush and Clinton) but in our tax code. In fact this preference was established in national law with the initiation of the income tax on corporations (1909) even before being incorporated in the laws relating to personal income (1917). However, the principle of exemption of nonprofit organizations from public taxation became more complicated after the Tax Reform Act of 1969 sharply delineated the formal concept of 'private foundation', and intensified the distinction between foundations and other charities that were defined as public (in effect publicly supported) under the Internal Revenue Code (Brilliant, 2000).

Nonetheless, and despite a strong tradition to the contrary, the exemption from taxation or public intrusion which is afforded voluntary institutions has been subject to almost continuous questioning since the 1950s and even before.[4] To begin with, fear of foundation power and challenges to blanket tax exemption influenced the outcome of the 1969 Tax Reform Act, which for the first time established an excise tax (then set at 4 per cent) on the income of 'private foundations'. Congress also attempted to place more rigid limitations on political and advocacy activity by foundations in comparison with other nonprofit organizations. Since business (private-for-profit) activity was at that time allowed almost absolute freedom in lobbying, control over organizational freedom to lobby seemed to depend on the nature of private and public monied interests, and in determinations related specifically to tax exemption and tax expenditures. In the event, charitable foundations as repositories for private wealth – even though dedicated to defined public purposes – were singled out for negative attention.

The notion of tax expenditure was promulgated in the 1960s by Stanley Surrey, a professor of taxation and tax policy at Harvard Law School. Surrey, who served as Assistant Secretary of Treasury for Tax Policy in the Democratic administrations of Kennedy and Johnson, formulated the concept that tax forgiveness or exclusions provided for certain categories of goods and activities, were not only a tax incentive for specific private activities, but constituted a direct cost to the government, and should be defined as tax expenditures (Surrey 1970; Surrey and McDaniels 1985). In effect, to opponents of this view, private contributions were being defined as public money. The whole story is too long (and too complex) to be told in this chapter, but the idea of tax expenditures was so powerful, and Surrey so persistent, that it influenced the outcome of the 1969 Tax Reform Act and was formally mandated to be part of the Federal Budget in 1974 (Brilliant, 2000; Surrey and McDaniels 1985). The idea evidently struck a receptive note with a variety of stakeholders, including progressive liberals who were concerned about inequities in tax policies, and ideologues on the left and right who resented the power of foundations that created programmes opposed to their views.

Recent efforts to tax the property or activities of nonprofit organizations at the state and local level can be considered as another aspect of the same philosophical position concerning tax expenditures. So also must efforts to eliminate tax provisions that allow charitable gifts of appreciated property (e.g. paintings or stocks) to avoid taxation on increased value. Proposals for a federal 'flat tax' suggest that this kind of tax benefit for contributions would be reduced or eliminated. In effect, proponents of such views are also challenging the basis for charitable tax deductions. Indeed, states and localities are asking: Why shouldn't nonprofit organizations be taxed? Moreover, if, as Salamon has argued, charitable organizations have become increasingly commercialized, by charging fees for service, or conducting for-profit business activities that amount to as much as half of their revenues, why should they be tax-exempt? (Salamon 1993). Why should contributors to such organizations receive a deduction from income for donations to entities that may no longer even be fully charitable, and in fact are becoming increasingly like businesses with for-profit activity?

Civil society or whatever it is

Although, like many others who are interested in the nonprofit sector, I believe in the value of a civil society, I also note that the concept is enshrouded in ambiguity and in some respects seems to be as much an article of faith as a precise term of reference. In fact, during a conference of the Association for Research on Nonprofit Organizations and Voluntary Action (November 1997) considerable controversy broke out over use of the term 'civil society', and even whether it necessarily carried with it an underlying conservative view of consensus and reduced political activity. In any case, the idea has a venerable history; it was shaped by influential political thinkers like John Locke and Jean-Jacques Rousseau, and is related to notions of citizenship. In the decade of the 1990s it has been used frequently in connection with the emerging democracies of Central and Eastern Europe; however, as one study of civil society in these countries noted, the term 'is open to widespread interpretation throughout the world' (Siegel and Yancey 1992: 73). Although Siegel and Yancey do not define the term 'civil society' concisely, the analysis in their monograph *The Rebirth of Civil Society* starts with the essential nature of alternative institutions to the state (of the nonprofit sector) and relates these organizations to critical concepts of citizenship, pluralism and diversity.

Robert Putnam, who has certainly been a centre of the debate in the United States, has used the words 'civic community' to encompass these four elements which in effect embodied his conceptualization of the civil society (Putnam 1993: 86–91):

1   Citizenship in a civic community is marked, first of all, by active participation in public affairs.
2   Citizenship in a civic community entails equal rights and obligations for all.
3   Citizens in a civic community are more than merely active, public-spirited and equal. Virtuous citizens are helpful, respectful, and trustful towards one another even when they differ on matters of substance.

4   The norms and values of the civic community are embodied in, and influenced by, distinctive social structures and practices.

Putnam (1993: 90) then goes on in greater detail about these associations as follows: 'Participation in civic organizations inculcates skills of cooperation as well as a sense of shared responsibility for collective endeavors'. Throughout we are reminded of Aristotelian concepts.

Lester Salamon and Helmut Anheier somewhat complicate the picture by suggesting that an effective relationship among all three sectors, business, government and voluntary, is a necessary part of the definition of a civil society, which they define as:

> a society that contains three distinct sectors – government, business, and not-for profit – but that fosters active cooperation among them in addressing societal needs.
>
> (Salamon 1997: 57–8)

On the whole, with the exception of the Salamon and Anheier definition, there seem to be two essential aspects basic to most views of civil society: first, that there is a considerable range of choice in association, accompanied by a diversity of institutions which embody this right of free association; and second, that these institutions offer protection for people from tyrannical rule, and that associations of opposing viewpoints exist which enable citizens to participate more meaningfully in political activity and in electing their governments. Thus these basic constructs embody democratic choice, but are not tied to any numerical dimension. In fact, although financial resources are certainly necessary for organizations to survive in a modern capitalistic state, it is not at all evident that merely increasing the number of organizations or the pot of money allocated to them necessarily strengthens civil society.

Questions have already been raised as to whether there is such a thing as an independent sector, in the sense of independent from government or business. In this regard the source of money to support these organizations may make a difference, and particularly in relation to the type of recipient organization: for example, the choice of the journal *Ms.* not to accept commercial revenues from advertising, or the advancement of the mission of the Metropolitan Museum with the aid of the enormous revenues from sales in its gift shop. Evidence is emerging that proprietary auspice in hospitals does affect the mix of services offered, and managed care certainly determines the nature of care patients receive in critical matters: length of stay in the hospital, choice of doctors, permitted medications, etc. On the other hand, relying totally on private contributions for support of large or medium-sized formal institutions, whether museums or family service agencies, is certainly no longer possible, and even where contributions are a significant factor, fundraising involves increased completion, marketing and business-like practices.

Probably no-one would suggest that the idea of civil society can be tied solely to the development of larger museums or more funding for private universities or hospitals. Indeed, although it is not always evident in the debate, we know that small grassroots groups and community-based organizations are essential to the preservation of those opposing voices necessary for a democracy. Nevertheless, because these do require increasing amounts of money, policy analysts and researchers are in constant danger of using the amount of financial gifts to these institutions as a surrogate for something else: for example, proof of cultural enhancement or the free exchange of ideas. But we have to be careful that we do not substitute the appearance for the real thing; in effect it is not an increasing amount of contributions, but a well educated, informed and responsible electorate that should properly be considered the most significant sign of an effective civil society. Furthermore, in the voluntary sector, as with governmental actions, the variety of benefits provided to ensure the general welfare of people may also be a mark of the true civil society – but as we know, the benefits of activities in the voluntary sector are even harder to measure than those of government, and face great difficulties (Clotfelter 1992).

Accountability and abuse

Discussions leading to the passage of the Tax Reform Act of 1969 (including earlier attacks of Congressman Wright Patman against the foundations) in essence articulated two levels of argument. The first suggested that there was a group of foundations (although the numbers and extent were debatable) that violated the intent and the practice defined as permissible activity in the IRS Code prior to 1969, particularly in regard to self-dealing by foundation officials or business-related activities (US Treasury Department 1965).[5] The second was a broader concern – that the phenomenon of foundations as a whole presupposed the existence of a powerful group of elite leaders who were able to use personal and business wealth to effect public policy in ways determined by their own interests, and without accountability to anyone but themselves (Domhoff 1979; Lundberg 1968; Subcommittee no. 1, Select Committee on Small Business 1962). Provisions in the 1969 Act were in effect written to address both of these issues: in the first case by mandating more reviews by the IRS and penalties for abuses in regard to defined activities (which were both financial and political) of foundations; and in the second case by setting more specific limits on foundation control of businesses or dealings between self-interested parties and foundations, as well as by mandating higher payouts of foundation funds (General Explanation of the Tax Reform Act of 1969–70).

Despite the initial shock after the passage of the 1969 Act, foundations in this country continued to flourish and arguably became stronger than ever. However, on the whole, it appears that discussion in connection with the Act excluded from equal consideration similar questions in regard to the larger group of 501 (c) (3) public charities, probably because they were able to protect themselves through more effective lobbying efforts, while the foundations seemed to lack a dedicated constituency group (Friedman 1973). Nonetheless, troublesome issues of accountability in the world of the public charities remained: among them the fundamental question about to whom a charitable institution is accountable. Despite the pressure to diversify, to what extent are the boards of directors of many important public charities, like those of private foundations, still mostly self-perpetuating elitist groups? What impact do the increasing amounts of public money (with some exceptions continuous through the mid-1990s) have on the policies and programmes of these public charities? And finally, how could the IRS ever be expected to monitor the activities of so many diverse and scattered organizations when they produce little direct revenue for the government and therefore are hardly central to the purposes of the IRS? What is the role of the states in monitoring nonprofit organizations which in fact are generally incorporated by them, and for whose activities they presumably have some responsibility?

Major issues of accountability in the nonprofit sector remain unanswered even now, thirty years after the Tax Reform Act of 1969. Many of these issues were addressed not only by the Peterson Commission but also by the Filer Commission; they were analysed in volumes of *Research Papers* published by the Filer Commission (1977) and have been the subject of extensive research by scholarship on the sector that has expanded since that time. In late 1999 a Division of Tax Exempt and Governmental Entities was established within the IRS; nonetheless researchers and the public still believe there to be difficulties in accessing information, and with evaluating the IRS monitoring of nonprofit organizations. In fact, at the end of the 1990s, there was an echo of the discussion of the late 1960s about whether the IRS is really the proper place for such an overseeing, and there were proposals for restructuring the IRS generally (McIntyre 1997), as well as specific questions about its monitoring of the nonprofit sector (Stevenson 1997).

Furthermore, in the past few years, there has been a renewed focus on the role of state regulation and monitoring. In response to anticipation of increased state responsibilities generally, as well as to numerous local attacks on tax privileges, there has been a movement to create state nonprofit associations; these are now reported to exist in about half of the states.

In short, there is still a range of accountability issues that remain troublesome for the American nonprofit sector and for the American public more broadly. As an example, there were dramatic problems of failed accountability faced by the long-established and prestigious central organization of United Ways, the United Way of America (Barringer 1992). In that case, and beyond the personal peccadilloes of the executive, William Aramony, the larger question was never really pursued – what was the board of governors of the organization doing while these abuses were happening? This is not the only example of such difficulties; but here I will only mention these other well publicized situations: the case of the treasurer of the National Episcopal Church, and the New Era Foundation in the mid-1990s (*Chronicle of Philanthropy* 1996) and, in 1999, the serious problems of the United Way of Santa Clara, California.

It may be suggested that these situations are few and far between, and indeed that may be so. Given the general lack of public oversight, we can not be sure.

However, the lack of information indicates that questions about how the sector can (or should) be monitored or who is guarding the guardians (*Quis custodiet ipsos custodes?*) merit far more public discussion than they are currently receiving. What should be the role of the states, and how can the public be assured that the board of governors of any given organization is acting in the public interest? These questions suggest an important research agenda, but they also raise issues which need open debate and discussion well beyond the halls of Academe and the nonprofit practitioner.

Where do we go from here?

The argument in this paper was conceptualized within the framework of a conference concerned with the state of a nonprofit sector facing a critical turning point in its development. If not at an actual crisis point, the sector seems undeniably to be at least at a crossroads. In that context, I have raised a number of troublesome issues affecting the future directions of the nonprofit arena:

1   the question of what the numbers really mean;
2   the collapse of distinctions between the three 'formal' sectors of American life;
3   the conceptualization of tax expenditures and the complicated meanings of public and private; and
4   the problem of determining the locus of accountability for nonprofit activity.

Although public airing of problems is in itself problematic, particularly when the essence of the voluntary sector – and the charitable subsector within it – is supposed to lie in its independence, I would argue for the need for greater public debate on these issues. The incidence of recently renewed attempts to limit crucial freedoms for advocacy or lobbying, such as that proposed in the Istook Amendment (1995) reminds us again that the price of a civil society is also vigilance.

There are grounds for questioning both the character and degree of the independence that is claimed to characterize the third sector. Indeed, as we know, the third sector cannot really be free from public opinion, public support (an indeterminate term) or even government regulation. Elsewhere I have argued that to a significant extent institutions of the third sector are not in fact independent of business nor of business interests (Brilliant 1990). At this point perhaps we should question the nature of sector regulation, or how much advocacy for it is needed, or put differently: What level of government or what private means should be involved? In any case, certainly the issues being raised are as much value-based as they are matters of empirical research, and they valorize matters of enormous consequence for the democratic polity in which we live.

In an earlier paper about the Peterson and Filer Commissions, I concluded that the Commissions played an important part in highlighting policy issues and in affecting some legislative outcomes (Brilliant 1996). I also suggested that it may now be time to consider establishing another commission concerned with philanthropic institutions and their relationship with other institutions in our country. Since then, a National Commission on Philanthropy and Civic Renewal has issued a report which criticizes private philanthropy (1997), at the same time placing a particular twist on the relationship between more philanthropy and less government aid. In addition, in 1998 the American Assembly of Columbia University sponsored a conference on the voluntary sector, which concluded, among other matters, that the sector should give more attention to the needs of the poor. However, neither report has received widespread public attention, nor become a focus for public policy. And meanwhile the events of 1996–9 once again confirm explicitly the degree to which the economic health of the independent sector is connected to the economic prosperity of the country; and we are at another crossroads.

It seems, therefore, that it may be time now to 'bite the bullet' and in fact create a national commission to consider the role of the third sector, and indeed to do so in the context of the interaction of the three sectors, business, government and nonprofit, and with consideration of what they mean to community and civil society in America. In doing so, of course, we should be careful not to repeat errors of the White House Conference on Families under the Carter administration (1980), which, in order to avoid offending anyone, became bogged down in decentralized meetings and multiple mini-conferences, with no place for central discussion and policy recommendations. We have only to contrast that effort with the national US Privacy Protection Commission (1977) or reports of various earlier advisory commissions with members appointed by the President. Even allowing for the possible risks in creating a public or quasi-public commission at the federal level, it would seem that a true overview of the problem for public policy in our country can only be articulated effectively at that level. Focusing on state-level activity in the United States appears to put the debate in the position of defensive action rather than focusing on the national character of significant public policy formulation.

If the national administration is not willing to create a public citizen's commission, or if the current climate seems to make such a locus problematic, there are other possible alternatives. For example, we can certainly look at models of private commissions like those of the Carnegie Corporation or the two earlier Rockefeller-initiated commissions. Perhaps we could find a benefactor who believes such exploration is sufficiently valuable to support such an effort. Otherwise, without a broad airing of critical issues, the nonprofit sector may be relegated to fighting rearguard actions in a never-ending battle that only delimits the degree of public interest it embodies, and which could indeed precipitate the crisis we are now discussing so calmly.

Notes

1 The Commission on Foundations and Private Philanthropy is generally dubbed the Peterson Commission after its chairman, Peter G. Peterson (at that time also the CEO of Bell and Howell). The Commission on Private Foundations and Public Needs,

referred to below as the Filer Commission, was chaired by John H. Filer, CEO of Aetna Life and Casualty.

2 The 501 (c) (3) group of organizations is generally referred to by the term 'charitable' (in the broadest sense); as used in the IRS Code the category includes religious, scientific, educational, literary and some other public-regarding activities, in addition to those explicitly labelled as 'charitable'. The category includes service providing agencies, as well as private foundations and other funding organizations.

3 The last time personal giving reached this percentage was in 1973 (AAFRC 1999: 10). It should also be noted that given the mandated 5 per cent payout requirement for foundations, contributions and grants to nonprofit organizations would rise with a rising stock market.

4 The number of registered 501 (c) (4) organizations was at a high of 142,573 in 1992; thereafter the number declined steadily to the low of 139,451 (1995) before the slight increase of 1996.

5 Two congressional committees of the early 1950s (the Cox Committee and subsequently the Reece Committee) attempted to show communist domination of the foundation world, in line with the general ideological attacks of the McCarthy era. The first exonerated the foundations; the second ended in dissension. But many years before (1913–15), in the middle of the Progressive era, a commission headed by Frank Walsh investigated the relationship between foundations and industrial power, with particular reference to the Rockefeller Foundation. The position that only a few foundations violated then existing provisions of the Internal Revenue Code of 1954 was incorporated in the foundations' coordinated testimony before the Senate Finance Committee in October 1969 (Testimony on Title I 1969).

References

AAFRC Trust for Philanthropy, A. E. Kaplan (ed.) (1997) *Giving USA: The Annual Report on Philanthropy for the Year 1996*, New York: AAFRC Trust for Philanthropy.

——(1999) *Giving USA: The Annual Report on Philanthropy for the Year 1998, Executive Summary*, New York: AAFRC Trust for Philanthropy.

Anheier, H. K. (1992) 'An elaborate network: profiling the third sector in Germany', in B. Gidron, R. M. Kramer and L. M. Salamon (eds) *Government and the Third Sector: Emerging Relationships in Welfare State*, San Francisco: Jossey-Bass.

Association for Research on Nonprofit Organizations and Voluntary Action (Arnova) Twenty-sixth Annual Conference 1997, 7–9 November, New York, plenary session and panel discussion.

Avery, R. B. and Rendall, M. S. (1993) 'Estimating the size and distribution of baby boomers' prospective inheritance', paper delivered at a meeting of the American Statistical Association.

Barringer, F. (1992) 'United Way finds pattern of abuse by former chief', *New York Times*, 4 April.

Brilliant, E. L. (1973) 'Private or public: a model of ambiguities', *Social Service Review*, 47, 3: 384–96.

——(1990) *The United Way: Dilemmas of Organized Charity*, New York: Columbia University Press.

——(1996) 'Looking backward to look forward: the Filer Commission in perspective', in *Toward A Stronger Voluntary Sector: The 'Filer Commission' and the State of Philanthropy* (proceedings of the National Board of Visitors of the Indiana University Center on Philanthropy, New York City, 8 December 1995), Indianapolis: Indiana University Center on Philanthropy.

——(2000) *Private Charity and Public Inquiry: A History of the Filer and Peterson Commissions*, Bloomington and Indianapolis: Indiana University Press.

Chronicle of Philanthropy (1996) 'Federal Grand Jury indicts founder of new era philanthropy fund', *The Chronicle of Philanthropy*, 17 October: 33–44.

Clotfelter, C. A. (ed.) (1992) *Who Benefits From the Nonprofit Sector?*, Chicago: University of Chicago Press.

Domhoff, G. W. (1979) *The Powers That Be: Processes of Ruling Class Domination in America*, New York: Vintage Books.

Filer Commission (Commission on Private Philanthropy and Public Needs) (1977) *Research Papers Sponsored by the Commission on Private Philanthropy and Public Needs*, Washington DC: US Treasury Department.

Friedman, Richard E. (1973) 'Private foundations/government relationships', in American Assembly of Columbia University (ed. Fritz F. Heimann) *The Future of Foundations*, Englewood Cliffs: Prentice-Hall.

General Explanation of the Tax Reform Act of 1969 (1970) Pub. 1. no. 91–172, Washington DC: Government Printing Office.

Ginsberg, E., Hiestand, D. L. and Rubens, B. G. (1965) *The Pluralist Economy*, New York: McGraw-Hill.

Hansmann, H. B. (1987) 'Economic theories of nonprofit organizations', in W. W. Powell (ed.) *The Nonprofit Sector: A Research Handbook*, New Haven: Yale University Press, 27–42.

Hodgkinson, V. A., Weitzman, M. S., Abrahams, J., Crutchfield, E. and Stevenson, D. R. (1996) *Nonprofit Almanac 1996–1997: Dimensions of the Independent Sector*, San Francisco: Jossey-Bass.

Hopkins, B. R. (1992) *The Law of Tax-Exempt Organizations*, 6th edn, New York: Wiley.

IRS (Internal Revenue Service of the United States) (1997) *1997 Data Book*, Washington DC: US Treasury Department.

Kahn, A. J. (1977) 'A framework for public-voluntary collaboration in the social services', *The Social Welfare Forum 1976*, New York: Columbia University Press.

Levitt, T. (1973) *The Third Sector*, New York: Amacom.

Lundberg, F. (1968) *The Rich and the Super-rich: A Study of the Power of Money Today*, New York: Lyle Stuart.

McIntyre, R. S. (1997) 'A big tax blunder', *New York Times*, 12 September.

National Commission on Philanthropy and Civic Renewal (1997) *Giving Better/Giving Smarter: Renewing Philanthropy in America*, Report of the NCPCR, Washington DC: National Commission on Philanthropy and Civic Renewal.

NCCS (National Center for Charitable Statistics) (1999) 'The Urban Institute, table of changes in total finances 1992–7 (public operating charities), May 1999' (data supplied to author by the Center).

Nielsen, W. H. (1972) *The Big Foundations*, New York: Columbia University Press.

Peterson Commission (Commission on Foundations and Private Philanthropy, Foundations, Private Giving and Public Policy) (1969–70) *Foundations' Private Giving, and Public Policy Report and Recommendations of the Commission on Foundations and Private Philanthropy*, Chicago: University of Chicago Press.

Phelps, E. S. (ed.) (1965) *Private Wants and Public Needs: Issues Surrounding the Size and Scope of Government Expenditures*, revised edn, New York: W. W. Norton.

Pifer, A. (1970) 'The jeopardy of private institutions', in *Annual Report Essays 1966–1982*, New York: Carnegie Corporation of New York.

Piven, F. F. and Cloward, R. C. (1977) *Poor People's Movements: Why they Succeed, How they Fail*, New York: Pantheon Press.

Putnam, R. D. (1993) *Making Democracy Work: Civic Traditions in Modern Italy*, Princeton: Princeton University Press.

Reagan, M. D. (1963) *The Managed Economy*, New York: Oxford University Press.

Salamon, L. M. (1993) 'The marketization of welfare: changing nonprofit and for-profit roles in the American welfare state', *Social Service Review*, 67, 1: 16–39.

——(1995) *Partners in Public Service: Nonprofit Relations in the Modern Welfare State*, Baltimore: Johns Hopkins University Press.

——(1997) *Holding the Center: America's Nonprofit Sector at a Crossroads*, New York: Nathan Cummings Foundation.

——(1999) *America's Nonprofit Sector: A Primer*, 2nd edn, New York: Foundation Center.

Schultz, C. L. (1977) *The Public Use of Private Interest*, Washington DC: Brookings Institution.

Siegel, D. and Yancey, J. (1992) *The Rebirth of Civil Society: the Development of the Nonprofit Sector in East Central Europe and the Role of Western Assistance*, New York: Rockefeller Brothers Fund.

Smith, B. L. R. and Hague, D. C. (eds) (1971) *The Dilemma of Accountability in Modern Government: Independence versus Control*, New York: St Martin's Press.

Smith, D. H. (1997) 'The rest of the nonprofit sector: grassroots associations as the dark matter ignored in prevailing "flat earth" maps of the sector', *Nonprofit and Voluntary Sector Quarterly*, 26: 114–31.

Staples, L. (ed.) (1984) *Roots in Power: A Manual for Grassroots Organizing*, New York: Praeger.

Stevenson, R. W. (1997) 'Congress sets investigation of tax audits for groups', *New York Times*, 25 March.

Subcommittee no. 1, Select Committee on Small Business, US House of Representatives (1962) *Tax-Exempt Foundations and Charitable Trusts: Their Impact on the Economy*, report of the Subcommittee, first instalment 31 October, Washington DC: Government Printing Office.

Surrey, S. S. (1970) *Tax incentives: Conceptual Criteria for Identification with Direct Government Expenditures* (symposium conducted by the Tax Institute of America, November 1969) Lexington: D. C. Heath.

Surrey, S. S. and McDaniels, P. R. (1985) *Tax Expenditures*, Cambridge MA: Harvard University Press.

Testimony on Title I of the Tax Reform Act of 1969 (1969) *Foundations and the Tax Bill*, New York: Foundation Center.

US Treasury Department (1965) *Report on Private Foundations, Senate Committee on Finance*, Washington DC: Government Printing Office.

Wedel, K. R., Katz, A. J. and Weick, A. (1979) *Social Service By Government Contract*, New York: Praeger.

Weisbrod, B. A. (1988) *The Nonprofit Economy*, Cambridge MA: Harvard University Press.

Wolch, J. R. (1990) *The Shadow State: Government and Voluntary Sector in Transition*, New York: Foundation Center.

13 NGOs and their vulnerabilities during the time of transition

The case of Poland

Joanna Regulska

Introduction

To claim that nongovernmental organizations (NGOs) in Poland, as well as in Central and Eastern Europe more generally, are a new post-1989 phenomenon, would be to deny the long history of formal and informal social and political engagements that citizens of these countries have exhibited over the centuries (Les 1994: 7). At the same time, the events of 1989 and 'the possible impact of this political reconfiguration on the position and prospects of its voluntary sector' (Les 1994: 5) have changed drastically the meaning, purpose and conditions under which NGOs operate. Not only has the new political and economic framework determined the sector's scope of activities, but it has also set the conditions for NGOs' development, as it shaped their internal and external challenges. At the same time, the legacy of the past continues to surface in multidimensional ways and to affect how and where NGOs develop, grow and mature. These tensions and relationships between past patterns of socio-economic development and past political ideology, and the new ones resulting from the transition produce and reproduce uneven conditions for the development of NGOs.

This paper will attempt to show how past conditions set by the authoritarian regimes and new circumstances introduced by the transition have intersected to produce a specific environment within which Polish NGOs have developed over the last decade. The analysis will look at four connected, but analytically distinct, scales: the level of NGOs' own 'internal' resource base and dynamics; and 'external' influences or forces at three levels: local, national and international.

The internal dynamic of NGOs

A basic lack of organizational and professional skills hinders many groups. This occurs to a far greater extent in smaller towns and in areas located in remote parts of the country (so-called 'Poland B') than in those located in urban areas or in close proximity to them (Grochowska and Graham 1996; Bienkowska and Pacholarz 1996). These legacies of the past, represent but one of the forces that set the present conditions for NGO development. While uneven development has not been an exclusively socialist phenomenon, what makes it different from capitalist formations is the fact that it often remained hidden and unrecognized, as it was produced in the name of eradication of difference, and ideologically fostered desire for social and spatial equality. Under new social and economic conditions, paradoxically, the old patterns of intermittent landscape are being forcefully reproduced.

Surveys of NGOs have repeatedly indicated that groups located in urban-industrialized areas have more opportunities to access information, funding or professional expertise, while those located in small towns or rural communities are isolated from such support (Klos 1994; Grochowska and Graham 1996; Wygnanski 1997). Lack of these resources forces many small NGOs to pay disproportionately high costs (psychological and financial) during their incuba-tion periods. This was the case of several of those NGOs working to assist unemployed people in the early 1990s (Klos 1994: 12), and continues to be the case now, with newly emerging groups in many small towns (Zakrzewska *et al.* 1998). Klos, in her assessment in 1994, argued that not only the lack of public-sector-readiness to work with NGOs, but also the actual weaknesses of NGOs themselves should be faulted for these failures (Klos 1994: 12). From research conducted in selected Polish small towns during 1993–4 and 1996–7, the internal weaknesses of NGOs (lack of ability to organize, to write proposals, to obtain funding, to set clear priorities, etc.) and their inability to collaborate with other local actors seems to represent the greatest obstacle to their survival (Grochowska and Graham 1996; Zakrzewska *et al.* 1998). This is not to say that NGOs in the larger cities are not faced with similar or even greater problems. Yet the large proportion of all NGOs that function in urban settings (Wygnanski 1997: 91–2) is suggestive of the advantages that such locations provide.

Another way in which struggles between past patterns and the new oppor-tunities are manifested at this level is through experience with volunteer mobilization. In a climate of fiscal austerity, many groups need to develop a large and steady base of volunteers to sustain their activities (Wygnanski 1997: 94). Unfortunately, there is little systematic data available on the nature of volun-teerism in Poland. However, from the evidence that is available, it is clear that citizens are more willing to give money and goods than time (CBOS 1997a: 7). Analysis of the CBOS survey also showed that the better the financial situation of the respondents, the greater their willingness to give money – but the lower the level of commitment to volunteer on behalf of others. Even among those with potentially more time to give – retired people, and people with disabilities – the survey showed that more than half were more willing to give money than time.

These low levels of volunteerism seem likely to reflect attitudes and beliefs inherited from the old regime. Under the latter, forty-five years of imposed top-down 'volunteerism' had been systematically controlled by ideology, and encourages scepticism about this new form of 'participatory democracy'. This negative influence of the past on current dispositions towards volunteering sur-faces most clearly when the institutions seeking to involve volunteers are in some way connected with the old regime. In particular, in Fuszara and Kurczewski's

(1995) data on foundations, a disproportionately high proportion of 'old' foundations – those created before 1989 – were experiencing difficulties with volunteer recruitment. This could be indicative of the desire of citizens to sever the links with the past by avoiding organizations associated with the old regime.

However, the legacy of the past provides only a partial explanation of these patterns. Currently, NGOs often simply do not have the skills to recruit and motivate interested individuals to work for them. In addition, leaders often do not know how to separate and delegate tasks for both staff and volunteers, yet good management is required to create initiatives, assign small tasks, and motivate. These skills, which become necessary as more NGOs seek a greater degree of professionalism, are still in great demand (Roczniak 1997).

A further way in which tensions between past and present exert an influence over NGOs' internal struggles is through the issue of financing. With some notable exceptions (e.g. the Batory Foundation, the Water Supply Foundation, and the Foundation in Support of Local Democracy), NGOs in Poland have extremely small funding bases. While theoretically NGOs have a variety of ways to gain funds – from the state, the business community, through private giving, or from foreign sources – in practice, some of these sources appear unready to provide funding, while others are highly selective. For example, as far as private giving is concerned, a recent survey found that over two thirds of funds raised were channelled to just two recipients – the Church, and a high-profile nation-wide initiative, 'Big Orchestra for Holiday Support' (CBOS 1997b). The failure of most NGOs to access significant amounts of private giving reflects in part a lack of basic fundraising skills in such areas as writing funding proposals; constructing a realistic, working budget; and maintaining long-term relationships with funders and potential funders.

Financing of NGOs is further complicated by the legal framework so far set in place by the Polish state, since new legislation concerning the sector can appear ambivalent. For example, a new law permitting the establishment of endowments appears to offer opportunities for the sector, including organizations operating at local level. But the associated regulations fail to offer clear fiscal incentives for individuals or businesses to give, and the subsequent patterns of philanthropy have been disappointing.

In sum, it is vital to underline the importance of historically and politically shaped localized conditions. These are only partially the result of current changes, as they also strongly reflect previous socialist patterns of development, socialist practices and resentment towards the past regime. These difficulties can often reinforce each other, as they result in the self-selection of those who have greater skills and organizational management, and greater access to information and resources.

Local level politics

As a newly established political actor on the local scene, NGOs have found themselves needing to affirm their identity and presence, establishing a variety of external relations with other local partners (local governments, other NGOs, citizens or the business community) and building alliances to assist them in achieving their goals. A survey of NGOs conducted in 1994 points to an interesting combination of new alliances, desires for new partners and tensions that are inherent in the construction of local political and social space (Wygnanski 1995: 120). Despite a number of difficulties discussed below, local government is emerging as the sector's primary collaborator and helper (in 35 per cent of cases). Links are also being cultivated with the business community and central and regional government. Political parties and the Church score relatively low, both in terms of number of contacts, and of their perceived desirability as partners. This is suggestive of a clear stand to maintain autonomy and distance from those institutions which may be motivated to exert overt ideological influence on NGO activities.

Many of these partners, like NGOs themselves, are attempting to claim power and to position themselves to gain greater access to resources, widen local constituencies, and establish connections with political elites. The growing complexity of post-1989 local space is confirmed by the often visible, and still confrontational rather then collaborative, dynamic of these relationships. The points of conflict between NGOs and other local actors are diverse, as they connote different struggles and signify each partner's different location within the local political and economic hierarchy. Some of them remain generally invisible, only emerging when actual confrontation over material goods or financial resources takes place (as with struggles over property, land and state subsidies). Others materialize as competition or rivalry. As Wejcman argued 'Competition exists at all levels of functioning within the independent organization sector: competition among groups of participants within the organizations, competition among organizations within the non-governmental sector, and competition between organizations and the public administration' (1997: 50). Yet he believes that competition is especially 'intense at the point of contact between the third sector and the apparatus of power' (the state) as 'nongovernmental organizations constitute an alternative to the state social assistance system' (1997: 51).

NGOs and local governments indeed represent new sets of local institutions that did not exist in their current form before 1989. They struggle with, and yet collaborate with each other more than with any other public or private institution. Their emergence manifests regime change: the devolution of power, democratization of practices and greater institutional responsiveness to local needs. Still, the past images of each other retain their hold, as they often do not perceive themselves as partners, but rather as adversaries representing two different constituencies: authorities and citizens, who locally confront each other in their struggle for resources and power. As Wejcman (1997: 52) surmises, the perception is of 'different approaches to problem solving and [experience] of uncomplimentary treatment by legislators' (see also Sekutowicz 1997). Moreover, adding further complexity to these conflicts is the fact that 'The new elite of local authority continues certain behaviours of the previous bureaucracy and does not pay enough attention to the need for delegating power' (Toczycki 1997:

40). As a result, local government officials often do not understand the role played by NGOs, and NGOs often perceive local government actions negatively, feeling that they are being used instrumentally.

More recently, however, both sides have begun to recognize that their relationship needs to move 'from protest to proposal', involving 'principles for the performance of public tasks by NGOs and on the other hand, minimum material guarantees (finances, premises) for these organizations' (Toczycki 1997: 42). The move towards a more constructive relationship is time-consuming, however: the eight years of joint working between NGOs and local government officials in the city of Lodz provides an example. It involved a transition from an initially purely demanding stance, through to a more conciliatory one, and finally achieved a mutual understanding and desire to collaborate – an example of the form of constructive relationship which can be achieved (Lechowicz 1997).

In sum, the local space represents a laboratory – a testing and learning ground, where post-1989 Polish democratization and decentralization intersect, struggle, and collaborate. How successful NGOs will be in establishing local networks and in generating local support, will not only be indicative of their individual strengths and the degree to which they participate in the democratic transition, but will in fact reflect the extent to which the consolidation of democracy has taken place. As Linz and Stepan have argued, in their recent analysis of the consolidation of post-authoritarian democracies, the existence of conditions for the development of civil society represents the first five conditions that are necessary for consolidation to be achieved (Linz and Stepan 1996: 7). Thus the existence of formal and informal groups, associations and movements, and their ability to mobilize and advance their interests, is a necessary pre-requisite (although not the only one) for Poland to complete the consolidation process, the first signs of which will be visible at the local level.

NGOs and the state

The democratization and decentralization of political power in Poland, as much as in the countries of Central and Eastern Europe (CEE) more broadly, has undoubtedly resulted in less control being exercised from the centre. At the same time its policy making arena has not always kept pace with political restructuring and policy making as experienced by NGOs, and has often been characterized by ambiguity, lacking a clear focus and agenda. Yet as Valenzuela argues, 'without the ... formal democratic procedures at the nation-state level a democracy cannot be said to exist' (1992: 61). The state can exercise a large degree of power in securing NGO autonomy (for example, providing for clear registration procedures that could protect NGOs from partisan politics), developing democratic mechanisms for the distribution of fiscal resources (that would benefit diversified groups of NGOs rather than selective few), or encouraging NGOs' role in the formulation of public policy (Jordan 1997: 83–4). One may, however, raise the question as to the extent to which the state should be relevant to the development of NGOs. While the important role of the state in the sector's development has been demonstrated by numerous studies (see Kuhnle and Selle 1992; and Les 1994 for European countries), the nature of the state itself, the degree to which the state intervenes, and the mode of that intervention, requires careful deconstruction. In these respects specific conditions mediate the development of the NGO sector in Poland, which seem to set it apart from its counterparts in consolidated democracies.

Of relevance in this context is the design of the rules seeking to regulate state/NGO links, and the implications they carry for the distribution of power and financial resources to NGOs. Kuhnle and Selle have argued that in Western Europe, where the demand and need for NGO services grew out of the critical views of the welfare state, 'from the very beginning, organizations have cooperated closely with public authorities. Cooperation rather then conflict has been the rule' (1992: 32). As a result relations with the state have been relatively stable, often 'cozy', and less volatile in terms of being subject to changing political winds. This is not the case, however, in countries where democratic transition has been abrupt, often violent, and with a clear goal of overthrowing the ruling regime – not just in CEE countries, but also in Southern Europe, Latin America, and many Asian or African countries. In these countries, rules are only now being developed, and questions pertaining to the new roles of the public and private sectors in meeting social needs, and to the type of policies that need to be enacted in order to allow desired roles to be fulfilled, remain to be answered.

The state's policy towards the NGO sector in Poland is confused. In the context of a high rate of government turnover – nine governments have presided over the last nine years – the attitudes of elected and appointed officials towards NGOs have also oscillated. Several Polish prime ministers and their governments, for example, felt obliged to take a public stand regarding NGOs; and with each sending different signals, a clear policy is yet to be established. Various fiscal and financial provisions have been introduced, only to be either withdrawn shortly afterwards, remain unimplemented, and/or to be hampered in implementation by excessively bureaucratic procedures (BSiAKS 1995a; 1995b; Roczniak 1997).

Instability and inconsistency have also been a consequence of partisan politics. This was the case with the Office for Cooperation with Non-Governmental Organizations. Established in mid-1993 in the Ministry of Labour and Social Policy during Prime Minister Suchocka's term, it was closed down when Prime Minister Pawlak's government put post-communist SLD leader Leszek Miller in charge of that ministry in 1994. As Boczon rightly pointed out 'The establishment of such an agency at a high level was quite important for the sector because it increased the sector's status, at the same time giving a positive signal to foreign observers' (1997: 33). Its closure therefore sent precisely the opposite message! Parallel struggles have also unfolded within Parliament itself. On one hand, the development of some of the legislative initiatives (taxation of subsidies, a new law on foundations, a proposal for new certification arrangements for NGOs) appears to have been stymied by a lack of political will on the part of the *Sejm* (BSiAKS 1995b; Jordan 1997). On the other hand, the Senate's conference on 'Building

Civil Society – The Role of the Non-governmental Organizations' attempted to counter these efforts and provide the forum for more comprehensive discussion on the role of NGOs and the challenges that they face (BSiAKS 1995a).

To summarize: unclear tax laws, ambiguous legal regulations regarding financial and charitable activity, and cumbersome financial reporting regulations (this latter necessary to maintain transparency and accountability) have often limited NGOs' ability to grow and function effectively (Fuszara and Kurczewski 1995; Roczniak 1997). While the need for audits and reviews is unquestionable, a general lack of transparency, and the sporadic use of regulatory tools in a way that seems to be politically motivated – even when legally justified – has created an atmosphere of censorship, partisan struggle and confrontation (BSiAKS 1995a; 1995b).

NGOs and the global community

From the perspective of CEE, one effect of globalization has been the opening of unprecedented access for NGOs to the international community. This development has been of great significance in providing NGOs with opportunities to act as advocates at the international level, while at the same time conducting most of their operational activities locally. However, acting on the international stage has proved problematic.

Participation and representation provides an example of the nature of the challenge for Polish NGOs and NGOs from other parts of CEE. While often welcomed in principle on the world stage, they have faced major difficulties in securing inclusion in the concrete existing regional structures of international organizations. Thus, at the 1995 NGO Forum and the Fourth World Conference on Women in Beijing, women's NGOs from CEE found themselves representing a 'non region' as far as the United Nations was concerned. They had neither a place to meet during the regional NGOs' caucuses in Hairou, nor were they given a place during the official regional presentation programme in Beijing. (In fact, during the conference, a statement was made by representatives of NGOs from CEE but only because another group gave up the time officially assigned to them by the UN.) The issue of inclusion and exclusion of CEE NGOs will soon be revisited as the European Community attempts to 'integrate' and 'enlarge' its membership. Here the rhetoric of enlargement is likely to be translated into the practice of exclusion as many CEE countries and their NGOs will find themselves outside of the 'New' Europe.

The issue of financing is equally significant (see also Kuti, Chapter 14 in this volume). Private foundations, international organizations and even many foreign governments have vigorously supported Polish NGOs over the last decade. This has made possible a wide range of projects and programmes which otherwise could not have existed, and for this reason foreign funding has often been desired not only by recipient NGOs, but by the state, which welcomes the additional resources to address or manage national and local problems. However, the initial influx of foreign funding has created major problems of its own, and in the long run may have contributed towards the vulnerability of the newly emerging sector. Difficult issues include over-dependency on foreign funding; its short-term duration; insufficiency of infrastuctural funding; inadequate tailoring to local conditions and inappropriate reliance on foreign staff; and a failure of funding programmes to stretch beyond larger urban areas (Cochran 1993; Les 1994; Regulska 1998; Osborne and Kaposvari 1998: 20).

Despite these difficulties and tensions, the position of Polish NGOs *vis-à-vis* the international community is undoubtedly stronger than *vis-à-vis* national government. The initial, international, steady flow of ideas, contacts and exchanges of people and information has permitted many NGOs to legitimize their own existence and often to gain a stronger position within their own local environment. These connections, in turn, often provided NGOs with very much needed acceptance and approval that they could not have received from state-level institutions. Under these circumstances, in the countries of transition, the local/global connections appear to be of greater significance than would be the case in Western democracies.

Conclusions

The development and growth of NGOs is seen as vital for the democratization process and the development of an active citizenry. The review, presented in this paper, of the pressures and support experienced by Polish NGOs and originating at multiple levels, reveals a great diversity of challenges. NGOs do struggle with their internal shortcomings, and yet they are increasingly supported by local government and the business community (even though both of these constituencies have a long list of criticisms and complaints regarding NGOs). Citizens, while they believe in the power of groups that can act on their behalf (as indicated through the large number of new citizens' initiatives), are not too eager to support these groups through their volunteer work, although they are willing to provide financial contributions.

At the level of the state, its stance has been characterized by ambivalence. Finally, at international level, the picture is also unclear but more approving, with two parallel tendencies unfolding. On the one hand, globally united voices have become increasingly powerful (largely due to the financing of their activities by the international donors' community); while on the other, these fiscally dominated relations have constructed a dependency that may, over time, weaken the sector's stability.

Of overarching importance in the Polish case, it has been argued, is the way in which the political past, and the current and future regimes, will mediate these forces by enhancing or inhibiting the growth and position of NGOs. In his review of the challenges facing the US nonprofit sector, Salamon (Chapter 2 in this volume) focuses our attention on the fiscal, economic, effectiveness and legitimacy crises. While on the surface these appear to have some resonance with the conditions described here, there are fundamental differences between them: the most obviously contrasting being the historical legacy, which we have tried to show continues to influence current developments; the chronic instability of the state's ideology and orientation towards the sector in the Polish case; and the distinctive way in which local, national and international conditions and influences are constituted in Poland.

References

Bienkowska, D. and Pacholarz, P. (1996) 'Regionalne zroznicowanie aktywnosci obywatelskiej, partycypacja obywatelska w życiu społeczności lokalnej: stan, bariery, rekomendacje', *Studia i, Analizy I*, Kraków: Fundacja Miedzynarodowe Centrum Rozwoju Demokracji, 57–80.

BSiAKS (Biuro Studiów i Analiz Kancelarii Senatu) (1995a) *Budowa Społeczeństwa Obywatelskiego: Rola Organizacji Pozarządowych w Polsce*, seminar, 12 June 1995, Kancelaria Senatu, S-14 RP, Warsaw, 85.

——(1995b) *Doniesienia Prasowe O Dzialalnosci Fundacji W Polsce*, WA-122, Warsaw.

Boczon, J. (1997) 'The role and place of intermediary structures in third sector development', *The Known-Unknown Sector, Roczniak*, 1: 31–6.

CBOS (Centre for Research on Public Opinion Surveys) (1997a) *Ocena Działalności Instytucji Publicznych*, BS/113/113/97, Warsaw.

——(1997b) *Aktywność Charytatywna Polaków*, Warsaw: BS/31/31/97.

Cochran, T. (1993) 'Envisioning nonprofit missions in dynamic contexts: democracy, devolution, markets and the growth of civil society', closing address to the workshop on Management of Non-Profit Organizations at the European Institute of Business Administration, November, Fontainebleau.

Fuszara, M. and Kurczewski, J. (1995) 'Fundacje O Sobie: Wyniki Badań Ankietowych', *Biuro Studiow i Analiz Kancelarii Senatu*, OT-155, Warsaw.

Grochowska, E. and Graham, A. (eds) (1996) *Jak Wziac Sie Do Dziela? (How To Begin?)* a resource guide for citizens' action, Warsaw: Foundation for Local Democracy.

Jordan, P. (1997) 'Non-governmental organizations and the public administration: cooperation or separation?', *The Known-Unknown Sector, Roczniak*, 1: 79–84.

Klos, B. (1994) 'Status, rola i miejsce organizacji pozarządowych realizujących zadania z zakresu polityki społecznej państwa', *Informacja*, 232, I-232, Kancelaria Sejmu, Warsaw: Biuro Studiów I Ekspertyz.

Kuhnle, S. and Selle, P. (1992) 'Government and voluntary organizations: a relational perspective', in S. Kuhnle and P. Selle (eds) *Government and Voluntary Organizations: A Relational Perspective*, Vermont: Ashgate.

Lechowicz, K. (1997) 'Samorząd: a organizacje pozarządowe', *Asocjacje*, 8, 71: 1–2.

Les, E. (1994) *The Voluntary Sector in Post-communist East Central Europe: From Small Circles of Freedom to Civil Society*, Washington DC: CIVICUS.

Linz, J. J. and Stepan, A. (1996) *Problems of Democratic Transition and Consolidation: Southern Europe, South America, and Post-communist Europe*, Baltimore: Johns Hopkins University Press.

Osborne, S. P. and Kaposvari, A. (1998) 'Nongovernmental organizations, local government and the development of social services: managing social needs in post-communist Hungary', Discussion Paper 4, Local Government and Public Service Reform Initiative, Budapest.

Regulska, J. (1998) 'Building local democracy: the role of western assistance in Poland', *Voluntas*, 9, 1: 39–57.

Roczniak (1997) *The Known-Unknown Sector*, vol. 1, Warsaw.

Sekutowicz, K. (1997) 'Cooperation: an opportunity, or a necessity for non-governmental organizations?', *The Known-Unknown Sector, Roczniak*, 1: 58–69.

Toczycki, W. (1997) 'Disrespect or immaturity: about the attitude of communes towards NGOs', *The Known-Unknown Sector, Roczniak*, 1: 37–47.

Valenzuela, J. S. (1992) 'How long? Consolidation and its problems', in S. Mainwaring, G. O'Donnell and J. S. Valenzuela (eds) *Issues in Democratic Consolidation: The New South American Democracies in Comparative Perspective*, Notre Dame: University of Notre Dame Press.

Wejcman, Z. (1997) 'Competition in the activities of non-governmental organizations', *The Known-Unknown Sector, Roczniak*, 1: 48–57.

Wygnanski, J. J. (1995) 'Raport o organizacjach Public Policy Oriented (PPO)', *Sektor Znany-Nieznzny, Roczniak*, 0: 97–127.

——(1997) 'Basic statistics concerning the scope of activities of non-governmental organisations in Poland', *The Known-Unknown Sector, Roczniak*, 1: 86–100.

Zakrzewska, A., Regulska, J. and Graham, A. (1998) *Jak Byc Aktywną w życiu Publicznym (Being Active)* Warsaw: Wydawnictwo OSKA.

14 Different Eastern European countries at different crossroads

Éva Kuti

Introduction

Lester Salamon's paper (Chapter 2 in this volume) invites us to raise the question whether challenges and crises facing the nonprofit sector are similar or different on the periphery of Europe. In this context, all countries of Central and Eastern Europe belong to the periphery (Wallerstein 1983). For this reason, a region-wide analysis seems to be appropriate even in the absence of sufficient information and reliable empirical evidence about the Eastern European voluntary sectors.

When Salamon states that the American nonprofit sector faces a 'significant' crisis (Salamon 1997), he speaks of what is often regarded as the strongest nonprofit sector in the world. The four crises he identifies are obviously prevalent in many other countries as well, and they can be particularly dangerous in regions where the newly emerging voluntary sectors are much weaker and must face not just these four, but several other challenges.

In order to develop a sensible strategy to respond to this situation, it is absolutely necessary to be able to answer a number of basic questions. Who are the main actors? In what circumstances are they operating? What are their aims, values, motivations and behavioural patterns? Which rules are they following? And what are the actual results and impacts of their actions? The main objective of this paper is to take an initial step towards a better understanding of the complex set of pressing problems that need to be addressed by the Eastern European nonprofit sectors and their supporters in the near future.

The policy crisis

Since the renaissance of the Eastern European nonprofit sectors is closely connected to the denationalization process, public policy has a significant impact on their development perspectives. Whether they have an explicit policy towards voluntary organizations or not, governments do influence at least the general regulatory framework and economic conditions under which NPOs work. Policy makers pursue lots of different political, social, economic or spiritual, global, national, organizational or individual goals, while their knowledge of the diverse and rapidly changing nonprofit sector is quite poor. There is reason to believe, then, that public policy towards the nonprofit sector is predominantly the outcome of these various intentions and endeavours, rather than a set of deliberate government efforts clearly targeted on a well defined voluntary sector (Anheier and Seibel 1998).

In most Eastern European countries there are several explicit and implicit government policies influencing nonprofit organizations, and they often lack consistency. This is also true of the general attitude of legislative bodies and government authorities. The explicit, publicly expressed policy can be supportive. But at the same time, the practical measures and implicit policies developed at different policy levels may be harmful for the nonprofit community. There can be divisions between the legislative and executive bodies, within the national government and between national, regional and local government.

It happens quite frequently that democratic principles, including the importance of the identity and distinctiveness of civic organizations, have more influence on legislation than on practice of government policy. Consequently, regulation at the constitutional level can be significantly different from actual policy at the operational level. Since the substantive ministries (e.g. of welfare, education and culture, etc.) or local governments are mostly interested in providing welfare services on the ground, the quality and availability of these services may have priority for them over macroeconomic considerations. They are likely to pay little attention to the overall costs, including direct costs and the lost tax revenues of the central budget. For their part, government agencies responsible for the overall performance of the economy (e.g. treasuries and finance ministries) are probably more concerned about the lack of information on the size and efficiency of direct and indirect support going to the nonprofit sector. For lack of comprehensive data, they may perceive that abuse is more frequent in this sector than in other parts of the economy. Their reaction can be a diffuse suspicion, and sometimes even a hostility, which may result in cuts of tax allowances and other economic restrictions.

In short, public policy toward nonprofits is a complicated set of particular and more-or-less contradictory policies developed by different legislative and government bodies. Open and fully consistent hostility between the state and the nonprofit sector is the exception rather than the rule in the Eastern European region. The experience has been mixed, even in Slovakia where the policy environment for the sector was most hostile during the Meciar period. While the government did initiate a really oppressive foundation law, it was opposed not only by the nonprofit umbrella organization and the numerous supporters of the Third Sector SOS Campaign, but 'The President of the Republic returned the legislation to Parliament with a request that it not be adopted' (CIVICUS 1997: 122). In much less dramatic ways, the same divergence could also be detected between presidential and governmental policies towards nonprofits in the Czech Republic until the fall of the Klaus government (Quigley 1997).

The policy crisis which seriously threatens the Eastern European nonprofit sectors is fuelled largely by the lack of a comprehensive knowledge of the sector and of clear political intentions of cooperating with it. This lack of information and clarity is much more dangerous and harmful than the occasional political attacks against it.

The identity crisis

The lack of a consistent policy is obviously related to the fact that 'despite an enormous upsurge of voluntary organizations after the breakthrough of 1989 and their growing capacity as service provider, formally they are still not conceptualized in terms of a separate and independent sector, similar to the public and private sectors' (Les 1997: 146).

Both researchers and nonprofit activists have made several efforts to map different kinds of nonprofit organizations (Bocz *et al.* 1998; Horváth and Deák Sala 1995; Hyatt 1998; Kuti 1996; Les 1994; Siegel and Yancey 1993) and give an overview of the various roles they play in the economy and society (Abzug and Webb 1996; Coury and Lucanin 1996; Gassler 1991; Jenkins 1995; Wunker 1991). In spite of these efforts, we still do not have reliable information either about the size or, especially, the structure of Eastern European nonprofit sectors, let alone how well the general public is informed about them. We know that many different types of nonprofit organization are present in the region, ranging from small, mainly recreation-oriented membership groups to service providers, grantmakers and lobbying organizations. We group them together as a nonprofit (or third, or voluntary, or non-governmental) sector, but one can hardly claim that they would really act or identify themselves as a sector.

An institutional field can gain collective identity if its members tend to move in concert. The lack of such coordinated movements is one of the most difficult problems in the Eastern European nonprofit sectors. The different roles they play create some 'natural' divisions between nonprofit organizations. Advocacy groups frequently resent the pragmatism and opportunism of service providers, while the latter think that their activities are much more important and useful than the ones in which other agencies are engaged. Recreation clubs and membership organizations feel neglected and discriminated against. In addition, there is a deep political conflict between the old-fashioned, formerly government-controlled voluntary associations and the new institutions of civil society. The relatively well trained and well paid leaders of the large grantmaking foundations pay little attention (if any) to the problems of the small groups or the sector as a whole. There is some tension between different political groups, and also between the heads of government-funded and foreign-funded organizations. Very few activists based in small organizations seem to perceive their organizations as belonging to a sector, nor their problems as challenges to be faced in cooperation with their counterparts.

Developing identity and sector-wide cooperation is clearly a responsibility of the nonprofit community itself. Paradoxically enough, governments help this process mainly through political attacks and restrictive economic measures, when they appear as a common enemy (Jenkins 1995: 196), thus pushing NPOs into building coalitions in order to protect themselves. As the above-mentioned Third

Sector SOS Campaign has proved, such an attack can even contribute to foster regional and international cooperation.

Strengthening sectoral identity and developing both national and regional cooperation are crucially important for the future development of the state/nonprofit partnership. This partnership may become critical for the sustainability of several nonprofit sectors in Central and Eastern Europe in the very short run.

The sustainability crisis

Though there is precious little empirical information available, the anecdotal evidence seems to suggest that many nonprofit sectors in the region are highly dependent on foreign funding (Table 14.1). The euphoria following the collapse of the Soviet empire in 1989 created an unprecedented flow of grants. Many foreign donors decided to support the democratic transition, and several Western NGOs opened offices and established local NPOs, support centres and even umbrella organizations in order to accelerate the democratization process in Eastern Europe.

This foreign aid was quite useful in the western part of the region, where the indigenous nonprofit sectors were developed enough to absorb these unexpected funds without seriously disturbing their organic evolution. By contrast, in other countries – for lack of civic organizations rooted in national traditions – the foreign grants could not build on an existing local nonprofit sector. Consequently they created new, more-or-less artificial and outlandish institutions which have remained extremely dependent on foreign funding (Fowler 1995; Lazar 1996; Regulska 1998).

As an American observer has stated, 'one of the overarching criticisms of Western assistance is that it has artificially created or strengthened certain organizations, organizations that do not necessarily respond to the interests or needs of a local constituency' (Cornell Gorka 1996: 28). For organizations which are not rooted in the local culture it is extremely difficult to raise local support and become relatively independent of foreign funding. Their dissolution or slow decline would weaken all nonprofit sectors of the region, especially those of the Balkans and the former Soviet Republics. If the experts quoted in Table 14.1 are not seriously wrong, in some Eastern European countries the majority of the third sector's revenues come from abroad. Thus reductions in foreign grants can potentially destroy or at least paralyse these nonprofit sectors.

The sustainability crisis will probably be much less profound in countries where the share of foreign funding is lower, but it still may have a harmful impact on some fields of the nonprofit sector. The figures for Hungary (Table 14.2), where the nonprofit sector has a relatively low general level of foreign funding, seem to prove that the extent of some nonprofit activities' dependence on foreign support is alarming even there. This would suggest that the sustainability crisis must be really deep in other countries of the region.

Table 14.1 Dependence on foreign funding

Albania	*Rasim Gjoka*: 'Financial and technical assistance from foreign CSOs are the mainstays of most Albanian CSOs' (p. 1).
Bulgaria	*Valentin Mitev*: 'No reliable statistics are available on the resources of Bulgaria's civic sector, but most funding comes from foreign sources' (p. 18).
Georgia	*Ulana Trylowsky abd Jesse Doiron*: 'In Georgia today, CSOs are heavily reliant on outside funding and grants to sustain their activities' (p. 56).
Moldova	*Lydia Spataru and Ilya Trombitsky*: 'Most CSOs in Moldova currently rely on funding from international aid organizations or foundations established by international organizations such as the Soros Foundation of Moldova' (p. 99).
Romania	*Lorita Constantinescu and Stefan Constantinescu*: 'International aid makes up 52 per cent of the total financial resources available to Romania's civic sector' (p. 114).
Poland	*Ewa Les*: 'Sixteen per cent of Poland's CSOs receive financial support from international nongovernmental organizations' (p. 110).

Source: CIVICUS (1997)

Table 14.2 Foreign support of the Hungarian nonprofit sector, 1996

Field of activity	Share of organizations supported by foreign donors	Foreign support as percentage of total income
Culture	4.8	1.5
Religion	12.5	17.0
Education and research	4.7	9.1
Health and social care	6.6	9.0
Sports and recreation	0.7	0.2
Economic and professional advocacy	1.6	1.6
Economic development	14.0	27.1
Philanthropic intermediaries	6.4	22.4
Other	7.0	9.0
TOTAL	3.7	8.0

Source: Bocz *et al.* (1998)

For the least developed Eastern European nonprofit sectors, it is crucial that foreign donors prolong their support and shift them towards 'indigenous' voluntary organizations. It seems clear that the latter are more likely to meet local needs and become financially sustainable, than are the creatures of international bodies and foreign nonprofit organizations (Hyatt 1998). Fortunately, there are some indications (McCarthy 1995; Siegel and Yancey 1993; Vajda 1997) that several Western donors are tending to increasingly turn their attention to indigenous skills and needs, and shifting from technical assistance to work with grassroots organizations.

The fiscal and economic crises

The fiscal and economic crises described by Salamon are also present in Eastern Europe, but against a different background: that of a transition economy.

The politically motivated renaissance of the Eastern European voluntary sectors can hardly be followed and consolidated by steady growth without a significant development of nonprofit service provision. Most nonprofit organizations are aware of this necessity, and make efforts to enlarge their services. These efforts are in line with the governments' intention to 'privatize' a large proportion of public services, in line with transforming a state-socialist welfare system into a mixed economy.

Whoever is the service provider, one of the most important sources of financing public services is the state budget. This state support comes through grants, subsidies, statutory and fee-for-service payments and/or indirect tax advantages. It is crucial for the development of the Eastern European nonprofit sectors if an important role in meeting citizens' needs and shaping a new model of the welfare state in their countries is sought. Unfortunately, the financing obligations are far from clear. The population is much too poor to buy the services at market price, or to finance their nonprofit provision through private giving. Governments are rather ambivalent. They realize that there is some qualitative and quantitative shortage in the market of welfare services, and that nonprofit organizations may contribute to the solution of this problem. But governments also have to face increasing budget deficits and serious economic difficulties. They are therefore reluctant to finance the delivery of new, additional services, and prefer to confine themselves to subsidizing nonprofit services which substitute for some public service provision.

The practice tends to be chaotic and contradictory. The tax system is under 'reconstruction'. Neither government authorities nor taxpayers have satisfactory information about the actual performance of the emerging new taxes, such as value added tax or personal income tax. Tax exemptions and tax deductibility are considered to be possible techniques of government support, and have already been introduced in some countries of the region. However, their mechanisms and effects are not yet sufficiently understood. Consequently, they are the subject of much debate and criticism, and subject to frequent changes. In the short run they are therefore an erratic and unpredictable basis of funding and cannot become a source of support upon which nonprofit organizations can firmly rely.

As far as direct state support is concerned, the situation is not much clearer or better. The arm's length and subsidiarity principles are not rooted in the Eastern European political culture. They are 'imported', they represent an attractive element of a recently developed vocabulary which fits, in best case, the ideology, but not the behavioural patterns of Eastern European governments. Competitive tenders are extremely rare. For lack of impersonal rules, informal social networks play an important role in the distribution of public funds. If nonprofit service providers wish to secure state subvention or government contracts, they must convince public authorities that their services are of high quality, necessary for the public, and innovative, while the large state-run service delivery networks (e.g. the national healthcare system) regard service providing NPOs as competitors and massively lobby against contracting out public services.

The crises of effectiveness and legitimacy

As Kramer (1992: 50) states:

> Using NPOs as service providers offers welfare states ... an acceptable way of dealing with the decline in the legitimacy ascribed to government, and the decreased confidence in its capacity to provide economic, equitable and effective public services. This policy also has considerable ideological appeal because it can be presented as a form of privatization and the promotion of voluntarism, both of which are highly valued in many countries.

If this is true in the developed welfare states, it is even more relevant in the post-socialist countries which have many more serious problems to be solved. Nevertheless, we must raise the question of whether nonprofits engaging in service provision will not face the very same decline in legitimacy and confidence from which the government, as a service provider, has historically suffered.

It is extremely difficult to accept that there are several human and social problems which cannot be solved. Losers are inevitable products of a competition-based market economy; mentally, psychologically, socially handicapped, marginalized persons are inherent parts of any, even the most humane society. Their problems can be alleviated, but not really solved by government or nonprofit agencies. This does not necessarily mean that these latter are inefficient (though they can be and quite frequently are), but makes them particularly vulnerable to criticism.

Given this vulnerability, the Eastern European nonprofit sectors should be more cautious about their rhetoric because it can easily turn against them. Ironically enough, this rhetoric is much more influenced by an Eastern European image of the highly developed countries' NPOs than by local experiences or by the self-image of Western nonprofit sectors.

As Lester Salomon states (in Chapter 2 of this volume):

> significant elements of the American public ... remain wedded to a nine-teenth-century image of charity and altruism, of small voluntary groups ministering to the needy and downtrodden. The nonprofit sector is thus being hoisted on its own mythology. Having failed to make clear to the American public what its role should be in a mature mixed economy, the sector has been thrown on the defensive by the revelations that it is not oper-ating the way its own mythology would suggest.

What happens in Eastern Europe is exactly the opposite. Much less developed nonprofit sectors, mainly consisting of small grant-seeking and membership organizations, claim that they are legitimated by their service provision role and the relatively high efficiency of their services. These poorly documented claims of high effectiveness, together with the somewhat mystifying civil society argu-ment, cause more harm than good because they are not confirmed by everyday experience. When the overwhelming majority of nonprofit organizations are not able to fulfil their mission for lack of sufficient income, well trained staff and satisfactory infrastructure, when some big NPOs are seriously discredited by highly publicized scandals, then solemn testimonies reflecting wishful thinking can only result in a legitimacy crisis.

Concluding comment

The different nonprofit sectors of Central and Eastern Europe have experienced the crisis reviewed above in different situations and to different degrees, and are therefore at different crossroads. Roughly speaking, three different groups can be distinguished among the countries on the periphery of Europe.

First, there is a small group of countries (e.g. Belarus, Serbia) where even the freedom of association and the very existence of an independent nonprofit sector are threatened. Open government attacks and hostile regulatory measures constitute the general environment for the everyday life of civic organizations in these countries.

Second, a much bigger group of the Eastern European nonprofit sectors (consisting of the Balkan and the former Soviet republics) is characterized by a dependence on foreign funding. The very likely decrease of this foreign support (Hyatt 1998; Lazar 1996; Quigley 1997) will result in a sustainability crisis in the near future, thus the development of indigenous, community-based voluntary organizations is a question of vital importance for these nonprofit sectors.

Third, in the most developed part of the region (i.e. the Visegrad countries) the main elements of the present crisis are the fiscal, economic, effectiveness, identity and legitimacy problems, which have something in common with the challenges that threaten the much more mature nonprofit sectors of the devel-oped world.

In short, while all three groups of the Eastern European nonprofit sector have many similar problems, they each have to cope with a different combination of challenges. To bear in mind these differences is important for both local nonprofit leaders and foreign supporters, if they want to find appropriate answers to real needs, and to develop strategies which can contribute to the organic development of local civil society.

References

Abzug, R. and Webb, N. J. (1996) 'Another role for nonprofits: the case of mop-ups and nursemaids resulting from privatization in emerging economies', *Nonprofit and Voluntary Sector Quarterly*, 2: 156–73.

Anheier, H. K. and Seibel, W. (1998) 'The nonprofit sector and the transformation of societies: a comparative analysis of East Germany, Poland and Hungary', in W. W. Powell and E. S. Clemens (eds) *Private Action and the Public Good*, New Haven and London: Yale University Press.

Bocz, J., Emri, I., Kuti, É., Mészáros, G. and Sebestény, I. (1998) *Nonprofit szervezetek Magyarországon 1996* (*Nonprofit Organizations in Hungary 1996*), Budapest: Központi Statisztikai Hivatal.

CIVICUS (1997) *The New Civic Atlas: Profiles of Civil Society in 60 Countries*, Washington DC: CIVICUS.

Cornell Gorka, K. (1996) 'US support for nongovernmental organizations', in M. Lazar (ed.) *Fortifying the Foundations: US Support for Developing and Strengthening Democracy in East Central Europe*, New York: Institute of International Education.

Coury, J. M. and Lucanin, J. D. (1996) 'Mending the social safety net after state socialism: "Dobrobit" – one nongovernmental organization in Zagreb, Croatia', *Nonprofit and Voluntary Sector Quarterly*, 3: 283–301.

Fowler, A. (1995) *Strengthening The Role of Voluntary Development Organizations: Policy Issues Facing Official Aid Agencies*, Washington DC: Overseas Development Council.

Gassler, R. S. (1991) 'Non-profit enterprise and Soviet economic reform', *Voluntas*, 2, 1: 95–109.

Horváth, I. and Deák Sala, Zs. (1995) 'A Romániai magyar egyesületek és alapítványok szociológiai leírása' ('A sociological overview of the Hungarian voluntary associations and foundations in Romania') *Korunk*, 11, 23–57.

Hyatt, J. (1998) *From Transition to Development: The Non-Profit Sectors of Central and Eastern Europe*, London: Charities Evaluation Services.

Jenkins, R. M. (1995) 'Politics and the development of the Hungarian non-profit sector', *Voluntas*, 6, 2: 183–201.

Kramer, R. M. (1992) 'The roles of voluntary social service organizations in four European states: policies and trends in England, the Netherlands, Italy and Norway', in S. Kuhnle and P. Selle (eds) *Government and Voluntary Organizations: A Relational Perspective*, Aldershot, Brookfield MO, Hong Kong, Singapore and Sydney NSW: Avebury.

Kuti, É. (1996) *The Nonprofit Sector in Hungary*, Manchester: Manchester University Press.

Lazar, M. (ed.) (1996) *Fortifying the Foundations: US Support for Developing and Strengthening Democracy in East Central Europe*, New York: Institute Of International Education.

Les, E. (1994) *The Voluntary Sector in Post-communist East Central Europe*, Washington DC: CIVICUS.

——(1997) 'The role of nongovernmental organizations in service delivery for the elderly in Poland', in V. Gáthy and M. Yamaji (eds) *A New Dialogue between Central Europe and*

Japan, Budapest and Kyoto: Institute for Social Conflict Research and the International Research Center for Japanese Studies.

McCarthy, K. D. (1995) 'From government to grass-roots reform: the Ford Foundation's population programmes in South Asia 1959–1981', *Voluntas*, 6, 3: 292–316.

Ners, K. J., Palmer, M. and Fyfe, A. (1998) *Assistance: To Accession and beyond*, Warsaw: Policy Education Centre on Assistance to Transition.

Quigley, K. F. F. (1997) *For Democracy's Sake: Foundations and Democracy Assistance in Central Europe*, Washington DC: Woodrow Wilson Center.

Regulska, J. (1998) 'Building local democracy: the role of western assistance in Poland', *Voluntas*, 9, 1: 39–57.

Salamon, L. M. (1997) *Holding the Center: America's Nonprofit Sector at a Crossroads*, New York: Nathan Cummings Foundation.

Siegel, D. and Yancey, J. (1993) *The Rebirth of Civil Society: The Development of the Nonprofit Sector in East Central Europe and the Role of Western Assistance*, New York: The Rockefeller Brothers Fund.

Vajda, Á. (1997) 'Citizens' initiatives in a middle-size Hungarian town', in V. Gáthy and M. Yamaji (eds) *A New Dialogue Between Central Europe and Japan*, Budapest and Kyoto: Institute for Social Conflict Research and the International Research Center for Japanese Studies.

Wallerstein, Immanuel (1983) *A modern világgazdasági rendszer kialakulása: A tőkés Mezőgazdaság és az eurólpai világgazdaság eredete a XVI században* (*Evolution of the Modern World-System: Capitalist Agriculture and the Origins of the European World-Economy in the Sixteenth Century*), Budapest: Gondolat.

Wunker, S. M. (1991) 'The promise of non-profits in Poland and Hungary: an analysis of third sector renaissance', *Voluntas*, 2, 2: 89–107.

15 Civil organizations in Mexico

Recent evolutions and current prospects

José Luis Méndez

This chapter begins by identifying how, as a result of the confluence of a number of factors, civil organizations (COs) in Mexico have shown an exponential development in the last fifteen years. However, it is argued that COs are suffering a fiscal crisis, and, in some sense, an economic one, provoked by the political reaction of the government towards this growth. At the same time, there is no crisis of legitimacy; their increasing levels of social support suggests a trend in the reverse direction. However, the legitimacy attributable by the population to nonprofits seems to be due to the novelty of this socio-political actor in the context of a disappointment with more traditional ones including government and political parties – as opposed to an endorsement of their proven capacity or efficiency in solving the problems of development. To take advantage of what seems to be a golden opportunity for its positive development, in addition to changing the unfavourable economic environment, it is argued that the sector has to face the challenge of thinking in its long-term interest and ensuring as much as possible that it is positioned to act capably and efficiently.

Introduction: the background and development of civil organizations in Mexico

The field of civil organizations (COs)[1] has a long history in Mexico – one which continues to have important implications for the current contours of the sector, and to condition the attitudes of the state towards it. One prominent group of organizations is the 150 or so *institutos de asistencia privada* (IAPs), that is private assistance organizations, distinguished by their origins between the nineteenth century and the 1950s, and their relatively closely controlled, and privileged treatment in law. These human service organizations are closely linked to the hierarchy of the Mexican Catholic Church, and enjoy tax-exempt status on the grounds of their 'public utility'. Their legal status is framed by the private assistance law of each state (*Ley de Asistencia Privada*) as well as the National Constitution (Article 27, which describes their status, rights and duties as 'moral social persons'). The former set up Councils to enforce detailed arrangements for the monitoring of donations and activities.

Two other broad groups have contributed to the recent 'explosion' of NGO activity (CEMEFI 1995). First an internally heterogeneous group comprising organizations marked by their shared origins from the 1950s onwards, but with a particular burst of growth from the 1970s until the present time. Most of these operate in social services fields (Fernandes 1994: 60; CEMEFI 1995), although health, education, environment and human rights are also major activities (Córdova 1996). Included are NGOs and DSOs (cf. note 1 above) which have eschewed registration as IAPs in order to avoid the monitoring and control of the state Councils, and tended to operate as civil associations (ACs), acquiring legal status through state civil codes. This involves a markedly more ambiguous and less supportive legal framework than that which is available to IAPs (see below).

Some of the most important factors shaping these organizations' dramatic growth have been their role as carriers of ideology for new social and popular movements, from the time of the 1968 student uprisings onwards; the withdrawal of the state from the social area, and the weakening of traditional exclusionary corporatist structures from the time of the 1982 economic crisis onwards, which opened up a wider political and social space in which COs were able to operate; the mobilizing effect of natural disasters, most prominently with the 1985 earthquake in Mexico City; and the interest of international funders in supporting these agencies (see Hernandez and Fox 1994; Aguayo and Tarrés n.d.; for parallels in other parts of Latin America see Thompson 1992; Fernandes 1994; VOLUNTAS, 7, 4).

A third category worth distinguishing typically has the most recent origins: political development support organizations (DSOs). After the strongly questioned elections of 1988, when Carlos Salinas became President amidst nationwide accusations of fraud, several COs and later networks of COs were created to promote clean and transparent elections. In 1995 a legal framework for some of these organizations was established. On the other hand, after the rebellion in the southern state of Chiapas in 1994, several peace organizations emerged, and other previously created political COs acquired greater national presence. We could in fact argue that it was in 1994, with this rebellion and a few months later national elections, that COs as a group consolidated their national relevance as a result of the activities of these high-profile political DSOs.

Beginning mainly in the 1990s, many of the second and third type of organization began to organize into formal networks of COs in specific fields (such as environment, and health) as well as spanning fields to form 'networks of networks'. Overall, this high rate of creation of COs and their networks suggests that the sector has been gaining legitimacy among the population in recent years. However, there is no indication that such legitimacy has its origins in a knowledge of the capabilities or efficiency of this sector; more likely it is connected with disappointment and disillusionment with other actors, including the government and political parties.

Recent developments in the legal and fiscal regime and government policy

In the light of this extraordinary burst of CO activity, reform of the legal framework for COs has been an important part of the congressional agenda in Mexico since 1995. The Chamber of Senators was charged with examining the position of IAPs, while other COs' legal treatment has been the responsibility of the Chamber of Deputies. While little progress has been made in the former, the Chamber of Deputies established the Citizens Participation Commission led by a well regarded human rights activist, which, after extensive consultations, presented a draft bill in 1997 – which failed to become law. Modified proposals are, in fact, currently still under discussion (see next section).

A number of factors seem to have stalled the 1997 legislation, illustrating some of the tensions and conflicts within the Mexican political elite in its positioning towards this part of the sector. According to some commentators, the idea of a 'new federalism' may have impeded the Congress from enacting a federal law that would have restricted states' sovereignty.

Others have suggested that the Office of the Presidency blocked the new law, because of the elections which were upcoming at the time. It is certainly the case that hostility exists within some factions of Mexico's elite towards the perceived political orientation of some COs, which may have contributed to this situation. Many COs fighting for the respect of political rights are seen as allies to, or even disguised members of, opposition parties or even the Zapatista movement in the southern state of Chiapas. As many of the most critical COs have had similar causes to the opposition centre-left party (Partido de la Revolución Democrática or PRD), some factions within the long-incumbent Partido Revolucionario Institucional (PRI) of President Zedillo, and even the conservative party (the National Action Party or PAN, somewhat close to the Church), deeply distrust them.

In the absence of new legislation, the status quo involves a number of government agencies with regulatory and fiscal responsibility for the sector. The Secretariat of the Interior is the entity of the Executive in charge of coordinating overall government policy towards COs, and has been to some extent supportive of efforts to bring in new enabling legislation. Also with an important stake in developments – because of the fiscal character of the state's policy towards the sector – has been the Finance Ministry. In fact, as early as 1989, Congress had passed an initiative drafted to the Secretariat of Finance to change the Income Tax Law (*Ley del Impuesto Sobre la Renta*), so that DSOs would be unambigiously treated as for profit organizations, paying income tax and the 2 per cent 'assets tax'. Overturning this decision has been a major goal of the sector's lobbyists ever since, but only partial and piecemeal exemptions have been achieved for certain subcategories of DSO. The role of the Secretariat of Foreign Affairs should also be mentioned, because it has been vocal in calling for much closer monitoring of COs' activities in the light of their receipt of funding from overseas – which has been seen in some quarters as potentially subversive.

Finally, the position of the state towards the third sector in Mexico also reflects the interests of national ministries funding COs, and working with them on the ground. The most important examples include the Secretariat of Social Development (SEDESOL) and the developmental bank (Nacional Financiera), whose relations with the sector have significantly widened and improved since Zedillo's election. Under Salinas' leadership (1988–94), broadly speaking, we can say that central government's social policy tended to displace DSOs, generating an environment of distrust between both sectors (Piester 1997: 485; Coulomb and Herrasti 1998). In more recent times, SEDESOL and the National Indigenous Institute have been trying to promote their participation in social policy (Contreras 1997). For example, the new social policy framework promoted by SEDESOL appears less clientelistic than the previous one, while experiences of succesful collaboration between the development bank and DSOs in nurturing microbusinesses have fostered goodwill (see for example Méndez and Ríos 1997).

The response of the third sector

The limited reforms of the 1989 tax law referred to above had been achieved in part by an organization formed in 1990, Convergencia de Organismos por la Democracia (Convergence of Organizations for Democracy) (Hernández and Fox 1994: 235; Salazar *et al.* 1996). However, from 1995 onwards, in the context of the formation of the Citizen Participation Commission, CO leaders formed an alliance with researchers (including the author) in an attempt to persuade the government to adopt more constructive policies towards the sector. One important strategy was to point out that Mexican COs experienced a relatively punitive fiscal regime compared to that prevalent in other parts of Latin America (see *Voluntas*, 7, 4). Most recently, another innovation has been to couple potentially acceptable solutions to perceived problems, rather than simply rehearsing the latter. In particular, often expressed concerns by state officials about the lack of mechanisms for accountability in the sector and the scope for tax evasion within it, have been recognized in new proposals suggesting COs' rights be closely tied with the clear demonstration of fulfilment of responsibilities, with a hierarchy of such rights and responsibilities depending on organizations' size and stage of development. At the time of writing, it remains to be seen if the new Congress accepts this project.

COs' fiscal and economic crises

COs in Mexico face both problems and opportunities. The lack of systematic and assured tax privileges referred to above effectively amounts now to a crisis in the light of Mexico's not-too-low rate of income tax (World Economic Forum 1997: figs 2.16–2.18), as well as its unfavourable positioning in terms of value added tax and corporation tax.

The unfavourable tax environment has no doubt created a poor climate for giving, reflected in corporations' and individuals' reluctance to make donations.

However, other reasons also seem relevant. First, the relatively low level of inter-personal trust in Mexico and in Latin America in general probably has knock-on effects for COs (Méndez 1997b). Second, the absence of a clear legal framework enforcing honesty and responsibility in CO behaviour may also deter giving. While this may not amount to a legitimacy *crisis*, COs may consequently suffer from legitimacy 'insufficiency' in relation to business and wealthy individuals.

More positively, Mexican COs, like other NGO sectors in the developing world, have the advantage of being placed to tap international funds. COs in Mexico have received funds from a variety of foreign sources, such as the World Bank, the Interamerican Bank and the European Union, whose expenditure on the sector has increased significantly in recent years in such areas as economic development, assistance to refugees, human rights and, increasingly, democratization.

However, in Mexico this beneficial situation has begun to change. This is the case because from the start, the Salinas administration presented Mexico as a country under rapid development – implying that Mexican COs no longer needed support – a trend exaggerated when Mexico became an OECD member in 1994.

Concluding comment

Of the four crises identified by Salamon (Chapter 2 in this volume), Mexican COs could be said to be suffering a fiscal crisis and approaching an economic one, for the reasons described above, which include an unfavourable tax treat-ment situation, a lack of clarity over legal provisions, and problems around securing support both from Mexicans themselves, Mexican companies, and more recently the overseas philanthropic community.

The question of legitimacy, conversely, seems to be more about 'insufficiency' than crisis – at least if we interpret this as a diffuse, social support among society as a whole. This shortfall appears to be predicated more on disappointment with traditional government and politics, as opposed to a positive endorsement of the benefits of the sector. Relatedly, as far as effectiveness is concerned, since very little is known about the sector's actual performance, it seems that for the time being the issue has remained off the agenda.

Note

1 'Civil organizations' is a term used to collectively refer to what in Mexico are known as nongovernmental organizations (NGOs) or development support organizations (DSOs); intermediary organizations; foundations; and assistance organizations. These have in common that they are usually formed by upper- or middle-class people inter-ested in providing services to poor people. The term is slightly narrower in coverage than the structural-operational definition developed by Salamon and Anheier (1997) in excluding political parties, churches, and trade unions and professional associa-tions. See Méndez (1997a) for a discussion of definitions and concepts, and the location of civil organizations in a broader six-level typology.

References

Aguayo, S. and Tarrés, M. L. (undated draft) *Las Enigmáticas ONGs Mexicanas: Una Caracterización*, Mexico City: DF.

CEMEFI (Centro Mexicano para la Filantropía) (1995) *Perfil de las Fundaciones en México*, Mexico City: CEMEFI.

Contreras, A. (1997) 'La política social hoy', in J. Cohen and J. Rogers (eds) *Associations and Democracy*, London: Verso.

Córdova, I. (1996) 'Necesario reglamentar la actividad de las ONGs', *El Nacional*, 22 July; in Paulina González Rubalcaba (1997) 'Análisis socio-jurídico de las organizaciones no gubernamentales en México', unpublished dissertation, Mexico City: UNAM.

Coulomb, R. and Herrasti, M. L. (1998) 'ONGs y políticas habitacionales en México', in J. L. Méndez (ed.) *Organizaciones Civiles y Políticas Públicas en México y Centroamérica*, Mexico City: Miguel Ángel Porrúa.

Fernandes, R. C. (1994) *Privado aunque Público: El Tercer Sector en America Latina*, Washington DC: CIVICUS.

Hernández, L. and Fox, J. (1994) 'La difícil democracia en México: los movimientos de base, las ONG y el gobierno local', in Ch. Reilly (ed.) *Nuevas Políticas Urbanas: Las ONG y los Gobiernos Locales en la Democratización Latinoamericana*, Arlington VA: Fundación Interamericana.

Hulme, D. and Edwards, M. (1997) *NGOs, States and Donors: Too Close for Comfort*, Basingstoke: Macmillan.

Méndez, J. L. (ed.) (1997a) *Organizaciones Civiles y Políticas Públicas en México y Centroamérica*, Mexico City: Miguel Ángel Porrúa.

——(1997b) 'The Latin American administrative tradition', in *International Encyclopedia of Public Policy and Administration*, Boulder CO: Westview.

Méndez, J. L. and Ríos, R. (1997) 'OCs y la política de promoción de microempresas; el caso de ADMIC', in J. L. Méndez (ed.) *Organizaciones Civiles y Políticas Públicas en México y Centroamérica*, Mexico City: Miguel ángel Porrúa.

Piester, K. (1997) 'Targeting the poor: the politics of social policy reforms in Mexico', in D. Chalmers, C. M. Vilas, K. Hite, S. B. Martin, K. Piester and M. Segarra (eds) *The New Politics of Inequality in Latin America*, Oxford: Oxford University Press.

Salamon, L. M. and Anheier, H. K. (1997) *Defining the Non-profit Sector: A Cross-national Analysis*, Manchester: Manchester University Press. A previous shorter version in Spanish of some their ideas can be found in L. M. Salamon and H. K. Anheier (1995) 'En busca del sector no lucrativo: la cuestión de las definiciones', *Umbral XXI*, special issue 1.

Salazar, A., Godoy, E. and Reygadas, R. (1996) 'Nuestra propuesta de ley para ONG', *Rostros y Voces de la Sociedad Civil*.

Secretaría de Gobernación (1994) *Directorio de Organizaciones Civiles*, Mexico City: DF, Secretaría de Gobernación.

Thompson, A. (1992) 'Democracy and development: the role of the nongovernmental organizations in Argentina, Chile and Uruguay', in K. McCarthy, V. Hodgkinson and R. Sumariwalla (eds) *The Non-Profit Sector in the Global Community*, San Francisco: Jossey-Bass.

World Economic Forum (1997) *The Global Competitiveness Report*, Geneva: World Economic Forum.

16 Beyond the crossroads
Policy issues for the Philippine nonprofit sector

Ledivina V. Cariño

Introduction

For the Philippines as a whole, as much as for its nonprofit sector, *the* significant crossroads was encountered in 1986 when the 'People Power Revolution' toppled the dictatorship of Ferdinand E. Marcos. Since then, the Philippine state has generally provided a supportive environment for the growth of nongovernmental organizations – NGOs – and civil society as a whole. This paper starts with a depiction of the formal and effective policies affecting the NGO sector during the Marcos period, its role in the transition to redemocratization, and the policies promulgated after leaving that crossroads. The challenges that the sector is now facing are then analyzed. Reference is made throughout to the 'NGO sector' rather than the 'nonprofit sector', since the main policy debates centre on the sector's relations with the state rather than with the market. As the former term is understood in the Philippines, we are therefore referring to 'private, nonprofit organizations engaged in development activities for society's disadvantaged sectors' (Quizon 1989: 3).

NGOs during the Marcos period

Philippine NGOs have always been mechanisms of grievance against the state. The first known NGOs were composed of peasants who organized in the 1900s to protest against concentration of land ownership and other agrarian problems (ANGOC 1984). NGOs emerged in great numbers in the late 1960s, triggered by the worsening poverty situation and increasing political repression. They faced additional difficulties during the martial law period (1972–86). Superficially, because its official credo envisioned 'a new society,' the martial law government paid frequent obeisance to the principles of popular participation and state sharing of power with the people. In reality, however, many NGOs were considered subversive and security risks, and were objects of suspicion, hostility and outright violence.

Policies after the dictatorship

The miracle of February 1986 was that Filipinos massed at Manila's major thoroughfare, Epifanio de los Santos Avenue (EDSA), in a non-violent, fiesta-like four days and in so doing drove a dictator away. The secret is that while many came individually, the bulk of 'people power' was composed of organized and disciplined groups. The NGOs were ready because they had been tested in dire times when adversity gave wing to their initiatives as alternative delivery systems, channels of popular discontent, and models of a desired relationship between state and people.

A government installed by people power could not turn away from these organizations. The principle of respect for, and encouragement of, NGOs and people's participation is enshrined in several sections of the Constitution of 1987. The constitutional emphasis is on the role of NGOs as guardians of the public interest. Subsequent laws have provided for NGO representation in Congress and in local special bodies. Various national departments operate NGO desks. NGOs are also invited to special policy summits called by the government.

Registration and accreditation systems, tax and funding incentives to NGOs, and other privileges have also been instituted (Quizon 1989; Brillantes 1991). Registration rules promulgated by government agencies have been quietly followed and have not stirred protests among NGOs. In addition, NGOs have started their own self-accreditation mechanism.

NGOs seek accreditation from government agencies to receive certain benefits. The tax incentives granted NGOs and other nonprofit corporations include duty- and tax-free foreign donations, and exemption from income tax. Donors receive exemption from donor's gift tax and income tax deductions under certain conditions.

The general picture that emerges is of a state providing an enabling and facilitating environment for organizations of civil society to exist. However, two factors tend to weaken this conclusion. First, bills to formally recognize NGOs have been pending since 1988 (when the first Congress under the redemocratizing period opened). This suggests that, although still enjoying widespread acceptance, the role of NGOs has slipped from the centre of the nation's consciousness.

Second, although consultation mechanisms are in place throughout government, genuine NGO participation is not necessarily taking place. For instance, laws initiated following supposedly popular consultations do not bear the mark of NGOs' policy influence (Quizon 1989; Hofileña 1997). There have also been instances of repression or abuse by the civilian government and the military of NGOs representing the urban poor or cultural minority sectors (Quizon and Reyes 1989; Alegre 1996).

Nevertheless, the gap between official and actual policy is not as wide, nor are relations between NGOs and government as hostile, as during the dictatorship. The efforts of the state to reach out to NGOs have been rewarded by their continued attempts at cooperation.

Challenges confronting the NGO sector

The challenges facing the Philippine NGO sector are similar to those of the list provided by Salamon (Chapter 2 in this volume): legitimacy, effectiveness, and economic and fiscal challenges. However, the ways these challenges are defined, and even the approaches to meet them, differ from the American situation.

The legitimacy challenge

The challenge of legitimacy may be phrased in this way: In the face of myriad organizations occupying the entire spectrum of ideologies and possibilities, how can any NGO claim the mantle of being able to speak for the people? Once in the corridors of power, how can it maintain its difference from the state? How accountable would it be to the people?

Representativeness

NGOs include both progressive and conservative organizations, are focused on one or several sectoral concerns, and are composed of middle-class change agents or the marginalized people themselves. Despite such a broad spectrum, a large part of the citizenry remains unorganized and uninvolved in NGOs.[1] NGOs claiming to speak for the people are therefore, in effect, self-appointed and self-proclaimed.

To legitimize NGOs as true people's representatives, the Philippines uses two mechanisms – appointment by appropriate officials, and elections. Leaving the choice to the concerned national or local official has led to many problems. For instance, many mayors choose NGOs headed by their wives to sit on the local development council. National officials may select the NGOs of their friends as their consultants on policy boards.

To prevent situations like these, NGOs have demanded that accreditation include criteria of representativeness rather than just viability as is the current government standard.[2] This would limit the discretion of the government entity concerned so as to enhance the chances of choosing an NGO representative who can speak for the people.

The more direct approach is through including as representatives in the Congress those NGOs which manage to secure a mandate through the country's mainstream electoral process. The idea here has been to include NGOs alongside elected individuals because it has been feared that relying purely on the latter would result in inadequate representation of the interests of the poor, since only wealthy candidates could afford to run for election, and these would be unwilling or unable to argue on behalf of the disadvantaged. To this end, the 1987 Constitution instituted a modified election mechanism called the 'party list' system, which sought to involve NGOs as representatives of otherwise marginalized people. Each voter has selected one organization from the party list as their representative, in addition to voting for a regular congressman. In theory, an

NGO can have as many as three representatives if it receives at least 6 per cent of the votes. The 'party list system' could potentially give as much as 25 per cent of national Congressional seats to NGO representatives.

However, when the scheme was actually used for the first time in 1998, traditional politicians joined long-standing organizations to form instant 'party-list NGOs'. Over one hundred groups (identified only by their acronym) were listed in the ballot. This resulted in the election of groups that did not come from the marginalized sectors for whom the scheme was devised. It is therefore widely argued that both the appointment and the party list systems need to be revised to secure more genuine participation. In the language being used here, such reforms would seek to address the legitimacy challenge.

Maintaining difference from the state

Another legitimacy question concerns NGOs retaining their distinctiveness from the state: not necessarily to be adversarial, but to bring to the consciousness of government officials different or new perspectives and approaches to policy. This requires a level of autonomy and independence that may be hard to maintain in a situation where the state is friendly and provides much facilities and support to NGOs.

Accountability to the people

If an NGO is conscious that it is the people's representative, it will accept responsibility to a constituency and not just to its own membership. A representative is duty-bound to consult with the sector presumed to be represented, or to make an independent personal judgement of what is in the public interest. This may be different from the stand of his or her own NGO. Accountability and representativeness may thus push in different directions on certain occasions.

The effectiveness challenge

The challenge of effectiveness is about NGOs being able to deliver what they promise. Their problems as the people's representatives were discussed above. This section will deal with the service delivery of NGOs.

NGOs' efforts at service provision do not constitute a simple market role of delivering desired services at affordable prices. Rather, they are viewed relative to the state: as an alternative to or in competition with government, as a complement to its services, or as a partner or collaborator of the bureaucracy (Cariño 1991). Delivery of services is a means to a higher end, 'empowering the people to actually engage in transforming their communities to a more just and humane society' (Soliman 1985: 57).

NGOs play a substantial role in delivering services in agriculture, fisheries, forestry, credit, education and training, housing, and appropriate technology. They serve people's organizations through training in community organizing, management and technical skills and nonformal education. They also help local economies by channelling funds to their areas (PHILDHRRA 1985).

Claims concerning the effectiveness of NGOs as delivery mechanisms in the Philippines are primarily made on three bases. First, their activities are rooted in communities and thus have a greater potential to be responsive to their needs. Second, they have committed staff and volunteers who view NGO programmes as their outlet for missionary zeal and idealistic change-agency. Third, they can be less tied to 'the establishment' and thus less shy about making not only technical innovations in a narrow sense, but also structural analyses and critiques of the current social and political situation.

NGOs have their share of weaknesses too (Salamon 1987), a number of which stand out in the Philippines context. First, they may put too much emphasis on process, and hence underestimate the value of indicators, targets and objective results. Second, they have often been led by charismatic individuals who can so subtly dominate the supposedly collegial organization that it may not survive their departure from the scene.

Third, the credibility of NGOs as alternative delivery systems may also become strained as they expand. Brillantes (1991: 121) warns that 'the growth in scope and assumed responsibilities actually outpaces the development of internal capabilities, not to mention … [the need for] a major reorientation about the so-called "vision and mission" of the NGO'. Because few NGOs have the resources to go beyond a small area, scaling-up may require collaboration with government. Unless their visions and mandates are similar, such an interconnection may breed conflict, to the detriment of those needing services.

Many NGOs are undergoing the transition from the original founders to second-generation leaders. This routinization of charisma may involve a certain amount of bureaucratization that young NGOs have managed to avoid. Making procedures more regular, keeping records, and paying more attention to results rather than just processes entails sea changes in current NGO management.

Fourth, there are also human resource management problems. For instance, Liamzon and Salinas (1989) report a high turnover of staff because of poor remuneration and benefits. The lack of a career path and frequent turnover of staff lead to problems in project management that can directly affect the effectiveness of the NGO. Capacities should also be developed in conflict management and negotiation. Professionalization of NGO staff is a felt need (Alegre 1996; David 1997) that has led the University of the Philippines to establish graduate programmes in voluntary sector management.

Economic and fiscal challenges

Funding is a major problem for NGOs, both in meeting programme costs and in paying for administrative and overhead expenses. Three major sources have been tapped: government, philanthropy, and self-generated income.

Government support

Government support is provided through tax exemption and other incentives, direct grants, and help in tapping Official Development Assistance (ODA). Government policy encourages providing these to NGOs. Worrisome issues relate first to their allocation to different organizations. Political expediency, for instance, may prevail over rational criteria in distributing grants so that a relatively new, untested NGO may receive funds ahead of others. Even discounting the possible bias of a decision-maker, needy but small organizations may be left behind by bigger and more experienced organizations because of their lack of information on funding possibilities, poor capacity to make project proposals, or lack of social marketing skills (Quizon and Reyes 1989: 23, 27, 62, 96; Wui and Lopez 1997: 19). This has led NGOs to upscale their initiatives to cover more communities and groups, and to develop projects led by networks and consortia (Alegre 1996: 43).

When funds have been given, the next problem is their effect on the independence and autonomy of the receiving NGOs. A government agency may find it hard to accept policy critiques from NGOs otherwise beholden to it for their survival. Conversely, the NGOs themselves may consider it ethically and culturally incorrect to bite the hands that feed them. Among organizations that cut their teeth on protests and dissent from government, funds from it may be seen as a sell-out (Quizon and Reyes 1989: 34, 80, 96, 129).

A third problem is the accountability of NGOs for those funds. Everyone who receives funds from government is subject to audit. For many NGOs, accounting for these funds is a burden, as even the smallest amount is expected to have receipts and documentation on demand. On the other hand, NGOs are also notorious for their disregard of these rules, creating, this time, problems for their supporters within the government agency (Creencia 1994).

A special type of government funding is ODA, which is support from another government. Depending on how the different countries arrange them, some of these, especially embassy funds, allow access to smaller NGOs. They are also generally directed towards social development programmes, coinciding with the thrusts of many NGOs. In that sense, they are similar to funds from international and local philanthropic foundations. Nevertheless, a common complaint is their ability to sway organizations towards the needs perceived by the donor rather than the recipient. 'Donor-drivenness' can lead to displaced goals, and activities which do not address real needs of Filipinos (Aldaba 1993).

Private philanthropy

Private philanthropy is not well developed in the Philippines. Wealthy families tend to take care of their own relatives and to give in personalized ways. Providing gifts for causes and to impersonal institutions like NGOs has yet to become ingrained. Thus, to a great extent, Philippine philanthropy is corporate rather than individual. Donations by corporations effectively decrease their pre-tax income, making this a rational business proposition, together with fulfilling social responsibility.

Membership fees and income-generating projects

Finally, NGOs may try to be self-sufficient through membership fees and income-generating projects. However, many NGOs face an ideological problem in generating income from their own projects: they find it difficult to accept that they must produce profit from their activities, having been reared on principles of socialism and equity rather than capitalism and accumulation (Alegre 1996: 62). There is also the management problem of finding a product that would sell, producing enough to generate a profit, and then determining how to use the proceeds to suitably match organizational goals.

Beyond the crossroads

In many ways, the NGO sector has an enviable position *vis-à-vis* the state sector in the Philippines. It is seen as the embodiment of the 'people power' that was the catalyst in toppling the dictatorship. The state has since developed an enabling and facilitating environment for NGOs to survive and prosper, and the path is now much less tortuous than it was before the crossroads of 1986.

The sector must continue to play a strong political role even though it is now an accepted and even glorified form. It cannot turn its back on its original mission of representing and serving the people – yet the dangers are apparent even now. The general popularity of the NGO form has already given rise to frauds which could undermine the legitimacy of civil society organizations as a whole.

The next challenge is effectiveness. NGOs must continue to deliver what they have promised – better alternative service than the state's – even as they manage their growing internal organization, expansion and institutionalization. They must do so in the face of difficulties of raising resources, and where resources are available, in the face of enticements to forget goals in order to access funds.

These challenges are interrelated. The legitimacy of NGOs is tied up with their effectiveness and their ability to meet the economic challenges. Thus NGOs have the task not only of raising funds through philanthropy, but also of nurturing the growth of philanthropy through their responsible use of these donations.

Born in adversity, the sector managed to outlive threats to its survival by the martial law regime. Now regarded as an indispensable part of society, it can nevertheless weaken as it succumbs to co-optation and forgets the reasons that have made the people accept it as a countervailing power to the state. It must therefore work out a more sophisticated relationship with government, some-times cooperating and reinforcing it, while at other moments dissenting, competing and providing better models of representation and service. The state/NGO relationship that must be forged is one that will guard the democratic gains of Philippine society while improving the system of delivering services to the people.

Notes

1 National College of Public Administration and Governance, University of the Phillipines. Correspondence should be addressed to Dr Ledivina V. Cariño, University Professor and Dean, National College of Public Administration and Governance, University of the Philippines, Diliman, Quezon City, Philippines 1101. e-mail: *ledivina@yahoo.com*
2 In Quizon's article, culled from six NGO sector studies and discussions among their researchers, it was recommended that government use the proximity of prospective NGOs to the problem addressed, and the credibility of NGOs among target communities, as indicators of NGOs' representativeness (Quizon 1989: 35).

References

Aldaba, F. T. (1993) 'The role of NGOs in Philippine social transformation', *Philippine Politics and Society* (Journal of the Ateneo Center for Social Policy and Public Affairs) 2–57. Kluwer-Plenum.

Alegre, A. G. (ed.) (1996) *Trends and Traditions, Challenges and Choices: A Strategic Study of Philippine NGOs*, Quezon City: Ateneo Center for Social Policy and Public Affairs and the Philippines-Canada Human Resource Development Programme.

ANGOC (Asian NGO Coalition for Agrarian Reform and Rural Development) (1984) *Status Papers on NGO Involvement in Rural Development: A Perspective of Ten Countries in Asia*, Makati, Metro Manila: ANGOC.

Brillantes, A. B., Jr (1991) 'NGOs as alternative delivery systems: the Philippine experience', in R. B. Ocampo and O. M. Alfonso (eds) *Alternative Delivery Systems for Public Services*, Manila: Association of Development Research and Training Institutes of Asia and the Pacific (ADIPA).

Cariño, L. V. (1991) 'Complements, competitors or collaborators: government–NGO relations', in R. B. Ocampo and O. M. Alfonso (eds) *Alternative Delivery Systems for Public Services*, Manila: Association of Development Research and Training Institutes of Asia and the Pacific (ADIPA).

Creencia, F. V. (1994) 'The accountability of nongovernmental organizations', *Philippine Journal of Public Administration*, 38: 224–36.

David, K. C. (1997) 'Intra-civil society relations: an overview', in M. C. Ferrer (ed.) *Civil Society Making Civil Society*, Quezon City: Third World Studies Center, University of the Philippines.

Hofileña, C. F. (ed.) (1997) *Policy Influence: NGO Experiences*, Quezon City: Ateneo Center for Social Policy and Public Affairs and Konrad Adenauer Stiftung.

Liamzon, C. M. and Salinas, M. A. (1989) 'Strategic assessment of NGOs in agrarian reform and rural development', in A. B. Quizon and R. U. Reyes (eds) *A Strategic Assessment of Non-Governmental Organizations in the Philippines*, Makati, Metro Manila: Asian Non-Governmental Organizations Coalition for Agrarian Reform and Rural Development (ANGOC).

PHILDHRRA (Philippine Partnership for the Development of Human Resources in Rural Areas) (1985) *Rural Development Cooperation: The Philippine Perspective*, report of the tripartite workshop between government agencies, NGOs and donor agencies, Metro Manila: PHILDHRRA.

Quizon, A. B. (1989) 'A survey of government policies and programmes on non-governmental organizations in the Philippines', in A. B. Quizon and R. U. Reyes (eds) *A Strategic Assessment of Non-Governmental Organizations in the Philippines*, Makati, Metro Manila: Asian Non-Governmental Organizations Coalition for Agrarian Reform and Rural Development (ANGOC).

——(1989) 'A summary of NGO issues on GO/NGO relationships and collaboration', in A. B. Quizon and R. U. Reyes (eds) *A Strategic Assessment of Non-Governmental Organizations in the Philippines*, Makati, Metro Manila: Asian Non-Governmental Organizations Coalition for Agrarian Reform and Rural Development (ANGOC).

Quizon, A. B. and Reyes, R. U. (eds) (1989) *A Strategic Assessment of Non-Governmental Organizations in the Philippines*, Makati, Metro Manila: Asian Non-Governmental Organizations Coalition for Agrarian Reform and Rural Development (ANGOC).

Salamon, L. M. (1987) 'Partners in public service: toward a theory of government–nonprofit relations', in W. W. Powell (ed.) *The Nonprofit Sector: A Research Handbook*, New Haven: Yale University Press.

Soliman, M. C. (1985) 'The role of ACES in rural poverty alleviation', in PHILDHRRA, *Rural Development Cooperation: The Philippine Perspective*, report of the tripartite workshop between government agencies, NGOs and donor agencies, Metro Manila: PHILDHRRA.

Wui, M. A. and Lopez, M. G. S. (eds) (1997) *State–Civil Society Relations in Policy-Making*, Diliman, Quezon City: Third World Studies Center.

17 South Africa

Anti-apartheid NGOs in transition

Adam Habib and Rupert Taylor

From the 1980s, as a result of the former apartheid regime's liberalization initiatives and greater funding being made available by international organizations, foreign governments and philanthropic foundations, the South African non-governmental organization (NGO) sector experienced phenomenal expansion. Moreover, this expansion continued into the 1990s in the context of the replacement of apartheid with democracy. South Africa thus provides an ideal setting in which to investigate how state/NGO relations change when countries undergo a transition from authoritarian to democratic political systems; and to assess the opportunities and challenges for NGOs in newly democratizing societies.

The focus of this chapter is on those particular NGOs that opposed apartheid, and which under apartheid were more appropriately called anti-government organizations, namely, nonprofit organizations that provided research/policy, socio-economic developmental, or welfare services with 'some indication of a social and political orientation which was non-racist or anti-racist and on the side of the poor and oppressed' (Walters 1993: 11). In particular, this chapter investigates how the democratic transition transformed the relations between the state and these NGOs in South Africa. It also highlights the challenges that have been generated by these new state/NGO relations, and their implications for the issue of NGO accountability to the poor and marginalized in developing societies.

Transforming state/NGO relations

At all levels, relations between the South African state and the NGO sector have changed dramatically in the last three decades. Prior to the 1980s, the political and legal system was only supportive of NGOs directed to serving the white community and the racial order. By contrast, NGOs critical of apartheid, of which there were only a handful, were subjected to continuous harassment and 'banning'. This political environment was transformed with the liberalization of the South African polity and economy in the early 1980s. Although not supportive of anti-apartheid NGOs, the P. W. Botha regime allowed many to emerge, organize, and serve the disenfranchized and marginalized majority black population.

This newly liberalized political environment, and the influx of funds – especially from Scandinavian countries, the European Union, and US foundations – encouraged a proliferation of anti-apartheid NGOs during the 1980s (the uniqueness of the South African situation under apartheid was that foreign funding was channelled directly to NGOs rather than being channelled through government). Generally, the result was a massive growth in the NGO sector to the point where, by 1990, it was estimated that there were some 5,000 NGOs pursuing developmental work in the country (Bernstein 1994).

It was in this context that most NGOs emerged, being created and run by professional people aligned to the anti-apartheid cause and concerned about giving assistance and support to the struggle. Such organizations constituted a self-mobilized and heavily interlocked network that undertook a number of roles, but which, broadly speaking, can be divided into two distinct groups. First, there were those such as the Urban Foundation, Black Sash, South African Institute of Race Relations (SAIRR), and the Institute for Democratic Alternatives in South Africa (Idasa) that conceived of themselves as liberal-oriented organizations and positioned themselves somewhere between the ideological extremes of Afrikaner and African nationalism (consider Hellmann 1979; Spink 1991; Jaster and Jaster 1993; Lazerson 1994). Second, there were NGOs such as the National Education Crisis Committee, the Legal Resources Centre, the Transvaal Rural Action Committee and the Trade Union Research Project, that more openly associated themselves with the African National Congress (ANC) and serviced the mass-based people's organizations of the national liberation movement (principally the United Democratic Front and the Congress of South African Trade Unions). Altogether, these NGOs worked to weaken and undermine National Party rule; they made up the core of an emerging non-racial democratic society independent of, and set against, the apartheid state (Taylor *et al.* 1999). Collectively, NGOs provided a non-racial social service delivery function for the disenfranchised, offering a kind of shadow (alternative) welfare system in support of the mass-based movements and the poor (Taylor *et al.* 1998).

During the 1980s under apartheid, the relationship between the anti-apartheid NGO network and the South African state can be described as having been antagonistic and adversarial. This operated on two levels. First, the administrative and legal environment, including the tax laws, were hostile to corporate sponsorship of the NGO sector as a whole (Lee and Buntman 1989). This prevented the development of a philanthropic and corporate social investment tradition in South Africa, thereby undermining the foundation for a vibrant and well resourced NGO sector. In addition, the Fund Raising Act of 1978 made it 'a crime to solicit or receive donations from the public unless this has been authorised by the Director of Fundraising. Any donation received from outside South Africa was deemed from the public within South Africa' (Budlender 1993: 86). This forced anti-apartheid NGOs, most of whom received the bulk of their funding from external sources, to develop a range of administrative measures that would camouflage their funding sources.

Second, the political and security environment was hostile to the operations of NGOs. Although the National Party's liberalization programme facilitated the emergence of anti-apartheid NGOs, it did not allow them to operate without any restrictions. Almost all anti-apartheid NGOs experienced some degree of confrontation with the state during the 1980s. NGO leaders and activists were subjected to banning, arrests, detentions without trial, death threats and assassination attempts, and having their homes and cars petrol bombed. NGOs were subjected to general Security Police harassment by having their telephones tapped, post intercepted, meetings disrupted and structures infiltrated. The apartheid state also sponsored counter-organizations to compete with and discredit anti-apartheid NGOs. Finally, the state utilized its censorship laws to continually ban publications produced by anti-apartheid NGOs. In sum, the political and security environment was a repressive one that curtailed and restricted the operations and activities of the anti-apartheid NGO sector (Taylor *et al.* 1998).

The repeal of apartheid legislation and the end of National Party rule changed all this. The conflictual relationship between anti-apartheid NGOs and the state was transformed with the transition to democracy in South Africa. The 1994 elections, in which the ANC gained 63 per cent of the vote, ushered in a new era and forced a shift from the politics of resistance to a politics of reconstruction (Marais 1998). NGOs and state institutions were now seen as partners in a national project – the Reconstruction and Development Programme (RDP) – to redress a society in which it is estimated that some 17 to 19 million black people are living below the poverty line (ANC 1994; Marks 1998: 26).

The resources of NGOs have been carried into the transition process in three main ways:

1   Many NGOs have been absorbed into, or fused with, the institutions of the new state, and important policy positions, key personnel and the majority of funding has moved into the state.
2   NGOs that were closest to the mass-based movements – and have survived the impact of assimilation into state structures – have, often by building on personal networks, repositioned themselves as NGOs with a complementary role to the new state by undertaking partnerships with government departments, developing policies, or providing welfare and development services.
3   NGOs that have been liberal in orientation have recast themselves as NGOs, taking up positions as 'watchdogs' of the new state, advocating various policy positions and asserting their independence from the state with the intent of strengthening civil society.

Nelson Mandela (1996) has written: 'Non-governmental organizations played an outstanding role during the dark days of apartheid. Today, many people who received their training within the NGO sector play important roles in government.' In fact, to some, the acronym NGO is taken to stand for Now Government Official. In some respects the former shadow state has become the new state. Nonetheless, although prime responsibility for reconstruction rests with the state, it has been acknowledged that 'irrespective of how much a government may regard itself as being a "people's government", implementation of its programme and projects, without participation of the civil society, will tend towards a top-down approach, with its inherent disadvantages' (Currin 1993: 168). Accordingly, the value of NGOs concerned with people-centred development, socio-economic uplift and service delivery has been recognized. Beyond this, NGOs that have turned to playing the part of watchdog over democratic practices have been supported by a range of donors (such as the US Agency for International Development, USAID) concerned to strengthen civil society through 'democracy and governance' programmes (consider Clayton 1996).

Overall, there has been a move to develop carefully constructed programmes and projects (often demand driven) and to address policy issues. During the 1990s, as the transition unfolded, a number of NGOs shifted their attention to policy research, first for the ANC and subsequently for the Government of National Unity (see Kraak 1995). Here, NGOs have been involved in the formulation of government green and white papers, as well as the work of parliamentary portfolio committees and government commissions (Kihato and Rapoo 1999). In particular, there has been much concern about land issues, labour reforms, what the post-apartheid social services (health, education, safety and security) should look like, and the structure of the Truth and Reconciliation Commission (TRC) (see van der Merwe *et al.* 1999, for a detailed study of the relationship between NGOs and the TRC).

To facilitate and consolidate the new state/NGO relations, the ANC-led Government of National Unity introduced a new legal environment and established new political institutions. In July and August 1995, the government released two versions of a draft nonprofit bill that was intended to coordinate and manage state/NGO relations in post-apartheid South Africa. Both versions of the bill provoked an outcry from NGO activists and leaders because it provided government with the authority to subpoena employees and intervene in the management of NGOs where there was some evidence of misconduct or mismanagement (consider Kane-Berman 1996).

In response to these criticisms the bill was revised, and a new nonprofit organization bill was submitted to the cabinet in August 1997 and enacted in December 1997. One of the more significant features of the new Act was its repeal of the 1978 Fundraising Act, which had limited NGO abilities to raise funds. The Act provided for a system of voluntary registration and provided benefits and allowances for NGOs and community-based organizations (CBOs). It also established a Directorate for Non-Profit Organizations, which was to be responsible for the coordination of, and development and implementation of policies in the nonprofit sector. Finally, the Act also required NGOs to keep a proper book of accounts and to submit audited statements to the government. The Act thus goes some way toward creating a positive legal environment for NGOs in South Africa.

Government also reorganized the political environment for NGOs. They were provided with access to the fourth chamber of the National Economic Labour and Development Council, the country's premier corporatist-style consensus-building agency (Habib 1997a), on condition that such representation occur through a single body. Given that this would provide access to the official policy making process, NGOs moved very quickly to establish the South African NGO Coalition (Sangoco) in August 1995 (Naidoo 1997), which now serves as a representative umbrella body for around 6,000 affiliated NGOs. Sangoco's primary role is that of advancing the interests of the poor. It is also concerned with developing an enabling environment for the NGO sector, especially through lobbying for tax reforms, and providing an arena for mutual monitoring (*NGO Matters* 1997).

In addition, in late 1994, in an effort to resolve the funding crisis of NGOs that arose as a result of the decision of foreign donors to channel funds directly to the RDP, the Transitional National Development Trust (TNDT) was established as a crisis, quick-step funder responsible for developing and funding NGOs and CBOs in the short term. The TNDT opened its doors in March 1996, after a delay of two years, and its initial R120 million (around US $20 million) budget (comprising R70 million from the European Union and R50 million from the South African government) has been used to fund education and training, health, and rural development projects.

In April 1996, through Deputy President Thabo Mbeki, the government established an Advisory Committee to assist it with determining the appropriate relationships and structures that should be established with organs of civil society. The Advisory Committee (1997) supported the idea of a new independent statutory body, the National Development Agency (NDA), with a publicly nominated board. The NDA is now the main state institution responsible for mobilizing government and other international and domestic resources to support NGOs and CBOs. It is also charged with the task of assisting government with policy formulation and implementation for, and monitoring and evaluation of, all registered organizations in civil society.

In sum, South Africa's democratic transition has transformed the political and legal environment for all NGOs. Whereas many state/NGO relations were adversarial and conflictual a decade ago, they are now much more collaborative. The post-apartheid government also has moved to promulgate new laws and establish new institutions to consolidate this partnership with the NGO sector. This, however, has not been an easy process; and it has generated problems with serious long-term implications for NGO accountability to the poor and disadvantaged in South Africa.

Impending crisis?

Relations between the new state and NGOs have been problematic. Despite its importance, the ANC-led government has been slow to develop coherent thinking on the NGO sector. There has been a lack of consistent policy on state/NGO relations (Kraak 1996), and the 1997 Advisory Committee (1997: 26) recognized the lack of clear policy and connecting points with government, and went so far as to remark that 'since the 1994 elections the sector is facing a crisis'. Many NGOs have found it difficult to access government support, set up partnerships, and obtain funding (CASE 1996). Some NGOs have felt marginalized; for example, to some, 'the biggest failure of the TRC to date has been its inability to build a strong working relationship with civil society as a whole' (Hamber *et al.* 1997: 5–6). There have been problems with tendering procedures, and funding has been caught up in the bureaucracies, which have been slow to confront the challenges facing the new South Africa. Some government departments have been riddled with corruption; others have been more concerned about pursuing government by the rules rather than by results.

Not surprisingly, the RDP has been seriously undermined by all of these problems. In fact, in March 1996, the RDP office was abolished (with foreign funding henceforth channelled through the International Development Cooperation unit of the Department of Finance). In June 1996 the government, under the influence of the World Bank and the International Monetary Fund (IMF), moved to endorse neo-liberal economic policies, shifting from RDP to GEAR (growth, employment and redistribution strategy). GEAR places emphasis on private-sector investment to create jobs, thereby putting economic growth ahead of state-led redistribution (Department of Finance 1996). And yet, as Alex Boraine, Deputy Vice-Chairperson of the TRC, stated in an interview with the present authors (5 December 1998), 'the transformation of the economic and social order ... that hasn't happened. The lines of wealth and poverty are still as stark as they were' (see also Pilger 1998).

From the perspective of NGOs, the heart of the problem is the shortfall in organizational capacity, the seriousness of which has been compounded by many NGOs having to face the problem of high staff turnover as skilled staff move into government and state-run institutions: according to Sangoco, 'the sector as a whole lost more than 60 per cent of its senior staff to government and the private sector since 1990' (*Mail & Guardian*, 22–28 August 1997). Just as serious is the dire funding situation. Since the 1994 elections, the foreign donor community has begun to channel funding directly to the government, and now the 'obsession with IMF/World Bank structural adjustment means financial cutbacks which are cutting swathes through NGOs' (Southall and Wood 1998: 224–5; see also Bernstein 1994; Kraak 1996: 79; Turok 1996).

Although, as noted, the government set up the TNDT and has now established a National Development Agency to address this financial crisis (a fifteen-person board was approved and funds allocated in August 1999), it is unlikely to compensate for the shortfall of funds from the international community. Moreover, even in cases where foreign donors have continued funding, such funding has become much more project-specific (as for example stipulated by USAID and the Ford Foundation). This has, during the 1990s, led to marked organizational growth for the liberal NGOs such as Idasa and SAIRR, and has promoted more streamlined managerial structures and a degree of professionalism in NGOs which, although welcome for raising issues of financial accountability and impact (under apartheid, overseas funding arrangements often did not require very stringent accounting reports), nevertheless tends to encourage commercialization.

Commercialization is prompted not only by the donor community. The financial crisis prompted the more farsighted NGOs to move away from donor funding to self-sufficiency. Many NGOs have sought to deal with the funding crisis by selling their services to the government and corporate sector. The Community Agency for Social Enquiry, for example, is now entirely self-sufficieny, and the Independent Mediation Service of South Africa attained around 75 per cent self-sufficiency prior to its closure in 2000. Given the wide-scale poverty in South Africa, such self-sufficiency could not entail local communities paying for services. Rather, self-sufficiency has meant that either NGOs become the voice of privileged sectors of the community (such as business) or that they tender for government and other transnational and donor contracts against other commercial firms. This has tended to blur the distinction between for-profit and nonprofit agencies (see in particular Price 1995).

This, of course, poses serious questions about the accountability of NGOs. The existing literature on the nonprofit sector is replete with suggestions that NGOs are institutions that service the interests of the poor and marginalized (see for example Korten 1987), but can one really argue this when NGOs become so commercially oriented and dependent on the resources of overseas donors and the government (see Habib and Owusu-Ampomah 1997, for a critical case study)?

NGOs' recent relations with government can work to strain their commitment and lines of accountability to the poor. NGOs' dependence on state funding and their newly formed 'client' relationships with government must lead one to question their autonomy and whether they can avoid being mere appendages of state institutions. Working as 'private subcontractors' of government and with funds from overseas governments, NGOs are increasingly no longer non-governmental. Will the one who pays the piper call the tune? Given that the South African government has adopted a rigid monetarist policy that inhibits its ability to deliver services to the poor and marginalized, this may well prove to be the case (Habib 1997b). Will this crisis of delivery not taint the NGO sector? Will the NGO sector's effectiveness not come into question as a result of its recent relations with the state?

Anti-apartheid NGOs were seen clearly as agents of change. Today, formerly progressive NGOs face the danger of being seen as agents of control, of being co-opted to neo-liberal agendas, of becoming the 'community face' of neo-liberalism (Ashley and Andrews 1998; see also Petras 1997). Hein Marais (1998: 213) has already noted that 'under the canopy of economic policies like GEAR, NGOs' roles tend to harmonize with standard neo-liberal logic as they toil in the wake of development and welfare responsibilities shirked by the state'. This is a disturbing prospect, because the reality is that, over seven years into democratic rule, the task of reconstructing South African society has barely began.

Conclusion

South Africa's anti-apartheid NGOs moved into the transition on a strong footing; their role in the anti-apartheid struggle, and their relations with the ANC, provided them with a large degree of popular legitimacy. However, the current NGO funding crisis and the turn to commercialization to address this crisis have created relations with donors and the state that ultimately, in a neo-liberal economic climate, could lead to a moral crisis of legitimacy and effectiveness. Nelson Mandela (1997) has already questioned the legitimacy of NGOs when he accused some, at the ANC's national conference in December 1997, of following the agendas of foreign governments. However, it should be added that the legitimacy of NGOs also can be undermined by the kind of client relationships Mandela's – and now Mbeki's – government has sought to establish. The financial crisis and commercialization of the new NGO sector in South Africa thus could evolve into a full-blown crisis of legitimacy and effectiveness. In this sense, the crisis of the nonprofit sector in the United States (Salamon, Chapter 2 in this volume) might simply prefigure the future of South Africa's own NGO sector.

References

Advisory Committee (1997) *Structural Relationships between Government and Civil Society Organisations*, report prepared for the Deputy President, Thabo Mbeki, South Africa.

ANC (African National Congress) (1994) *Reconstruction and Development Programme*, Johannesburg: Umanyano Publications.

Ashley, B. and Andrews, M. (1998) 'Warning: handle with extreme caution', *Reconstruct* (supplement to the Johannesburg *Sunday Independent*) no. 17, 28 June.

Bernstein, A. (1994) 'NGOs and a democratic South Africa', *Development and Democracy*, 7: 55–66.

Budlender, G. (1993) 'Overview: the legal and fiscal environment of voluntary organisations in South Africa', in A. M. Micon and B. Lindsnaes (eds) *The Role of Voluntary Organisations in Emerging Democracies: Experience and Strategies in Eastern and Central Europe and in South Africa*, New York: Danish Centre for Human Rights and Institute of International Education.

CASE (Community Agency for Social Enquiry) (1996) *Tango in the Dark: Government and Voluntary Sector Partnerships in the New South Africa*, Johannesburg: CASE.

Clayton, A. (ed.) (1996) *NGOs, Civil Society and the State: Building Democracy in Transitional Societies*, Oxford: INTRAC.

Currin, B. (1993) 'Summing up: civil society organisations in emerging democracies', in A. M. Micon and B. Lindsnaes (eds) *The Role of Voluntary Organisations in Emerging Democracies: Experience and Strategies in Eastern and Central Europe and in South Africa*, New York: Danish Centre for Human Rights and Institute of International Education.

Department of Finance (1996) *Growth, Employment and Redistribution: A Macroeconomic Strategy for South Africa*, Pretoria: Government Printer.

Habib, A. (1997a) 'From pluralism to corporatism: South Africa's labour relations in transition', *Politikon*, 24, 1: 57–75.

——(1997b) 'South Africa: the Rainbow Nation and prospects for consolidating democracy', *African Journal of Political Science*, 2, 1: 15–26.

Habib, A. and Owusu-Ampomah, K. (1997) 'Report on the Institute for Democracy in South Africa (Idasa)', unpublished report prepared for the International Study of Peace and Conflict Resolution Organizations, South Africa.

Hamber, B., Mofokeng, T. and Simpson, G. (1997) 'Evaluating the role and function of civil society in a changing South Africa: the Truth and Reconciliation Commission as a case study', paper presented at seminar on The Role of Southern Civil Organisations in the Promotion of Peace, Catholic Institute for International Relations, London, 10 November.

Hellmann, E. (1979) 'Fifty years of the South African Institute of Race Relations', in E. Hellmann and H. Lever (eds) *Conflict and Progress: Fifty Years of Race Relations in South Africa*, Johannesburg: Macmillan.

Jaster, R. and Jaster, S. (1993) *South Africa's Other Whites: Voices for Change*, London: Macmillan.

Kane-Berman, J. (1996) 'Leave well alone: the role of NGOs in the process of democratization', in H. Kotzé (ed.) *Consolidating Democracy: What Role for Civil Society in South Africa?*, Stellenbosch: University of Stellenbosch and Konrad Adenauer Stiftung.

Kihato, C. and Rapoo, T. (1999) *An Independent Voice? A Survey of Civil Society Organisations in South Africa, their Funding and their Influence over the Policy Process*, Research Report 67, Johannesburg: Centre for Policy Studies.

Korten, D. C. (1987) 'Third generation NGO strategies: a key to people-centered development', *World Development*, 15: 145–59.

Kraak, G. (1995) *An INTERFUND Briefing on Development, Education and Training in South Africa in 1994/5*, Johannesburg: Development Update.

——(1996) *An INTERFUND Briefing on Development and the Voluntary Sector in South Africa in 1995/96*, Johannesburg: Development Update.

Lazerson, J. (1994) *Against the Tide: Whites in the Struggle Against Apartheid*, Boulder: Westview.

Lee, R. and Buntman, F. (1989) *The Future of the Nonprofit Voluntary Sector in South Africa*, Research Report 5, Johannesburg: Centre for Policy Studies.

Mandela, N. (1996) *Message from President Mandela on the Occasion of NGO Week*, 2–6 December, Rand Afrikaans University, Johannesburg.

——(1997) *Political Report of the President, Nelson Mandela, to the 50th National Conference of the African National Congress*, Mafikeng, 16 December.

Marais, H. (1998) *South Africa, Limits to Change: The Political Economy of Transformation*, London: Zed Books.

Marks, S. (1998) 'Social change, order and stability in the new South Africa', in F. H. Toase and E. J. Yorke (eds) *The New South Africa: Prospects for Domestic and International Security*, London: Macmillan.

Naidoo, K. (1997) *South African NGOs: The Path ahead*, London: CIIR.

Petras, J. (1997) 'Imperialism and NGOs in Latin America', *Monthly Review*, 49, 7: 10–27.

Pilger, J. (1998) *Apartheid Did Not Die*, television documentary, London: Carlton International.

Price, M. (1995) 'Some reflections on the changing role of progressive policy groups in South Africa: experiences from the centre of health policy', *Transformation*, 27: 24–34.

Southall, R. and Wood, G. (1998) 'Political party funding in Southern Africa', in P. Burnell and A. Ware (eds) *Funding Democratization*, Manchester: Manchester University Press.

Spink, K. (1991) *Black Sash: The Beginning of a Bridge for South Africa*, London: Methuen.

Taylor, R., Egan, A., Habib, A., Cock, J., Lekwane, A. and Shaw, M. (1998) 'Final Report: International Study of Peace and Conflict Resolution Organizations – South

Africa', presented to the 3rd International Conference of the International Society for Third Sector Research, University of Geneva, 8–11 July.

Taylor, R., Cock, J. and Habib, A. (1999) 'Projecting peace in apartheid South Africa', *Peace and Change*, 24, 1: 1–14.

Turok, B. (1996) 'Why are NGOs struggling?', *Johannesburg Mail & Guardian*, 29 November–5 December.

Van der Merwe, H., Dewhurst, P. and Hamber, B. (1999) 'Non-governmental organisations and the Truth and Reconciliation Commission: an impact assessment', *Politikon*, 26, 1: 55–79.

Walters, S. (1993) *Continuity and Change in Community Organisations: Trends in Greater Cape Town from 1989 to 1991*, CORE Working Paper 1, Cape Town: University of the Western Cape.

18 Conclusion

The third sector at the crossroads? Social, political and economic dynamics

Jeremy Kendall and Helmut K. Anheier

The contributions to this book explore central questions about the third sector's current position and future development in a broad cross-section of countries, with a particular emphasis on its role in public policy debate. These questions are being asked against the backdrop of an array of complex economic, political and social changes. At the turn of the millennium, we have witnessed the continuation of long-term trends in economic growth, at least in the developed and newly industrializing world, but accompanied by a more uneven distribution of wealth in many countries, coupled with concerns about sustainability. At the same time, shifts in the distribution of political power between different tiers of state, changing international relationships, and the fundamental change from an industrial to a post-industrial society, with its massive implications for labour markets and social security institutions, add to a sense of profound transformation.

These changes have been accompanied by a major re-appraisal of the roles of government, market, third sector and the family. In large part, this re-appraisal reflects changes in the values, beliefs and expectations of populations, as well as awareness of new and diverse needs and problems associated with long-term demographic trends as diverse as increased longevity, greater social and geographic mobility, and growing cultural diversity and co-existence.

Struggling to come to terms with these changes, policy makers from institutions as diverse as the World Bank, the European Union, national governments and local public administrations have turned to the third sector more than ever before. Privatization efforts, renewed attention to both the responsibilities and rights of citizenship, the search for innovations in social welfare delivery, and the quest to find ways of integrating vulnerable or socially excluded people into society have all led policy makers to the third sector. The sector has experienced a rapid transition from obscurity and assumed irrelevance to almost unseemly endorsement and lavish political acknowledgement. And while some chapters in this volume point to gaps between political rhetoric and actual policy making, the sheer level of activity among policymakers to encourage its development signal that there is more to this than simply 'hot air.'

Policies have followed a variety of courses. As we have seen, in some countries (the Netherlands being the clearest example), policy makers and many researchers tend to see nonprofit organizations less as a 'sector' as such but rather as 'discrete' actors in 'vertical' fields like education, social services, training and employment, or the environment. In other countries, however, a more strategic, 'horizontal' agenda is emerging, which does correspond explicitly to the notion of a separate sector that cuts across otherwise balkanized vertical policy fields. At a minimum, this amounts to a recognition that these organizations can and do face a large number of shared legal and fiscal considerations simply by virtue of their common nonprofit-distributing character and constitutional separation from the state (see Salamon and Anheier 1997). The state's efforts to adapt and redesign legal frameworks and fiscal treatments can thus be seen as a crucial aspect of the shaping of the third sector's policy environment. Sector-specific policies going beyond legal and tax policies have also emerged. These range from the modification of state bureaucracies to include specialized, relatively low-visibility personnel and departments dedicated to cross-cutting 'horizontal' issues such as volunteering and 'infrastructure' (as in the US and the UK), to incorporation into the world of high politics, as with the extraordinary involvement of NGOs as 'representatives of the public interest' in the Filipino Congress (see Cariño, Chapter 16 in this volume).

Whatever combination of *de jure* and *de facto* actions underpin this 'mainstreaming' of the third sector (Kendall 2000a), a result is that 'the state' looms very large indeed for third sector organizations. Increasingly, nonprofit organizations are finding themselves part of private/public partnerships that enlist them in complex networks of responsibilities, financial obligations and accountability requirements *vis-à-vis* different stakeholders. These can involve not only multiple tiers of the state as funders and regulators, but also non-state actors as providers of private finance, and users or beneficiaries of services – not to mention traditional private donors, volunteers involved in governance, resource acquisition and services, and paid staff, too. Reconciling these diverse and sometimes conflicting constituencies can be a fraught and exhausting process (see Anheier 2000; Hudson 1999).

To thicken the plot further, while these organizational and relational dilemmas have generally been managed in the context of overall third sector growth as emphasized throughout this volume, this trend conceals ongoing changes in its composition, which in turn seem to reflect an ongoing rebalancing of interests in civil society at large. For example, many countries see a decline in traditional social organizations such as work-based and class-oriented associations, major churches, and political parties; and many established forms of voluntary organization still rooted in theory and practice in pre-modern and industrial era forms of organizing are experiencing falls in membership, and are losing the political clout and integrative capacity they once had.

At the same time, the third sector's growth as a whole demonstrates the extent to which other forms of voluntary action seem to be thriving in both developed and developing countries, and to an extent that more than compensates for this decline in traditional forms. Examples include user-controlled and self-help groups expressing more assertive and diverse citizen collective action, and the formation and defence of new identities; organizations addressing ecological and environmental concerns; entities formed specifically to respond to global problems of social development; agencies geared towards innovation in services and successfully mobilizing the expertise of professionals, or the experiential knowledge of local people; hybrid forms of agency created to circumvent obstructive public sector regulations or to meet particular needs judged incompatible with the maximization of shareholder value; and organizations which have been created out of the new networks facilitated by modern technological and communicative innovation, sometimes representing new alliances of socially excluded groups and their empathizers catalysed by 'social entrepreneurs' (Leadbetter 1999; Giddens 2000).

Against this rapidly changing and turbulent backdrop, the contributors to this volume tend to emphasize not one set of crossroads but many different ones. In particular, the process of applying Salamon's 'four crises' template, as a launchpad for organizing accounts of national policy situations in some of the chapters in this volume, reveals the extent to which economic, fiscal, effectiveness and legitimacy concerns are pervasive, but tend to have different meanings in different countries, and rarely have sufficient salience to amount to a full-blown 'crisis' in each case. Moreover, even where they are seen to be significant individually, they do not always seem to jointly cumulate in a 'systemic' crisis, but instead hang together loosely, without any underlying connectedness or interdependence being recognized by the policy designers, implementers and researchers who together form each country or region's 'epistemic community' (Haas 1992).

In sum, using the 'crossroads' and 'crises' cues as a device for exploring shared policy questions in the context of significant overall expansion has served to underline the third sector's much heralded diversity. By demonstrating how third sector policy problems are constituted differently in different countries and regions, are open to varying interpretations, and have generated contrasting policy responses, we can begin to reveal more fully than has been possible before the richness and depth of third sector activity.

Ultimately, however, simply demonstrating diversity in the context of quantitative growth within and between different countries is hardly a satisfying endpoint. Concluding that each case is 'unique' in how economic, fiscal, effectiveness and legitimacy problems are constituted, and in the policy responses to such problems being discussed or adopted, cannot gratify the thirst for understanding of any of the third sector's primary stakeholders. Third sector researchers must rise to the challenge of looking for 'fundamentals' and common structures that constrain and enable third sector policy across more than just one country to look to underlying forces operating at the regional, and ultimately even global, level. To do this necessitates at least two steps. First, scholars must try to expose below-the-surface processes of change and transformation (van Til 1988). To take this road is not to deny the relevance of country-specific cultural, historical and institutional factors in shaping the development of national third sectors, but rather to suggest it is worthwhile scoping out more 'seismic' constraints and influences which provide the backdrop against which more immediate and visible national changes are played out.

Second, we must take seriously the role of supranational institutions and agencies which span borders and boundaries. This is so not only because such institutions increasingly form a supplementary arena for direct policy making in their own right – as has been suggested most prominently here in the chapters dealing with the EU's painfully emerging posture towards the third sector of its own member states. But it is also true because the possibilities for domestic policies are indirectly constrained by the economic and political climate created by such institutions, as the experience of the developing world and economies in transition underlines perhaps most dramatically.

In the remainder of this chapter, we therefore tentatively seek to sketch out some significant dimensions of underlying institutional and structural change.[1] The analytic dimensions are: *social*, interpreted as relating to the third sector's role in relation to welfare systems, and where our account is primarily retrospective; *political*, where we look to the possible future impacts of changes in the 'layering' of polities; and *economic*, where we consider ongoing changes in the third sector's contribution to economic life, considered in relation to alternative organizational forms such as market firms. While these dimensions are clearly bound up with one another in complex ways, we treat them separately – not to deny this inter-dependency, but purely as an analytic device to make it easier to tease out underlying trends and processes. By way of conclusion, in each case we summarize our argument in the form of propositions to guide further research.

The social dimension: a retrospective view on the third sector's role in welfare system 'structural adjustment'

Many of the chapters in this volume stress how the social contributions of the third sector can only be understood as part of public welfare systems for social protection, finance and regulation that states have developed (cf. Kuhnle and Selle 1992; Salamon 1995). Logically therefore, to understand the nature of the social pressures facing it, one has to understand how *welfare states* themselves are having to respond to ongoing changes in the social, economic and political contexts in which they find themselves. Although the social dimension of third sector organizations is not reducible to those activities pursued in and around 'welfare states', this does at least give us a point of departure for addressing one centrally important aspect of the third sector's social role.[2]

Moreover, it is in the welfare sphere of social activity that writers have most systematically attempted to build theories attending to underlying structures and processes. Yet despite much talk of 'crises' in writings on the welfare state in the last quarter of the twentieth century, one of the most striking aspects of the more considered recent 'stocktaking' literature on developed welfare states has been its acknowledgement that the 'crisis' in which influential writers of the New Left and New Right argued it was structurally implicated has not materialized.[3] In contrast to developing countries and transition economies, the welfare systems of Western market economies have not experienced crises-induced catastrophic collapse. To the contrary, they have weathered the storms generated by exogenous shocks (such as the 1970s oil crises), internal 'contradictions' and other theoretically destructive systemic tendencies. Moreover, in those Western states where it has deeper historical roots, welfare state spending has tended to stabilize at least in terms of its aggregate share of GDP, and overall remained reasonably popular with citizens (C. Pierson 1998). In general, as Mishra has recently surmised, the 'incremental reform package [represented by welfare capitalism] has not only not been a failure, rather it has been highly successful' (1999: 112).

Following Chistopher Pierson (1998), instead of 'crisis', the best label we can probably use to portray developments in established Western democracies, at least up until the early 1980s, is as involving 'structural adjustments' whereby extensive *qualitative* changes have taken place in both the internal character of welfare states, and the way they relate to their political, economic and social environments while leaving the aggregate picture relatively secure.

Writers such as Pierson who have drawn attention to and sought to explain this unanticipated resilience have tended to focus on a number of contributory factors which *incidentally* affect the third sector, without drawing out the latter's role in this process. These include the redistribution of spending programmes within aggregate budgets in line with populist priorities, and concomitant cuts to the eligibility and entitlements of groups seen as 'undeserving'; the adoption of quasi-market and more contractual styles of service delivery in attempts to deliver publicly funded services at lower cost; political and ideological shifts facilitating such reordering, perhaps driven by the economic climate; and a new emphasis on 'active' labour market policies to push traditionally welfare-dependent citizens back into jobs, and thus limit the systemic costs of unemployment as far as possible.

The chapters on the US, UK and German experience in particular reflect how some of these trends, and particularly the first two, have fed through to deeply affect third sector service providers involved in welfare service delivery systems. But the point to emphasize here is that the third sector's response to these changes, however many strains and stresses those have created for *that* sector, can also be understood as *facilitating* a much wider process of social structural adjustment. Whether or not the third sector has now reached its own internal crisis point, an equally important social phenomenon to be explained must be its relative contribution in preventing a wider systemic crisis up until the last decade of the twentieth century.

A central question of particular relevance for both welfare state and third sector theorists then becomes: What is it about the third sector that allowed it to facilitate crisis avoidance through incremental reform or 'structural adjustment' in the 1970s and 1980s? We are thus discussing this question in the context of a time period prior to the marked recent intensification of pressures associated with economic globalization on welfare systems.

Broadly speaking, there seem to be four ways in which the third sector's activities in and around welfare states could be said to result in the 'smoothing over' of systemic change processes.[4] First, and perhaps most obviously, the third sector can be a desirable ally for the state to the extent that it mobilizes human and financial resources that otherwise would not be available to it. Accessing voluntary inputs in the form of volunteer contributions and private giving for welfare tasks is evidently one way in which the state can avoid financial responsibilities which otherwise would add to the expense of operating the welfare state (with its assumed deleterious knock-on effects for private capital), especially when economic conditions are unfavourable. In addition, however, one could argue that even when the third sector does not secure 'added value' from independent private sources, but instead essentially blends resources from different tiers of the state and varied state agencies over time, it also undertakes an adjustment role.

This is so because different state tiers and agencies may be differently vulnerable at different stages of the economic cycle, and the third sector may be well positioned to carry over surpluses earned from generous state payments in one time or service area, in order to support activities in more lean times and in other service areas. In addition, the third sector is often well placed in the first place to strategically access budgets from across different functional state departments. Indeed, the *raison d'être* of many third sector organizations is to respond to such 'messy', otherwise unmet needs. For example, in the UK, third sector organizations have been purposefully formed by a mixture of independent and state initiative to address in an integrated way the sorts of social needs which call for a multiple intervention, because housing, social and health needs are interwoven with one another (Wigglesworth and Kendall 2000).

Second, it is now widely argued that the portrayal of welfare state expenditures as tending to be 'unproductive' unless directly and unambiguously tied to the interests of capital is grossly misleading. Historically, elites have often justified these expenditures on welfare as 'investments' to improve the capabilities of the citizenry. More recently, economists have emphasized how pervasive and cumulative market failures provide an efficiency-based rationale for such state interventions, particularly in health and education, so as to ensure more appropriate levels of investment in human capital than would otherwise be the case (Barr 1993; Esping-Anderson 1994).

Public social expenditures on the third sector in these fields can similarly be portrayed as productive for the economy as a whole through their enhancement of human capital. But resourcing for third sector activities more generally has recently also been argued to be productive through its positive impact on levels of *social* capital too. To the extent third sector organizations contribute to bonds of trust and norms of reciprocity which facilitate efficiency and effectiveness in economic life (Putnam 1993; Pharr and Putnam 2000), state support for the third sector may be significant in contributing to, rather than undermining, the smooth mutual functioning of the economy and welfare systems, perhaps particularly at crucial times of stress and transition.

Third, some writers have pointed to the ambiguities that often reside in third sector organizations' structures, policies, purposes and financial relations with the state (Seibel 1990; Billis and Glennerster 1997). This 'open', indeterministic character can be used as an advantage if 'muddling through' is required during times of change. Seibel (1990) even explicitly characterized the third sector as a safety valve or 'shunting yard' for insoluble social problems. By this logic, it matters not whether the third sector functions efficiently and effectively. Indeed, Seibel rehearses a range of reasons why we should expect *in*efficiency and *in*effectiveness: what is important is that the impression is given that 'something is being done'. In this sense, the third sector helps to create a sense of welfare system legitimacy even if it does not actually enhance its performance in either the short or longer term.

Finally, an important aspect of many traditional diagnoses of welfare crisis, but especially those of the New Right, was the supposed tendency of welfare capitalist systems to generate more and more 'vested' or 'sectional' interests, defending their own pet programmes and public expenditure priorities. Both 'insiders' such as service professionals, public bureaucrats and publicly funded employees, and 'outsiders', particularly single-issue pressure groups, were charged with 'irresponsibly' claiming resources for their own advantage, without taking into account the diffuse interests of the many, in particular, taxpayers.

The result, so the argument goes, was that aggregate public expenditure on social welfare tended over time to move away from its optimal level as demands on the state accumulate, with private market activities crowded out both directly in the production of goods and services, and indirectly by the adverse affects on financial and monetary markets. A number of ways can be suggested as to how the third sector's activities may have helped to prevent this process spiralling out of control. First, the third sector has often acted as an important pioneer of new services, and incubator of innovation in the social services field, often prompted by time-limited small-scale public financial support (Kramer 1981; Knapp *et al.* 1990; Osborne 1998).

By acting as a 'test bed' for new public initiatives, the third sector has offered state decision-makers an intermediate possibility between complete policy inaction on the one hand and unconditional commitment of public resources on the other. The state thus has a wider policy repertoire than it would otherwise have had: new demands for social welfare services *may* go on to be absorbed by the state as full blown financial responsibilities, but this is not *necessarily* the case, and valuable time can be bought in the meantime. This may of course be particularly relevant in times of economic under-performance, when a more buoyant situation is anticipated as likely to emerge in the medium or longer term.

While this aspect of the third sector's involvement suggests the possibility of 'stalling' and the short-term avoidance of public financial commitment in line with a given set of public expectations, it can also be argued that features of the third sector allow it particular influence in actually changing public expectations. Given the apparent success of welfare systems (Mishra 1999), we need to look for routes by which the third sector has played a role in ensuring expectations have tended towards 'realism' rather than 'irresponsibility'. A number of theoretical possibilities suggest themselves. First, this position is adopted in the literature on '(neo) corporatism'. Such a system involves state and third sector 'peak associations' in institutionalized and semi-institutionalized contexts in ongoing dialogue and negotiation which can involve mutual accommodation and learning as part of the 'concertation' process (Streeck and Schmitter 1985; Cohen and Rogers 1995). To the extent that such arrangements foster 'realism' in expectations, the downward adjustment by 'peak associations' of their demands on the public purse, in response to a combination of information from and persuasion by state actors, could be a highly relevant outcome.

However, focusing on the possible advantages of neo-corporatist arrangements provides a relatively rather limited explanation of the third sector's role in the adjustment of social expectations. Such institutional structures are limited to a number of countries (most famously, the consociational democracies of Northwestern Europe; see Lipjhart 1999). Moreover, even in those countries in which they do function, they are feasible only under rather strict conditions, since they can operate only in professionalized fields involving members whom peak associations are able to 'deliver' for the state. In unprofessionalized or semi-professionalized fields without hegemonic membership-based peak associations or dominant public bureaucracies with whom to liaise, any third sector's role in the adjustment of expectations must involve other processes.

It seems plausible to suggest that, absent corporatist structures, third sector involvement in welfare systems can contribute to 'realism' in expectations in two primary ways. First, to the extent third sector organizations are required to have an explicit commitment to the public good as a condition for achieving fiscal and legal privileges, in making demands on public budgets they are required in law to 'present their case' in as balanced and 'objective' a fashion as is feasible. The information disseminated by 'public good' third sector organizations can significantly shape expectations around social conditions or problems, and frame issues in particular ways. In some countries this even extends to the requirement that such evidence be 'non partisan' or 'not political' (Randon and 6 1994; Salamon and Toepler 2000).

A second source of 'realism' may stem from the practicalities of third sector engagement as implementers of social welfare policies particularly on a routine, ongoing basis. Such involvement necessitates continuous, low-visibility communication between public officials and third sector organizations. Even if such discussions are formally around technical issues of implementation for given policies rather than broader questions of policy design or budgetary allocation, they can provide opportunities for informal mutual learning and hence expectation adjustment in third sector-relevant policy contexts. Such engagement may be more associated with government/third sector relations than government/for-profit sector ones, even where the latter are also involved in policy implementation, because perceptions of shared value bases, priorities and even more general world views facilitate communication and constructive discourse (Wistow 1996; Kendall 2000b).

Finally, as a counterpoint to the importance of vertical professional hierarchies as transmitters of policy-relevant expertise to public officials emphasized by theorists of corporatism, an inclusive understanding also requires recognition of the important role of 'useable knowledge' in problem solving (Lindblom and Cohen 1979). To the extent that third sector organizations are repositories of lay understandings of community level problems, perhaps reflecting their origins in horizontal community networks and relationships (Milovsky 1987), they can bring crucial experiential knowledge to the policy process. While these inputs may be less formalized or visible than those transmitted via corporatist style arrangements, they nevertheless can enhance the 'intelligence' of policy making in terms of the concomitant 'realism' of policy actors' expectations.

We summarize our discussion of the social dimension of third sector policies with the following proposition :

> *Proposition 1: The third sector has played a heretofore underestimated dynamic social role, allowing welfare systems in developed democracies to successfully achieve 'structural adjustment', thus avoiding the lurch into 'crisis' predicted by some welfare state theorists.*

As we have seen, important aspects of this process follow from the ability to mobilize additional resources; enhance national stocks of human and social capital to improve economic functioning; sustain system legitimacy by 'keeping up appearances'; and the capacity to increase the intelligence of policy processes, particularly by fostering realism in social expectations via both formal and informal routes.

How does the situation in developing and transition countries differ from the scenario sketched out above for Western welfare capitalist economies? Of course, a much more detailed analysis would be needed to identify the full range of factors at work. But we can speculate that the chronic weakness of state structures and frequent regime failures in many developing countries, which have so limited public sectors' capacities to support the third sector there (Anheier and Salamon 1998), has in turn fed back to generate severe adverse consequences for the public sector. Because public sector/third sector partnerships have typically not had the opportunity to mature, the third sector's capacity to contribute to long-term structural adjustment processes for the mutual advantage of both sectors has been severely constrained. Welfare systems in the developing world have often, therefore, experienced uneven and abrupt patterns of change over time, rather than the relatively smooth incremental reforms characteristic of Western systems. Similarly, in transition economies, in part because of the deep institutional schism between state socialism and market reform, relations between state and third sector have tended to remain weak, underdeveloped and overly short-termist. In these cases too, it has also typically not been possible to capture the potential gains that only durable and mature relations can bring.

The political dimension: the emergence of supranational components to third sector policy

The fundamentally different situation of the third sector in welfare domains in developing countries and transition economies when compared to most Western countries, also seems to apply to its positioning in the realm of politics more generally. In part because of the financial weakness, fragility and unreliability of national public sectors (not to mention domestic private sectors) as sponsors and supporters, the third sector has systematically looked to the international donor community for succour.

The domestic deficit has therefore been overlain by an emerging sphere of internationalism, and a growing presence of supranational governmental and non-governmental actors. If one of the most important traditional policy dilemmas for the third sector has been 'How and on what terms to engage with an unpredictable and ineffective domestic state?', the third sector in transition economies and developing countries alike also now confronts a new challenge: 'How and on what terms to respond to the economic and political power wielded by international organizations like the IMF and World Bank?'. The last two decades of structural adjustment programmes (in their usual sense) in many parts of the developing world suggests that international organizations now seem to rival the political influence of national governments in a significant number of cases, so in some countries this second question is already just as salient as the older one.

Turning back to the Western developed world, it is in the EU countries where the implications of the ongoing redistribution of power for the policy competences of national and supranational political authorities has received most scholarly attention (Richardson 1996; Wallace and Wallace 2000; Rosamond 2000). As far as the specifics of third sector policy are concerned, a debate about the respective roles of national and supranational government has rather belatedly started to gather momentum, although the fault lines of this still-emerging policy field are far from clear. Indeed, at first sight, there seem to be major barriers to the emergence of any EU policy engagement with the third sector at all. First, most European third sectors' activities are concentrated in fields which lie at or close to the core of 'welfare states', and this has been a policy terrain which national political elites have jealously protected from EU competence.[5] Second, with the notable exception of the policy sub-field of overseas development and relief, there is no evidence of European general public opinion in favour of policy proactivity on the part of the EU institutions, nor obvious impetus provided by national labour movements or employers.

Third, the resource capabilities of the EU for policy action seem extremely limited. In terms of financial resources, a climate of austerity prevails in the context of the ongoing and planned reforms to reorganize the governance and enhance the effectiveness of the Commission, and in anticipation of the costs that follow as enlargement takes place. Third sector policy seems poorly placed to claim scarce resources because, by its very 'horizontal' nature, it does not fit with any one of the single 'vertical' traditional policy fields and associated interests, as reflected, for example, in the various Commission Directorates-General or European Parliament committees. The question of the appropriate 'institutional home' to act as a focal point for sector-wide policy remains a matter of considerable debate, at both national and European levels, and seems to have inhibited policy making.

Finally, as we reported in Chapter 10 of this volume, there still remains a basic lack of agreement in Europe as to what the third sector actually is, and therefore how the problems to which policy might react should be understood. In particular, a fault line in understanding exists between the two most active protagonists in the world of high politics, where supportive policy has to date involved largely symbolic policy statements. French actors have emphasized both third sector connectedness to the economy *and* its social embeddedness, while German policy entrepreneurs have sought to characterize it as, in essence, a 'social' rather than 'economic' matter. This tension and ambiguity was an important ingredient of the policy inertia and political stalemate which characterized the 1990s in this field.

However, set against this are increasingly persuasive, and ever more widely accepted reasons for taking the European dimension of third sector policy seriously in the new millennium in the longer term. First, the literature on the development of European social policy alerts us to the sense in which national welfare states are, in fact, '*semi*-sovereign'. In particular, to the extent that quasi-market type reforms are adopted in fields such as health and social care, and third sector organizations are the providers of those services, the European Court of Justice (ECJ) has competence in enforcing 'market compatibility' requirements (Leibfried and Pierson 1995).

Indeed, the ECJ has recently cast judgement on the legality of arrangements in one member state for privileging nonprofit over for-profit provision in a regional quasi-market in social services (nursing care for older people), which involved cross-border activities (European Court of Justice 1997). In addition, even in those countries where quasi-market style reforms have not explicitly driven policy redesign, sector-spanning 'partnerships' as a strand of 'horizontal' social exclusion oriented policies, particularly in the area of urban policy, have increasingly been promoted by alliances of local, regional and European-level actors.

Second, because third sector organizations are significant economic actors more generally (Salamon *et al.* 1999) and not just in quasi-market situations, they are *de facto* affected by both EU labour market and fiscal policy. Moreover, this economic activity is not entirely confined to within-country transactions. Not insignificant financial flows originating in and/or destined for the third sector now pass across borders in the case of at least two EU member states, the UK and Germany (Nahrlich and Zimmer 2000; Kendall *et al.* 2000).

Third, as we emphasized in our opening chapter, despite the inertia of high-profile political actors, there has been room for manoeuvre within the EU institutions for creative low-visibility bureaucrats to start to build, from the bottom up, a sector-specific agenda (see Anheier *et al.*, Chapter 1 in this volume). For their part, NGOs have been increasingly active lobbyists on the European stage (Thomas 1999; Cullen 1999; Warleigh 2000). These joint efforts have yielded, *inter alia*, transnational network creation and mobilization along specific 'vertical' issue lines, with considerable potential to form the building blocks for more, cross-cutting 'horizontal' alliances between third sector actors; the establishment of new, albeit for now small, sector-specific budget lines; and attempts to 'bend' existing structures and regulations so as to provide a place for the third sector where none previously existed.

Finally, in the world of high politics, while support has still remained essentially rhetorical, its basis has recently broadened and deepened. Within the Commission, the Employment and Social Affairs Directorate-General has continued to lobby for the development of an explicitly 'horizontal' third sector policy to secure greater 'coordination' and 'coherence' (Commission of the European Community 2000) supported by more active interest from the Secretariat-General, building upon its earlier joint initiative with what was then DGXXIII (Commission of the European Community 1997). The Economic and Social Committee has increasingly added its voice to the debate. What is perhaps even more significant is the recent European Council's unprecedented explicit recognition of a potential role for 'civil society ... and NGOs as ... partners' in implementing its agreed strategic goal of sustainable economic growth and social cohesion (European Council, Lisbon 2000: para. 38).

This joint rhetorical recognition from the national heads of government and the head of the Commission had been preceded by a call from the President of the European Parliament to mobilize the third sector in order to support vulnerable citizens; and has been followed up by the Commission Vice-President with allusions to the important but largely unspecified role foreseen for civil society in the future Europe. This seems to suggest a new order of political will to seriously develop a meaningful European policy towards the third sector, capable of tackling entrenched 'vertical' interests in the context of the Vice-President's wider ongoing programme for root-and-branch reform in the Commission, is now in place for the first time.

> *Proposition 2: In the developing world and economies in transition, the third sector is already significantly engaging with supranational agencies in addition to nation states. In contrast, in the EU, national (and sub-national) governments continue unambiguously to be the* primary *levels of the polity to which the third sector, and particularly its welfare core, relates. This will continue to be the case in the immediate future. However, over time a range of* de facto *and* de jure *pressures will result in the emergence of significant supranational policy competence relating to the third sector's welfare services core in the EU.*

The economic/organizational dimension

Having looked at social and political dynamics, we now examine the economic/organizational dimension. What light can prevailing economic theories of the nonprofit sector shed on recent developments and future prospects?[6] These theories focus our attention on the influence of economic forces in terms of the interaction of supply and demand conditions (Anheier and Ben-Ner 1997). By interpreting human interactions in all sectors with the aid of this market analogy, they have sought to explain how knowledge of particular 'technical' properties of goods and services, together with market structure considerations, can help us identify economic activities in which the nonprofit form has a 'comparative advantage' over for-profit and public sector alternatives. Most attention has focused on the choice between the for-profit and nonprofit form. In particular, for given incomes and tastes/values (defined as the relevant constraints and preferences on both the demand and supply/entrepreneurship side), dimensionalizing goods and services in terms of their degree of publicness (nonrivalry and nonexcludability), the extensiveness of problems of information asymmetry, and perhaps their 'relational' content can, some theorists argue, uniquely determine whether the nonprofit or for-profit form is the more efficient choice of auspice (Ben-Ner and Gui 2000).[7] By looking at how advances in technology change the dimensionality of goods and services and the repertoire of institutional responses to the associated 'failures', in the context of increasing income, education and concomitant value shifts, predictions for changing sectoral divisions of labour can be made for each industry (with its particular dimensionality). The picture for the economy as a whole can then be portrayed by aggregating these individual scenarios, and analysing developments through this theoretical lens suggests the third sector's economic contribution overall may stagnate or even decline in coming years, with the for-profit sector making up the difference (Ben-Ner 2000).

This is a complex line of argument, to which we cannot do justice here, but one example, concerning how change along one of the dimensions, that relating to the information asymmetry, can change the identity of the 'preferred' sector, can be used by way of illustration. A decade ago, Hansmann (1990) showed how the US savings and loan industry, including parts of the banking and insurance sector, underwent a fundamental transition from predominantly nonprofit to for-profit status as government regulation and industry supervision came into place. Prior to this transition, the nonprofit form, by blunting incentives to act opportunistically (to make profits), acted as a crucial signal of trustworthiness, without which customers would have been worse off. Yet with the introduction of an increasingly sophisticated regulatory regime, technological innovation worked to effectively prevent the systemic abuse of clients. With information asymmetry addressed and consumers less vulnerable, the nonprofit form *per se* was 'less needed' to signal trustworthiness relative to other institutional arrangements, and the balance of comparative advantage shifted in favour of other 'solutions'.

Most importantly, these changes make possible (and efficient) both an increased presence of for-profit providers – through new entrants and status 'conversion' – and a greater reliance on market-type revenue across all sectors. This pattern of for-profit penetration in traditionally nonprofit (and public) dominated fields is a familiar one, particularly in the US and UK. Moreover, once the precedent of for-profit provision in previously 'no go' zones of the economy for profit-oriented firms has been established, 'reputation effects' and demand side learning can kick in to the benefit of those (nominally) for-profit suppliers which seem to be operating in a non-opportunistic fashion (Forder *et al.* 1996; Kendall 2000b).

Yet the multidimensional 'comparative advantage' logic also alerts us to the extent to which a wide range of other factors can also come into play to ensure that the nonprofit form remains the 'efficient' option for a wide range of types of service. In particular, the other dimensions discussed may be less amenable to technocratic 'solution'. The emergence of new needs involving a range of vulnerabilities and hence new informational problems (by definition not overseen by state regulation because of their novelty) and the technically insurmountably public and relational character of some existing provision (including environ-mental actions and activities with a strong 'sociability' or 'processual' component) are particularly noteworthy.

Moreover, the spiralling of citizen expectations, leading to ever more varie-gated and complex demands, can mean that state regulators are chasing a 'moving target' as far as quality standards in particular are concerned: the gap between what is capable of being regulated and consumer aspirations is far from easy to close. This can leave attributes of goods and services of significance to those who demand them unaddressed by the systemic confidence that comes with regulation (Sako 1992), even in such apparently well regulated fields as nursing care in the United States (Weisbrod and Schlesinger 1986; Spector *et al.* 1998). All these factors mean that there are still considerable technical limits to the sorts of services and market niches open to for-profit penetration, and that many economic activities will remain a 'best fit' to the nonprofit sector, although as we have seen, Ben-Ner has claimed that the net effect will be contraction rather than growth.

In sum, this framework can offer us an ambitious and systematic 'technical' account of the economic strengths and weaknesses of each of the traditional sectors. However, in abstracting from the *political* economy of decision-making in the interests of parsimony, the approach neglects at least two important consid-erations which seem relevant in taking a prospective view regarding possibilities for the third sector's relative economic contribution. In this sense at least, it does not provide a sufficient explanation of economic developments.

First, implicit in the approach is an image of the state as an 'objective', neutral, benign and capable regulator. Not only is the state assumed to act as an enforcer of the non-distribution constraint of nonprofits themselves, and thus be central in safeguarding that form's relative trustworthiness (and by implication its comparative advantage in handling information asymmetries); it is also required to operate smoothly, efficiently and 'objectively' at the industry (multi-sector) level, in order to enable for-profit penetration to be feasible as described above. If the state's willingness and ability to act in these ways is constrained or absent, then the explanation is simply not applicable, at least in its conventional 'legal-istic' form.[8] The material in this volume seems to suggest that in both the economies in transition and the developing world, the state tends to operate neither as a reliable, trust-enforcing regulator at sector level, nor with the requi-site amount of sophistication at industry level. It therefore seems clear that in the economies in transition and the developing world, the trajectory of nonprofit field initiation, followed by a combination of state field-level regulation and for-profit penetration, is less likely to unfold, at least in that sequence for those reasons. This explains why theorists on economies in transition, for example, have looked to different paradigms and alternative arguments predicated on rather different assumptions about the character and role of the state in economic life (see in particular Sokolowski 2000; Böröcz 2000).

Moreover, even in the developed world, while reasonably durable and reliable arrangements for generic third sector regulation do typically seem to be in place or in the process of introduction, industry-specific regulations may either be relatively underdeveloped, or not always of the type that allows for-profit penetration.[9] The former, involving incompleteness in terms of coverage or simply implementation failures, may flow from resource constraints in the context of public fiscal austerity (or even 'crisis'): while regulation may be less resource-intensive than direct provision (Majone 1996), it still makes significant claims on public budgets.

As far as regulatory design is concerned, two ingredients seem relevant. First, regulations may be framed which do not explicitly exclude for-profits, but which implicitly disfavour them. This could happen on one hand, by emphasizing aspects of performance either with which compliance is easier in the nonprofit sectors; or, conversely, which are so minimalistic in generating systemic confidence trust that a large degree of reliance on sector-signalled trustworthiness remains than might be 'technically' optimal. Second, in some cases, regulations may even explicitly forbid for-profit operations because of claims or beliefs that profit making is inherently incompatible with the activity in question, regardless of any apparent 'technical' argument to the contrary.[10]

Supporters of such 'for-profit unfriendly' regulation may of course include the very third sector organizations who pioneered the services in question. These may often be particularly significant actors in the regulatory aspects of policy design, for the reasons discussed earlier in this chapter. To the extent they use this positioning to pursue 'vested interest' goals (protecting institutional territory), consciously or otherwise (*despite* any of the legal-institutional pressures noted earlier to operate in the 'public interest') this may serve to limit for-profit sector involvement in fields where 'technically' it may have a 'comparative advantage'. To treat such powerful countervailing forces as merely transitory 'institutional inertia' seems to understate considerably the influence third sector organizations may wield by virtue of their 'insider' status as far as policy design is concerned.

The above arguments are essentially speculative: remarkably little is known empirically about the political economy of regulatory design in third sector-relevant industries, and little has been written to elaborate the theme conceptually. However, a second difficulty is both more fundamental and more general, and highlights the extent to which the sector model used as the launch pad for the above analysis is inherently problematic. At an empirical level, an increasingly widespread observation that prompts this concern is that, in recent years, there has been a proliferation of organizational arrangements which transcend the three sector (public, private, third) model in the sense that they cannot be uniquely assigned to any one sector. Rather, they involve 'hybrid' or multiple sector 'partnership' arrangements which significantly combine the features traditionally associated with each of the sectors (Weisbrod 1998). Put differently, sectoral 'blurring' or 'fuzziness' is significant *and* increasing (Kendall and Knapp 1995; Kramer 2000; Moulton and Anheier 2000). Analysis which focuses on economic activities (traditional) sector by (traditional) sector, and seeks to uniquely allocate them accordingly, is inherently unable to treat such developments within its scope of explanation.

One apparent way of responding to this issue, without jettisoning the logic of technical comparative advantage, would be simply to specify additional hybrid 'sectors' at the interstices of the public, private and third sectors. These might then tend to be 'best fits' in the case of goods and services with mixed or 'intermediate' characteristics able to combine strengths and weaknesses (and hence net comparative advantage) *across* sectors. Increased blurring or hybridization could then be understood as the result of some combination of a greater supply of, and increased demand for, goods and services with such intermediate features.

Such a modification offers considerable potential. However, it seems unlikely to provide a full explanation for the economic emergence of 'hybrids'. This is because ultimately there are limits in the extent to which goods and services can be uniquely assigned to sectors simply by an 'objective' reading of their technical characteristics. Why is this the case? First, our above analysis of the issues of political economy at stake in regulatory design indicated the importance of acknowledging the constraints and pressures on, and limitations of the state in, that specific aspect of policy. Such difficulties seem likely to also be relevant with regard to policy more generally. In particular, the definition of the public good which underpins policy and hence permeates decision-making in choice between sectors (however many are identified!) may deviate significantly or 'bend' in response to (innocent or strategic) political pressures. This could result in fewer or more 'hybrid' organizations emerging than the theory would suggest.

Second, we have recently been forcefully reminded of the limitations of any approach claiming to allocate goods and activities definitively as 'public' or 'private' – or by extension, unambiguously to a place on the continuum somewhere between (Mansbridge 1998; Calhoun 1998). By this logic, even after controlling for all the influences outlined in the 'technocratic' account and settling on a quite specific place and moment in historical time, the same economic activity could be viewed as 'in the public benefit' (to a certain degree) by one constituency but not so for others. This would be the case whether the method of definition was essentially 'utilitarian' (technocratic), or was influenced by more explicitly political concerns, as referred to above. Different constituencies and interests, shaped by social, cultural and political experiences and world views, will hold fundamentally different, contested views as to the amount of 'publicness' in a given good or service.

If we wish to understand the direction of change, we then need to ask if the extent to which the meanings of 'public' and 'private' are contested seems to be increasing or decreasing over time. Hybrids proliferation could then be seen as constituting a sort of 'tension field' (Evers 1993), providing arenas for the creative synergies between opposing understandings and approaches, and playing an important part in resolving or managing such apparent conflicts in a mutually beneficial way.

We would point to a number of reasons why this contestation is increasing, with a concomitant growth of cross-sector hybrids. First, there are the social/structural shifts referred to by Wolch (Chapter 4 in this volume). Trends towards social fragmentation and increasing citizen assertiveness, bound up with wider shifts in identity politics, may all contribute in this regard to an increased willingness to define and defend one's own definition of interests. Such trends seem to have taken place not just in the US, but in a significant number of other countries too, as reflected not least by the emphasis of contributors to this volume on the role of social movements. While some may steer clear of developing collaborative efforts with the for-profit or public sector for ideological or political reasons, many see such arrangements as a chance to push their own agendas, and engage in constructively critical dialogue.

Another reason is that in some countries, such as the UK, national legal frameworks and structures (including those relating to the third sector) still reflect formulations of 'the public good' which are widely seen as outdated and inappropriate for the twenty-first century. This has fuelled a frustrated desire for root-and-branch reform, in the absence of which policy innovators have looked for and endorsed cross-sector approaches (Mulgan and Landry 1995; Deakin 1995; Chapter 3 in this volume).

Third, there has been increasing awareness, fuelled by research and the cross-national exchange of expertise, that organizing activity through hybrid forms can work by playing to the strengths of the involved sectors (Giddens 2000; Kramer 2000). Consequently, the modern *zeitgeist* has involved an increasing willingness to 'think outside the box' in terms of looking beyond single sector solutions.

> *Proposition 3: A range of demand and supply side factors come together to explain the economic contribution of the 'traditional' third sector, which reflect such 'technical' attributes as degree of publicness, informational asymmetry and relational components. Taking into account these factors in the context of technological change and regulatory innovation, for-profit penetration may be anticipated in many fields in which the third sector has traditionally dominated. However, there are technical limits to this process. Political considerations may also serve to limit the entry of profit-oriented provision in significant parts of the economy. If we consider cross-sector 'hybrid' arrangements as within scope too, moreover, then economic growth of the third sector, inclusively defined, seems set to continue apace.*

Concluding comment

We live in a world of rapid social, economic and political change, and third sector policy scholars, as well as public policy analysts more generally, must increasingly find ways of attending to these processes in building their frameworks for analysis. In this context, we have noted the strategic importance of deepening our understanding of welfare system transformation and adjustment by accounting for the third sector's role therein; sought to identify pressures for change in their political context, in EU countries in particular; and noted how and why economic growth seems to have been accompanied by compositional change in terms of organizational form. The challenge ahead is to make sure that public policies safeguard the rich diversity of third sector life at all levels, support the emergence and development of new organizational forms, and facilitate the transition of existing ones.

Notes

1 These dimensions and the associated propositions as they relate to EU countries are discussed in more detail in Kendall (2000c).
2 We have in mind the service provision, advocacy and participation functions of the third sector in and around the core 'social welfare industries' of education and training, health, social services, housing and income maintenance. We therefore consider out-of-scope for the purposes of what follows other third sector activities such as recreation, culture and environmental action, all of which also have important social aspects.
3 As emphasized above, our remarks on the social dimension are backward-looking, and we seek to interpret developments roughly until the mid-1990s: arguably, more recently and into the future 'globalization' pressures transform the *problématique*, and prospective analysis will need to take into account the raft of issues associated therewith (Rhodes 1996; C. Pierson 1998; P. Pierson 1998; Mishra 1999; Scharpf 2000).
4 While mainstream welfare state crisis theorists such as Habermas, Offe and Gough from the left, and Olsen on the right, virtually ignored the role of third sector organizations – at least as simultaneously service providing and advocacy oriented actors – in their accounts, Wolch (1990) has provided an imaginative attempt to integrate third sector theory with this tradition of New Left theorizing on the welfare state. But in her reductionist moves to portray all but specialist advocacy third sector organizations as necessarily functional for capital and completely integrated into the 'para-state apparatus', she seems to deny any independent role for multiple-function third sector organizations.
5 Outside its social welfare oriented core, in particular policy fields, the third sector has engaged with the EU to a major degree. Most obviously, this has been the case with overseas development (see Kendall and Anheier, Chapter 10 in this volume); and environmental activity (Lowe and Ward 1998; Rootes 1999).
6 Economics has arguably been the most productive disciplinary terrain for theorizing the comparative role and contribution of the nonprofit form over the past twenty-five years or so. The approach of Ben-Ner and Gui (2000), used as a launch pad for what follows, seeks to synthesize and integrate a variety of the well known theories, including government failure (Weisbrod 1977; 1988); contract failure (Hansmann 1980; 1996); and supply-side and entrepreneurship oriented analysis (James 1987; Badelt 1997a).
7 The co-existence of the same sectors in a given field is then explained either by claiming that only one form of auspice is 'efficient', and that the other (inefficient) forms are there because of 'institutional inertia' and will disappear in the long run; or by arguing that the 'given field' is itself internally heterogeneous and characterized by dimension-relevant product differentiation. This way, sector co-existence in what appears to be the same field or type of service can be efficient if providers in

different sectors are actually inhabiting different sub-markets, which in turn vary in their dimensionality from what is typical for the field as a whole (cf. Anheier and Kendall 2000).

8 The theory also looks to stakeholder control as an explanation for the nonprofit form's trustworthiness advantage. However, it does not make clear the extent to which such a mechanism can be assumed to function in the absence of a legally enforced non-distribution constraint to underpin it.

9 While third sector-specific regulation may be relatively mature in the developed world, however, it is often still argued that there is major scope for improvement within those countries; for example, on the US case, see Fleishman 1999.

10 For example, Badelt (1997b) explains how social democratic parties in continental Europe have traditionally argued that profit making is inconsistent with caring in welfare services, a claim also still made by some trade unionists (but not the New Labour government) in the UK. Historical experiences rather than rarefied ideology can also be a factor. In the UK, state support for 'social housing', accompanied by a dense regulatory regime, has been limited to the nonprofit sector, at least in part because of memories concerning the 'exploitative' activities of for-profit landlords in the inter-war years (Wigglesworth and Kendall 2000).

References

Anheier, H. K. (2000) 'Managing non-profit organisations: towards a new approach', Civil Society Working Paper 1, Centre for Civil Society, London: Centre for Civil Society, London School of Economics and Political Science.

Anheier, H. K. and Ben-Ner, A. (1997) 'Shifting boundaries: long-term changes in the size of the for-profit, non-profit, cooperative and government sectors', *Annals of Public and Cooperative Economics*, 68, 3: 335–53.

Anheier, H. K. and Kendall, J. (2000) 'Trust and voluntary organisations: three theoretical approaches', Civil Society Working Paper 5, London: Centre for Civil Society, London School of Economics and Political Science.

Anheier, H. K. and Salamon, L. M. (eds) (1998) *The Nonprofit Sector in the Developing World*, Manchester: Manchester University Press.

Badelt, C. (1997a) 'Entrepreneurship theories of the nonprofit sector', *Voluntas*, 8, 2: 162–78.

——(1997b) 'Contracting and institutional choice in Austria', in Perri 6 and J. Kendall (eds) *The Contract Culture in Public Services: Studies from Britain, Europe and the USA*, Aldershot: Arena.

Barr, N. (1993) *The Economics of the Welfare State*, London and Oxford: Oxford University Press.

Ben-Ner, A. (2000) 'On the boundaries of the mixed economy: the nonprofit sector between the private and public domains', paper presented at ICTR, University of the Negev, March; and Centre for Civil Society, London School of Economics, June.

Ben-Ner, A. and Gui, B. (2000) 'The theory of nonprofit organisations revisited', in H. K. Anheier and A. Ben-Ner (eds) *Advances in Theories of the Nonprofit Sector*, publisher and place unspecified.

Billis, D. and Glennerster, H. (1997) 'Human services and the voluntary sector: towards a theory of comparative advantage', *Journal of Social Policy*, 27, 1: 79–98.

Böröcz, J. (2000) 'Informality and nonprofits in East Central European capitalism', *Voluntas*, 11, 2: 123–40.

Calhoun, C. (1998) 'The public good as a social and cultural product', in W. W. Powell and E. Clemens (eds) *Private Action and the Public Good*, New Haven: Yale University Press.

Cohen, J. and Rogers, J. (eds) (1995) *Associations and Democracy*, London: Verso.

Commission of the European Community (1997) *Promoting the Role of Voluntary Organisations and Foundations in Europe*, Luxemburg: Office of Official Publications of the European Communities.

——(2000) *The Commission and Non-Governmental Organisations: Building a Stronger Partnership*, discussion paper, Brussels: European Commission.

Cullen, P. P. (1999) 'Coalitions working for social justice: transnational non-governmental organisations and international governance', paper presented at the American Socio-logical Association Annual Meeting, Chicago.

Deakin, N. (1995) 'The perils of partnership: the voluntary sector and the state, 1945–1992', in J. D. Smith, C. Rochester and R. Hedley (eds) *Introduction to the Voluntary Sector*, London: Routledge.

Esping-Anderson, G. (1994) 'Welfare states and the economy', in N. J. Smelser and R. Swedberg (eds) *The Handbook of Economic Sociology*, Princeton: Princeton University Press.

European Council, Lisbon (2000) presidency conclusions, retrieved from press release library, the internet (*http://europa.eu.int*).

European Court of Justice (1997) Sodemare SA, Anni Azzurri Holding SpA and Anni Azzuri Rezzato Srl *v.* Regione Lombardia: Freedom of establishment – Freedom to provide services – Old people's homes – Non-profit-making, Case C-70/95, European Court of Justice.

Evers, A. (1993) 'The welfare state mix approach: understanding welfare pluralism systems', in A. Evers and I. Svetlik (eds) *Balancing Pluralism: New Welfare Mixes in Care for the Elderly*, Aldershot: Avebury.

Fleishman, J. (1999) 'Public trust in not-for-profit organisations and the need for regula-tory reform', in C. T. Clotfelter and T. Ehrlich (eds) *Philanthropy and the Nonprofit Sector in a Changing America*, Indianapolis: Indiana University Press.

Forder, J., Knapp, M. and Wistow, G. (1996) 'Competition in the English mixed economy', *Journal of Social Policy*, 25, 2: 20–221.

Giddens, A. (2000) *The Third Way and its Critics*, Cambridge: Polity Press.

Haas, E. (1992) 'Introduction: Epistemic communities and international policy coordina-tion', *International Organisation*, 46, 1.

Hansmann, H. (1980) 'The role of non-profit enterprise', *Yale Law Journal*, 89, 5: 835–901.

——(1987) 'Economic theories of nonprofit organizations', in W. W. Powell (ed.) *The Nonprofit Sector: A Research Handbook*, New Haven: Yale University Press.

——(1990) in H. K. Anheier and W. Seibel (eds) *The Third Sector: Comparative Studies of Nonprofit Organizations*, Berlin and New York: DeGruyter.

——(1996) *The Ownership of Enterprise*, Cambridge MA: Harvard University Press.

Hudson, M. (1999) *Managing Without Profit*, London: Penguin.

James, E. (1987) 'The nonprofit sector in comparative perspective', in W. W. Powell (ed.) *The Nonprofit Sector: A Research Handbook*, New Haven: Yale University Press.

Kendall, J. (2000a) 'The mainstreaming of the third sector into public policy in England: whys and wherefores', Civil Society Working Paper 2, London: Centre for Civil Society, London School of Economics and Political Science.

——(2000b) 'The third sector and social care for older people in England: towards an explanation of its contrasting contributions in residential care, domiciliary care and day care', Civil Society Working Paper 8, London: Centre for Civil Society, London School of Economics and Political Science.

——(2000c) 'The third sector in the EU: social, political and economic dynamics', European University Institute Discussion Paper 2000/C/3.9, European University Institute, Florence.

Kendall, J. K., Comas-Herrera, A. and Passey, A. (2000) 'United Kingdom', in H. K. Anheier and R. List (eds) *Cross-border Philanthropy: An Exploratory Study of International Giving in the United Kingdom, United States, Germany and Japan*, West Malling: Charities Aid Foundation.

Kendall, J. and Knapp, M. R. J. (1995) 'A loose and baggy monster: boundaries, definitions and typologies', in J. Davis Smith and R. Hedley (eds) *Introduction to the Voluntary Sector*, London: Routledge.

Knapp, M. R. J., Robertson, E. and Thomason, C. (1990) 'Public money, voluntary sector: whose welfare?', in H. K. Anheier and W. Seibel (eds) *The Nonprofit Sector: International Comparative Perspectives*, Berlin and New York: de Gruyter.

Kramer, R. M. (1981) *Voluntary Agencies in the Welfare State*, Berkeley: University of California Press.

——(2000) 'A third sector in the third millennium?', *Voluntas*, 11, 1: 1–24.

Kuhnle, S. and Selle, P. (1992) *Government and Voluntary Organizations: A Related Perspective*, Aldershot: Avebury.

Leadbetter, C. (1999) *Living on Thin Air: The New Economy*, London: Viking.

Leibfried, S. and Pierson, P. (1995) 'Semisovereign welfare states: social policy in a multi-tiered Europe', in S. Leibfried and P. Pierson (eds) *European Social Policy: Between Fragmentation and Integration*, London: Brookings Institution.

Lindblom, C. E. and Cohen, D. K. (1979) *Usable Knowledge: Social Science and Social Problem Solving*, New Haven: Yale University Press.

Lipjhart, A. (1999) *Patterns of Democracy: Government Forms and Performance in thirty-six Countries*, New Haven: Yale University Press.

Lowe, P. and Ward, S. (1998) *British Environmental Policy and Europe: Politics and Policy in Transition*, London: Routledge.

Majone, G. (1996) 'A European regulatory style', in J. J. Richardson (ed.) *European Union: Power and Policy-making*, London: Routledge.

Mansbridge, J. (1998) 'On the contested nature of the public good', in W. W. Powell and E. S. Clemens (eds) *Private Action and the Public Good*, New Haven: Yale University Press.

Milovsky, C. (1987) 'Neighborhood-based organizations: a market analysis', in W. W. Powell (ed.) *The Nonprofit Sector: A Research Handbook*, New Haven and London: Yale University Press.

Mishra, R. (1999) *Globalisation and the Welfare State*, Aldershot: Edward Elgar.

Moulton, L. and Anheier, H. K. (2000) 'Public-private partnership in the United States: historical patterns and current trends', Civil Society Working Paper 16, London: Centre for Civil Society, London School of Economics and Political Science.

Mulgan, G. and Landry, C. (1995) *The Other Invisible Hand: Remaking Charity for the 21st Century*, London: Demos.

Nahrlich, S. and Zimmer, A. (2000) 'Germany', in H.K. Anheier and R. List (eds) *Cross-border philanthropy: an exploratory study of international giving in the United Kingdom, United States, Germany and Japan*, West Malling: Charities Aid Foundation.

Osborne, S. P. (1998) *Voluntary Organisations and Innovation in Public Services*, London: Routledge.

Pharr, S. J. and Putnam, R. D. (2000) *Disaffected Democracies: What's Troubling the Trilateral Countries?*, Princeton: Princeton University Press.

Pierson, C. (1998) *Beyond the Welfare State: The New Political Economy of Welfare*, University Park: Pennsylvania University Press.

Pierson, P. (1998) 'Irresistible press, immovable objects: post-industrial welfare states confront permanent austerity', *Journal of European Public Policy*, 5, 4: 539–60.

Putnam, R. D. (1993) *Making Democracy Work: Civic Traditions in Modern Italy*, Princeton: Princeton University Press.

Randon, A. and 6, P. (1994) 'Constraining campaigning: the legal treatment of non-profit policy advocacy across 24 countries', *Voluntas*, 5, 1: 27–58.

Rhodes, M. (1996) 'Globalization and west European welfare states: a critical review of recent debates', *Journal of European Social Policy*, 6, 4: 305–27.

Richardson, J. J. (ed.) (1996) *European Union: Power and Policy-making*, London: Routledge.

Romanelli, E. (1991) 'The evolution of organisational forms', *Annual Review of Sociology*, 17: 79–103.

Rootes, C. (1999) 'The Europeanisation of environmentalism', paper prepared for the conference 'L'Europe des Interêts: Lobbying, Mobilisation et Espace Publique Européen', Maison Française and Nuffield College, Oxford, October.

Rosamond, B. (2000) *Theories of European Integration*, London: Macmillan.

Sako, M. (1992) *Prices, Quality, and Trust: Inter-firm Relations in Britain and Japan*, Cambridge and New York: Cambridge University Press.

Salamon, L. M. (1995) *Partners in Public Service: Government–Nonprofit Relations in the Modern Welfare State*, Baltimore: Johns Hopkins University Press.

Salamon, L. M. and Anheier, H. K. (1997) *Defining the Nonprofit Sector: A Cross-national Analysis*, New York: Manchester University Press.

Salamon, L. M., Anheier, H. K., List, R., Toepler, S., Sokolowski, S. W. and associates (1999) *Global Civil Society: Dimensions of the Non-profit Sector*, Baltimore: Johns Hopkins University Press.

Salamon, L. M. and Toepler, S. (2000) 'The influence of the legal environment on the development of the nonprofit sector', Center for Civil Society Studies Working Paper 17, Baltimore: Johns Hopkins University Press.

Scharpf, F.W. (2000) 'The viability of advanced welfare states in the international economy: vulnerabilities and options', *Journal of European Public Policy*, 7, 2: 190–228.

Seibel, W. (1990) 'Organizational behavior and organizational function', in H. K. Anheier and W. Seibel (eds) *The Nonprofit Sector: International Comparative Perspectives*, Berlin: de Gruyter.

Sokolowski, S. W. (2000) 'The discreet charm of the nonprofit form: service professionals and nonprofit organizations (Poland 1989–1993)', *Voluntas*, 11, 2: 141–59.

Spector, W., Seldem, T. and Cohen, J. (1998) 'The impact of ownership type on nursing home outcomes', *Health Economics*, 7: 639–53.

Stiglitz, J. (1998) Wider Lecture, Helsinki, January.

Streeck, W. and Schmitter, P. C. (1985) 'Community, market, state – and associations? The prospective contribution of interest governance to social order', *European Sociological Review*, 1, 2: 119–38.

Thomas, C. (1999) 'Non-governmental organisations as a lobbying force in the European Union: myths and realities', paper presented at the 6th Biennial Conference of the European Community Studies Association, Pittsburgh, June.

van Til, J. (1988) *Mapping the Third Sector: Voluntarism in a Changing Social Economy*, New York: Foundation Center.

Wallace, H. and Wallace, W. (2000) *Policy-making in the European Union*, Oxford: Oxford University Press.

Warleigh, A. (2000) 'The hustle: citizenship, practice, NGOs and "policy coalitions" in the European Union – the cases of Auto Oil, drinking water and unit pricing', *Journal of European Public Policy*, 7, 2: 229–43.

Weisbrod, B. A. (1977) *The Voluntary Nonprofit Sector*, Lexington: D. C. Heath.

——(1988) *The Nonprofit Economy*, Cambridge MA: Harvard University Press.

——(1998) *To Profit or Not to Profit? The Commercial Transformation of the Nonprofit Sector*, Cambridge and New York: Cambridge University Press.

Weisbrod, B. A. and Schlesinger, M. (1986) 'Public, private, nonprofit ownership and the response to asymmetric information: the case of nursing homes', in S. Rose-Ackerman (ed.) *The Economics of Nonprofit Institutions*, Oxford and New York: Oxford University Press.

Wigglesworth, R. and Kendall, J. K. (2000) 'The impact of the third sector in the UK: the case of social housing', Civil Society Working Paper 9, London: Centre for Civil Society, London School of Economics and Political Science.

Wistow, G. (1996) *Social Care Markets: Progress and Prospects*, Buckingham: Open University Press.

Wolch, J. (1990) *The Shadow State: Government and Voluntary Sector in Transition*, New York: Foundation Center.

Index